Business Ethics

DAMIAN GRACE STEPHEN COHEN

Business Ethics

CANADIAN EDITION • William R. Holmes

OXFORD
UNIVERSITY PRESS

Oxford University Press is a department of the University of Oxford.
It furthers the University's objective of excellence in research, scholarship,
and education by publishing worldwide. Oxford is a registered trade mark of
Oxford University Press in the UK and in certain other countries.

Published in Canada by
Oxford University Press
8 Sampson Mews, Suite 204,
Don Mills, Ontario M3C 0H5 Canada

www.oupcanada.com

Library and Archives Canada Cataloguing in Publication
Grace, Damian, author
Business ethics / Damian Grace, Stephen Cohen & William
R. Holmes. — Canadian edition.

Includes bibliographical references.
ISBN 978–0–19–542528–4 (pbk.)

1. Business ethics—Canada. 2. Business ethics. I. Cohen,
Stephen, 1947–, author II. Holmes, William R., author III. Title.

HF5387.5.C3G73 2013 174'.40971 C2012-906475-0

Cover image: Andy Roberts/Getty Images
Introduction opener: Zoonar/Thinkstock; Chapter 1 opener: Hemera/Thinkstock;
Chapter 2 opener: iStockphoto/Thinkstock; Chapter 3 opener: Pixland/Thinkstock;
Chapter 4 opener: Sadeugra/iStockphoto; Chapter 5 opener: Zoonar/Thinkstock;
Chapter 6 opener: Photodisc/Thinkstock; Chapter 7 opener: Photodisc/Thinkstock;
Chapter 8 opener: iStockphoto/Thinkstock; Chapter 9 opener: iStockphoto/Thinkstock;
Chapter 10 opener: Otmar Winterleitner/iStockphoto; Chapter 11 opener:
Zoonar/Thinkstock; Chapter 12 opener: Fuse/Thinkstock

This book is printed on permanent (acid-free) paper ♾.

Printed and bound in Canada

2 3 4 — 16 15 14

Contents

CONFIDENTIAL

Cases

Acknowledgements

We wish to express our gratitude to a number of people who assisted in the completion of this work. We thank Kaz Kazim, John Cheong Seong Lee, Shirley Cohen, and Greg Goodman for their assistance and advice. Karen Hildebrandt of Oxford University Press provided good counsel for this edition, as did the editorial wisdom and meticulous care of Tim Fullerton, who greatly assisted us in improving the text.

We wish to thank the following colleagues who made comments on the earlier editions and suggestions for improvement: Andrew Brian, Pam Byde, Ted Cohen, Conal Condren, Glyn Hardingham, Kathleen MacDonald, Bryan Maher, Ian Marsh, Michaelis Michael, Noel Preston, and members of our classes in the Graduate Programs in Professional Ethics at the University of New South Wales.

Thanks are also due to Saatchi and Saatchi, Toyota Australia, Fairfax Media, Style Counsel, Chrysler Corporation, Bozell Worldwide Inc., and Behrens Brown for supplying material and allowing its reproduction.

A number of the analyses, arguments, explanations, and modes of presentation in this volume have benefited from presentation at academic and industry forums. In particular, the Roads and Traffic Authority of New South Wales (RTA) has encouraged us and provided invaluable feedback through its various ethics workshops and seminars. We especially thank Peter Houston and Rob McCarthy from the RTA.

Damian Grace and Stephen Cohen

Many thanks must go to Damian Grace and Stephen Cohen for their original concept and ideas for this book, their original approaches to problems, and their original analyses of ethical situations. Without those foundations this adaptation would not have been possible. Much gratitude and thanks goes to Jennifer Holmes for her patience and understanding. Lisa Peterson of Oxford University Press provided magnificent support and counsel.

William Holmes

About the Authors

Damian Grace was an associate professor of philosophy at the University of New South Wales. Since 2010 he has been an honorary associate in the Department of Government and International Relations at the University of Sydney. Aside from his work in business ethics, Damian has published in the area of history of political philosophy.

Stephen Cohen is the director of Graduate Programs in Professional Ethics at the University of New South Wales, and an associate professor of philosophy. Stephen has published widely in the areas of business ethics, professional ethics, ethics in the public sector, and moral theory and moral reasoning. Stephen also consults to public and private sector organizations and to the professions on matters of ethics, values, and moral reasoning.

Together Damian and Stephen founded the Graduate Programs in Professional Ethics at the University of New South Wales. Damian and Stephen have been working together for a number of years. Aside from this text, they have jointly published a number of essays in business and professional ethics. They have also designed and presented many workshops to the public sector. The photo of them here was taken on top of the Sydney Harbour Bridge and shows them in what was a team-building exercise for a large public sector organization in New South Wales.

William R. Holmes is the dean of the Faculty of Business at the Sheridan Institute of Technology. His career has spanned the corporate and educational sector and has included assignments in Europe, Asia, and the Middle East. William holds a Doctor of Business Administration from the University of Southern Queensland, an MBA from the University of British Columbia, a Master of Philosophy (Ethics) from the University of Waterloo, and undergraduate degrees in economics and philosophy, also from the University of Waterloo. He is a certified management accountant (CMA) and a certified human resource professional (CHRP).

Introduction

Business as Usual?

One of the most significant aspects of the global financial crisis of 2008–9 was the attribution of moral failure as a cause. Greed was identified by presidents and prime ministers as the root of the problem, and amid the wreckage of venerable financial houses, such as Lehman Brothers and the Royal Bank of Scotland, this seemed indisputable. Executives continued either to receive large salaries or to walk away from failed companies with lavish payouts. Excess still seemed in fashion and restraint a foreign concept to many business leaders. In the United States in 2008, Merrill Lynch reported a fourth-quarter loss of more than $15 billion. Somehow, this loss did not seem to affect $3.6 billion in bonuses that Merrill Lynch paid to its executives just before being rescued by Bank of America—with direct government assistance of $20 billion and a further guarantee of $100 billion to secure risky assets. John Thain, the chief executive officer (CEO) who paid the bonuses, spent $1.2 million on renovating his office, including $87,784 for a rug, $35,115 for a toilet, and $1,405 for a garbage can. Thain promised to repay the money to Bank of America, and later the bank dispensed with his services.[1] The New York attorney-general was repelled enough to investigate the bonuses.[2] Citigroup lost

$28.5 billion but received $345 billion in government funds and guarantees, so it decided to go ahead with the purchase of a new 12-seat corporate jet for $50 million.[3] At the same time as Royal Bank of Scotland losses of $34.5 billion were announced, the pension package of the bank's former boss, Sir Fred Goodwin, was revealed as being £693,000 for life.[4] In October 2008, the former chairman and CEO of Lehman Brothers, Richard Fuld, took full responsibility for the collapse of the merchant bank while declaring that his decisions "were both prudent and appropriate." In January 2009, Fuld took another prudent decision: he sold his half of the Florida family mansion (purchased in 2004 for US$13.75 million) for US$10—to his wife. Fuld, it seems, wished to continue at least some business as though times were not unusual.[5]

Who could fail to be shocked by the lack of shame exhibited by corporate chiefs when hundreds of thousands of people were losing their jobs and their life's savings? Well, maybe the greed and excess of executives have something to do with the kind of work they do—with the fact that investors don't like to see returns on their investments reported in red ink. Consider the view of Michael Lewis, published four years before the crash. Lewis suggests that a CEO might

> genuinely want to make the world a better place. He may genuinely dislike his moral climate. But the atmosphere created by investors for investors requires him continually to mollify these awful, greedy little people who have done nothing but put up some money and who care about nothing except next quarter's earnings.[6]

Lewis's conclusion is not that corporate excesses are justified, but that responsibility extends beyond the top levels of management. In the face of demands from investors for robust returns, is it surprising that executives "exhibit less-than-ideal ethical standards? . . . The pressure applied to people who run public corporations almost requires them to forget how to be good."[7] In the context of the global financial crisis four years later, this argument had resonance. Yes, corporations were imprudent in their remuneration and spending, but perhaps that became the price of giving investors what they wanted. At least Lewis moves us beyond the simplification that the greed of a bunch of jet-setting executives brought the world financial system to its knees.

These responses to the financial meltdown tell us a number of things. First, ethics matters to business. As we argue in this introduction, business is not morally neutral—amoral—and business people are no more ready to accept ethical defeat than anyone else. Second, there is something to *know* about ethics—it's not intuitive—and that means there is something to teach and something to learn. Learning something about ethics can assist you in the articulation of judgments and give you a systematic approach to dealing with ethical issues in business. Finally, ethics matters to everyone—to investors and governments as well as to those who run businesses. It happens that the moral judgments passed on many executives in the 2008–9 financial crisis were justified, but sometimes media moralizing clouds the issues and subverts sound ethical appraisals. As Lewis reminds us, addressing such moralizing is more complex than learning the formalities of ethics, but such an education is a very good place to start.

Why Study Business Ethics?

Why should business students study ethics? What good might be expected to come from such a study? Apart from the customary jokes about the brevity of a course on business ethics and its oxymoronic nature, there are serious reasons to doubt the benefits of such courses. For example, it is hardly the case that students in business schools are being taught unethical practices. Now that such courses have been running for many years, particularly in the United States, what difference can be observed in the behaviour of business people? And, given that almost all of those undertaking business courses will not be in a position to shape the policies and directions of corporations until they have gained substantial industry experience, what use is it to them to learn about the ethics of Enron or WorldCom? There was also some justified skepticism about using morality to make business look good after the failures and excesses of the 1980s. Beyond these reservations, however, there persists what might be called "social discomfort" about the public discussion of ethical issues. After all, is not ethics a matter of personal belief, preference, and values? How could one talk of business ethics when there is so much disagreement about ethics in general, let alone in one particular area? Are there reliable surveys to tell us what most people want from business ethics? Why is it important to bring up children with a proper grounding in ethics and morality if the morality they learn from their family, neighbours, school, and peers is not good enough to serve them in life? What will we have next: shopping ethics, sports ethics, nightclub ethics?

These questions illustrate some of the most common kinds of objections to business ethics, but none of them has slowed the development of the subject and its incorporation into the curriculum of business courses. It is worth taking such questions seriously not only because they remain current, but also because the justification for business ethics provides a useful way of introducing the subject.

It is odd for teachers to argue that ethics education makes no difference to behaviour: one might as well argue that teaching organizational behaviour or marketing will make no difference, or that any form of education is flawed if it does not turn out preformed products. No one would seriously argue that books, films, or television programs that portray certain modes of behaviour never affect people or that they do not give them cause to consider their own behaviour. As any student or educator knows, education is more than reading and writing. To avoid explicit discussion of ethical issues in a field of study is to send a message that ethics is dispensable. That message is not one that responsible educators or business would want to risk sending today. People cannot be "made good" by telling them to do X or to avoid doing Y, but standards of conduct and acceptable values can be entrenched in people and in organizations, and people can be put in a position where they make informed choices in the professions and occupations in which they work. This is the minimum ethical education that a student of any practical course has a right to expect.

In this respect, business has for too long been short-changing itself. While degrees for the professions have had requirements for ethics to be included in their courses, business degrees have lagged. What has been regarded as standard in medicine, law, social work, nursing, veterinary science, engineering, and architecture has, until recently, been seen as optional in commerce. If some in business think that this is acceptable, they will quickly find that the public will not tolerate ethical indifference. More than ever before, business is expected to be accountable, not only to shareholders but also to society.

The view that ethics is superfluous assumes that people will act as they must and will leave the idealism to the classroom. Perhaps, but that implies that ethics has nothing but idealism to offer. Sometimes, however, it is the case that people of goodwill do not know what the ethical thing to do is in a complicated situation. Particular ethical studies, whether in accounting or medicine, engineering or marketing, should at least offer some clarification and perhaps even some answers. An important point here is that ethics should help a person in making a decision, and further, ethics should help people live with themselves and their society even after a tragic decision. Ethics is not a salve for the bruises of life, but it places in perspective the moral problems, which, after all, affect only those who are already concerned with this aspect of their conduct. Ethics will not make people good by some magic, but what good reason could there be for keeping people in ignorance of the ethical demands society makes of business or, more adventurously, for keeping business professionals from exploring the possibilities and problems that will confront them at a time of great technological and social change? In short, why would business practitioners not wish to advance the professional status of their occupation?

This reference to business as a profession is not casual; the term is not meant as a synonym for occupation. The point about professions is that they serve and are responsive not only to clients but also to other interested sections of society, nowadays called "stakeholders," the topic of chapter 3. Professions rely on conceptual thinking and embody their distinctive ways of doing things in what are called "practices." It is common to hear talk of architectural practice, psychological practice, legal practice, engineering practice, and so on. It is important to note that this is not just a fancy way of describing what these professions do. Take, for example, surgery. We do not say that "surgery" was practised on the prisoners of war who were the subjects of medical experiments, even though the operations were performed by surgeons, sometimes with great skill. There is such a strong distinction between treatment and experimentation that it can be difficult even for critically ill patients to be treated with drugs that are still experimental. This distinction between experimentation and treatment is based upon the idea that the respect to which people are entitled forbids their being used as a means to some other good. People are goods in and of themselves; they have value as people per se. Treatment is directed to securing that good. To ensure that the paths to this good remain clear and unconfused by ulterior and ignoble objectives, the medical profession has assumed and codified a body of ethics. This code is a shorthand way of indicating a commitment to a morality of practice. If a practice like surgery entailed simply the knowledge and skills necessary to operate, then there would be little to distinguish the experimenter from the surgeon. In fact, we do not recognize experiments on involuntary subjects, such as prisoners of war, as medical practice because basic human values are attacked by such experiments and, in the case of prisoners of war, because there is a failure to respect the value of humans as such. There is a failure to regard the value of individual humans as other than instrumental in the achievement of other values or goals. It is the ethical direction of the accomplishments of a profession (particularly its regard for the individuals who are subject to its activities) that entitles the profession to a certain status and power, such as self-regulation, and other marks of social recognition. And that is why unprofessional conduct usually refers not merely to competence, but to conduct and decorum in a wider sense— to doing the right thing with one's knowledge and skills and using them to serve rather than to take advantage of people.

"Practice," then, is a very useful notion, for at its heart is a conception of human good that directs the application and use of the competencies that it embodies. Central to a practice is an ethical commitment, not just a skilled way of doing a job, and the practice of business is no different from the practice of other professions in this respect.

Like the professions, business is conceptual, intellectual work. It is not simply a matter of routine, repetitive tasks. It cannot be reduced to mere administration. The signs of a successful business are keeping employees, customers, and the tax man happy and taking a profit at the end of the day. Making these very different things happen is the real vocation in business. It takes skill, knowledge, and practical wisdom to secure the future of a business and make it grow. Successful business does not happen by chance; it is the product of skill and intelligence.

One major implication of this view is that business needs a stock of concepts. This stock embraces concepts from law, accounting, marketing, industrial relations, and many other areas, as well as concepts relating to the kind of industry with which the business deals, such as medical supplies or software sales. All of these concern human values. Business is about meeting the needs and desires of human society and is therefore about human goods and the best means of providing them. And this is where ethics comes in. Ethics is concerned with the identification of human goods (ends) and their pursuit (means), including the direction and constraints that might be involved in their pursuit.

Whether or not ethics is explicitly considered in its various functions, it is inescapably part of business. In dealing with ends and the means to those ends, business is making ethical decisions, even if such decisions are not perceived by managers and boards in this light. This book provides an ethical perspective on the appraisal of means and ends in business life, and thereby enriches the stock of concepts recognized as necessary to it. If there is no conception that a decision entails ethical considerations and if there is no adequate conceptual vocabulary to make sense of ethical requirements, then reasonable ethical standards in business become a matter of luck. In this respect, we claim to be contributing to the stock of conceptual tools that are useful in doing business successfully.

People do not have to take a moral philosophy course to be ethical. Ethics is expressed in the lives of people who have never heard or uttered a philosophical syllable in their lives. We do not always need to be acquainted with the theories of academics to get on with life. This point has been well made by non-academic critics of modernity and the domination of life by theory. One of the most famous paintings of the great surrealist painter René Magritte, *The Treachery of Images*, depicts a tobacco pipe under which is the caption "*Ceci n'est pas une pipe*" (This is not a pipe). This caption startles with its obviousness: we are so used to a theoretical understanding of the world that we are apt to confuse the representation of things with the things themselves. And so it is with theories of ethics. There is no substitute for the practice of the thing itself. Conversely, just as Magritte's picture has its own value, so does ethical theory.

Of course, a strong objection to business ethics might be inferred from the following line of reasoning—namely, that most business has gotten by ethically for a long time without the help of jargon about concepts and, in general, without the analytic input of academics. Why worry about formal business ethics and conceptual thinking? This objection has truth but it is also partly false. It is false in that traditional business virtues and conventional ethical concepts have hidden a spectrum of injustice. For example, the labour of women and children was, and in some cases still is, unjustly exploited, and the rights of indigenous people have too often simply been ignored in the pursuit of mining and pastoral wealth. But the social environment has changed. Traditionally, people were brought up in the family business and learned to be proficient by way of a kind of apprenticeship. Few would find that satisfactory today. Now proficient business requires the ability to deal conceptually with all aspects of the business environment, and one aspect of that environment is ethics. The social context in which business occurs today is one in which concern for ethics is not merely an option.

People may well display high levels of personal integrity but remain unaware of the demands of institutional ethics. How would they deal with questions of social responsibility, equity, and accountability? Would they even be able to conceptualize what the issues at stake are? The importance of such questions has been underlined not only by the ethical failures of the 1980s, but also by the demands of the social agenda. While the 1980s were not unique in raising critical ethical issues, they provided a wealth of illustrations of the damage that ethical ignorance as well as unethical behaviour can do. Unless managers are aware of ethical issues, know how to think about them conceptually, and can devise justifiable solutions, they will fail to institutionalize ethics in corporate life. Ignorance can be as pernicious as malice; the dictum that "greed is good" goes hand in hand with the "myth of amoral business," as Richard De George calls it.[8] Both slogans are excuses for unacceptable business practices, but only the latter claims the dignity of ignorance.

Bluntly, ethics is not an option. If a company or industry cares nothing for ethical requirements, it may expect from government a policy and legislative response that imposes standards and practices. This is already happening, and some of these pressures are discussed in chapter 10.

Already this suggests a kind of negativity about ethics that can be distorting. Just as fine cooking is not a response to fast food, so business ethics is not only a response to ethical failure. There happens to be great scope for ethical repair work, but if we take seriously the notion that business is conceptual work, there is greater scope for using ethics to promote excellence in business. At its simplest, ethics is a normal part of everyday conduct, a normal part of business. At its best, ethics is about human excellence. A survey of thousands of accountants between 1994 and 2000 revealed a positive correlation between the implementation of written corporate codes of ethics and the effective implementation of ethical practices and the organizational success and reputation of their respective companies. Ethical conduct of a company was measured by evaluating respondents' ratings of the effectiveness of their employers with respect to practices that included conducting operations in a manner consistent with the company's ethical standards, providing ethics training, consideration of ethical standards in long-term decision-making, and rewarding ethical actions. Organizational success of the companies surveyed was evaluated by analyzing factors such as profitability, productivity, sales volume, growth, and asset utilization.[9] There is a clear relationship here between excellent management inputs into companies and excellent outcomes. A concern for ethics is part of this drive to excel. It should lead to a proactive stance by business on ethical issues and a greater preparedness for the crises that will inevitably emerge in the business community, just as they did in the 1980s. Being well brought up is a fortunate basis on which to build good ethical practice, but it is not the only way and not a sufficient way of achieving this.

About This Text

Most business ethics texts begin with a smorgasbord of ethical theories, followed by topics and cases in specific areas. Readers are often invited to choose a theory to apply to a topic in order to resolve an ethical problem. This can suggest a kind of "off the shelf" approach to ethics, which we eschew. Certainly the philosophers who have developed each of the major positions did not regard them as substitutable by rival theories; they argued for them because they believed they were true or in some other way preferable to other theories. So, while it is important to have some familiarity with the main theories of morality, this would be more in the interests of understanding the conceptual language of contemporary ethics than of providing some kind of algorithm for the solution of ethical "dilemmas." Indeed, chapter 2 shows that often there are no clean solutions—that no matter how well people try to act, they can still end up with "dirty hands."

Hence, in seeking to acquaint readers with widely used ethical vocabularies, we are not suggesting that ethical solutions are simply about making the right choice of theory and applying it to a problem. In order to avoid confusion and a false sense of choice in moral theory, we deal with this matter only in a summary fashion. We do, however, set out a theory of reflective equilibrium that we believe provides conceptual tools for considering and resolving ethical problems. Further, it will be clear from this introduction that we believe that people espousing different moral theories and religious views can exhibit the same virtues, can meaningfully and fruitfully discuss ethical problems with each other, and, indeed, can often agree on practical solutions to moral problems. In this respect, we suggest in chapter 1 that a commitment to "moral pluralism" or to "relativism" does not stand as a barrier to fruitful ethical discussion.

Near the end of chapter 1, we say a word about the benefits of approaching a study of business ethics through case studies. We note that sometimes our purpose is to call attention to something that has gone wrong (or right) and sometimes it is to call attention to some ethically problematic aspect of behaviour or organizational structure. Given that we are dealing with case studies that often have the nature of vignettes only, we recognize a limitation, a constraint, and a danger that is also important to signal. In "telling stories" to illustrate various themes or problems, we are concerned to present salient features that are relevant to the points we want to make. And, while we certainly do not wish to distort facts and do believe that we provide reasonable accounts, we do not provide "full" accounts of all the cases. Further, we would allow the possibility of another side of the story. In this respect, we invite the reader to approach the cases as problematic in more ways than one. Perhaps you know of, or could imagine, additional facts that would be relevant to a moral appraisal of the situation. Perhaps you could suggest possible solutions to the ethical difficulties presented. That the context be seen as Canadian and the problems recognized as real and serious is important. Beyond that, whether or not an illustrative example is itself factual is relatively unimportant. It is worth repeating, however, that we do attempt to give factually correct accounts of the cases.

What This Text Is and What It Is Not

This text is not a catechism or a "deuteronomy" for business and professions. It is not a handbook of exhaustive questions about, and definitive answers to, moral problems that arise in those contexts. Sometimes issues are clear and sometimes they are not. Sometimes there is a clear solution and sometimes there is not. The most important aspect of the text is its argument that we can think through ethical problems and ethical issues systematically and that we can arrive at an answer or a response that has integrity. There are conceptual tools to help us do this. A response should be justifiable and should not shy away from offering justification, even if it is not the only justifiable response. Sometimes for reasons of "dirty hands" (see chapter 2) and sometimes for other reasons, the response is not something that can simply be "ticked off" and from which we can move on. Ethical problems sometimes need to be revisited and reconsidered. Ethical decision-making often lacks the certainty we might desire. This does not make it wishy-washy, soft, unimportant, or unsystematic. Our aim is to make this clear in the chapters that follow.

An important consideration in a book such as this is to present an appropriate balance between, on the one hand, theory, principles, and conceptual tools and, on the other, practical examples and case studies. We do, in fact, make a comment about that near the end of chapter 1. This edition is the first Canadian edition of the book. As with previous editions, this one strives to maintain the balance between theory, principles, and conceptual tools and the supporting practical examples and case studies. The Canadian edition presents the theory, principles, and concepts found in the earlier editions, but within a Canadian context. The major changes and additions to this edition focus on the replacement of, or addition to, the examples and case studies with either Canadian examples or high-profile international ones. Apart from adopting the Canadian context, a new chapter on the role of ethics in corporate governance has also been added.

Responses to earlier editions indicated a desire by students to get a better grounding in, and have the opportunity to think more precisely about, the area of theory, principles, and conceptual tools. We have taken these as indications not that a chapter in this book should include more about moral theory and moral reasoning, but rather that a different book—concerned only with those things—would be helpful. One of us, Stephen Cohen, has written such a book (also published by Oxford University Press).[10] People who are interested in further exploring ideas about moral theories and, in particular, the structure and process of moral reasoning might be interested in having a look at that book.

1

Ethical Reasoning in Business

Chapter Outline

Business ethics covers the whole spectrum of interactions among firms, individuals, industries, society, and the state. In other words, business ethics is as complex as business itself. It is not an optional accessory to business life or a mere enthusiasm of philosophers and moralists; business ethics is about how we conduct our business affairs, from the basest fraud to the highest levels of excellence. It is about individuals and the institutions with which they deal. And it is about the expectations and requirements—including the social and economic requirements—of society.

Such a scope suggests that individuals might have a limited role in ethical matters. After all, if they have a limited range of business responsibilities, they will not be in a position to make much of an ethical impact. An important way of looking at the responsibilities of individuals is to examine their roles. Company directors, for instance, have fiduciary responsibilities to act in the best interests of shareholders. Does that entitle them to ignore ethically suspect practices that benefit shareholders? Sometimes people's role in business is itself the problem. Should their occupational role diminish their moral responsibility for actions done in the name of their company or employer? If so, where do individual conscience, character, and choice come in?

The same kinds of questions might be asked not only of individuals, but also of firms and industries that operate under socially determined legal and economic constraints. What are the ethical responsibilities of "non-natural persons"—legal entities that have no character or conscience in the usual sense and are persons only in law? How is ethics to be made part of the fabric of institutions? Should ethical standards be imposed in a market economy?

What Is Ethics?

ethics *the study of the theoretical foundations of moral principles governing individual behaviour and the practical application of those principles*

If **ethics** were only a matter of rules, customs, and contracts, such questions would be relatively straightforward. We already have abundant procedures, instruments, conventions, and regulations ranging from law to etiquette. It is important to note that ethics does not duplicate these things; nor can its importance or scope be measured by them. Ethical issues are often grey; ethical reasoning is not as concrete (or sometimes as precise) as legal reasoning; and people can differ on the subject of ethics as they may not on the laws of physics or the facts of geography. Although these are facts about ethics, they are not reasons for believing that ethics is conceptually soft or trivial. Ethics is not poor reasoning, vague law, indeterminate custom, or an ideological form of social control, but one of the most important sources of motivation and guidance in human conduct. It occupies an important field of knowledge in its own right.

Aristotle gave a view of the matter in a famous passage of his *Nicomachean Ethics*:

> Our account of this science (ethics) will be adequate if it achieves such clarity as the subject-matter allows; for the same degree of precision is not to be expected in all discussions. . . . Therefore in discussing subjects, and arguing from evidence, conditioned in this way, we must be satisfied with a broad outline of the truth; that is, in arguing about what is for the most part so from premises which are for the most part true we must be content to draw conclusions that are similarly qualified . . . it is a mark of the trained

> mind never to expect more precision in the treatment of any subject than the nature of the subject permits; for demanding logical demonstrations from a teacher of rhetoric is clearly about as reasonable as accepting mere plausibility from a mathematician.[1]

Ethical reasoning, according to Aristotle, is not a matter of applying the appropriate algorithm to a situation and mechanically calculating the correct moral result, the correct moral prescription. Ethical reasoning is more subtle, less precise, often more difficult. Not all ethical thinkers have agreed with Aristotle. Some have tried to put a much more precise formulation on moral duties. Nevertheless, given the kinds of debates about ethical problems in Canada, it is clear that lack of precision is not the problem, or at least not the major problem, in solving them. In order to gain a clearer grasp of what ethics is and is not, consider the film *The Godfather*.

ethical reasoning *the reasoned application of ethical theory or theories to a given situation*

The Godfather

At the beginning of the film we are disgusted by the violence and absence of humanity in the Mafia. As the story progresses, however, we come to see the internal rules of "the Family" at work and realize that although they are contrary to the rules of normal society, they make their own kind of sense. At the end of the film, the anti-hero, Michael, is attending the baptism of his nephew in a church while his henchmen systematically kill his rivals for leadership of the Family. This is how life is in the Mafia. This is what we understand to make sense in that kind of culture. The Mafia has its own ethos, its own rules and mores. This is a dark parallel to the ethical values of the wider society, and it is this parallel, rather than the ruthlessness and violence per se, that causes *The Godfather* to be shocking.

The Godfather raises all kinds of ethical questions that apply equally to society and business. Is just any system of binding rules, norms, and duties a system of ethics? Is it possible to say that one system is better than another? Does not moral luck determine the circumstances of people's birth and development and therefore the attitudes they bring to life? The importance of these questions is readily apparent. If people born in the American South in the early nineteenth century believed wholeheartedly in slavery, how can they be blamed? If a person grew up as a white child in South Africa during the Vorster regime, why should he or she be blamed for having white supremacist attitudes? And who is to say that one system of social beliefs and customs, even if racist, is worse than another? These are real questions, requiring thought and careful consideration.

If **cultural relativism** is the case, then business must adapt to the norms and practices of the cultures in which it operates. What is unethical in Canada might be good manners in one of our trading partners. What would be poor working conditions here might be superior working conditions overseas. Sharp practice[2] might well be the norm elsewhere. Surely we would be mistaken to try to universalize our standards of right and wrong in our dealings with other countries. Or would we?

cultural relativism *the view that behaviours and values are relative to particular cultures; that behaviours are dependent on the accepted norms of the particular culture or society in which they take place*

Defining Ethics

What is ethics? What does it mean to have an ethical point of view or an ethical opinion or to behave ethically? A definition will not solve the problems raised but will go some way towards clarifying what is at stake.

The term "ethics" owes its origins to ancient Greece, where the word *ethikos* refers to the authority of custom and tradition. When Cicero sought a similar word in Latin, he chose *mos*, from which we derive the terms "moral," "mores," and "morale." So it seems that "ethical relativists" have at least a good historical basis for their views: ethics and mores originally referred to the customs, habits of life, or traditions of a people. We shall consider **ethical relativism** in our discussion of ethical reasoning, but a relativist could say that we have as much right to condemn the customs of the Mafia or apartheid as we do to condemn any foreign system of behaviour—that is, none. Or rather, we can condemn them in terms of our moral system, but we should not and cannot insist that others who do not share our values listen to our complaints.

ethical relativism *the view that moral values are relative to particular environments; moral behaviours are dependent on the accepted ethical norms of the particular culture, society, or environment in which they take place*

Plainly this will not do. A definition of ethics that dignified any and all customs would not answer to a common-sense understanding of the term. The Mafia, slavery, and apartheid are objectionable, and not just because most people think so. The nineteenth-century German philosopher Georg Wilhelm Friedrich Hegel distinguished between ethics as the customary norms and ways of behaving in a society, and morality as a reflection on those norms and the deliberate generation and adoption of principles that may well modify them. On this distinction, the ethos or ethics of a particular culture might require reverence for older people or assign special responsibilities to the oldest son. Examples of moral thinking would be the growth in recognition of human rights and the greater sensitivity to suffering in animals. Another example can be seen in the deliberate study of professional and business ethics. In this sense, then, morality is the missing part of ethics that as modern people, rather than as villagers regulated by custom and tradition, we often take for granted. In fact, so familiar to us is reflective, conceptual thinking about ethical issues that customs and traditions are often ignored or dismissed as irrelevant. Both custom and reflection are part of ethics.

By and large there is no reason to make a distinction in meaning between "ethical" and "moral." There is certainly no difference in meaning that could be attributed to their etymological roots. Sometimes some moral philosophers, or "ethicists," distinguish these words from each other, but not all philosophers do; and those who do distinguish them from each other do not all distinguish them in the same way. Some have distinguished "moral" and "ethical" in the manner of Hegel, but others have distinguished them in a variety of different ways. It is recommended here that the words be considered as synonymous except in some peculiar usages. We will see later, in discussing codes of ethics, that there is an issue about whether or not the use of "ethics" in "code of ethics" is a specialized use or whether it is even there synonymous with "morality." We will suggest that, in that context, "ethics" is a specialized use and should not be confused with "morality." That is the only exception to our use of these words as synonymous.

What is ethics? What kind of thing is a moral reason? What is being considered when one considers the "moral dimension" of a problem? What makes this different from the non-moral aspects of a situation? Is there anything peculiar about moral reasons? These questions themselves have been debated among moral philosophers. Without entering into the debate or prejudicing a position, we can say something about what ethics is. We can offer a "minimalist" description that offers only the bare bones of what must be involved in something being a moral concern. It is then arguable whether perhaps something more must also be involved in a consideration being an ethical one. Keep in mind that for now we are not talking about what is involved in the correct moral opinion, but rather about what it is for an opinion to be a moral opinion at all, be it correct or incorrect, or whatever.

- Considering something ethically requires that one go outside, or beyond, one's self-interest alone in reaching a decision. Moral opinions, then, are not opinions based only on the promotion of one's self-interest. Moral opinions are impartial.
- An ethical judgment is one that can be "universalized." It is one that is perceived to apply to everyone in similar circumstances and not only to oneself.
- Ethical opinions must be capable of being defended with reasons. This requirement distinguishes ethical opinions from biases and mere preferences for which one might have no reason at all for having: "I don't have a *reason* for liking vanilla ice cream more than chocolate raisin; I just do. I *prefer* its taste."
- Ethical opinions are not subject to a "vote" in the way that political opinions and decisions are. A moral opinion is not just whatever a majority decides it is. An opinion or a position on something does not become moral in virtue of popular support for it. In this respect, moral opinions are non-negotiable.
- Moral opinions are centrally "action-guiding." They are not only of theoretical or academic interest. They are centrally concerned with *behaviour*. They are concerned with evaluating behaviour and with prescribing ways in which people should behave. To at least some extent, this requires that one thinks about the consequences of one's actions.

Here are some examples of what some philosophers have said that ethics amounts to:

> [M]orality is, at the very least, the effort to guide one's conduct by reason—that is to do what there are the best reasons for doing—while giving equal weight to the best interests of each individual who will be affected by one's conduct.[3]

> [M]orality amounts to "guidelines that set the boundaries of acceptable behavior"—concerned with harming others, paying the proper regard for others' well-being, and treating persons with respect.[4]

> [M]orality is concerned with "rules, principles, or ways of thinking that guide actions" . . . it refers to "values, rules, standards, or principles that should guide our decisions about what we ought to do."[5]

> The notion of living according to ethical standards is tied up with the notion of defending the way one is living, of giving a reason for it, of justifying it. . . . Ethics requires us to go beyond "I" and "you" to the universal law, the universalizable judgment, the standpoint of the impartial spectator or ideal observer, or whatever we choose to call it. . . .

> In accepting that ethical judgments must be made from a universal point of view, I am accepting that my own interests cannot, simply because they are my interests, count more than the interests of anyone else.[6]

Where do ethical principles come from? Are they matters of religion, society's inculcated beliefs, universal rational truths? Are they principles that are formed as a result of a bargain that individuals reach in order to live together, all having their own welfare as their top priority, but realizing that in order to successfully advance their individual self-interests, they must operate according to mutually acceptable principles? These very important questions will not be dealt with here. They are by no means easy, and there is no universal agreement about what their answers are. However, although we should be aware of them, it is possible to proceed without answering them.

Elements in Moral Thinking—Broad Strokes

golden rule *the maxim accepted by the vast majority, if not all, of the world's cultures and religions that states that one should treat others as one would like others to treat oneself*

utilitarianism *the contention that the greatest good comes from choosing the alternative that provides the greatest aggregate level of satisfaction*

ethical dilemma *a situation involving the conflict between moral imperatives where to comply with one necessitates the transgression of the other*

When we appreciate a problem as a moral problem and come to deal with it, our appropriate concern involves consideration of rules (for example, the **golden rule**, "be fair," or "tell the truth") and also consideration of achieving outcomes or consequences of our action or decision (for example, **utilitarianism**, producing the most good, avoidance of offending someone). Most **ethical dilemmas** and serious ethical concerns involve clashes between these different types of considerations. And then there's more—for instance, the ethical requirements that come into play for an employee or professional or for someone in a role of any kind (for example, requirements of independence, attendance to the interest of the client, to the interest of the profession, loyalty to the firm, and so on). These considerations, as well, can conflict with regard to ethical rules and ethical outcomes.

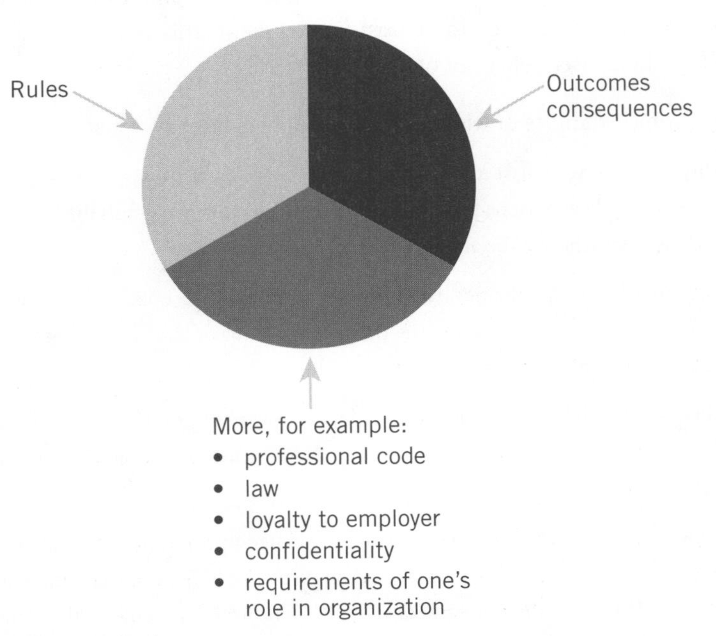

Figure 1.1 The moral pie

In facing and dealing with an ethical issue, we recognize different types of moral considerations at work. Here are a few:

- In this case, what does truth-telling (a rule) require?
- And what about the promise (a rule) I made to them yesterday?
- What course of action could I take here that would most benefit these people (an outcome)?
- Would that be fair (a rule)?
- In this situation, what is required by my remaining independent in the advice that I give (a professional requirement)?

There can be different—and sometimes conflicting—answers to these questions. For example, "In this case, if I am open and truthful in telling these people about our plans for the development, I can't benefit them as much as I can if I hide the truth from them, at least for a while." There is no mechanical or formulaic recipe for coming to a resolution in many cases. That does not mean, however, that in cases of conflicting ethical considerations, just anything at all will be ethically okay or that anything will be ethically as acceptable as anything else. What is required here is good judgment. We will have more to say about this later in the context of the various moral factors involved and the satisfactory justification for the decision that is made.

Descriptive and Prescriptive Ethics

There are many ways of studying ethics, but a vital first distinction is between **prescriptive** theories and **descriptive** theories of ethics. Descriptive ethics is, as the name suggests, the study of ethics in particular groups and societies. It is an empirical investigation that might be conducted by a sociologist or anthropologist or social psychologist of what happens when people follow or deviate from social norms. It could also be an account (a description) of what particular ethical beliefs a person or group holds. It makes no judgment of the rightness or wrongness of the events studied, but merely describes them.

prescriptive theories of ethics *theories that allow for the judgment of an act as right or wrong; recommending and forbidding certain types of conduct*

descriptive theories of ethics *the non-judgmental empirical study of ethics in particular groups or societies*

Prescriptive ethics is about judging an act to be right or wrong. It recommends or forbids certain types of conduct. It would, for example, prohibit robbery, fraud, and injustice while requiring honesty, truthfulness, and fairness. The way we are using the term "prescription" here means simply anything with "should" or "ought" involved in it: for example, "You should lead a good life." Prescriptive and descriptive ethics can become confused when people believe that the way things are done is, for that reason alone, the way they should be done. If fraud and dishonesty were commonplace, it would be an ethical error to recommend them on that basis. We are all familiar with the confusion of descriptive and prescriptive ethics found in the old excuse "Everybody's doing it." Now, this excuse might be genuine as a factor in our psychology, but it will not make a wrong act right. That is, the example of most people might count as an excusing reason for an individual doing the wrong thing, but it does not make the act right. Take the example of corporal punishment in schools. This was a widespread practice until relatively recently, but this fact about it did not make it right. It might, however, excuse the teachers who applied corporal punishment unthinkingly, perhaps, or in the belief that it was beneficial in the long term to school pupils.

A variation on this confusion of descriptive and prescriptive ethics is the commonly held view that if something is legal, it's ethical. That is, if there is no legal prohibition on an act, then I can do as I choose. This view will be revisited below.

Ethical Reasoning

We are concerned with three central points in this book:

- that there are moral concerns
- that you should address them
- what it means to address moral concerns.

Very few people would deny that there are moral concerns in their lives. In this respect, then, it takes little or no convincing that there are moral concerns. We will be presenting some moral concerns to you, indicating what there is about them that makes them moral and then dealing with them in a systematic way. In presenting moral issues, we have a few key matters in mind, not all of which can be dealt with in each instance. Sometimes we call attention to something that is clearly a moral impropriety and then proceed to discuss what exactly is wrong and how it might be rectified or, more importantly, how it might have been avoided. We are equally concerned, however, to call attention to some matters that are problematic and that, for that reason, should generate thought and argument in the context in which those matters occur. Serious, genuine analysis is called for, and people in business or in the professions should not avoid devoting some time to it.

As an individual or as an organization or as an individual occupying a position (a role) in an organization, you should address moral issues. Why? There are a number of answers to this question, ranging from a theoretical interest in moral philosophy to a purely pragmatic and self-interested concern. At the most theoretical level, the question "Why should I be moral?" is one to which philosophers have offered an array of answers since the time of Plato, more than 2,000 years ago. Some theories have urged that rational behaviour and rational thinking themselves require people to be moral. Other theories have referred to morality as empirically compelling, and others have made reference to a feeling people have about what they regard as moral. Many arguments suggest that we should be moral because that is what we want to be if we could find the moral thing to do in any particular situation. Suppose, however, that at the theoretical level such answers left you cold. What more could be said? When we discuss codes of ethics specifically, we will urge that, given the amount of public awareness and accountability required these days, coupled with the possibility (or threat) of governmental regulation over many aspects of business conduct, the climate in business is such that it is in people's interest to pay attention to moral, not simply legal, requirements. There is a good deal of truth to the practical dictum "Good ethics is good business." Perhaps purely self-interested motives for adopting a moral point of view are not noble—or not as noble as compassion or a sense of fairness or other motives that are not themselves based on one's own welfare and concern for advancing one's own interests ahead of those of others. Still, there can be no denying that requirements of public accountability are greater today than they have ever been before and that public awareness of, interest in, and demands concerning the conduct of businesses and the professions are very great, perhaps enlightened. Clients, customers, shareholders, or society at large will not tolerate professional or business conduct that is perceived to be unethical.

There is an important analogue to the question "Why be moral?" as it arises in this context. Political philosophers and philosophers of law often discuss the question of whether or not people should obey the law. This question, "Why should I obey the (legal) law?," is, in those discussions, most significantly directed to looking for a moral reason to obey the law. However, at another level, an appropriate answer to the question is a resounding, "Yes, I should obey the law, because if I don't, I'm going to get into trouble with the law." This is an answer that cannot be ignored when we consider why we should be moral in business as well.

Top-Down and Bottom-Up Approaches

If we recognize that there are moral concerns and we appreciate that we should address them, then what is it to address them? What is the nature of moral reasoning? Consider a couple of possibilities.

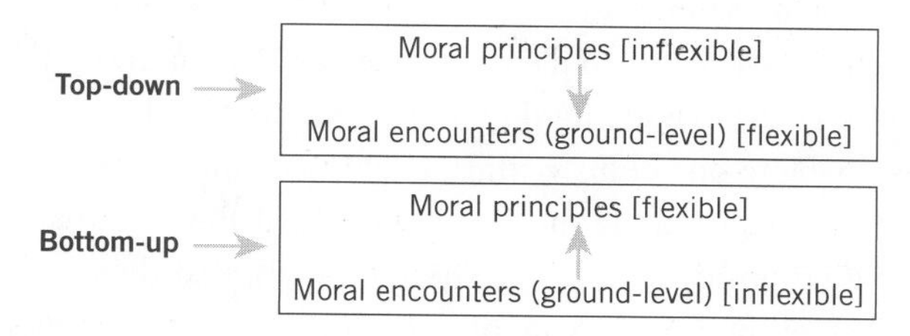

Figure 1.2 Top-down and bottom-up reasoning

The first is a **top-down approach** according to which the first principles of moral reasoning are general or universal moral principles that can be applied to specific situations. This conception of moral reasoning envisages the reasoner approaching a moral situation armed with general principles: for example, "Tell the truth," "Advance people's welfare," "Keep your promises," "Honour **fiduciary relationships**," and a number of others, all of which rest on some kind of general foundation. Moral reasoning, then, consists of applying the appropriate principles to the situation and overlaying those principles onto particular types of situations as those situations arise. For example, when faced with a moral choice, a committed utilitarian might engage in tallying up and comparing the amount of welfare that would be produced by the various alternatives. The act likely to produce

top-down approach to ethical reasoning *general or universal moral principles, which are inflexible and non-negotiable, are applied to specific situations in order to determine the ethically justifiable decision*

fiduciary relationship *a legal or ethical relationship of confidence or trust between two or more parties where one person or party (the fiduciary) acts at all times in the best interests of another person or party*

utility *level of satisfaction or happiness*

the most **utility** would be the one that the utilitarian principle would direct be performed. The principle—in this case the utilitarian principle—drives the reasoning, and its application to the particular situation determines the correct, ethical result. According to the top-down approach, the task for moral reasoning is to bring particular moral judgments or intuitions about particular situations into harmony with overarching general principles.

bottom-up approach to ethical reasoning *the moral judgments we make personally through moral intuition or reactions we have to particular situations*

According to a **bottom-up approach**, on the other hand, the first principles of moral reasoning are the moral judgments we make personally—perhaps moral intuitions or reactions we have to particular situations. It is these ground-level judgments—perhaps intuitions or feelings—themselves, rather than overarching principles, that are the first principles of moral reasoning. This conception of moral reasoning sees moral encounters as situations in which the reasoner is struck by the nature of the situations themselves and need look no further to appreciate the moral dimension that is present and arrive at a moral decision. If one were interested in doing so, it might be possible to enunciate general principles that are consistent with the intuitions that emerge from the particular situations to which we react. The starting point and the foundation of moral principles in this approach, however, rest with the evaluation of the particular situations.

Ethical Defeat

At times, we question the sincerity of people claiming to be ethical. Perhaps we should be equally suspicious of people who claim to be amoral or indifferent to ethics. The predatory businessman David Tweed dismisses questions about the ethics of his targeting the old and vulnerable in what are frankly disgraceful offers to buy their shares. He has been reported as saying to one of his victims, "I didn't do morals at school."[7]

ethical defeat *the admission that a person's actions have no positive ethical justification; that a person's actions are completely immoral*

People are reluctant to admit complete **ethical defeat**—that is, to grant that their acts have no positive ethical justification at all, that their acts are completely immoral, bereft of any positive moral elements. This is an important feature of human nature. It shows that, by and large, people do not dismiss ethics as an unimportant concern. Sometimes they get it wrong—sometimes their acts are immoral—but seldom do the agents themselves dismiss morality altogether. This is important. People do not simply admit to being caught with the smoking gun, with nothing to say for themselves. We are not oblivious—or impervious—to moral argument about what we do. In this respect, we do not need to be convinced to enter the moral arena for the purpose of evaluating potential courses of action. They are already there, even though they might be perceived as not "correct." This point was vividly illustrated many years ago in a newspaper report about drug trafficking in New York City: a heroin dealer pointed out to the reporter that he only sold good dope and that he never sold to kids.[8] Even at this level, the dealer is hearkening to the moral defensibility of some aspect of what he is doing. He is not oblivious to the importance of such a concern, even though, in his case, it was particularly misplaced. Consider another case.

Rationalizing a Crime

In 2008 in the Austrian town of Amstetten, the appalling story came to light of a woman, Elizabeth Fritzl, and her three children who had been imprisoned in a cellar by Elizabeth's father, Josef, for 24 years. Fritzl had kidnapped and imprisoned his daughter when she was 18 and raped her repeatedly over the following two and a half decades. Of the seven children he had fathered upon her, three—Kerstin, 19, Stefan, 18, and Felix, 5—had spent their entire lives in the cellar. Three others had been adopted by Josef Fritzl, and one had died. What could prompt such vile conduct is a matter of speculation for psychiatrists,[9] but even after admitting his crimes, Josef Fritzl sought to affirm something of his humanity. When Kerstin became severely ill with a form of epilepsy related to incest, he admitted her to hospital as his granddaughter whom he found ill on his doorstep. Eventually, Elizabeth Fritzl was able to persuade her father to let her visit the hospital and the full story was revealed.[10] Fritzl insists that this proves he's no "monster." "I could have killed them all," he said. "Then there would have been no trace. No-one would have found me out. . . . If it weren't for me, Kerstin wouldn't be alive today. It was me who made sure she was taken to hospital."[11]

The moral of these stories is simply that the answer to a question such as "Who cares about ethics anyway?" is "Nearly everyone." And, if this is the case, then it is unnecessary to spend much time trying to convince people that they should be interested in the moral aspects of what they do. However, there is, of course, much work to do in determining exactly what those aspects are and what course of action one should take, or what courses of action are permissible.

It is not infrequent that invitations—or pleas—to business and the professions to engage in moral reasoning carry with them the suggestion that the reasoners might choose whatever moral principles they want, recognizing that they might well be attracted to different and disparate principles. Such invitations allow the possibility of **moral pluralism**: the presence of a number of different, perhaps incompatible, moral principles. The point of such invitations is to get business people and professionals to recognize that there is a moral dimension to the problems they face, and to urge that this dimension not be ignored but dealt with systematically by the various practitioners. The invitation is for people to engage in reflective moral consideration and to confront the notion of "principled action," which requires consideration of principles (to which the whole idea of principled action refers).

moral pluralism *the presence of a number of different, perhaps incompatible, moral principles*

In routine matters, routine ethics can work quite well. In critical situations that are other than routine, however, managers have to fall back on character rather than rules. In this sense, character and the virtues that inform it serve as repositories of moral knowledge and wisdom. It is these—not overarching principles—that lead to individual moral judgments. This might be seen as a feature of the bottom-up approach.

In a similar vein, Jonsen and Toulmin have argued that agreement on ethical issues is more likely to come from the consideration of concrete cases than from a dispute about principles.[12] People might agree about particular matters for different reasons; that people of good faith might differ in their principles need not preclude a workable ethics being shared among them. Argument from cases is more likely to secure this than a battle fought to secure commitment to a philosophical position or overarching principle.

Reflective Equilibrium

A third approach regards neither particular judgments nor general principles as first principles. Both are important, and the interplay between them is what drives moral reasoning. In 1970 John Rawls introduced the phrase "**reflective equilibrium**."[13] As he used it, the phrase refers to beliefs about justice. However, the notion has been discussed as having an important role to play in understanding the nature of moral reasoning and moral theorizing in general. As such, it refers to the state of a person's beliefs when their moral principles and moral judgments are in harmony. Notice that "reflective equilibrium" refers to a result, or end state. A reflective equilibrium is something to be achieved. "Top-down" and "bottom-up" approaches both clearly refer to processes aimed at arriving at a result. It would make sense to say that they, too, would be aiming at a result where principles and judgments are in equilibrium. As it is used, however, the phrase "reflective equilibrium" is also a view about *how* to establish this result—a process—not just the result itself. Roger Ebertz has written,

reflective equilibrium *the state of a person's beliefs, reached by interplay between principles and judgments, when his or her moral principles and moral judgments are in harmony*

> I find it helpful to speak also of "the reflective process" to refer to the activities which lead one to reflective equilibrium. These include carefully considering individual beliefs, comparing them with one another, considering the beliefs of others, drawing out consequences of beliefs, and so forth.[14]

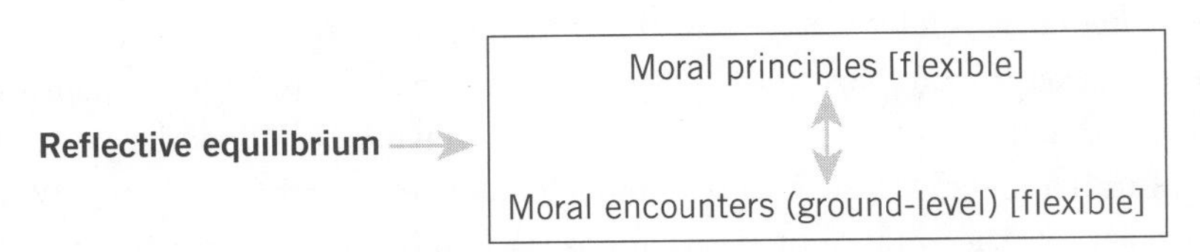

Figure 1.3 Reaching a reflective equilibrium

According to this view, neither particular judgments nor general principles are pre-eminent. Further, this view allows us to skirt the question of whether there are any immutable moral facts or whether there are any objectively true moral propositions. Moral reasoning is a matter of bringing into harmony, or consistency, various particular judgments with one another and with the principles that we hold. In this respect, moral reasoning is seen to be centrally neither top-down nor bottom-up. Rather, it works in both directions, with the goal of reaching an equilibrium among the principles to which one subscribes and the particular judgments that one makes. Moral reasoning is also concerned to achieve consistency among one's particular judgments (relative to each other) and among the various principles to which one subscribes (relative to one another).

Reaching a reflective equilibrium is essentially a dialectical process that involves a give and take of principles and intuitions. Neither the principles nor the intuitions are immutable; reaching a reflective equilibrium involves "massaging" both. It is important to us to have a consistent set of beliefs. Notice, for instance, that when we argue with others, our strongest arguments are in terms of allegations that the other party is failing to be consistent.

(a) Reflective equilibrium between principles and judgments

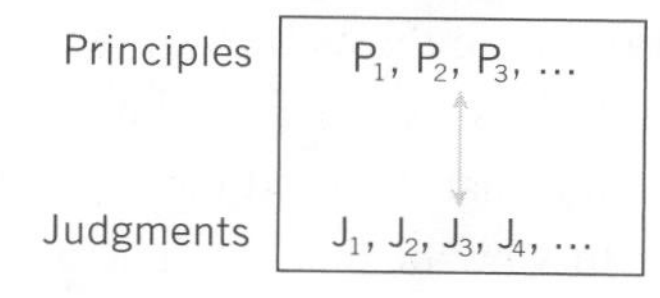

(b) Reflective equilibrium among principles

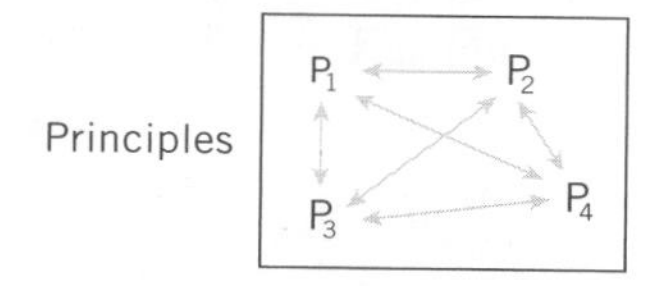

(c) Reflective equilibrium among judgments

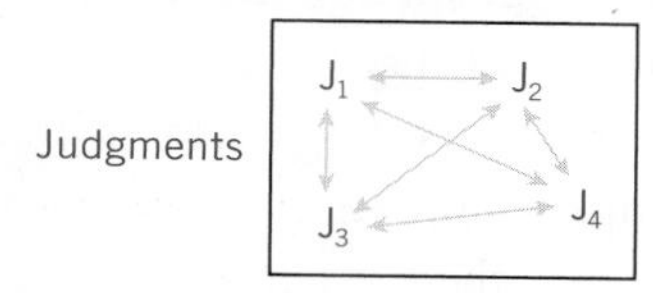

Figure 1.4 Elements in reflective equilibrium

Suppose that, for whatever reason, I am attracted to some moral principle. For example, I think that I should try to maximize utility. Suppose also that I think that in a particular situation I should keep my promise to drive a friend to the airport, even though it appears that I could produce more utility by doing something else. Here, there is an apparent conflict between a principle to which I am attracted and a particular judgment that I feel is correct. I might argue that keeping the promise will maximize utility, or I might argue that my commitment to the utilitarian principle is modified by some other (theoretical) commitments, the result of which is that I am not being inconsistent in believing that I should keep my promise on this occasion. It will be important to me not to be a hypocrite about the situation, however. It will be important to me that my ground-level judgment not conflict with my purported theoretical commitment. It will be important to me to resolve the apparent conflict.

In considering my position on both the practical and theoretical levels, I allow that there can be interplay between the two levels and that my beliefs, commitments, or intuitions about something at either level are subject to review in the light of my beliefs, commitments, or intuitions about something at the other level, as well as in the light of my beliefs about something at the same level. That is, it is important to me to strike a reflective equilibrium between the principles to which I subscribe and the judgments that I make. And it is important to me that my judgments are consistent with each other, and that I can consistently maintain a commitment to the various principles to which I subscribe. If I offer apparently inconsistent judgments on some occasions, it is important to me either to correct this inconsistency (and so alter my judgment or some aspect of my theoretical commitment) or to "distinguish" the situations so that the apparent inconsistency is revealed to be only apparent, not actual. For example, on one occasion, I thought it was permissible for me to break my promise, whereas on another I thought that it was not. When pressed (either by myself or by someone else), I might perceive that on one of the occasions the promise was to a workmate and on the other occasion it was to a business acquaintance and that it would have disastrous consequences for my business if I kept the promise. In view of this, I might try to articulate the principles according to which these individual judgments are not inconsistent with each other, and neither of them is inconsistent with the principles to which I subscribe. The process of moral reasoning allows for modification and revision of the principles to which one subscribes, as well as of the particular judgments that one makes.

Consequentialism

consequentialism *a moral outlook that evaluates actions or behaviours according to the consequences of those outlooks or behaviours*

Consequentialism refers to a moral outlook that evaluates actions or behaviour according to the consequences of that behaviour. According to this outlook, the moral rightness or wrongness of an act is due to its producing some specified type of consequence—for example, happiness, welfare, pleasure, or knowledge. Moral appraisal of a mode of conduct, then, is a matter of judging how well that conduct produces the relevant consequences. The most well-known form of consequentialism is utilitarianism. The effective founder of utilitarianism was Jeremy Bentham (1748–1832), an English thinker and social reformer. His guiding moral principle was that the ethically right thing to do is that act which produces a greater sum of utilities than any other act could. In Bentham's case, that meant producing in one's acts a greater amount of pleasure than pain, because he believed that pleasure and pain were the two driving forces of human action. Of course, a puzzle immediately arises here: if humans are driven by pleasure and pain, then why do they need a moral theory to tell them to act to maximize pleasure and minimize pain? After all, other animals are not in need of such guidance. A simple answer to this question is that, as a moral requirement, utilitarianism prescribes that people look not merely to their own pleasure. They should be concerned to maximize pleasure wherever that can be achieved. As a moral prescription, utilitarianism requires agents to be concerned not merely with the consequences that impact upon them, but also with a wider view of pleasure and pain effected more generally.

It is because humans do not act merely from instinct (and that humans can choose to act one way rather than another) that moral theory has a place at all. Later utilitarians, notably Bentham's protégé, John Stuart Mill (1806–1873), refined Bentham's theory, and many twentieth-century followers have since modified it. As to the requirement that individuals look outside themselves, Mill commented,

> [T]he happiness which forms the utilitarian standard of what is right in conduct is not the agent's own happiness but that of all concerned. As between his own happiness and that of others, utilitarianism requires him to be as strictly impartial as a disinterested and benevolent spectator.[15]

Bentham's simple notions of pleasure and pain have come to be replaced with other measures of utility, such as intrinsic goodness, satisfactions, preferences, desires, and second-order desires. Whatever meaning we might ascribe to "utility," the basic idea is to maximize benefits and to minimize costs.

In Bentham's vision the greatest happiness of the greatest number was a moral and a democratic principle. The happiness of one person ought not to count for more than the happiness of another. This view accords very well with political liberalism and a free market economy: we choose our lawmakers, our consumables, and our pleasures freely. No one is better than another politically, in the market, or morally. There are no intrinsic moral norms except the maximization of pleasure and the minimization of pain.

There are difficulties with using this formula to solve human ethical problems. It seems to put all kinds of pleasure seeking and pain avoidance on the same footing. Bentham was a radical and did not mind challenging conventional ideas about morality and politics, but his view would have destroyed notions of altruism and self-sacrifice, virtues such as courage, and elementary principles of morality such as telling the truth for its own sake. It would also have put minority and individual rights at risk; it allowed the ends of any act to justify the means in an unqualified way; and as John Stuart Mill pointed out, it gave no recognition to human dignity or any spiritual quality in humanity. Mill, while still defining "utility" in terms of pleasure, believed that utilitarianism could accord these important human characteristics their proper due. Mill argued that not all pleasures are on the same footing, that some kinds of pleasure—those requiring intellect—are qualitatively better than others.

It is already clear that there is a great deal of utilitarian thinking in the ways in which business justifies itself ethically. Philosophical discussion, as noted earlier, is present in world affairs. This is not at all surprising. Human goods are always at stake in any moral practice. A theory that did not take account of them would be grossly deficient. Our actions have consequences, and it is part of being morally responsible to include some appraisal of them in our assessment of conduct. If we could not do so, we would be at least partially blind to the morality of our acts. Business and any other practical activities must pay attention to results to remain viable and to remain ethical.

Modern utilitarianism no longer deals in the somewhat crude measures of pleasure and pain or of intrinsic and extrinsic goods. It is more likely to argue that preferences are to be accommodated as fully as possible. This avoids making value judgments about the interests of others as though there were an independent platform for morally appraising the world. If a business meets the preferences of most of those likely to be affected by its actions—the stakeholders—without disproportionately thwarting the preferences of others, then it should have a right to call its actions ethical. After all, every day decisions have to be made in business that are not to the advantage of all. To take care of the interests and preferences of most stakeholders would clearly be the mark of an ethical enterprise for utilitarians.

So much of utilitarian theory seems common sense that it can be difficult to see how rival accounts of morality have a place, but deontological ethics is also a familiar moral outlook.

Nonconsequentialism

nonconsequentialism (or **deontology**) *a moral outlook that evaluates actions or behaviours according to something other than the consequences of those behaviours*

Consequentialism identifies the moral worth of conduct in terms of how well that conduct produces some effect. In this respect, consequentialist reasons are "forward-looking." They look to the future (the expected consequences that would result from the various actions open to an individual to perform) in order to determine what a person ought to do. In contrast to this, a nonconsequentialist moral outlook is either "backward-looking" or "present-looking." **Nonconsequentialism** is often called "deontology," from the Greek etymological root *deon*, meaning "duty." Nonconsequential—**deontological**—reasons look to the past or to the present. According to a deontological outlook, an act's being morally right or wrong is due to something other than its consequences. Perhaps, for example, the rightness of an action depends on that action being a matter of keeping a promise that one made (backward-looking). Perhaps the rightness depends on the fact that the other party is a personal friend of yours (present-looking). Deontological ethics requires people to do the right thing simply because it is the right thing to do—regardless of the consequences. What makes a thing right is something other than its consequences; for the deontologist, consequences can never be an adequate ethical justification for an act. The most famous deontologist was the great German philosopher Immanuel Kant (1724–1804). Arguments for a deontological outlook (albeit a non-Kantian one) have been advanced strongly by defenders of individual rights and liberties.[16] Kant's view was that morality is a matter of doing one's duty, regardless of consequences, and that duty itself is determined not by reference to consequences, but by reference to consistency and the requirements of rationality.[17] Consistency is certainly one of the things expected from moral behaviour. If we do not lie to our friends and family, are we being inconsistent and hence immoral if we lie to strangers? Is "lying" the operative notion here (Kant thought it was), in which case it is clearly a case of being inconsistent, or should some moral weight be given to the fact that on one occasion it is a friend who is the target and on another occasion it is a stranger? If we do not cheat our neighbours, then are we being inconsistent if we cheat people from other cities, states, or nations? Kant claimed a very tight connection between morality and rationality and, in particular, logical consistency. He believed there could be a science of morals just as there is a science of the physical world.

How could this be possible? And if it is possible, how could people disagree about morality in ways they do not disagree about physics or geology? Kant believed he had developed an argument that answered these questions. He believed that a science of morals is possible because humanity has the use of freedom and reason. We can and should choose our own morality—the subjective part of morality—but we have available an independent objective standard against which to measure our subjective choices: the moral law. When we do any act, we act with an intention, and our intention includes a maxim, a general principle. For example, if I intend to give to charity, there is in my intention an implicit maxim that one ought to give to charity. That maxim may be tested against a standard of morality that Kant called the "**categorical imperative**" and that he formulated in a number of ways, the first of which is "Act only according to that maxim by which you can at the same time will that it should become a universal law."[18] This test is a thought experiment that involves generalizing an action: What would it be like if everyone behaved like this? Would it be possible? Would it be desirable? For example, say it was my intention to lie for a good cause. Could I universalize the maxim that it was justified to lie for a good cause? Kant would say no, because my lying involves people believing that I am telling the truth; generalizing my intention to lie would undermine the very institution of telling the truth. In other words, the inconsistency involved is destructive of the moral institution on which lying depends. Suppose I am considering not helping someone who is in need. Could I will that the maxim of not helping become a universal law? Kant says I could not: I can imagine a world in which no one helped anyone else. There is no logical inconsistency involved. But I cannot see it as desirable; I could not will it. For one thing, I cannot but believe that occasionally I will need help myself. And, of course, I will want help on those occasions. A universal law of people not helping each other would be inconsistent with this. Kant produced a second formulation of the categorical imperative, which perhaps is more familiar and certainly very important: "[A]ct so that you treat humanity, whether in your own person or in that of another, always as an end and never as a means only."[19] This is sometimes expressed as respect for persons. This is a meaningful requirement for business relationships as well as for individual interpersonal relationships. In business, it means that management and owners should not see employees simply as human resources on the analogy of natural resources: they are first and foremost people deserving of respect. The same would hold for customers, suppliers, creditors, and others involved in some way with the conduct of business. This should not be seen as pious theory without the experience of real life to bring it back to earth. Kant does not say that we should not use the abilities of others to make profits. He says that in our dealings with others we must never treat them merely as means to our ends. People should not be treated as objects or as mere instruments to be used to achieve our goals. In all dealings with people, they must be treated as persons and accorded respect for their dignity as such.

categorical imperative *an ethical principle developed by Immanuel Kant that requires, without exception, that a person "act only according to the maxim by which you can at the same time will that it should become universal law"*

Kant's theory of duty is not about our following an imposed list of duties (such as might be found in the armed forces), but about our being autonomous and rational agents who make choices for which we are responsible. Kant's theory effectively provides an intellectual justification for the golden rule (treat others as you would wish to be treated). His argument demands universality, consistency, and reversibility. Treat all other people justly without discrimination, just as you would have them treat you. The moral law treats all people equally.

Considering only these two formulations of the categorical imperative,[20] it is clear that Kant has offered an important counter-consideration to consequentialist theories of morality. Moreover, the categorical imperative fits in well with current views about rights and unfair discrimination, such as sexism and racism. The notions of respect for persons and the autonomy of moral agents have played prominent roles in moral reasoning and moral theorizing, and can illuminate an understanding of business conduct without forcing a particular ethical theory on anyone. A requirement of maintaining respect for persons can be expressed in a number of moral theories, albeit with varying degrees of success.

Both consequentialist and deontological ethical theories are relevant to business. It is necessary for business to make a profit in order to survive, but not at any cost. And it is necessary for business to take into account interests and consequences other than profit. There are necessary restrictions on what can be traded—cigarettes, alcohol, drugs, and weapons, for example—and there are necessary occupational health and safety laws governing working conditions. We still call our markets free despite these and other restrictions, such as anti-discrimination legislation, the prohibition of child labour, and taxation. Utilitarian considerations are tempered by respect for persons and their rights. It should be remembered that Adam Smith believed that the pursuit of individual gain could occur only in an environment regulated by ethics and social controls.[21] It is arguable that business requires deontological as well as utilitarian principles if it is to operate as more than a ruthless struggle for wealth. There is a more positive way of putting this: business must respect rights and assume its appropriate duties if it is to meet the expectations of society and enjoy the confidence of its stakeholders. Making a profit is not the only criterion by which business is judged.

What duties does business have? It is easy to spell out a list of specific duties—such as not deceiving, being frank and fair with shareholders, treating colleagues and employees justly—that will save people thinking this question through, but perhaps that is not the most desirable way in which to raise ethical awareness. Even a succinct hierarchy of duties, such as that proposed by William Frankena, will be better than a list of specific duties at revealing why it is important to reason ethically in business. Frankena's hierarchy of duties is this: do no evil, prevent evil, remove evil, and do good.[22] These duties, of course, are general in nature; they apply to everyone. So how are they to be connected, if at all, with the conduct of business? Within business, which of these four general duties apply, and when?

In one way it is easy to answer these questions and in another way it is very difficult. It is easy to see that certain professions, as part of their practice, are obliged to do things that others are not. If a medical practitioner sees someone knocked down on the road, then she or he should render the kind of assistance that passersby cannot give and therefore cannot be obliged to give. If social workers are as sure as possible that a child is at risk in a family, then they might report the matter or take personal action; but if inexperienced or self-righteous people took it into their heads to act on their own views about what is good for children, they might do a great deal of harm. There is in this case not only no duty to intervene, but also a duty not to. In this type of situation it is significantly true that "it is none of their business." In our kind of society, no one demands that an individual should be a certain kind of professional. But if anyone takes on a particular area of professional expertise, then extra social obligations may follow. This is the easy answer, at least in the sense that there are social expectations to be met. Exactly what sort of expectation is attached to any particular profession or professional and whether anything is similarly required of business per se will have to remain as questions here.

The difficulty in applying this kind of reasoning to business is that the roles of business people are not as obviously directed at social goods in the manner of the professions. And yet this view seems to suggest that the creation of wealth, employment, and a taxation base for the provision of social benefits such as education, health, defence, and welfare is not a legitimate social role. This is not the case at all; the problem is that the boundaries of business are not as clearly defined as those of the professions. And, according to classical economic theory, it is by paying attention to the success of its own enterprises that a business furthers the common good. To abandon good business practice in order to satisfy the kinds of obligations that are attached to medicine or social work would, it seems, be self-defeating.

Virtue Ethics

Since the 1970s, there has been a revival of **virtue ethics**, a conception of ethics that dates back to Aristotle. Virtue ethics stresses the kind of moral abilities that put us in a position to act morally, whether after weighty deliberation or quick reaction. This view of ethics focuses on the character of the person performing the action and rejects the idea of dealing with moral problems by applying the correct theory, at least in any mechanical or algorithmic way.[23] Rather, it focuses on a person's response to a moral problem as that of a moral person—that is, one with the requisite character. Moral behaviour is seen in this way rather than as a conscious and conscientious application of moral theory to practical situations. One of the difficulties of the applied theory view of ethics is time. Say there is no time to consider an ethically important question. Is all ethical responsibility removed from people who do not have time to make calculations of a utilitarian kind? Clearly this is not so. This was recognized by John Stuart Mill, who defended utilitarianism from the charge that its calculations were too complex to allow ready responses to moral problems by referring to the many responses that are, or can become, second nature to us.[24] He might have been talking of virtue ethics.

virtue ethics *a moral outlook that bases the rightness of an action on a comparison to the response of a moral person or person with the requisite moral character*

In the discussion of moral reasoning, reference was made to a top-down approach. Perhaps this can be seen as an analogue of the applied theory view. The applied theory view is essentially "outside-in." The theory is imposed from without—for example, from objective rules, duties, rights, and constraints of utility—and applied as appropriate. A virtue ethics view sees the process more as "inside-out." Moral behaviour should be the result of, and flow from, a person's character. This is not to say that moral behaviour is only automatic or spontaneous. It can indeed involve difficult and perplexing thinking and deliberation. But, on a virtue ethics view, a person's character and the kind of person they are is integral to the way that person will perceive ethical situations and the way they will think about ethical matters. Cultivation of an ethical person, then, is very largely a matter of developing the right character.

It is commonly—and importantly—said that in order for a corporate plan, a mission statement, or a code of ethics to work effectively, it must be "owned" by all the members of the organization; it must emanate from within, rather than be imposed from without. And it must be part of the organization's soul, or character, rather than something of an appendage. It is fair to say that the virtue ethics concept of ethics sees the relation of ethical behaviour to an individual in general in this way: ethics is not just a matter of what people do; it is a matter of what people are.

As such, there are a couple of different ways in which we can conceive of virtue ethics. One is a straightforward way in which virtue is of value because it is effective in leading to actions that are morally correct in terms of the consequentialist or deontological theory that one accepts. The other way places value in the virtues themselves in terms other than those of being instrumental in doing what is morally correct on consequentialist or deontological grounds. The first sees virtues as valuable in terms of their being aids towards doing that which, on other grounds, is morally desirable. The second sees virtues as valuable at least partly in terms of their determining what is morally desirable.

It is important to see that it is only in a limited sense that the first conception of virtue ethics is an "alternative" or is in "opposition to" consequentialism and deontology. Consequentialism and deontology are both views about what makes right acts right. For the most part, virtue ethics is a view not about what makes right acts right, but about how to go about achieving whatever it is that gives something moral worth, whether it be the production of consequences of some kind or a deontological feature of the situation. A virtue ethics approach focuses on the qualities of the agent (or the organization) as the target for development because it is the qualities, or character, of the agent or the organization itself that will result in the morally correct behaviour, whether consequential or deontological. Or, simply put, virtues are virtues for some reason, and depending on a person's moral outlook, that reason will be consequential or deontological (or a mixture of them).

The second conception of virtue ethics, which is perhaps more interesting but also more problematic in terms both of theory and of practical application, can be expressed as "Virtue is as virtue does, and virtue does as virtue is." According to this concept of what determines the rightness or wrongness of an action, a particular act will be the right act precisely because it is the act that a virtuous person will perform. It is that which makes it the right act. It is not (simply) that a virtuous person will perform right acts that are right on independent (consequential or deontological) grounds; it is rather that what a virtuous person does determines the rightness of that behaviour. The fact that the act is what a virtuous person would do is what makes it right. Consider this suggestion using the following hypothetical situation:

Virtuous Mary

Mary is a virtuous person; honesty and benevolence are two of her virtues. Her character is such that she acts honestly and benevolently. Suppose that, on a particular occasion, if she tells the truth, some harm will result to the public, and if she is to provide for public welfare, she will have to lie. On this occasion, it is impossible for her to both tell the truth and provide for the public welfare. Not only can she not both provide for the public benefit and tell the truth in this situation, but it is also the case that either truth telling or provision for the public benefit will have to be sacrificed. What should she do? On this account of virtue ethics, the question is whether, given the situation, Mary could lie and still be an honest person, or whether she could avoid providing for the public benefit and still be a benevolent person. It will depend on the particular situation, and very importantly, it will depend on the perception of the situation by Mary herself. Given that her character really is honest and benevolent, it is she who will determine (not simply discover) what is the morally correct thing to do. The question will be whether, in this situation, she can lie and still be honest, or whether she can fail to provide for the public welfare and still be benevolent. This will be a matter not only of how she perceives the situation, but also how she would perceive herself. At least partly, it will be a matter of whether she could fail to provide for the public welfare and still perceive herself as benevolent.

It would be incorrect to describe Mary's situation as one in which either honesty or benevolence must be sacrificed. It is, rather, a situation in which the issue is what honesty and benevolence require. After all, for instance, to tell the truth in a situation where catastrophic effects would result would not exemplify honesty; it would be fanaticism. Such a case is an "exception which proves the rule" (that is what this phrase means).[25] It is not honesty that gives way; rather, lying in this situation is consistent with being an honest person—it is an exception. In this situation, the person is no less honest for failing to tell the truth.

Many problems are resolved using characteristic modes of behaviour, not as conditioned responses but as a kind of shorthand or use of rules of thumb. We see this in everyday tasks all the time. It is true also of morality. Often it is the case that even when we do deliberate over a moral difficulty, we still make our decision not according to a moral algorithm, but according to our character. Further, our character goes a long way towards determining even how we perceive the problem.

Some of these points about virtue ethics may be illustrated through the story of the Roman general Regulus presented in the next box.

Virtue ethics stresses the kind of moral abilities that put us in a position to act morally, whether after weighty deliberation or as a quick reaction. Both kinds of conduct are regarded as meritorious—or not. Both kinds of conduct are behaviour for which we are responsible. Consequentialism and nonconsequentialism are both centrally concerned

The Story of Regulus

Captured by the Carthaginians, Regulus was sent back to Rome under oath to exchange himself for certain noble prisoners of war held there. If he did not succeed, he was to return to Carthage and face death. Once in Rome, Regulus persuaded the Senate that it would not be in the interests of Rome to return these brave young warriors to their commands in exchange for the life of an aging general. So, in the face of his love for family and country, Regulus kept his oath and returned to Carthage to face death by torture. For him, keeping his word was an integral part of the character that made him the person he was. If he had broken his oath because of the commonplace, but for him narrow, conception of self-interest, he could not have lived with his shame.[26] He would have sacrificed an integral part of his character: he would have lost his integrity.

with the question "What should I do?" Different views in each of these camps propose different answers and different principles for deciding the answer to this question in any particular situation. A utilitarian, for instance, would propose utilitarianism as the general principle for deciding what to do, and the questions would be "What specific action in this specific circumstance does utilitarianism require? What action will maximize utility?" Virtue ethics (explained above as the "second conception" of virtue ethics) is not centrally concerned with "What should I do?," but rather with the question "What kind of person should I be?" It is centrally concerned with what virtues there are and with what a virtuous human being is like (what virtues that person will possess). Suppose, among other things, I should be courageous. Questions, then, for applied ethics will be around what is involved in being courageous (as something I might try to emulate and, one hopes, develop in myself), what can lead to my developing the virtue of courage as part of who I am, and what actions might a courageous person perform. Then I try to apply this to particular circumstances.

Relativism

As with our discussion of virtue ethics, where it was important to see that for the most part virtue ethics is addressing a question different from that addressed by consequentialism and deontology as moral outlooks, so it is important to appreciate the location of **relativism** on the moral map. Moral relativism does not stand opposed to any of those moral outlooks. It, too, is suggested (by those who advocate it) as an answer to a different question. As well, relativism is concerned with a matter different from that with which virtue ethics is concerned.

relativism *the view that moral values are relative to particular environments; moral behaviours are dependent on the particular culture, society, or environment in which they take place*

Moral relativism is a view according to which moral values are relative to a particular environment. Particular moral values are not universal and they are not absolute; for example, "When in Rome, do as the Romans do" because in Rome and according to

Romans, who are the correct moral judges for behaviour in Rome, that is the morally correct thing to do. Moral truths are relative. Perhaps this means that moral values differ from culture to culture, from society to society, from one time to another, or, in the extreme, from one person to another. And perhaps it means that any individual ought to behave in the manner seen to be moral within the environment in which he or she is operating (when doing business in Rome, then . . . , and when doing business in Japan, then . . . .) Or, when operating as a private individual, there are certain requirements, and those requirements are different from those that are present when a person operates as an official, an employer, or an employee.

It is important to see that moral relativism does not stand as an alternative to utilitarianism and deontology. Moral relativism is, rather, a view about the domain over which any moral position (for example, utilitarianism) ranges. "In this country, there's a moral duty to tell the truth." This claim does not invoke a position other than deontology; it identifies the domain relative to which a particular duty is present. Relativism stands in opposition to **absolutism**, a view according to which there is only one universally correct moral position.

absolutism *the view that there exists a universally correct moral position*

Relativism need not stand as a barrier to conversation between various perspectives and environments. A commitment to moral relativism should not prevent a person from being converted from one (relativistic) perspective to another (relativistic) perspective, and adopting it. We can allow the possibility of "moral pluralism" (more than one moral view, all of which are equally "correct") while still insisting that there can be fruitful moral discussion, argument, and conversion from one moral view to another.

There is a considerable philosophical literature on moral relativism that we cannot go into here.[27] Nevertheless, it is important to clear up some of the confusion that arises because people quite rightly believe in tolerating cultural difference and imagine that this toleration commits them to a position of indifference on ethical principles. Such confusion is descriptive and normative. The descriptive component is this: there is no reason to assume on the basis of present experience that, say, a universal ethics could not exist. For example, before the British settled in Australia, it was assumed in England that all swans were white. Further experience showed this to be false. The normative fallacy is this: ethics is a prescriptive matter, and to assume on the practice of many cultures that what is practised should be practised is to make a fallacious move from what *is* the case to what *ought* to be the case. The practical effect of this conceptual point may be illustrated by way of women's rights. The fact that women were not given equal career opportunities with men was used to deny them those opportunities; what was the case was used to argue that there should be no change.

However, it does not follow that because there are a variety of moral rules, there are no fundamental principles. From two different perspectives, Marcus Singer and John Finnis have argued that universal principles and goods can generate a variety of rules.[28] Thus a moral pluralism in the cultural sense could be grounded on commonly shared universal principles. The general argument is that although specific rules might differ from culture to culture, they are nevertheless grounded in the same overarching principles. We cannot take up the philosophical argument here, but it is important to signal that the argument is two-sided and that simplistic notions of moral relativism derived from cultural difference should not be used as an evasion of ethical reasoning, which requires justification and the other features noted earlier.

Relativism in business is most often discussed in terms of foreign trade or the conduct of operations in foreign states. Usually the argument comes to this: in country X you cannot do business by our rules. You have to realize that people in country X have different expectations and that the only way to deal satisfactorily with them is to play by their rules. What this kind of justification often amounts to is not respect for a host culture, but excuses for inducements, secret commissions, and bribes. If a person respects the religious and cultural conventions of a country that does not permit the consumption of alcohol, then excuses are not necessary. Genuine respect is almost self-explanatory.[29] But the payment of inducements is anything but self-explanatory; it requires excuses. What if everyone agrees that bribes are necessary to do deals? This was very much the case in the early European settlement of Australia when convicts were unlikely even to unload much-needed food unless they were persuaded with a measure of rum. In the Soviet Union, vodka was a similar kind of currency. Yet in neither case were bribes of alcohol recognized as legitimate. On the contrary, they were signs of a corrupt system generally.

A business is obliged to operate in a manner acceptable to the host country, both legally and morally. To claim the mantle of cultural difference to justify secret commissions is akin to racism. All kinds of demands are made on Canadian businesses in order to secure unjustified benefits. When the Lockheed Martin Corporation offered secret commissions—bribes—to Japanese government officials in order to sell jet airliners to Japan Airlines, who could think that this could be made acceptable by reference to cultural or moral relativism? When questionable pressures are placed on firms operating overseas, these firms must deal with them in the same way that they would handle similar pressures at home. Part, but only part, of what they should ask themselves is whether the person (or firm) applying the pressure believes that there is no moral impropriety in what they are doing. Other central questions they should ask themselves are these: Would the government and public of the host country countenance this kind of pressure? Would our shareholders welcome disclosure of our conduct and approve of us acceding to this pressure? Would we welcome disclosure to the government and public of secret commissions or other favours?

In other words, if you would not be ashamed to declare your actions to the world, you have probably not done anything that stands in need of an excuse. Cultural and moral relativity do not come into it. In fact, the normal hospitality and gift-giving that is part of business need no excuses or appeals to relativism. When the gifts become more substantial—such as trips to Fiji, or computers, or cars—then it is wise for a company to draft policies and procedures that are made known to clients and staff so that there is no room for misunderstanding. Again, this is common sense and does not necessitate reference to, or a special position for, relativism. "Relativism" is not synonymous with "ignore your own moral values." If anything, it is a requirement to recognize the legitimacy of moral views other than the one relative to you. It is not obviously a directive for you to become a moral chameleon.

Testimony to this is the United States Foreign Corrupt Practices Act of 1977. This law makes it illegal for any American citizen or resident to bribe or induce any foreign official or candidate for office to act corruptly to further the business interests of that person. This act was passed into law relatively quickly over the objections of business leaders, who asserted that payments were often extorted by foreign officials rather than offered as bribes and that the government should not intervene to prevent managers obtaining the best returns for their shareholders.[30] In the light of such objections, it is not surprising that Congress passed the Foreign Corrupt Practices Act into law so promptly.

Thinking about "What should I do?"

More often than not (and some would argue that this is the entire domain),[31] ethical considerations function as a constraint on what one may do. They function as a constraint on pursuing one's own interest. For example, suppose that I am thinking about performing some particular act because it will benefit me. I then recognize that doing this act would not be fair to the recipient of the act. Ethical considerations say not to do it. The reason any thoughts about ethics arose at all was, basically, because I asked myself whether or not it would be okay to pursue my interest in this situation. Ethical considerations constrain what I might otherwise do in the name of advancing my interest. Moral philosophers often contrast ethical reasons with prudential reasons. "Prudence" means looking after your own interests well. For most of us, the reason we think we should visit the dentist regularly has nothing to do with ethics, but rather is a matter of looking after our own individual well-being. We are being prudent. There is a "should" here (a prescription), but it is not a moral "should"; it is, rather, a prudential "should." The claim that moral considerations function as a constraint on the pursuit of self-interest, then, is a claim that moral considerations can conflict with prudential ones. It is a claim that in thinking about ethics, regard for interests other than one's own should come into the mix. How and when this is so—and whether there must be a conflict between these—will be a discussion point throughout this book (see, for example, the discussion of "good ethics is good business").

Talking about ethical considerations as a constraint and then talking about our trying to apply consideration of rules, outcomes, and more to our deliberations about ethical decisions and ethical actions points to the central question of what ethical thinking is all about—namely, it is geared to answering the question "What should I do?" Ethical thinking is a species of what is called **practical reasoning**—that is, reasoning for the purpose of action, reasoning for the purpose of doing something. With the discussion of ethical characteristics, or traits, notice that the focus is not on "What should I do?," but rather on "What kind of person should I be?" In this way of seeing the ethical landscape, the practical question becomes "What could I do to develop these characteristics in myself?"

practical reasoning *reasoning for the purpose of action, or for doing something*

These are important distinctions in philosophical discussions and analyses of the whole area of ethical inquiry. But they are also important in thinking about ethics within any organization. People encounter ethical issues, and they have to decide what to do. An organization itself can offer important assistance to people trying to make ethically justifiable decisions, not only by providing instruments (for example, ethical decision-making models) and rules, but also by establishing a culture that encourages ethical behaviour. Its culture can very much affect not only what it as an organization does, but also what its employees do. That is, the kind of organization that an organization is goes a long way towards determining what kinds of action it and its employees perform. There is an important connection between looking at ethics as a matter of "What should I do?" and looking at ethics as a matter of "What kind of person (or organization) should I be?" We will return to this distinction later.

The concern in talking about business ethics is not only to talk *about* business, but also to talk about moral reasoning *within* business. Particularly, with regard to moral reasoning and behaviour within business, it is worth spending some time talking about the point of it all. Systematic, organizational attention can be directed at improving ethical performance and moral judgment. Within business, there are, roughly speaking, four targets. Attention can be focused on each of them in reaching justifiable ethical decisions.

Requisite Considerations for Justifiable Ethical Decision-Making

1. Avoidance of "Moral Negligence"

moral negligence *failure to consider something that one should consider*

Moral negligence amounts to a failure to consider something that one should consider. This may result from a lack of awareness. Consider the model of "legal negligence." Suppose you are doing some construction work, and you manage to create a pothole in the footpath. You do not notice the damage you cause, and so do not do anything to warn pedestrians of its existence. A passerby stumbles in the pothole and suffers an injury. This person could sue you for negligence. You should have been aware of the danger, but you were not; and you should have warned pedestrians of it, but you didn't. As a result, a passerby was injured. You were negligent in not warning pedestrians.

2. Avoidance of "Moral Recklessness"

moral recklessness *failure to give adequate consideration to something; lack of attention due to haste or lack of due concern*

Moral recklessness amounts to a failure to give adequate consideration to something: dealing with it in too hasty a fashion, not paying enough attention, or not particularly caring to get it right. Thinking again of the pothole, imagine that you recognized that you had created this danger and that you thought you could manage it by just posting a general, cover-all-contingencies sign that said something like, "Beware of possible dangers and inconveniences caused by our construction." Again, you can imagine that passersby might stumble in the pothole and suffer an injury. They could sue. Legally, this would still be negligence, but we can appreciate a difference in the two cases. In this case, you did, in fact, realize the danger, but your way of dealing with it was not adequate; it was too cavalier.

3. Avoidance of "Moral Blindness"

Moral blindness amounts to a failure to see that there is an issue at all. A person might be looking in exactly the right place, but simply does not see that there is a moral feature or issue. By way of analogy, consider the pothole once again. Suppose that when you created this, you did, in fact, notice that it was there. But, say, you just figured that it's each person's own responsibility to determine whether or not they get tripped up and possibly injured by it. Here, you were neither negligent nor reckless—you did not fail to realize that it was there as a danger, and you did not fail to take care of it adequately. Rather, you were aware of it, but you just didn't see it as of any concern for you. (Again, as far as the law goes, this is negligence. But, for our discussion, it is helpful to see it as blindness.) As a remedy for this failure, ethical decision-making models like those described in section 4 below do not go very far. See Appendix 1 for specific examples of ethical decision-making models. These models can possibly do something, but they cannot go very far—for two reasons: (1) A person will only ever think of using an ethical decision-making model if they perceive there to be an ethical issue to reason about. If one is blind to the ethical dimension of a problem, then one would not consult an ethical decision-making model at all, and so would get no benefit from it. (2) A person might stare at an ethical consideration all day long, and simply not get it. They are not negligent or reckless in that they did, in fact, focus on the relevant consideration (it did not escape their attention), but when they did think about it, they were absolutely blind in their comprehension or appreciation.[32]

moral blindness *failure to see that a moral issue exists at all*

4. Cultivation and Exhibition of Moral Competence

The cultivation and exhibition of moral competence is difficult. Partly, it is the cure for moral blindness. Partly, it is not a cure for anything. It is the requirement for engaging in moral recognition, reasoning, and decision-making well. It involves developing adequate preparation, sensitivity, awareness, knowledge, and conceptual apparatus to deal with ethical issues. It is precisely in this area where the exercise of judgment is concerned. This means dealing in areas where situations are not black and white and where judgments are better or worse not because they are correct or incorrect, but because their justifications paint more attractive pictures or tell more attractive stories. They are better or worse because they reveal a more understanding and sympathetic appreciation for the situations that they are judging—not because they are truer or more correct. Judgments in these situations, and the explanations that one offers, will show an understanding of the situation and its ethical elements and will involve facility with appropriate moral principles and values. The involvement of principles will not be merely as a recitation of those values and values statements, but will also reveal an understanding of them and a facility in their application. These are the characteristics that are integral to moral competence. Encouraging, cultivating, and maintaining them throughout an organization are at the core of the creation and maintenance of an organizational culture that promotes and supports ethical excellence.

As a step towards addressing the dangers of moral negligence and moral recklessness, a number of organizations have used or developed their own "ethical decision-making

ethical decision-making model
a set of systematically organized trigger questions that take into account the differing perspective that anyone in an organization must be aware of in dealing with ethical issues

models."[33] An **ethical decision-making model** is a set of systematically organized trigger questions, "Have you thought about this? ... Have you thought about that? ... Have you considered these values? ..." These instruments are for the purpose of assisting the decision-maker in navigating through something that they have perceived to be an ethical issue.

Most ethical decision-making models take into account the different perspectives that anyone in an organization must be aware of in dealing with ethical issues. Aside from appreciating the conflicts between concern for ethical rules and concern for ethical outcomes, they typically also recognize that the ethical requirements of the particular organization—and the ethical requirements of being in an organization per se—might not be identical with people's own individual ethical outlooks. There are, in fact, nearly certain to be conflicts in this context. In any such case, people should certainly be aware of the conflicts that are present and must make up their mind accordingly. In facing an ethical issue as an individual, it will sometimes be appreciated that the requirements from within the organization should take precedence over one's own individual view, and sometimes it will be the other way around. In any case, among the points called to attention by an ethical decision-making model should be the possibility of this tension. And the ethical decision-making model should make it clear that whatever decision is ultimately reached, it will be the reasoner as an individual who reaches that decision. It will be the individual's responsibility. It will be their judgment that is at issue. Perhaps the decision will be to defer to the ethical perspective of the organization; perhaps it will be to buck the organization's perspective in favour of that of the individual. Whatever ethical conclusion is reached, it is important to appreciate that it is the reasoner as an individual who must reach it, and that it is the reasoner as an individual who must bear the responsibility for it. This is an important point in recognizing the complexities involved in conflicts between public and private morality.[34]

The categories "moral negligence," "moral recklessness," and "moral blindness" are not technical, and they are not particularly precise. Still, they can be helpful in recognizing and appreciating moral failures—or at least failures to deal with ethical situations or issues satisfactorily. Recognizing inadequacies is most usually a critical step towards rectifying them.

Business

Business could be called the world's oldest profession. Since the beginning of organized society, the buying and selling of goods and services have been important means of encouraging the production and distribution of social necessities. Because of the importance of individual initiative and competition in these processes, those who confer mythical powers on the market may overlook the social purpose of business. As with the mythical heroes of legend, great honour has been bestowed on entrepreneurs and their deeds, and the vocabulary of battle and chase has dramatized the mundane affairs of exchange. Of course, if business were like war, no society would or could tolerate it.

Business exists not because it suits certain individuals, but because it serves society and meets collective and individual needs.

This is not, of course, how business is usually presented. The traditional view is that the true market system is essentially free. Adam Smith's view that individual preferences combine to produce order from self-interest is no doubt comforting to rampant individualists, but implicit in all legitimate business transactions is a **social licence**.[35]

social licence *an intangible permission endowed by a society rooted in its beliefs, customs, traditions, and practices*

Free markets are a matter of choice, and from time to time societies—or, more usually, governments—have chosen to dispense with them and work through command mechanisms. Although command economies might not have been very successful, they retain a strong attraction for many people. Therefore, business in market economies needs to be mindful that it enjoys its position because society believes that the benefits of the system outweigh the costs. This is even more true of modern societies because of the dominant role of corporations and the privileges—such as tax concessions and limited liability—that they enjoy.

Two Hypothetical Cases: Failure to Reveal v. Concealment

Imagine that you are the distributor of a leading brand of desktop computers. You are expecting a big drop in price on your new top-line model in the next quarter, but you have a lot of old stock on hand. As news of the lower price on the more powerful model has not become public, you can continue selling its predecessor without discounting the price. If word were to get out, people would defer their purchases until the more powerful and competitively priced model came on the market, so you warn your staff to be very careful with such sensitive commercial information. One of your staff comes to see you to question this policy. He argues that it is taking advantage of people to deny them access to information that would allow them to make a proper purchasing decision. "What about your moral duty to the community?" he asks. Your sales manager replies that there is a difference between concealing and not revealing. "I am not at the moment revealing to you the theory of relativity, but I am hardly concealing it from you," she tells him. "There is no ethical issue here." Which of them is right?

Take another case. You are selling a house you have come to dislike. When a buyer comes to inspect it, you say nothing about its defects. The buyer makes no inquiries and seems perfectly happy to buy it as it is. Your sister cannot believe that the buyer has not found out about the problems with the house and asks how you can sell a house you know to be defective. "If you did that in your shop, you wouldn't have any customers and the authorities would be after you," she says. "If it's wrong to sell faulty merchandise, why isn't it wrong to sell a faulty house?" Your brother has a different view. "*Caveat emptor*," he says. "Let the buyer beware. No one can expect the vendor to do the buyer's job as well." While you have not disclosed the defects of the house, you have not concealed them. It is the buyer's responsibility to make the appropriate investigations before the purchase. Who is more correct here: your sister or your brother?

One response to the questions raised in the above cases is that silence per se is not concealment. Concealment lies in seeking your profit by keeping from others information in which they have an interest.[36] Unfortunately, such a definition of "concealment" does not help us resolve the issues in these cases. At an auction, buyers conceal the very thing that it is in the interest of other parties to know, namely the figure they are prepared to pay. Similarly, sellers at auction conceal the amount they are prepared to accept. Concealment is a more complex matter than simply calculating who profits from it.

While we have become used to the notion that certain acts are intrinsically wrong, the attempt to catalogue these for easy reference is shown in these cases to be flawed. It is not concealment per se that is wrong, but preventing others from making an informed contract. Quite simply, it is dealing with others on terms that are deliberately set up to disadvantage them. The vice of dishonesty is the thing to discern here, not the relatively simple matter of concealment, which in the case of a surprise party may be a necessary means to the realization of a good. These cases stop one or two steps before fraud and so are particularly interesting. Falling short of open fraud makes them morally debatable, thus revealing that something more than a simple moral algorithm is required to resolve them.

There would seem to be a prima facie case for some social responsibility on the part of business, and it might be assumed that debate would focus on the extent of that responsibility. But this is not how some writers see it. And it is in this disagreement that fundamental problems of business ethics arise. The standard non-interventionist position was once held by Peter Drucker.[37] He put the case with classic simplicity: society sets the ground rules for business, and business has no other duty than to follow those rules in pursuing its interests. It is not for business to usurp the democratic processes of public policy-making by taking decisions on the spurious grounds of social responsibility. Business ethics is a matter of observing the law of the land and acting fairly. It is not a matter of individual managers or boards assuming responsibilities foisted on them by people who believe that business should pick up the tab for schemes of social improvement.

Milton Friedman argued for an even stronger directive: not only does business not have a duty to have an eye towards social responsibility; business has a positive duty not to have an eye in that direction.[38] Friedman argued that the notion of social responsibility in business is objectionable. Managers and directors owe a fiduciary duty to shareholders, not to society or putative stakeholders. We elect legislators to make policy in democracies; for non-elected officials to do so violates the democratic mandate and allows the injection of private decisions, values, and priorities into public life. A legislator has to consider the reactions of many parts of society and seldom has the luxury of indulging personal whims, preferences, or values. By contrast, people of conscience (those who would include social responsibility as part of their job descriptions) have no constituency to answer to: they are defending their personal integrity, which, ironically, is accountable not to society but to themselves as individuals. This may be individually satisfying, but it is not, according to Friedman, socially justifiable. It is not mandated, and it is not democratic. There are, then, two things here: the first is the questionable fairness of placing the burden of social responsibility on individuals; the second is the wisdom of placing it on groups or organizations whose continuing benefits are important to society. In any case, the notion of social responsibility is hardly trouble-free. In a liberal society, the question immediately arises, "Responsible to whom?" While many accept that they belong to a society, this loose sense of belonging is at the very least questionable. Liberal societies are nowadays more legal communities than moral ones, and this makes public accountability in matters of ethics rather tricky.

The work of philosopher Jonathan Dancy suggests an interesting way in which the question of business accountability might be conceived. He distinguishes between values and moral reasons that apply to everyone generally and those that apply specifically to certain persons or to persons in certain situations. He illustrates the distinction in the following way. Imagine that you install a phone in your home that will give different rings for different members of the family. In addition to the usual phone number and ringing tone for the common family number, members each have their own number that gives a distinctive ring when their numbers are dialed. All the rings are audible to all the family, but unless the general number is dialed, only the person whose distinctive tone rings feels called to answer it. Others may answer it, just as they might answer an absent colleague's phone in the office, but there is not the same "obligation" or the same "call" to do so as when a person's own number rings. If someone is able to take a call and a message for another member of the family, well and good, but if that person is busy or resting, they might prefer to let the caller ring back. People do not feel called in quite the same way as when their own ring or the general ring is sounded.[39]

This is how it is in ethics. The fact that personal calls are directed to us does not mean that ethics is subjective. On the contrary, for much of the time others can hear our number ringing and may wonder why we do not answer it. Should we, in business, answer the call when it is the general number that is ringing? Should we, in business, pick up a call for someone else when they are not answering? In the following chapters we identify some of the distinctive moral calls to which business should respond. We can be sure that if business ignores these calls directed specifically to it, then others will decide to answer them to stop the phone ringing. And they might well be hostile to business for having to do so. It would at the very least be prudential, then, for business to heed well the call of ethics.

Moral Pluralism

Recently, a number of writers on ethics and ethical theory have seriously discussed and advocated **moral pluralism**.[40] There are different types of moral pluralism, and different writers have suggested different approaches. The general idea, however, is that no single moral theory or principle should be accepted as preferable to others; rather, different, diverse, and even mutually inconsistent ethical positions should be recognized, and there is not necessarily any single moral principle or set of principles that everyone should accept, either because they are true or because they are preferable in some other respect. Earlier, in Figure 1.1 and in an explanation of different

moral pluralism *the view that there is no single moral theory or principle that should be accepted as preferable to others; different, diverse, and even mutually inconsistent ethical positions should be recognized and considered*

types of moral considerations and different legitimate moral perspectives, we indicated that pluralism of some kind or other is, in fact, the moral stance that most people adopt. Moral pluralism is not the same thing as moral relativism, which, as we have been discussing, claims that moral correctness is relative to time, place, and people. Moral pluralism is not making a claim about relativities.

Good Ethics Is Good Business

Shortly after the publication of the first edition of this text, an article by Geoffrey Barker appeared in the *Australian Financial Review Magazine* that was partly a review of the book and partly an article on business ethics generally.[41] Barker understood the first edition to be largely neglecting the possibility that self-interested motives could, in fact, produce ethical behaviour and that often good ethics can simply be a matter of good business sense.[42] In this respect, Barker was accusing us of unnecessarily taking the moral high ground in the analysis of any moral problem while neglecting that good business sense can often coincide with ethical requirements and that, in many cases, even where the motives would be considerably different, the outcome is the same—namely, ethical business practice. Barker was urging that, in this context, we should not be so critical of self-interested motives. His concern is an important one. There can be no denying that many apparent ethical problems can be viewed as problems of good business management, *sans* ethics. But this is not the case with all ethical problems.

We should consider this a bit further.[43] The phrase "good ethics is good business" has been much discussed. Some have suggested that there is nothing peculiar about the issue of ethics in business, arguing that good business decisions as business decisions will, as a matter of course, be ethical and will certainly not be unethical.[44] That is, some have suggested that there is nothing additional to infuse into good business decisions in order to make them ethical—that a concern to do the ethically right thing need not be a constraint upon business decisions. In this respect, they have suggested, good ethics is good for the bottom line. There is nothing special about good ethics: ethically sound decisions will be sound business decisions; the two coincide.[45] We can call this "the Hobbesian view": the basis and sole concern of ethics are self-interest.[46]

At the other extreme, some have suggested that if all we are talking about is good business management, then we are not talking about ethics at all.[47] This group would suggest that it is not possible for good ethics to be good business. Rather, ethical behaviour functions as a limit or a constraint on, or a correction to, what business may do as business. Ethics and business naturally stand in opposition to each other. Further, decisions made for the sake of sound business management are not, properly speaking, ethical, even when they happen to coincide with ethical requirements. Ethical decisions are, properly speaking, ethical only when they are made in the context of their being in conflict with advantageous business decisions. It is this awareness that, in fact, makes the decision an ethical one. Perhaps we can call this "the Kantian view": to be an ethical decision, it must be made in the awareness of its conflict with self-interest.[48]

It is worth considering further the scope of arguments that good ethics is good business. Much of the discussion of this topic has seen the question too much in terms of polarization: either good ethics is directly and immediately good business or good ethics is not good business. Among other things, this view is too simplistic. Ethical behaviour can be related in a number of ways to furthering self-interest. Possible relationships between ethical behaviour and the bottom line are actually more varied than simply the two extremes of being immediately connected or not being connected at all.

At least for a while, we will ignore the suggestion that ethical decisions can occur only in matters of personal conflict and that ethical decisions must reflect a decision to forgo enhancing the bottom line (Kant's position). Consider the following five possible connections between ethical behaviour and the promotion of a business's self-interest.

1. Straightforward or Simple Coincidence

In some cases, doing the ethical thing (or avoiding the unethical thing) is actually the best course of action with respect to self-interest. There is a straightforward coincidence between ethical behaviour and the enhancement of one's interest; the two go hand in hand. For example, the shareholders will read about your activity in the newspaper, and your company's share prices will rise or fall accordingly. People do not want to do business with perceived immoral operators. Or, as Paul Simons has suggested, ethical decision-making will coincide with decisions that are straightforwardly good business decisions—decisions that are straightforwardly good in enhancing the bottom line.[49] Sometimes the enhancement is not immediate or short-term, but rather produces long-term benefits that are, all things considered, the best for the business. Here, one need not have an eye on ethical requirements for any reason other than their direct relationship to good business sense. It is not difficult to think of examples here. For instance, think about the business value of one's reputation for qualities like honesty, integrity, and conscientiousness. Here, then, are cases of a straightforward coincidence, a clear and direct connection between good ethics and good business.

2. Self-Preservation via Socially Created, Institutional Coincidence

Sometimes, doing the ethical thing will be the best thing to do for the sake of self-interest, but not because the ethical thing straightforwardly coincides with the best business decision. Rather—given the community's or society's interest in avoiding certain kinds of business conduct (or, more exceptionally, in fostering certain kinds of conduct)—if the business itself does not regulate its behaviour accordingly, then either the business or a particular mode of business activity will be made the subject of external regulation or will fall foul of already existing external regulation. Perhaps the simplest and grossest illustration of such conduct derives from a consideration of laws that do not apply exclusively to a particular area of business conduct. Usually it is in a business's self-interest not to engage in fraud—or at least society has tried to enact legislation so that it will be against a business's self-interest to behave in this way. The risks to self-interest and the penalties for so behaving are enough to outweigh the potential benefits of fraud. Therefore, it makes straightforwardly good business sense not to be unethical in this regard.

A business person does not need to have an eye specifically on ethics here; it is enough to have an eye on what is likely to be good (or bad) for business. Business also recognizes that, with respect to some of society's concerns about regulation and ethical behaviour, business itself is presented with two alternatives: either regulate its own conduct in a certain area (that is, make sure that it reaches some standard of ethical acceptability) or have that conduct regulated from without. And usually, from the perspective of self-interest, business finds it more appealing to behave ethically or to impose ethical requirements on itself than to have such requirements imposed from without. It is better for business's bottom line this way. Notice that the coincidence here is not a straightforward one. Rather, society has engineered this coincidence. Aside from considering specific laws, think, for instance, of the position of Canada's Competition Bureau, an independent law enforcement agency whose mandate is to ensure a competitive and innovative marketplace facilitating the prosperity of Canadian businesses and consumers.[50] The Competition Bureau's mandate is to enforce truth in advertising, prevent the abuse of market power, investigate cartels, and engage in fraud prevention. In the United States, the existence of the Federal Sentencing Guidelines takes into account the ethical environment in which a breach is committed. Perhaps society in general, though not business in particular, does have its eye on ethical behaviour per se, and it is because of this that good business sense in this area will produce ethical conduct. Nevertheless, from the perspective of the business person, situations like this require that he or she focus only on self-interest to appreciate that behaving ethically will be beneficial.

3. A Little Effort

In some situations, it can be in a business's self-interest to do the ethical thing, but only if it does more than simply the ethical thing. For example, if the business publicizes having done something with moral merit, it can get some bottom-line mileage out of its action. Chrysler Motors set up a car buyers' bill of rights, articulating the guaranteed quality of its products and the guaranteed performance of the company in certain areas. It also set up a formal consumer protection "tribunal" to ensure that performance (that is, ethically commendable performance) was up to scratch; if it was not, the tribunal was empowered to impose sanctions on the company.[51] By itself, establishing such a tribunal might or might not (and probably would not) have enhanced the company's bottom line. However, Chrysler used this ethical performance as the basis of an advertising campaign explaining why people should do business with them. And this was good for business. It was not the ethical behaviour by itself that accomplished this. It was, rather, the extra effort made by the company in publicizing that behaviour. Here, too, it is not difficult to come up with more examples. In Canada, BC Hydro brands itself as an environmentally responsible energy producer and supplier committed to clean energy. Similarly, Mountain Equipment Co-op is a Canadian outdoor-activity outfitter that promotes responsible enjoyment of the outdoors and publicizes its commitment to environmental causes and support of pro-environmental organizations. The Body Shop, with its promotion of its practice of not selling products that have been tested on animals, is a particularly well-known example.[52]

4. Lateral Thinking or Augmentation

Doing the ethical thing can be augmented (or protected) so that it serves the business's self-interest. However, without this augmentation, it is not clear that this would be so; indeed, it would appear not to be so. For example, a building company that had established a reputation for quoting accurately and completing its jobs on time found that its competitors were understating both time and costs—and winning contracts away from this company. The competitors' quotes were initially lower than this company could honestly offer, but then, within legally acceptable parameters, the construction times and costs of the competitors would increase once the jobs were underway. This, of course, had been anticipated by those competitors. To protect its virtues of honesty and integrity (to protect its ethical behaviour) in this atmosphere, the company decided to offer a bond along with its quotes. It said to its clients, "If we fail to deliver in terms of time and costs, the bond is forfeit. All we ask is that you ask our competitors to do the same."[53] The result was that the company successfully protected its moral behaviour and, with the augmentation of that ethical behaviour, turned its virtues into a benefit for the company's bottom line. This differs from position 3 above in that something extra is required here to prevent the ethical behaviour from actually being detrimental to self-interest. Here, it is a matter of engineering protection for the ethical behaviour (creating a situation in which the ethical behaviour will, in fact, be good for business), not merely publicizing its existence. In position 3, it is the ethical behaviour itself that can be promoted in such a way that it serves self-interest. In this case, however, it is not only a matter of promotion; it is also a matter of augmentation or protection.

5. Good for the Practice

Ethical behaviour might be opposed to self-interest in the short term while nevertheless enhancing the practice of business. The result is that, eventually, generically, it serves self-interest. Ethical behaviour can help to define or redefine what the practice of business (or a particular business) is about—perhaps by redefining the playing field. This can inform the argument that business should be more professional, for instance. This point is of vital importance in discussing the ethical constraints on, and goals of, business,[54] but it should not be confused with an aspect of position 1 above: that ethical behaviour does not produce an enhanced bottom line in the short term, but does enhance the bottom line in the long term (as in, for instance, short-term and long-term investments). The point here is rather more complex and contentious: it involves a change in the practice as well as in perceptions of what the practice is about. Simply put, changing the character of the practice from one thing to another (for example, changing it to a profession) creates an environment in which business can enjoy the benefits of that new status.

One argument for the creation of "the profession of business" is that if the practice of business is redefined, then ethical behaviour must be regarded as benefiting self-interest (at least in certain areas). Ethical behaviour and self-interest will coincide, though not in the simple way suggested in position 1.

Perhaps part of what becomes redefined here is the very notion of "self-interest" as well as the type of person or business practice that we are. Somewhere in this process, options for unethical behaviour can simply disappear. They do not occur to the practitioners of the practice; they are not consistent with what the practice is (or has become). Consider the following analogy. Angela is honest (perhaps to a fault). When put in a position in which some people might lie, she will not even consider whether she wants to lie (or whether it could be in her interest to lie). Rather, given the type of person she is, lying is not one of the options available to her. Telling the truth (or not) is not seen, or appreciated, by Angela as negotiable. In the same way, a practice becoming a different type of practice—with its attendant outlook and potential benefits—can produce a different ethical environment, a difference in character, and greater benefits in terms of self-interest. Just as some people are "more ethical," it can be argued that some types of practice are inherently "more ethical." This point is contentious, and we note it merely for your consideration. Much of what we try to illustrate throughout the book is based on professionalizing business conduct.

6. Not Good at All

This position is the polar opposite of position 1: in this type of case, there is no coincidence whatsoever between good business and good ethics. In such cases, doing the ethical thing is contrary to self-interest, no matter what. Some people have denied that this is a genuine possibility (certainly Hobbes did). It is certainly a view that would not be at all popular among those who advocate that good ethics is good business—and more particularly, among those who advocate that the reason *why* businesses would be ethical is *because* being ethical is good for business. Consider the following simple thought experiments, however.

Simple thought experiments

a. **The Ford Pinto case.** Let us assume that no one would ever have discovered this car's tendency to explode on impact. On this assumption, would it be ethically permissible to allow its production to continue? "No" is the answer. On the same assumption, would it have been a sound business decision—in the sense of enhancing the bottom line—to allow production to continue? Yes, of course.

b. **An Ok Tedi story.** Assume that in the early days, when the water contamination from BHP's Papua New Guinean mine at Ok Tedi was discovered by, and affected, just a few isolated people, it was possible to "resolve" the entire matter by annihilating a few families—no one else would ever know. Considering only the benefits for business, this would have been the course of action to take. A crass cost-benefit analysis would point in this direction. Would it be ethical to do this? No.

c. **Nestlé's baby formula.** When Nestlé sold its baby milk powder to Third World countries, it had the opportunity to get rid of its surplus and make some profit. While exploiting such an opportunity could be good for business, there are other reasons why a company should not behave in this way. Although these reasons might not coincide with self-interest, business should nevertheless pay attention to them. This is exactly the point.

The point in all these cases is that sometimes there need not be coincidence between ethical behaviour and the advancement of self-interest. The further point is that, even so, the right thing for business to do in each case is to take the ethical course of action, forgoing self-interest. Why?—because ethics requires it. That is the nature of ethics.

You might be thinking, in each of these cases, that as a matter of fact someone would find out, and so the business would suffer. (Maybe this could be called "the Aquinas position": even though you should do the ethical thing for ethical reasons, there will nevertheless be a coincidence with self-interest.)[55] But that is a different thought experiment. The thought experiment here involves supposing that people *do not* find out—and supposing they do not, then what? It is not ethically permissible in these cases to cover up or disregard the dangers. The ethically required action is simply not good for business.

It might seem as though these points border on the obvious. It is clear, however, that this kind of thinking has escaped many who believe that good ethics will always naturally coincide with good business—in one way or another—and that the task set in discussions of business ethics is to find the coincidence or ways to make them coincide. Further, this kind of thinking appears either to have escaped or to have been regarded as unacceptable by those who demand that the only convincing reason for behaving ethically is that it is good for business. These are two very separate concerns. As for the first—that ethics and good business must coincide—we have nothing more to say. As for the second—that the only acceptable or convincing reason for behaving ethically is that ethical behaviour also enhances self-interest—we will expand on it further.

If we were identifying the criteria for an ethical opinion (not necessarily a correct ethical opinion), as well as nominating features such as universality, justifiability, and possibly "overridingness," we would probably make reference to impartiality and the necessity of taking a broader perspective than self-interest.[56] For reasons such as this, moral philosophers most commonly think that **ethical egoism** (not to be confused with **psychological egoism**)[57] is an incoherent position: as an ethical position, it is a "non-starter," precisely because it identifies one's self-interest as the reference point for the moral world and the gauge of what is morally right and morally wrong. When it comes to thinking about individuals—and simply getting along in the world—it is generally accepted that doing the morally right thing will sometimes differ from acting in one's own interest. While serious questions are often asked about why one should adopt a moral perspective, rarely would we question the proposition that a moral perspective has a broader basis than self-interest alone. Given this, why should there be so much concern to say that the situation in business is different—that good ethics must enhance the bottom line (that is, that ethical behaviour must advance self-interest)? It would seem that those who have pushed this line so hard have ignored the situation for individuals—perhaps in their hurry to offer an easy, prudentially acceptable, and palatable reason for business to be ethical. For individuals, sometimes doing the morally right thing works in their interest, but not always. The situation for business is no different. Perhaps an insistence on the coincidence of ethics and self-interest is an attempt or demand to make the difficult ethical questions easier to comprehend and resolve than, in

ethical egoism *identifying one's self-interest as the reference point for the moral world and the gauge of what is morally right and morally wrong*

psychological egoism *the stance that people are always motivated by self-interest and selfishness*

fact, they are. The important and difficult question "Why should I be moral?" is no more easily answered for business than it is for individuals.

The search for the ethical-prudential coincidence in business could, in fact, lead to a different conclusion. One might take the view that morality is none of business's business. Perhaps we can call this "the Friedman view," after Milton Friedman's bold claims in the late 1960s and 1970s about the inappropriateness of allowing ethical concerns into the business arena.[58] From this perspective, business is seen as appropriately out of the moral realm altogether; it is a non-moral or an amoral operator in much of what it does and in much of what it should be thinking about and concerning itself with. Notice, however, that this is a significantly different proposition from the one that suggests that the activities of business are within the moral realm and that the carrying out of those activities should, or can be made to, coincide with the business's self-interest. The Friedman view is an important view to take account of, but it is completely different from—and largely irrelevant to—the discussion here, where it is recognized that business can engage in moral or immoral behaviour and it is urged that reasons should be moral. The plot has been lost when this point has been coupled with the expectation or demand that the only important reasons should be those that point to the coincidence of morality and self-interest.

It is perhaps worth comparing the situation regarding business and ethics to the relationship between law and ethics. Here, too, we can usefully look at the individual's relationship with the law in order to draw a parallel with business. In matters of individuals' behaviour, we do not think that the law covers the entire area of ethical concerns—and we do not think that it is appropriate for it to do so. Some things are morally wrong, even though they are not illegal (for example, common cases of lying or promise-breaking or breaches of trust). The fact that these modes of behaviour are not ones in which the law reinforces moral requirements by no means implies that there is therefore no reason to behave ethically in such situations. Indeed, this distinction lies at the very heart of ethical theorizing and discussion. Again, for someone who suggests that business ethics is completely covered by law (or else that there is no reason for behaving ethically), we should seriously ask why the situation for business should be regarded as different from that for individuals. The answer, we think, is that they should not be regarded as different from each other at all.

There is a serious danger present in "good ethics is good business" talk and in conceptualizing the situation so that this is, in fact, an appropriate way to speak about business and ethics and about reasons for business to behave ethically. Consider what the point is in making the claim that good ethics is good business. The point is to offer an answer to the question "Why be ethical?" The answer is "Because it's good for business." This sounds straightforward enough, but thinking of things in this way has a very worrisome implication—namely, that if some bit of ethical behaviour were *not* good for business, then it would be permissible (in whatever important sense that the listener is supposed to be taking account of) to *not* engage in that bit of behaviour. The idea that ethical considerations might counterbalance or act as a constraint on other considerations is simply dismissed. Ethics is considered to be on the same side of the scale as anything (else) that is good for business. There is no counterbalance at all.

The difficulty in seeing the business situation as one in which good ethics is good business is that this way of speaking invites one to place ethical behaviour on a scale—a scale measuring what is good for business. The idea, then, is to see where the heaviest weight lies. And this is precisely the danger. The implication is that if the heavier weight lay on the scale in opposition to ethical behaviour, then it is that non-ethical behaviour that should "win" and so be permissible (in whatever relevant sense), despite the fact of its being unethical. This way of conceptualizing the situation places ethical behaviour as just one of the many considerations to be taken into account, the focus of all of which is directed solely towards how good they would be for business. "Good ethics is good business" implies that the reason for behaving ethically is that such behaviour is good for business and that if it were good (or better) for business for one to behave unethically, then unethical behaviour would be permissible, perhaps even obligatory. The claim that "good ethics is good business" implies that ethical behaviour is of instrumental value only. If that were so, then on any particular occasion when ethical behaviour was not perceived to be instrumental towards the achievement of whatever *is* of value, there would be no rationale for behaving ethically.

A Note on Self-Interest

It is not uncommon for people to refer all conduct, including apparently altruistic acts, to self-interest. In business, this unexamined assumption has widespread popularity and has almost attained the status of a dogma. For the characters in films like *Wall Street* and *Bonfire of the Vanities*, drive and ambition are indistinguishable from greed and selfishness. "Self-interest" has become a shorthand term for both vicious and laudable motives in business, but this does nothing but confuse important issues.

First, self-interest is not identical to selfishness. Selfishness is an undue regard for one's own interests at the expense of regard for the reasonable interests of others. Self-interest may be expressed in observing the dress code at work, in eating a balanced diet, or simply in maintaining personal hygiene. None of these instances could be called selfish. Selfishness is an excessive preoccupation with one's own interests, possessions, and enthusiasms, even to the exclusion of a proper regard for self-interest. Some business people are so selfishly ambitious that they destroy the very thing they value. It was not, for example, in Conrad Black's interest for Hollinger International to collapse. Sometimes selfishness and self-interest coincide, but they are not conceptually identical. On the whole, it is not in a person's interests to behave selfishly or to be perceived as selfish, but some selfish people are heedless of their own best interests. They might, say, have a wealthier lifestyle, but this is not a good commensurable with other goods, such as friendship, respect, trust, and admiration. The absence of these goods cannot be compensated for by money: they are incommensurable. Selfishness is an inability to count another's good as a reason for acting. It is a socially disabling vice. Self-interest is not disabling in this way. It can be excessive, but it also enables us to live our day-to-day lives in a reasonable way. It is not to be devalued. It is, after all, the pursuit of one's own good, and as long as that good does not exclude the good of others, self-interest helps us not only to survive but to prosper and to spread that prosperity to others.[59]

Of course, if self-interest did explain all conduct, this would be something we could never know. This is because it is a view that cannot be falsified: there is no possible set of circumstances that could refute it, so we could never know that it underlies everything we do. In the light of this, claims that people are egoistic in all their acts look very weak, and we must seek a richer moral vocabulary with which to describe our ethical experiences.

Professional Ethics

professional ethics *the application of ethical principles to professional practice*

A person in a business can certainly behave "professionally"—they can be upright, behave with integrity, exhibit a great deal of competence, and be a number of other things. But that is different from being a "professional" in the sense of belonging to a profession. Among the features used to distinguish a profession from a business, these seem central:

- a specialized body of knowledge
- a credentialing body
- attention to the public interest (perhaps the public interest is paramount)
- a focus on the client's interest
- the exercise of judgment
- the presence of a code of ethics (including a requirement not to bring the profession into disrepute)
- regard for the public trust.

We want to focus for a moment on a few of these.

Consider the following two situations and the text that follows them:

Part A: Suppose you regard yourself as an important person and you would like to drive a car that is appropriate to your station. Suppose that you stop by a Ford dealership, explain to the dealer that you're important, and ask for his advice about what car you should be driving, explaining to him that you want the best. The dealer recommends the Taurus SHO with appropriate accessories. So, you buy this car. Not long afterward, while you are driving around, you happen to notice a really elegant-looking Lexus, the LS460, which you believe is unquestionably a classier-looking car than the Taurus you are now driving—it is certainly more expensive. You actually believe that the difference in class is obvious. So, you feel disappointed. Maybe you even feel somewhat angry about your choice. But (and this is the important part) you are not angry at the Ford dealer. You do not think that you have a claim against him because of poor advice. You realize that his position is to survey the entire Ford landscape and offer you the best that is there to satisfy your needs. (Maybe you would feel that you had a claim had he put you in a Focus instead of the Taurus, but not if he put you in a Taurus instead of telling you that you should be visiting the Lexus or the Mercedes dealers down the street.)

Part B: Suppose you went to your doctor about a health difficulty. After examining you and diagnosing your situation, the doctor prescribed a certain medication, and you began taking it. Not long afterward, you happened to learn that there was a better drug available for treating your condition but that the doctor did not prescribe it because he received a commission from the original drug company if he prescribed its products. In this case you would be not only disappointed with your situation, but also angry at the doctor, and you would believe that you have a claim against him.

There is a very important difference between being a member of a profession and working in a business. The professional—but not the business person—has a duty to survey the entire landscape, having the client's interest as the focus. The business person—here, the Ford dealer—has a duty to survey the landscape, but with (appropriate) constraints that are not present for the professional. He is, after all, a *Ford* dealer; *that* is the landscape that he needs to take into account. The difference is the ethical requirement relating to regard for the client's interest, and for some professions, it is also a matter of the ethical requirement of independence. The professional—but not the business person—also has a duty to focus on regard for the broader public interest. Regard for the client's interest and regard for the public interest are at the heart of a professional's consideration of values at play in dealing with ethical issues that may arise. And the presence of these values makes for a considerable difference between professions and businesses. They are, of course, not everything, but they are very significant in distinguishing professions from businesses. It is near universal (maybe completely universal) that the code of ethics for every professional body includes these three values (focuses):

- the client's interest
- the public interest
- the profession's interest: the duty not to engage in conduct that could bring the profession into disrepute.

Among other things, it is clear that these three values themselves can conflict with one another. Some professions have tried to indicate something of a hierarchy for these values, usually, for instance, placing the public interest above the client's interest (in law, for instance, a lawyer's duty to the court overrides the lawyer's duty to the client). Even here, however, there is usually no formulaic means of resolving conflicts. This is a matter of judgment, and to represent it in any other way is usually a distortion.

the public trust *the reliance of the public on the integrity of the public sector or of a given profession or professional*

The public trust is also an important feature of professions. The analogue in the world of business is "reputation." For the public sector and for professions, this is a matter of public trust. Reputation—or sometimes "brand"—is an intangible asset. If reputation is important, which it surely is, then considering only its vulnerability and its dollar value, it is certainly worth protecting and enhancing. It is worth spending time and resources on exactly this. It is fair to translate these facts about reputation into similar comments about the value and vulnerability of the public trust.

Professions are directed to good ends—to the benefit of clients—and ethics is integral to them. Professional ethics is not a special type of ethics but the application of ethical judgment in professional practice. This application can be difficult in business settings, as conflicting demands can arise. For example, lawyers working for corporations remain lawyers with obligations to the legal profession and the courts at the same time as they are working under the instruction of corporate managers. Engineers are expected to abide by their professional codes, but their liberty to do so can be limited by their employer. Doctors commonly work in medical centres run on business lines rather than on the old doctor-patient relationship. In areas where professional practitioners are employed, there is potential for a conflict.

Being a member of a profession does not exempt one from common morality. The requirements of professions add to, rather than replace, ordinary ethical obligations. Although there is debate about what constitutes a profession, one mark of a profession is commitment to some distinguishing values, typically expressed in a code and related documents. Professional practice requires of practitioners:

- adherence to the rules of their profession formally set down by the professional body and compliance with the directions of any regulatory authority established by the profession or the government;
- the exercise of professional skills and expertise on behalf of clients primarily for their benefit; and
- adherence to the principles of ethical conduct that govern professional practice; that is, to the minimal principles of professional ethics (Table 1.1).

Let us look a little further at the professional values that are built on these principles. Typically, professional codes and standards have a strongly deontological tone. They prescribe principles and they proscribe some kinds of conduct. This tone can seem to be impartial and exceptionless and to leave no room for caring. The point about care is that we care *for* someone or care *about* something. We are not detached observers when we care. We become involved with the concerns of people when we care about them.

Table 1.1 The minimal principles of professional ethics

Beneficence	Doing good
Non-malfeasance	Not doing harm
Confidentiality	Respecting the privacy of clients
Avoiding conflicts of interest	Keeping private interests separate from those of clients
Respectability	Behaving in ways that do not bring the profession into public disrepute
Competence	Keeping up with the latest developments in the profession, and carrying out work at an appropriately high level

Care

A famous study of the moral reasoning of women by Carol Gilligan found that they tended not to reason according to the impartial model of ethics and they did not seem as concerned with rules and principles as previous studies had found in men's moral reasoning.[60] They were more concerned with the impact of their moral decisions on relationships than with whether their decisions conformed to a set of rules. They put care above the traditional considerations of moral reasoning. Gilligan does not suggest that her findings apply uniformly to women or that women never consider morality in its traditional forms. Clearly they do, but Gilligan identified care as a missing element in traditional accounts of morality.

Gilligan's study calls our attention to an understated aspect of the traditional ethics we have been discussing. While it would be inappropriate to confuse professional and personal care, it is clear that care belongs to both spheres. A caring professional is likely to be more understanding of, and attentive to, clients' interests and to be a better practitioner.

Confidentiality

Confidentiality is a traditional value for the professions and one of the most important in professional ethics. One reason for this is that confidentiality assures the trust of clients. In order for a practitioner to provide a service, the client must disclose personal information. Confidentiality facilitates this disclosure. No matter what its significance to the practitioner, disclosure should be regarded as private. In effect, the practitioner makes the client an implicit promise to keep information disclosed in their relationship confidential. To break this promise is to act in bad faith and can even be legally actionable as a breach of fiduciary duty.

In our society, privacy is a legally protected but not unqualified right. The right to privacy provides another reason for confidentiality, but privacy and confidentiality are not identical. Privacy is a right of non-interference independent of any agreement made with a practitioner. Confidentiality pertains to the contractual terms upon which information is given and becomes available to others. A separate confidentiality agreement does not usually have to be made between practitioner and client, because the obligation of confidentiality is built into the professional relationship.

Confidentiality is often treated almost as an absolute principle, one that is binding, no matter what the consequences. Journalists often see their sources in this light and are willing to go to jail rather than breach confidences. While this can be a rule for individuals, it makes no sense for it to be a requirement of a profession. Professions serve their clients and the ends of their clients. Confidentiality is the restriction of information in the interests of serving a client professionally, but it is not an unqualified commitment not to disclose information acquired in the course of professional consultations. The principle is elastic enough to allow, for example, consultation with colleagues about a case or to meet the requirements of the law. Nor are all departures from confidentiality breaches. There are many exemptions. Not all breaches of confidentiality are equally serious: simple disclosure of information, for example, might not be as serious as its use for personal gain. For all its importance in professional ethics, confidentiality is not an absolute and exceptionless principle and, as with other principles, its proper exercise requires judgment.

It is important to maintain confidentiality in order to sustain client trust and the confidence of the public generally. All personal information about clients obtained, even inadvertently, in the course of offering professional services is subject to confidentiality. Confidentiality is not the same as secrecy. Secrecy prevents exchange of information except with express consent. It is intended to place holders of information under a strict obligation not to communicate the information to any third party. Confidential information may be shared with relevant colleagues for the benefit of the client, but not with others unless (1) it is required by law, (2) written consent is obtained from the client, and (3) in exceptional circumstances, the public safety and welfare require disclosure. Confidentiality means that client records are to be maintained properly and securely.

Responsibility and Accountability

Accountability imposes costs and constraints on practitioners. Accountability is, in this respect, like insurance: it provides protection for a profession and its members if something goes wrong. It is also a habit of mind that is a useful counterweight to professional autonomy. A practitioner who can account for her or his conduct is in a stronger position if a complaint is made, and a properly accountable profession will sustain public confidence in its services.

Responsibility should not be confused with accountability. Accountability, on a "tick and flick" model can require no more than "signing off" on a project. Formally, one can be accountable without being responsible for a decision. To be responsible is to engage in deliberative decision-making and the exercise of judgment and discretion. This is more than a formal or procedural or rule-bound requirement: responsibility involves initiative, empowerment, and trust. Responsibility should be thought of as a liberating notion. It is about being responsible: "Yes, I did it"; and about taking responsibility: "I'm going to do something about this." Accountability is about restraint: it is a limit on responsibility, but the two work together. Accountability cannot do the job of responsibility. Fully accountable people might end up producing nothing. Nor can responsibility displace accountability without becoming unduly risky.

Professional Judgment

The point of professional principles and standards is to enable good judgment. One should be able to give an account of such judgment, so the question "Could I explain this to my peers?" should be part of one's thinking. That is a sensible approach to accountability. If you cannot account for your behaviour, it is likely to be unjustified. On the other hand, professional judgment needs to be responsible, not only in the sense of making justified decisions, but also in the sense of being willing to engage with an issue—to be proactive in dealing with it.

One of the most widespread ways of thinking about moral obligation is through the notion of role. Is it my *role* to take responsibility for this decision or this person or this situation? And what happens when I have a number of roles that conflict? What should I do, for example, if professional demands require my services at a time when my child is in a school play? Although we might have several roles, we remain one person. Our values will ultimately guide our conduct, not a role that we unquestioningly assume. So, individuals will and should, on occasion, defy a code of conduct in the name of integrity *and* professional judgment; and they will have to answer for it if they go along with professional and organizational directives that violate their personal values. The attitude that takes loyalty to a profession or employer as the final word has been given a felicitous name: *malicious compliance*. This term was coined by Roger Boisjoly, famous for warning that the launch of the fated space shuttle, *Challenger*, posed an unacceptable risk.[61] If professional judgment is to mean anything, it has to be truly independent, but it also has to be properly accountable.

Case Studies and Moral Theory

What is the best way to present materials so that they will help people to think logically about practical matters? At one extreme, this question is answered thus: "Go heavy on the theory." The point here is that to reason well about practical moral matters, we must be well acquainted with moral theory. We might think of moral behaviour as principled behaviour. If this is so, then in order to reason about moral matters, we must be well schooled in moral principles: what they are and their various rationales. We must develop our own moral position. This extreme view would continue: "Once we've come to terms with moral theory, which itself can take years, we've done all the preparation that is necessary for getting out into the world and dealing with practical moral problems. Solid grounding in moral theory is, in fact, what is required for dealing with moral problems at any level." The other extreme advocates working through elaborate case studies as the way to help people reason about practical moral problems. The Harvard Business School's case studies are in this mould. This position argues that we don't need to deal with moral theory at all; what we need are detailed case studies. The idea here is that this is the way the real world comes to us: detailed cases, not packaged in theory. What we need practice in is ways in which to sort through and sort out the details with the aim of reaching a moral decision.

We do not favour either of these methods. Each has serious flaws. Briefly, although theory is very important, we do not think that, by itself, it is sufficient to help readers connect with practical moral matters. We have tried to indicate this in the previous discussion about what is at work in moral reasoning, which we suggested is not simply a matter of top-down reasoning. On the other hand, case studies, by themselves, do not reveal the proper importance of theory. In dealing with particular cases, our consideration should be "informed" by theory. There is another difficulty with elaborate case studies. A detailed case study often presents itself as a complete picture: no loose ends, no missing pieces, and no particular nuances that need further investigation or further interpretation. Very often, however, the moral world does not present itself in this way. There is more left to do, more left to speculate about—many things are unknown. And sometimes the environment in which the decision must be made is one in which such loose ends remain and cannot be tied up before it is incumbent on us to reach a decision. Generally, the moral world we encounter in real life is a good deal less clear and less complete than that of a self-contained case study.

What we present here are short—some are very short—case studies that we invite you to consider, being mindful that discussions should be informed by theory. We do not expect that the introduction to moral theory that we have provided in this chapter is where your thinking about moral theory will begin and end. We certainly do not think that the purpose of encountering moral theory is merely to enable you to label things properly. Similarly, the case studies are not the "be all and end all" of the factual situations that you should consider.

Why Case Studies?

The connections between ethical reasoning and business are best discussed in relation to cases. Case studies exemplify problems and allow for complexity and ambiguity, but above all they have the virtue of being believable. On the one hand, it is easy to dismiss talk in terms of principles as sermonizing or as having only academic interest. On the other hand, empirical surveys of beliefs and values might be useful in diagnosing a problem, but they do not tell us what to do. If we are content with our present ways of doing things, then surveys can confirm our beliefs. But we cannot find out what to do simply from looking at what we have done. Case studies tell us more than what we have done: they illustrate values, reasoning, reactions, decisions, and consequences. They tell us something of the character of a practice. Take, for example, the issue of whether what is legal is ethical. Very often there is a close alignment between the two, but often it is to the advantage of one party to insist on what is legal, to the detriment of what is ethical.

Review Questions

1. Is it clear what the attraction is to the idea that good ethics is good business? Is it also clear what the danger is with this idea?
2. Can you give an example from the field of business or the professions that reveals moral pluralism in approaching an ethical issue?
3. a) Is it clear that the ethical requirements of a profession cannot be rule-bound?
   b) Is it also clear that within this context it can be shown that an ethical requirement was breached?
   c) Can you give an example?

Suggested Readings

Cohen, S. *The Nature of Moral Reasoning: The Framework and Actiities of Ethical Deliberation, Argument, and Decision-Making*. Melbourne: Oxford University Press, 2004.

Friedman, M. "The social responsibility of business is to increase its profits." *New York Times Magazine*, 13 September 1970. Reprinted in T. Donaldson and P. Werhane, eds, *Ethical Issues in Business: A Philosophical Approach*, 2nd edn (Englewood Cliffs, NJ: Prentice Hall, 1983), 239–42.

Hinman, Lawrence, *Ethics: A Pluralistic Approach to Moral Theory*, 5th edn. Boston: Wadsworth Publishing, 2012.

Pojman, Louis P., and James Fiesher. *Ethics: Discovering Right and Wrong*, 6th edn. Belmont: Wadsworth Publishing, 2009.

Wiggins, David. *Ethics: Twelve Lectures on the Philosophy of Morality*. Hammondsworth: Penguin, 2006.

Suggested Websites

The Competition Bureau:
www.competitionbureau.gc.ca/.

Stanford Encyclopedia of Philosophy:
http://plato.stanford.edu/

Ethics Updates (by Lawrence Hinman):
http://ethics.sandiego.edu/

2
Dirty Hands

Chapter Outline

- Public Office and Business: Altogether outside Ethics?
- Different Perspectives: Public and Private Morality
- Public and Private Morality, and Dirty Hands
- Necessity
- Good Ethics Is Good Business—Again
- Review Questions
- Suggested Readings

> [T]here is such a gap between how one lives and how one ought to live that anyone who abandons what is done for what ought to be done learns his ruin rather than his preservation: for a man who wishes to make a vocation of being good at all times will come to ruin among so many who are not good. Hence it is necessary for a prince who wishes to maintain his position to learn how not to be good, and to use this knowledge or not to use it according to necessity.
>
> —Machiavelli, *The Prince*, chap. 15

This quotation illustrates a difficulty in business that may be called the problem of "dirty hands." The term is borrowed from political theory and relates to the ethics of role and the doing of what is necessary, even morally necessary, to fulfill that role. The classic expression of dirty hands can be found in a short, powerful, and even infamous work by Machiavelli, *The Prince*:

> [T]he experience of our times shows those princes to have done great things who have little regard for good faith, and have been able by astuteness to confuse men's brains, and who have ultimately overcome those who have made loyalty their foundation. . . . Therefore a prudent ruler ought not to keep faith when doing so is against his interest.

Moralists have thought this line of reasoning repugnant ever since it was written, nearly 500 years ago. But Machiavelli was articulating an ethics of public, not personal, life. Everyone wants to be ethical or at least to appear to be ethical, but as Machiavelli shows, such an aspiration can be self-indulgent in a bad world. People can be ethical at home in the bosom of their family with those they can trust, but to be ethical in this private sense while at work is to fail to notice the changed environment. Such private fancies can ruin a state for a ruler, or a corporation for a manager, and cost employees their jobs, stockholders their investments, and customers their supplies. In business, as in politics, ethics seems to be an option that is not always available.

This argument found classic expression in an article by Albert Z. Carr[1] that, despite echoing the views of Milton Friedman,[2] caused an unprecedented reaction from readers when it appeared in the *Harvard Business Review*. It remains one of the most cited articles from that journal. For Carr, business is a game-like activity. People do not exactly cheat, but they do not express personal virtues either. They perform as circumstances require and expect that others will do likewise. Hence there is no deception, but rather a shared expectation that all parties will exaggerate or bluff. This is not acceptable behaviour at home, but business is not family life and different rules apply. For example, when a fund-raiser comes knocking on your business's door asking for contributions to a political party you would never vote for, you give because that is the price of doing business. People can lie in business and politics and break promises too because, to quote Carr, "within the accepted rules of the business game, no moral culpability attaches to it." This is not a criticism of business activity. Rather, it is an expression of a difference in the moral hierarchy in business. It is an expression of a difference between public morality and private morality.

Public Office and Business: Altogether outside Ethics?

"Do as you would be done by"—the golden rule of Confucius, Saint Paul, and Kant—is alien to business on this account. To quote Carr again, "A good part of the time the businessman is trying to do unto others as he hopes others will not do unto him." It does not seem to Carr that if these are the accepted rules of the game of business, the golden rule must apply. For if people are prepared to do to other players what they would not like to have done to themselves, it is only a matter of time before they themselves are excluded from the game or other players behave as they do and the game collapses.

Carr clearly sees business practices as akin to Stephen Potter's "gamesmanship": a style of play exemplified by coughing just as a snooker opponent is about to hit the ball, disturbing the concentration of a chess player between moves, or interrupting someone's golf swing. These illustrations of gamesmanship are legitimate for Carr as long as the laws of the game are not broken, and the same applies in business. Why? Carr and Friedman would reply that business is about winning, about making a profit, and therefore any legal means to this end are fair. "The major tests of every move in business, as in all games of strategy, are legality and profit," writes Carr. Altruism belongs in people's private life, and there is no inconsistency between managers who are both tough at work and sensitive and caring at home. For Carr and others like him, business is a zero-sum game, and there can only be one winner. How different that is from the models of American corporate excellence that Peters and Waterman identify as collaborative, attentive, and values-driven.[3]

What Carr misses is that real people conduct business; it is not just a matter of deals but a matter of human relations involving belief in, and pursuit of, human values. People not only cannot leave their private values at home; they should not, or at least they should not leave ethics to their private life only. There is now a large management literature that would contest Carr's position, but we shall cite from just one well-known source: "The productivity proposition is not so esoterically Japanese as it is simply human . . . loyalty, commitment through effective training, personal identification with the company's success and, most simply, the human relationship between the employee and his supervisor."[4] In other words, Carr is very successful at building a model, but that model is not one of successful business. It reflects a narrow view of rationality and the belief that hard numbers trump values.

But is this being unjust to Carr? Have we misrepresented his case? Is he amoral? Have his views been unfairly criticized? Carr has faced a similar response to that accorded Machiavelli's *The Prince*, a work of political theory that has upset many modern interpreters. Machiavelli tried to show that a ruler must be prepared to take actions that we would never accept in non-political life. A ruler must be prepared to have "dirty hands"—dirty in the sense of common morality. Whereas common morality would object to lies, torture, deceit, murder, bribery, and so on, these strategies are necessary to the defence and survival of a state and the ruler's position within it. These are not personal matters in any sense; a prince who acts from personal motive will jeopardize the state. These are acts of political necessity.

Can't the same case be made for business? After all, there are actions necessary in business quite apart from the personal preferences of managers. Is it not sometimes necessary for a manager to write a report on a friend that is damaging to that friend's career prospects? Is not a manager sometimes forced to fire people?

These examples are perhaps not morally as significant as others suggested by John Ladd.[5] Ladd distinguishes personal actions from "social" actions. The former serve personal goals, the latter organizational goals. When managers, judges, or politicians pursue their personal goals in their official capacity, they are doing the wrong thing. They must take responsibility for the consequences of such actions individually. Only actions related to the goals of the organization are social, and only these are "owned" by the organization. Putting personal goals ahead of organizational goals is wrong, even if the personal goal is usually called moral. Private morality is a personal goal, not an organizational or official one, and therefore it is not one to be condoned. In this respect business is like a game, and Ladd is in agreement with Carr.

Games occur in contexts. We do not allow people to punch others in the street. This is assault. But we do permit the sport of boxing, an activity hedged by rules that state what counts as a fair punch and that require other conditions as well, such as medical certificates. So, too, with business, according to Ladd: "Actions that are wrong by ordinary moral standards are not so for organizations; indeed they may often be required."[6] Ladd gives examples of what he understands as secrecy, espionage, and deception, and argues that while a naval officer who grounds his vessel should be court-martialled for defeating the goals of his organization, an officer who bombs a village and kills innocent people should be praised for achieving the goals of the military. So much for war crimes. As Peter Heckman points out,[7] organizations can never do the wrong thing on Ladd's account. Their goals, by definition, fall outside the realm of private moral appraisal. This would mean that conventional, private morality should be abandoned as a guide to action in the public sphere, where it is appropriate to judge by criteria of public morality—hence the necessity for dirty hands in political and organizational life. Business cannot avoid such moral soiling if it is to succeed.

What Carr said could hardly have been new to his critics, so why all the fuss? One reason might be that business people did not like acknowledging the truth about themselves and their occupations. Perhaps they preferred to believe that they behaved in business as they would in private life. Instead of speculating, let us look at some of their replies to Carr. Alan Potter, a senior manager with Ciba, holds that

> it is not at all the case that businessmen do not expect the truth to be spoken. . . . The economic system would collapse without mutual trust on a practically universal scale among business executives.[8]

J. Douglas McConnell of Stanford Research Institute believes that it is impossible to insulate business from broader social judgments. Harry R. Wrage, manager of MEDINET at General Electric, takes the stakeholder position:

> Business is not a closed society, free to operate by special rules as long as all the players understand them. Nor does business want this status. The responsible businessman recognizes a great responsibility to non players in Mr. Carr's "game"—to employees and suppliers, to customers, and to the general public. . . . If we do not all meet all of these responsibilities all of the time, that is understandable, but this is not evidence of the existence of, or a need for, special and looser ethical standards for the business community.[9]

And from Mrs Philip D. Ryan of New Jersey:

> Plainly, the true meaning of a man's work escapes Mr. Carr. A man's work is not a card game; it is the sum of his self-expression, his life's effort, his mark upon the world.[10]

Carr has done a valuable service in bringing to the surface a widespread skepticism about business ethics, but he is in error in supposing that some kind of business necessity excuses dirty hands. Many situations in life are tragic, and because of the risks of business and the frequency of failure there are bound to be a fair number of business tragedies. But that does not mean that people have to invent a separate ethic to explain the tragic decisions that must be made. It is arguable that, depending on the context, different moral requirements have greater or lesser weight. Thomas Nagel, for instance, has argued that the context of holding political office is such that the officeholder acquires moral obligations that are not present in private life.[11] It is thus a moral requirement that these obligations be taken into account in determining the morally correct course of action to be taken in a person's role as a political officeholder. Further, Nagel suggests, having regard for consequences is morally more important in public, political life than in private life, where other moral concerns and other moral virtues carry greater weight. It is not only that there are different considerations and different moral requirements. It is also the case that there is an important difference in the ordering of those requirements.

Using the metaphor of a game in relation to business makes it acceptable to abandon ethics and normal standards of conduct. To claim that business has its own ethics and then fail to show that anything counts as ethics at all in business except results is precisely to exempt business from ethics, not to show that business is special. Look at the professions. What distinguishes them from one another and from other occupations is their values. But these values do not exempt professionals from normal standards of conduct; on the contrary, professions take on extra personal and social obligations—for example, *pro bono* work in law or rendering assistance at accidents for medical practitioners.

In his reply to his critics, Carr seems to retreat a little from his original position.[12] But plainly he is still muddled. Here is one disturbing defence:

> My point is that, given the prevailing ethical standards of business, an executive who accepts those standards and operates accordingly is guilty of nothing worse than conformity; he is merely playing the game according to the rules and the customs of society.[13]

The confusion here is that Carr accepts the prevailing standards of business as normative—as representing a standard not only of how businesses do behave, but of how they should behave. If we are playing tennis or Monopoly, of course we are bound by the current rules, but in the activities of life, this is not so. The game analogy misleads Carr into supposing that business people need to look no further than to established business practice and custom in order to discover what is morally required of them.

We do not want to discount altogether a view of morality that gives some weight to the opinions or feelings of a group as a determinant of moral conduct. As indicated in the discussion of moral reasoning, we do not want to insist that morality must be a matter of discovering a theory and then overlaying that theory onto practical matters of behaviour. Moral reasoning and moral commitment can very much be a matter of relating theory and practical intuition. In this way, having regard for a community's moral commitment to something is not irrelevant to suggestions of a "correct" moral position. The English jurist Lord Patrick Devlin has gone so far as to claim,

> If the reasonable man believes that a practice is immoral and believes also . . . that no right-minded member of his society could think otherwise, then for the purpose of the law it is immoral. This . . . makes immorality a question of fact . . . with no higher authority than any other doctrine of public policy.[14]

This very important question—about what morality is, and what the law should consider it as being—has received much attention. Lord Devlin advocates that (at least as far as the law is concerned) morality is a matter of anthropology or sociology: to be moral is to be felt as moral by the relevant group. This view has attracted a fair bit of criticism. First H.L.A. Hart[15] and then Gerald Dworkin[16] (and many others) offered objections to Lord Devlin's characterization of morality and, in particular, of what it is to recognize a group as having a morality or a moral view. While not endorsing Lord Devlin's view wholeheartedly, neither do we want to dismiss it altogether as inappropriate or inapplicable in the context of morality in business. However, recognition of the legitimacy of a view like Lord Devlin's certainly does not require acceptance of the type of *laissez-faire* view advocated by Carr.

And why would we assume that ethical conduct was not itself a legitimate goal of business? Of course, if we are doing business in morally dubious ways, it becomes difficult after a while to see the fault. And then, as some of Carr's critics suggest, business becomes degraded. In contrast, accounting, law, psychiatry, and many other professions sustain standards and prevent such degradation by striking wayward practitioners off their books. Is business to be the last refuge of scoundrels, where bad or unethical practice can survive as a norm? Given the central place of business in the creation of wealth in our society, one would hope for a more positive view of its aspirations.[17]

That compromise is the rule rather than the exception, and that dirty hands are sometimes unavoidable is no reason to abandon standards of conduct or to pitch them at the lowest level tolerable. Consider first a case offered by Sir Adrian Cadbury, chairman of Cadbury Schweppes.

Sir Adrian Cadbury's Grandfather

Sir Adrian's grandfather was a strong opponent of the Boer War. He was so strongly opposed that he bought the only British newspaper that shared his views so that he could reach a wider audience. But Sir Adrian's grandfather was also opposed to gambling and thus removed all references to horse racing from his paper. The circulation of the paper fell accordingly and defeated the point of buying it in the first place. An ethical choice had to be made: report on horse racing and acquire a large audience for moral arguments against the war or stick to principle, allow no help to gambling, and lose an anti-war voice. Sir Adrian's grandfather decided that opposition to the war was more important than offering some small encouragement to gambling, and the reporting of horse racing was resumed.[18]

The important point to note here is that even though Cadbury made a decision he considered ethical, it was not ethically cost-free. He had to sacrifice a principle, something that is as difficult for a principled person to do as sacrificing material goods is for one devoted to wealth. There was an inescapable ethical price to pay whichever way Cadbury chose. Significantly, he chose to compromise on a strongly held personal belief in favour of promoting an ethical principle of greater urgency and with more far-reaching consequences.

Take another case, this time fictional.

A Move into Tobacco Marketing

Suppose that you are chief executive officer (CEO) of the Healthy Life breakfast cereals company. You rose quickly to this position because your management skills positioned Healthy Life products at the top in a health-conscious market. In fact, you have made Healthy Life just the kind of company that might serve the diversification interests of a corporation trying to protect its future in an increasingly difficult environment. And so it is that Healthy Life is taken over by the R.J. Smudge tobacco empire. In the restructuring, you are offered control of a languishing tobacco products division with the specific mission of increasing market share, as you had done with cereals.

You now face an ethical dilemma. You do not like smoking and believe it to be harmful to the health of tobacco users and passive smokers. You did not resign when Smudge took over Healthy Life because you remained in the cereals division. If you are now moved sideways into tobacco marketing, you face the choice of resigning or marketing "unsafe" products. For some people there would be no problem: they would not market a product in which they did not believe or which they found morally objectionable. They would simply resign.

But is this not walking away from a problem rather than resolving it? After all, somebody will take the job, probably someone who does not have your scruples. If you do not do the morally wrong thing, someone else will. Does this not give you moral permission to do it? Moreover, the product is legal, and it is up to individuals to make the choice of whether to smoke or not. Your primary task would be to increase the wealth of R.J. Smudge and its shareholders, employees, and contractors by maximizing its share of a market comprised of people who have made a choice that is legitimately theirs: to smoke tobacco products. What if an alcoholic beverage company had taken over Healthy Life? Would you have faced the same kind of problem? How paternalistic is a person required to be—that is, how far should a manager let his or her private values impinge on a matter of public policy? Is it not a form of self-indulgence to take a principled stand that ignores the consequences of choices made for others?

The questions raised in the fictional tobacco-marketing case require reconsideration of the nature of the problem, for it is one thing to see it as a matter of public policy that it would be unreasonable to expect a marketing manager to solve, but quite another to see it as an issue of personal morality that invites a person to compromise morally or to behave inconsistently.

Different Perspectives: Public and Private Morality

We have seen that the great sixteenth-century Florentine political thinker Machiavelli held that a ruler ruled well who took account of political necessities and did not flinch from the hard tasks of government because these necessities conflicted with conventional morality. We mentioned that Thomas Nagel has held that the moral requirements are different and the moral hierarchy is different in public and private life. Bernard Williams has argued that in public life (particularly in politics) sometimes the "right" thing to do is something that is not moral and that sometimes this has the result of allowing that there is a "morally disagreeable remainder" even after one has done the right thing.[19]

> The possibility of such a remainder is not peculiar to political action, but there are features of politics which make it especially liable to produce it. It particularly arises in cases where the moral justification of the action is of a consequentialist or maximizing kind, while what has gone to the wall is a right: there is a larger moral cost attached to letting a right be overridden by consequences, than to letting one consequence be overridden by another, since it is part of the point of rights that they cannot just be overridden by consequences. In politics the justifying consideration will characteristically be of the consequentialist kind.[20]

While Nagel argues that moral requirements and the moral hierarchy are different in the private and public arenas, Williams argues that it is not that the hierarchy changes, but rather that in the public arena it is sometimes appropriate that something override the requirements of morality. Either way, this is often called the problem of dirty hands. Dirty hands are inescapable in life. Lawyers avoid questioning their clients too closely about their guilt or they will not be able to defend them. Justice is served by remaining ignorant of the guilt of the accused. Priests hear the confessions of child abusers and know that such people are likely to reoffend. Priests, unlike doctors, nurses, or social workers, will not notify the appropriate authorities. Journalists will expose malpractices in corporations, but will not reveal their sources, although this would allow people to prosecute for recovery of their money. Generals will send soldiers to capture a position knowing that casualties will be high. In the best of cases, dirty hands are simply soiled; in the worst, they are bloodied.

In the fictional case of R.J. Smudge, the manager is in a similar position to a ruler, lawyer, priest, journalist, or general. Like them, the manager must make decisions that he or she might not make in private life. It may be that the manager does not use the company's own products—such as tobacco—at home. But at work a different standard applies because the manager has fiduciary duties to the corporation, to shareholders, and, arguably, to the employees. The sphere of decision-making is circumscribed by the role of the manager in the corporation, by the corporation's articles of association, and by the law. The manager has an obligation to further the interests of the corporation. The problem for the ethical manager, then, is the reconciliation of private values with the duties of role and position. How can this difficulty be resolved?

At about the time that Machiavelli was writing *The Prince*, the English lawyer, diplomat, and intellectual Thomas More was writing an equally famous book called *Utopia*. In the first part of the book the problem of dirty hands is discussed. The main character, Raphael Hythloday, the wise traveller to the isle of Utopia, the best of all known societies, is asked why he does not serve some European rulers and thereby make more widely available the wisdom of the Utopians. His reply is that the rulers of Europe care only for new territories, not for the proper government of those they already have. If a wise counsellor were to advise them against war and to make better laws for their own peoples, he would be useless because rulers brought up on warfare and injustice are hardly likely to listen to a counsellor who advised them against following their inclinations. So the two courses for a virtuous and wise counsellor are either to agree with the evil schemes of kings or else to resign.

To this defeatist line, another important character, Morus, who understands the politics of dirty hands, replies,

> If you cannot pluck up bad ideas by the root, or cure long-standing evils to your heart's content, you must not therefore abandon the commonwealth. Don't give up the ship in a storm because you cannot direct the winds. And don't force strange and untested ideas on people who you know are firmly persuaded the other way. You must strive to influence policy indirectly, urge your case vigorously but tactfully, and thus make as little bad as possible. For it is impossible to make everything good unless all men are good, and that I don't expect to see for a few years yet.[21]

This is a beguiling solution to the problem, but does it hold good for the manager? Earlier, in the context of acceptable limits of non-disclosure, we briefly discussed an issue about concealing the relevant truth and about informed consent. Is Morus's concern similar or analogous to that discussion, or is it simply different? The role of the manager is not quite the same as that of the politician who might have to make a decision to go to war, to raise interest rates, or to cut public spending, or a general who knows that he will lose troops in battle. The reason is simple. The ruler is charged with protecting the interests of the whole community, whereas the manager is committed only to the welfare of the corporation.

There is enough in common between the political leader and the business manager, however, to warrant an analysis of the problems of business ethics through the issue of dirty hands, for both business and politics lay a stress on consequences, on getting a result. (As we have seen, both Thomas Nagel and Bernard Williams have regarded this point as particularly important in the context of political decision-making.) Business and politics are both driven by the imperative of success, and if that is the measure of conduct, it is easy to see why they share the problem of dirty hands. The rationales for action are similar: in the case of the politician, the welfare at stake is that of the state; in the case of business, it is the corporation or enterprise. In both cases, the appeal to a higher cause to justify action does not refer immediately to principle but to a good to be achieved. The good of the state or corporation is assumed to be an adequate justification, whereas self-interest usually is not. Sometimes, however, altruism is cited as a justification for dirty hands. Consider the situation depicted in the classic film *Arsenic and Old Lace*.

Arsenic and Old Lace

The classic comedy *Arsenic and Old Lace* is a good illustration of the point. Two old ladies kill elderly gentlemen to relieve them of their difficulties with aging, and measured by the standard they have assumed to represent good, their actions are not murder but kindness. The telling thing about this comedy is its prescience: it captures many of the moral issues facing modern society, such as euthanasia and the international arms trade. Moreover, it exposes the problem of defining right action solely in terms of some particular desired good. This is shown clearly in the actions of the kindly old killers. Does the problem arise here because they did not produce good? In their terms they did. They got their hands dirty, and they were a little crazy in killing their gentlemen friends; but their intentions were good and they were concerned about the welfare of others.

Raimond Gaita has called the type of altruism represented in *Arsenic and Old Lace* the RSPCA (Royal Society for the Prevention of Cruelty to Animals) view of human good.[22] It adopts a perspective according to which evil may be done that good may come, because its benevolent attitude assumes that the alleviation of misery is the prime object of human existence. If this is so, then what is done to others cannot be anything but good if it does them no physical or psychological harm. Harm is almost a synonym for pain here. The very notion that one is doing evil to produce good is ruled out definitionally. The ends are held to justify the means as long as the latter are in proportion to the former. Good ends make for good means. Consider the following:

A Few Good Men

In the film *A Few Good Men*, two marines at Guantanamo Naval Base in Cuba are charged with the murder of one of their fellow marines. The death of the marine occurred during the enforcement of an informal standard called "Code Red." Code Red is the internal correction of infractions of rules or good discipline—that is, the punishment of offenders by their peers rather than by superior authority. The dead marine was a victim of a Code Red action that went wrong. The man had a condition that was worsened by the attack on him.

Under cross-examination, the commandant of Guantanamo admits that he had ordered the Code Red, and the men are acquitted of murder but convicted of conduct unbecoming a member of the armed services and dishonourably discharged. One marine expresses amazement at this verdict and the punishment. "We did the right thing," he says to his companion. After all, they followed orders. The other marine knows the true gravity of his offence. The role of the marines was to protect the weak, and they had killed a weak man, even though under orders. They had corrupted the organizational aims of the marines. Even within the organization, obedience to commands is only one requirement. And this was a case where that requirement came into conflict with another, resulting in the verdict that the other requirement was such as to overrule this one. As for the commandant, he is arrested. He nonetheless can see nothing wrong in ordering a Code Red, in lying, or in deception and fraud because he sees himself defending lives. His hands must be dirty by the standards of common morality, but he has no time for such niceties. As he puts it, he has breakfast every morning less than 100 metres from the communist enemy. He believes that those who preach common morality do so from the safe cover provided by his protection and that the price of that protection is acknowledgment of a different kind of correct practice, one that involves Code Red disciplines, and loyalty to the unit and the Marine Corps even before God and country. In other words, he exhibits goal perversion.

Yet to regard the moral victory as going to the prosecutors is too simple, whatever the demands of the plot, since the commandant is expressing the values of agent relativity and this is also what is demanded of marines in general. For people in any occupation, the issue of agent relativity comes with the job. Agent neutrality is the position of the prosecutors and the audience, and that is the position that is affirmed. This is too simple, too black and white, too ready to cleanse dirty hands—or rather, too ready to declare that the hands are nothing but dirty, for, from the agent-relative position of the marines, they do have reasons to place the corps and country ahead of God, shocking though this seems from an agent-neutral position.

The problem of dirty hands is essentially one of whether evil may ever be done, not just in exceptional circumstances—which most people are apt to find excusable—but as an inevitable part of human life. Is the problem of dirty hands simply part of the human condition, an existential difficulty that cannot be resolved by any theory of morality because it is not a matter of simply making the right moves, but inescapably the horror of having to decide between two repugnant choices? In recent times it has been used to justify the carpet bombing of cities, nuclear weapons, abortion, genetic engineering, and some very odd business decisions. Of course, in the case of unusual circumstances it is quite common for the act in question to be defended in terms of choice of the lesser evil. The dropping of the atomic bombs on Japan is just such a case. In less dramatic circumstances, the dilemma is presented as almost unresolvable and inevitably tragic whatever decision is made. A poignant and much publicized case is that of a 14-year-old pregnant rape victim in Ireland who, in 1992, wished to travel to England for an abortion. Arguably, whatever choice she made, morally speaking it was not cost-free.

Public and Private Morality, and Dirty Hands

There are two issues to deal with here: one, the distinction between **public morality** and **private morality**; and two, the possibility of dirty hands. In the senses in which we are using these terms, "public morality" does not mean something like "that which you do in public as opposed to that which you do in private," and "private morality" does not mean something like "that which you do in the privacy of your home." Rather, "private morality" refers to morality and moral requirements and considerations present in one's personal affairs, whether or not those affairs are private. "Public morality"—sometimes called "role morality"—refers to morality and moral requirements and considerations present when one has a public persona, role, or position. Questions arise about whether there is a difference between the moral factors at work in these two arenas, and whether a hierarchy of moral requirements might be differently organized between them. For example, in the moral scheme of things in the personal conduct of individuals, the duty to keep one's promises probably occupies a fairly high position within a hierarchy of moral requirements. Some have argued that in the case of public morality, however, and particularly in the case of the political arena, keeping promises is not as high a moral priority as some other requirements that, placed in a private arena, would rank lower. This is not a claim about how politicians act, nor is it a criticism directed at the untrustworthiness of politicians. Rather, it is a suggestion about the correct ordering of priorities and about a difference in the correct moral ordering between the public and the private arenas.

public morality *the morality and moral requirements and considerations present when one has a public persona, role, or position*

private morality *the morality and moral requirements and considerations present in one's personal affairs, whether or not those affairs are private*

Dirty hands amounts to a situation that is something like, but not quite like, "damned if you do, and damned if you don't." It is a situation in which, even if you do the morally right thing, you have also done something that is morally wrong. Morally speaking, it is better that you did what you did, but that does not mean that in doing it you did not also do something immoral at the same time. That is, moral choices do not always amount to win-win situations. Sometimes there is a moral cost to doing the morally right thing. In some instances where moral values come into conflict, the situation is such that opting for one over the other is not only the right thing to do, but also involves no moral sacrifice. Sometimes, however, it seems that even when we do the right thing, there is still a moral cost. This is not quite a situation of "damned if you do, and damned if you don't." It is more like "damned if you do, and more damned

dirty hands *a situation in which, even if someone does the morally right thing, that person has also done something that is morally wrong. The moral wrongness does not evaporate simply in virtue of the rightness of the act.*

if you don't." That is, while the moral cost is not such that it then becomes a matter of indifference which choice you make, it is nevertheless the case that when you do the morally right thing, you are also responsible for something that is morally not good. For people who have seen this as an appropriate characterization of some moral choices, this is referred to as a matter of "dirty hands."[23] A dirty hands situation is one in which doing something that is right (morally good) carries with it something for which you are responsible that is wrong (morally bad), the wrongness of which, itself, does not evaporate simply because of the rightness of your act. Many moral philosophers have either denied that this is actually possible or denied that it is a good way to characterize the situation. On the other hand, many have considered the notion of dirty hands to be an important notion and the characterization to be an important insight into a particularly difficult and gut-wrenching area of moral decision-making. Consider this example:

Impossible Dilemma

Imagine that you are walking through the jungle in surroundings that look just right for a *Mission Impossible* adventure. You come upon a firing squad. The sergeant in charge looks at you, cigar in his mouth, assumes an evil grin, and says to you, "Okay, either I'm going to shoot these 20 people or else you take the gun and kill one of them. You choose."[24] What are you going to choose? What is it that you are thinking about when you are trying to decide what to do? And suppose you choose to shoot one. Will there be nothing of substance to the moral complaints of the parents of that person when they say to you that you murdered their child? Suppose that you decide to refuse to accept the option that would involve you in killing anyone at all. And suppose also that you deny that the blood of the 20 is on your hands. Even in thinking that you have done the morally correct thing, do you think there is anything of substance to a claim that might be advanced against you that you are nevertheless responsible for the occurrence of something morally untoward?

Here is another example:

Dilemma and Emotional Ties

Some children are in danger. You can save either your child or some other child; or you can save your child or two other children; or you can save five other children; or, indeed, you can save your child or all of the people in Toronto? What are you thinking about when you are considering what you should do in these cases? And do you think that even when you have made the correct moral decision, you are nevertheless open to legitimate moral criticism?

Is the following perhaps an example both of the distinction between public and private morality and of dirty hands? Legal ethics requires "legal professional privilege." This is a privilege on the part of a client and an obligation on the part of the lawyer. The lawyer has an obligation not to disclose information learned about clients or from clients for the purpose of giving legal advice or in litigation involving the clients, without the approval of the clients themselves.[25] Suppose a client tells the lawyer that he or she did, in fact, commit a murder. The lawyer cannot disclose this. Suppose a client tells the lawyer that he or she plans to go and rob a bank. It is clear that there is a legal duty not to disclose.[26] It is also clear that there is a professional or "ethical" duty (which in this context amounts basically to the legal duty) inasmuch as it forms part of the code of ethics for lawyers. It is arguable that there is moral duty as well.[27] We might argue that the legal system we use is morally valuable and that it requires that clients can speak absolutely confidentially with their lawyers. Allowing that it is morally permissible for lawyers not to maintain confidentiality with their clients, or even that there are exceptions to this duty, could damage the legal system. Although some moral harm might occasionally result from the maintenance of confidentiality, more moral harm would result from not strictly maintaining it. Therefore it is not up to lawyers to consider each individual case on its merits in order to decide whether, morally speaking, they should maintain confidentiality. Rather, it is that, morally speaking, confidentiality should be maintained without exception.

Suppose that we accept this argument. Let us note the points that bear on the discussion of public and private morality and dirty hands. The profession presents an obligation that is not present in private life. This obligation is present precisely because of a person's professional, or public, persona; and it is something different from that present in the area of private morality, where the maintenance of confidentiality has some moral significance, but is not the strict duty that applies within or for the profession. Perhaps this is a difference between public and private morality. Even if a lawyer has done the morally required thing in maintaining confidentiality, might there not be some moral (immoral) repercussions in allowing the client to perform some undesirable action because confidentiality was maintained? If the answer is yes, then this is to say that the lawyer has dirty hands, even though the lawyer did what should have been done professionally.

If there is a problem of dirty hands, what, theoretically, makes it possible for such a problem to exist? If the rightness of an action were simply judged by the overall happiness or welfare that resulted from that action (that is, if simple utilitarianism were the only moral consideration), there could be no problem of dirty hands. In this approach, if the overall result is a balance of happiness over unhappiness, then the act was right; if the overall result is a balance of unhappiness, then it was wrong. If, in the course of producing a balance of happiness over unhappiness, some unhappiness also results, that is just a feature of the production of the overall balance of happiness: "In order to make an omelette, you have to break eggs." This is one story. Suppose, however, that moral deliberation is not simply a matter of tallying up the consequences and reaching a sum total.

Suppose that the moral features of a situation involve other elements as well—for example, respect for rights, performance of obligations, and doing your duty. It is possible that there are conflicting obligations. It is also possible that rights can come into conflict with duties. In such situations, even if one of them outweighs the other (and it is clear what is required by morality), it might also be the case that the heavier one does not altogether eradicate the lighter one—it simply outweighs it. Perhaps it is thus possible that there remains an element of, say, "moral unpleasantness" because of the failure to satisfy the one obligation. There could remain a "moral complaint" against you, a moral uneasiness felt by you, even though what you did was morally correct. As mentioned earlier, Bernard Williams has argued not only that it is possible that there is a "morally disagreeable remainder," a resulting justifiable moral complaint, but also that it is sometimes appropriate for something (non-moral) to override moral considerations entirely (a point significantly different from that suggested here as creating the environment where dirty hands is possible).[28] It is exactly this that, according to Williams, creates a situation where there is a "morally disagreeable remainder" even when the correct act has been performed. What Williams addresses in the context of politics—the justifiability or desirability of putting political concerns ahead of moral ones—is very similar to a problem that occurs right at the centre of business ethics concerns, namely the justifiability or desirability of putting the business's welfare ahead of transparently moral concerns. For example, you might "know" that you are acting immorally but also that it is legal to do what you are doing. Or you might witness immoral behaviour within your company or, perhaps, the immoral behaviour of your company as a whole. Should you be willing to run the business into the ground in order to quell this behaviour? Is this a situation in which something other than moral concerns becomes paramount? Is it one in which different kinds of moral concerns come into conflict? Is this a problem of dirty hands?

The presence of different kinds of moral values—rights, duties, obligations, consequences—creates an environment in which it is possible that some morally important considerations must be forgone for the sake of others. Possibly the result is not dirty hands (that is, there is no moral remainder), but possibly there is a genuine moral remainder in such an environment. A terrible danger (for the moral theorist, as well as for anyone who comes face to face with moral decision-making) is that there are occasions on which different kinds of moral values are not only different, but also incommensurable—that is, they cannot be compared morally—so that a moral calculation cannot yield a result ("Do this!") in a situation in which two incommensurable values are involved.

You considered the jungle scenario and the other descriptions that might present the impression of a situation of dirty hands. What might make you think that there is a genuine moral remainder in these situations? Perhaps it is that you are unhappy with some of the features of the decision that you regard as the morally correct one. Perhaps you do not feel good about some aspects of the decision. Maybe that is the answer, but possibly it is not the answer at all. Perhaps the feeling of unhappiness (or whatever) is not a matter of recognizing the presence of a moral remainder, a moral complaint that persists even when the morally correct decision has been taken; perhaps it is, rather, a matter of being affected by other dimensions of the situation as well, one effect of which is that you confuse the moral dimensions with other aspects. These may not be situations of dirty hands; perhaps there are no situations of dirty hands. The point here is not to convince you either that dirty hands is a legitimate phenomenon or that it is not. Rather, the point is to call the possibility of dirty hands to your attention, because, as in war, it is used extensively in business to justify conduct that some people find morally objectionable.

Necessity

Sometimes it seems that behaving immorally is inescapable. If a business is to survive, some difficult decisions have to be made. People who do not have to face such basic challenges might view these decisions as unethical. If, say, a firm is operating in an environment where secret commissions are standard, how can it be expected to survive, let alone prosper, without doing the same thing? If a company is faced with cost pressures, how can it avoid firing staff or reducing wages? If a factory has overseas competitors who freely pollute the environment, how can it hope to keep its workforce employed, contribute to national income, and live to fight more cleanly another day if government regulations, levies, and other penalties apply? Perhaps these questions appear easy for the detached and disinterested moralist to answer, but for managers and owners they are not black and white problems.

Good Ethics Is Good Business—Again

As we stated in chapter 1, the slogan "good ethics is good business" has considerable persuasiveness. We would issue a caution, however, about reading it as "ethics is only good when it is good for business." At first sight this is just the kind of incentive that seems to be needed to get business to take ethics seriously. It appeals, or seems to appeal, to the profit motive and therefore is likely to be more convincing to profit-oriented business people than injunctions to do the right thing for its own sake. The public has an interest in ethical behaviour. And shareholders, the public at large, and the government all have a direct interest in the ways that businesses behave. If a business does not behave in what is perceived to be an ethical way, there is a strong likelihood that it will suffer. Share prices will drop, there can be a reaction against the business's products, and government may interfere in or regulate the business's activities. In short, there are strong prudential reasons for businesses to be ethical.

Overcoming the ethical reticence of business in this way, however, solves a practical difficulty at the expense of morality. If ethical conduct is held to produce good profits, then being ethical is a matter of prudence. It might be prudent to be ethical on two grounds: first, the market will ultimately punish unethical behaviour with failure; and second, if unethical practices abound, governments will legislate to protect consumers and to control trading. Both reasons appeal to self-interest. However, self-interest is not an ethical reason for acting. Hence, appearing ethical to enhance the interests of your business is not what ethical business conduct would prescribe. What is done by a corporation might well coincide with ethical practice, and this is not something that those doing business with that corporation would lightly dismiss. But a routine of transactions based merely on self-interest can never produce an ethic.

But more than these considerations is the issue of what end is to be served by ethical conduct. Ethics is not about self-serving; it is about doing the right thing despite the personal costs. So, if good ethics is good business, it cannot be simply in the sense of making sustained profits free of government interference and a tangle of regulations. Ethical considerations and ethical reasons can conflict with consideration of self-interest alone. These can be considerably different kinds of considerations—perhaps not always, but clearly sometimes.

We do not have to take a cynical view of ethics being good for business: ethics is good for everyone, and for too long business has been considered outside the agreed standards of common decency in some sense. This is no doubt due to a common attitude that blames business for many of the ills that beset society—for example, the banks for high interest rates. There is also the idea that markets have nothing to do with morals, that they are free in the sense of requiring no constraints apart from those that participants voluntarily impose on themselves through entering into contracts with others. This seems to set business off from those occupations that have acquired the status of professions.

The professions have core bodies of knowledge, clearly defined practices, and identities that distinguish them. Business is a more generic domain and is more varied in nature. Yet there have always been practices, knowledge, and norms in business that have exercised a shaping, if diffuse, influence. It is these norms and practices that are the object of ethical interest.

The fact that business is not a profession should not suggest that it has no need for ethics. Recall our earlier observation that unless business cleans up its own problems, the regulators will move in. The concern if regulation is increased or tightened is not only the cost and inconvenience this will cause entrepreneurs and managers, but also the potential for damage to the enterprise. Regulators commonly take a purely legal view of affairs, and they tend to be indifferent to matters such as morale, trust, and camaraderie. Regulators must live in a world of rules, formal requirements, and bureaucracy. Hence, business needs to be aware of the ethical dimension of its practices and to understand that mavericks can do immense harm by being morally negligent, reckless, or blind. The Sarbanes-Oxley reforms were a response to the collapse of Enron. When the US government bailed out American International Group (AIG) and other firms in danger of collapse in the 2008–9 global financial crisis, it expected old practices to be discarded. It was, after all, a crisis, a turning point, a departure from previous practices. Instead, AIG continued business as usual. It was not alone, but its decision to pay bonuses to its staff triggered outrage in the media and Congress. Those who received bonuses were pressured by New York Attorney-General Andrew Cuomo to return them voluntarily (but on pain of being named if they did not). Congressmen were not so flexible: the *New York Times* reported that "lawmakers began rushing to impose heavy taxes on bonuses paid to executives of companies receiving federal support. The House on Thursday voted overwhelmingly in favor of a near total tax on such bonuses."[29] This anger was not the most rational expression of ethical concern, but it would be a stupid business person who ignored it.

In 2010, President Barack Obama signed into legislation the Dodd-Frank Wall Street Reform and Consumer Protection Act in response to widespread calls for more stringent regulation subsequent to the financial crisis beginning in 2007 caused by the subprime mortgage crisis. (See accompanying box below for a further description of the subprime crisis.) Dodd-Frank is officially described as "An Act to promote the financial stability of the United States by improving accountability and transparency in the financial system, to end 'too big to fail,' to protect the American taxpayer by ending bailouts, to protect consumers from abusive financial services practices, and for other purposes."[30]

The Dodd-Frank Act delivers the most sweeping reforms to the US financial regulatory environment since the regulatory reform that followed the Great Depression.

The Subprime Mortgage Crisis[31]

The subprime mortgage crisis was the series of events that culminated in the financial crisis beginning in 2007 and the subsequent recessions in North America and Europe. Pooling mortgages, securitizing them, and selling the resulting mortgage-backed securities on the financial markets with the underlying mortgages as security was a way of diversifying the risk of mortgage defaults by spreading that risk among a large number of holders of these mortgage-backed securities. The rise in popularity of mortgage-backed securities created an increasingly robust market for mortgages.

This demand by securities firms for mortgages for the purposes of securitization led to aggressive mortgage lending by banks and mortgage lenders. In order to generate more mortgages, mortgage lenders began to offer mortgages to increasingly higher risk borrowers. Additionally, lenders initiated a subprime teaser interest rate for the first six to twelve months of the life of the mortgage to entice prospective homebuyers. The subprime mortgages were of increasingly lower quality and characterized by a much higher likelihood of default.

These aggressive lending practices increased the demand for mortgages by prospective homeowners and put upward pressure on real estate prices. The rising real estate prices created a false sense of security among borrowers who assumed that their properties would continue to increase in value: if they were forced to sell, they would still have accrued a capital gain on the value of their property, or if the mortgage payments got too onerous, they could always refinance their home based on its increased market value.

The default rate for mortgages in the United States started to increase as the teaser interest rates began to expire and the real mortgage rates took effect, often significantly increasing the borrower's monthly payments. As more and more homeowners defaulted on

continued . . .

their mortgages, the risk profile of the securities backed by these pooled mortgages increased. The risk that had been "diversified" among large numbers of investors had now become a systemic risk that spread throughout the entire financial system. Many of largest US financial institutions, not to mention a large number of international banks, held significant portfolios of mortgage-backed securities. As the increasing occurrence of mortgage defaults threatened the stability of the market for mortgage-backed securities and their associated derivatives, these assets became "toxic" or of such high risk that no one would touch them. This situation was further exacerbated by the extensive use of derivative instruments, such as credit default swaps, whose value was contingent on the underlying mortgage-backed securities. The systemic risk presented by these toxic assets came very close to causing the collapse of the global financial system and would probably have done so without the massive intervention by the United States and other governments to shore up financial institutions by purchasing many of these assets.

This situation also had the effect of driving a significant tightening in the availability of mortgages for prospective homeowners that, combined with the increasing number of houses hitting the real estate market subsequent to their repossession by the mortgage lenders due to default, resulted in a collapse of the housing market. This led to a drop in prices so drastic that up to one-third of all homes in the United States had mortgages greater than their market value, creating further incentive for borrowers to default on their mortgages and walk away from their homes.

The tightening of credit driven by the subprime crisis was the primary contributing factor to the subsequent recession in the United States and Europe.

Many lenders saw themselves as promoting the Clinton administration's aim of home ownership for all working families. Fannie May and Freddie Mac, the largest mortgage lenders in the United States, were originally established following the Great Depression by the US government, with the goal of supporting home ownership. An analysis of the subprime crisis from an ethical point of view, however, provides some sobering insights. While the diversification and spreading of risk is a valid strategy, many in the financial industry saw the pooling of mortgages as a way of growing their business, allowing them to increase their volumes and profits by taking on greater levels of risk. In providing mortgages to people who were clearly ill-equipped to meet their payment obligations, lenders were reaping short-term profits while turning a blind eye to the ramifications of their actions in terms of the risks to the borrowing homeowners and the investors in mortgage-backed securities on whose shoulders the risks would ultimately fall. The willingness of the mortgage lenders and the financial institutions that were pooling and securitizing these mortgages to ignore the systemic risks they were creating in the name of generating short-term profits is an example of just how far-reaching the negative consequences of operating with "dirty hands" can be.

Review Questions

1. Compare these two considerably different views about the position of business.
   a) Albert Carr: People can lie in business and break promises because "within the accepted rules of the business game, no moral culpability attaches to it."[32]
   b) Harry Wrage: Business is not a closed society, free to operate by special rules as long as all the players understand them.[33]

   Are you clear about the difference—and what difference it makes?

2. Consider the following view:

   > A dirty hands situation is one in which doing something that is right (morally good) carries with it something for which you are responsible that is wrong (morally bad), the wrongness of which, itself, does not evaporate simply by virtue of the rightness of your act. It is a situation in which even when you do the right thing, there is a "morally disagreeable remainder."

   Is it clear how this is a different view from the one that would instead offer a characterization in terms of "in order to make an omelette, you have to break eggs"—the view that if you have, in fact, done the right thing and some unpleasant fallout resulted from it or was attendant with it, then that's a shame, but it is nothing for which you should apologize? That is, there is no "morally disagreeable remainder"; there is only an unfortunate feature that accompanies doing the right thing in this case.

3. With reference to the material in chapters 1 and 2:
   a) Is it the case that business requires the kind of ethics that recognizes the realities of the marketplace?
   b) What could it mean (or could it make any sense at all) to say that a different kind of ethics is appropriate to the marketplace?

4. In what ways are the principles of ethics set out in chapters 1 and 2 relevant to business? Is there anything special or different about the way they apply to business? Give two or three examples.

Suggested Readings

Davies, H. *The Financial Crisis: Who Is to Blame?* Cambridge, UK: Polity Press, 2010.

Friedman, M. *Capitalism and Freedom.* Chicago: University of Chicago Press, 1962.

Machiavelli, N. *The Prince*. New York: Bantam Dell, 2003.

Muolo, P., and M. Padilla. *Chain of Blame: How Wall Street Caused the Mortgage and Credit Crisis*. Hoboken, NJ: John Wiley and Sons, 2010.

3
Stakeholders

Chapter Outline

Recent attempts to gain purchase on the problems of business ethics, especially to overcome the bias towards self-interest, have appealed to the notion of stakeholders. The term seems to have been coined in the early 1960s as a kind of pun on "stockholders"[1] and has found its way into common usage both in the business community and beyond it. In Canada, the term **shareholder** is more commonly used than "stockholder." For the purposes of this textbook, the term "shareholder" will be used.

shareholder *any individual, institution, or corporation legally owning shares in a public or private corporation*

stakeholder *the broad constituency served by business. As such, they have a deemed interest in what a firm does in order to earn profits.*

Stakeholder, as it is used in discussions of business ethics, has a meaning different from that which it has in discussions of law, conveyancing, and gambling. If a couple of people are shooting pool, they might want a stakeholder to hold the bet and then pass it along to whoever wins. If someone is buying a house from someone else, the purchaser might want a stakeholder (usually, the real estate agent) to hold the deposit for some period of time, until it is safe to pass it along to the vendor. In these contexts, a stakeholder is a disinterested third party, someone with no vested interest in the activity for which they are holding the stake. In another context, stakeholder means something very different. Often in discussions of topics relating to business ethics, professional ethics, and sometimes simply practical ethics, a stakeholder is someone who does have a vested interest in some activity or some situation, someone who is or will be affected by some outcomes.

The reach of the concept is deliberately broad, but there is a spectrum across which arguments about stakeholders are deployed. A widely held view identifies six groups of stakeholders: owners, employees, customers, suppliers, industry, and the community. This notion of stakeholders identifies those whose opposition to a company's operations or goals could seriously harm it: "Stakeholders do hold the power of life and death over an organization."[2] By contrast, Edward Freeman's definition places more emphasis on interdependence:

> Simply put, a stakeholder is any group or individual who can affect, or is affected by, the achievement of a corporation's purpose. Stakeholders include employees, customers, suppliers, stockholders, banks, environmentalists, government, and other groups who can help or hurt the corporation. The stakeholder concept provides a new way of thinking about strategic management—that is, how a corporation can and should set and implement direction.[3]

Stakeholders are the broad constituency served by business. As such they have a deemed interest in what a firm does in order to earn profits. While shareholders have a prima facie right to consideration in decision-making, it is not sufficient to negate the rights of society to a say in business dealings. As a former American executive put it, "Every citizen is a stakeholder in business whether he or she holds a share of stock or not, is employed in business or not, or buys the products and services of business or not. Just to live in American society today makes everyone a stakeholder in business."[4] In a word, the move towards a stakeholder approach is most frequently a bid for social responsibility in business.

When an individual or a group engages in some practice, the interests of the stakeholders should be taken into account. However, it is a topic of some debate whether or not all types of stakeholders should be taken into account. For example, religious zealots may well have a vested interest in some activity that a business is considering undertaking, but it is problematic whether that business should, morally speaking, take account of those interests in reaching a decision. In one view, although anyone with a serious interest is (by definition) a stakeholder, not all of their interests must be taken into account and not all of their moral standing warrants consideration by someone proposing to engage in an undertaking. In some contexts it would be important to distinguish genuine stakeholders from people whose interest is officious and to distinguish genuine stakeholders from those who might have a genuine interest but who are not affected sufficiently to give them the status of stakeholder. In some cases, for example, merely being offended by the presence of some practice or merely having a genuine concern for the well-being of others does not, by itself, render one a stakeholder in relation to the practice. An analogue here would be that of "standing," or "standing to sue," in court where only those who have standing can bring a claim against another party. In the present context this will not be particularly important. The more important point here has to do simply with taking genuine stakeholders' interests into account, regardless of how the notion of stakeholder itself is characterized or restricted.

What is it, then, to take account of the interests of stakeholders? The simple answer is that it is to calculate the impact of an action or a practice on stakeholders and to figure into the overall calculation the effect of the practice or action on them. Usually this is seen as a matter of calculating the utility or disutility of a proposed practice for the stakeholders, recognizing that various stakeholders (groups of stakeholders) have different stakes in the possible outcomes of some activity. Kenneth Goodpaster has made the important point that merely identifying a group as stakeholders in some activity does not, by itself, point towards a correct or appropriate ethical analysis of the activity.[5] It may be a significant prerequisite to moral reasoning, but it is not more than this. A stakeholder analysis by itself is not "strategic." Given the looseness of the notion of stakeholder, identifying some person or group as a stakeholder does not, by itself, say anything at all about how they should be treated. The phrase "stakeholder analysis" has had some currency in the literature. While it is an important notion, there is also a danger that, as a phrase, "stakeholder analysis" might simply become synonymous with "social responsibility" while presenting a misleading impression that there is some methodological substance to it as a particular type of analysis or that identification of the stakeholders itself implies something about taking others' interests into account and how to do this. This is a danger. Nevertheless, "stakeholder" is an important notion, and the injection of a consent consideration into a stakeholder analysis amounts to recognition of a very important element in moral reasoning.

Reaching a decision about whether a possible practice would be advantageous or disadvantageous to a particular group need not involve actual consultation with that group. Sometimes the options available and the choices to be made are such that it is not presumptuous for someone other than the stakeholders to decide what is in the stakeholders' interest. If a certain activity would endanger the health of a group of stakeholders and offer no prospects of advantage to them or to anyone else, it would not be presumptuous to calculate accordingly, without consulting with the stakeholders themselves. In such a case we probably would not consider that the decision not to endanger their health was being paternalistic. It would simply be deciding not to engage in an activity because of its possible harmful effects on some group—effects that are not offset by anything else.

In some cases, however, decisions about whether to engage in an activity might be based on trying to take account of the group's welfare in the context of competing claims about that welfare or at least in the context of advantages and disadvantages associated with the activity (for example, fluoridation of a community's water supply or stringing power lines over the homes of some of its members). Here, to decide to act one way or another because of the benefit to the group could well be to engage in a paternalistic decision: "We'll do this, because it'll be for their good," or "We'll allow this risk, because the likely benefits are such as to make it a risk worth taking," or "We'll do this because the disadvantages or losses are outweighed by the benefits that will accrue." In such cases, someone decides the matter for those who will be affected by the activity. This differs from the earlier case (where there was nothing but disadvantage) in that there was, in effect, nothing to decide in that case—given that the proposed activity had no benefits to offset its likely disadvantages. And it also differs from a case in which it is decided that the possible disadvantage to one group is outweighed by the possible advantage to another and where the original calculation was to sacrifice the disadvantaged group's welfare for something else.[6]

As an alternative to paternalistic decision-making by whoever has the power or the authority (governmental body, professional organization, business entity, or individual), it is important to keep in mind the possibility of taking account of the wishes or decision of the potentially affected group itself. It is important to recognize that stakeholders are not only to be taken account of but, when appropriate, to be given a voice. Sometimes this is so (or should be so) because the stakeholders can give a worthwhile opinion about the cost or benefit of the proposed activity. Sometimes there might be a real question of what that group would consent to. Given that there are some disadvantages or some risks associated with a possible gain for the group concerned, there might be a real question of whether incurring those disadvantages or risks is worth the possibility of that gain—whether it is worth this to them. And here it should be recognized that it is not always the case (perhaps it is hardly ever the case) that only one decision is the rational (or even the reasonable) one. That being so, there is something to be decided, some choice to be made, on grounds other than simply, say, the dictates of rationality. Here, very importantly, is an occasion for taking account of the interests of stakeholders. And it is an occasion where being informed of the actual view or opinion of the stakeholders themselves is important in order to properly take account of their interests.

The Problem with the Notion of Stakeholder

As already indicated, the notion of stakeholder is not trouble-free. Unreflective use of the notion can be dangerous. It can lead you to believe that you have moral responsibilities to any number of "interested" parties when, in fact, you have no particular obligation to them simply because they have taken an interest in your activities. An interest is not necessarily a stake. Even people who are affected by your activities do not necessarily have a stake in them. It is salutary to be mindful of Milton Friedman's view—mentioned briefly in chapter 1. It is probably not an overstatement to say that the entire literature on stakeholders has been a reaction to Friedman's view about the appropriate responsibility of business. His view—developed mainly in the 1960s and popularized mainly in the 1970s—is that the only appropriate interest of a business is its shareholders.[7] Aside from what is required by the law, a business has no business at all taking anyone else's interests into account. A company not only *need not* but *should not* have an interest in benefiting anyone else at all. To engage in so-called socially responsible behaviour or to have an eye on the interests of any erstwhile stakeholders is, in effect, to steal from the shareholders, who are the only ones with a rightful claim on the company's concern and its profits. We will not go further with arguments specifically for and against Friedman's view. We simply want to call attention to that view as a counterbalance to the extreme view that because someone or some organization could benefit from the attention of a business, therefore the business should direct its concerns towards producing that benefit.

The term "stakeholder" is useful, but you should be careful that you do not find yourself overcommitted simply by having used that word. On the whole, the literature takes the notion of stakeholder as a given. Yet a stakeholder's character is very much that of an asserted rather than a demonstrated proposition. Indeed, in much of the literature the use of the term is question begging: the social responsibilities of business are the thing to be proved, and talk of stakeholders as analogous with shareholders does not offer such proof. On the contrary, given that business starts from the premise that unfettered trade is a social good, the imposition of obligations beyond those of trade might be thought to stand in need of considerable justification.

Even this simple criticism exposes much that is wrong with using "stakeholder" to formulate a more inclusive definition of the responsibilities of business. As the quotations from Freeman and Leibig show, a concept that is over-inclusive is virtually useless. Why not just refer to all citizens rather than to stakeholders at all? Nor does the notion of stakeholder of itself present a clear ethical claim for consideration among many. Take the building of a paper pulp mill at a time of recession and unemployment. To some people advocating a stakeholder position, the interests of stakeholders mean the interests of environmentalists. To others they are the interests of the unemployed, of the community in which the mill will be located, and of the nation through exports. All are right, and this means that the notion of stakeholders does not do more than shift the argument to the question of who are the "real" stakeholders, or to the utilitarian question of which of the stakeholders is greatest, can generate the most good, and so on. In other words, a broad notion of stakeholder adds nothing to the discussion of business ethics.

"Stakeholder" is used to connote an interest in business, usually in a particular business. The problem with this is that while society's interest in business as a whole is intelligible and can even be the source of ethical principles, it is difficult to extrapolate from this general social interest to specific interests in particular businesses. Identifying the moral claims of stakeholders in IBM or BCE is potentially a confusing, unproductive, and inefficient means of judging the merits of claims.

So while the term "stakeholder" is a striking contrast to "shareholder," it is most peculiar conceptually. For if the term means something different from simply anyone with an interest, then how does one acquire a stake? It is clearly quite like a property holding without explicitly being one: it trades on its similarity to and difference from shareholder. In the sense that stakeholding implies a moral footing with serious claims against property holders, how is such a holding to be justified?

Robert Nozick is quite clear about this. People acquire a holding not through being affected by an activity but by a proper consensual procedure—that is, not by accident.[8] Even in those cases where business is transacted between parties, this must of necessity be limited to the agreed matters if business is to be done at all. For if every dealing were potentially open-ended, there could be no clarity about responsibility, liability, and other matters pertaining to fairness and justice. Even in consensual matters there is a limit on the deemed involvement of parties to the matters covenanted.

In a very general sort of way, creditors, employees, suppliers, customers, banks, and local, state, and central governments have an interest in businesses. They stand to gain from their success. They might even stand to lose from their failure, but such losses are properly described as proximate rather than direct, for shareholders invest in a corporation as a risk, while those trading or dealing with it do so as part of more general activity; no single deal is all or nothing, although unpaid bills are an unfair burden on any business activity. In other words, shareholders have made a commitment—even risking the whole of their investment—but those who benefit indirectly, like small retailers in a mall whose major tenant is a crowd-pulling retailer, have not put anything directly into the business. Nor have governments, creditors, or banks. Stakeholder claims seem, then, to be asymmetrical: they apply only when self-interest is at stake, not when some sacrifice is required. Clearly, whatever is owed to the associates of a business must be covered by agreements as well as ethical responsibilities; it is not adequately covered by a notional obligation to them as stakeholders.

Can the same point hold true for employees? This is connected with the very old question of the rights of employees. A view that held that employees were no different from others associated with a corporation would see the sale of labour as no different from the sale of raw materials or services or credit facilities, and would give the employees of a firm in difficulty no priority over the employees of creditors who might also be adversely affected by a corporate collapse. That is, the addition of the term "stakeholder" to the term "employee" confers no special rights. Employees are entitled to risk their capital in their place of employment by buying its shares, but a corporation's liabilities extend no further than the legal requirements of the land and the contracts it has freely entered into. Nor should employees be especially privileged, for this must be at the expense of other interested parties, principally shareholders.

The case of employees, however, provides a good illustration of what is wrong with a stakeholder view of business: if one party is to benefit, it will often be at the expense of the others. The stakeholder theory does not by itself rank or give different interests their due. It is a misconception of stakeholder theory that it completes the moral analysis of a situation. This disturbs the long-established view that rewards are tied to contributions. Such a conception seems to give a spuriously democratic, egalitarian hue to the world of business, but only at the expense of the rights of all parties.

All this can be obscured by talk of stakeholders. Shareholders who do not know the extent of liability of the firm they are investing in are not in a position to assess the risk of their investment. On one interpretation, the notion of stakeholder makes business potentially liable to claims against it in an open-ended way and thereby asks people to risk their capital with even less assurance of a return than the usual vicissitudes of market and nature provide. The notion might allow that any officious interest, anyone affected in any way by an activity, is therefore a stakeholder in the activities of that organization. In short, the notion of stakeholder might be superfluous or dangerous. The reasonable aspects of stakeholder analysis are generally covered by other requirements anyway. The notion of stakeholder adds nothing positive, and it provides a blind for an ambush on a company and the assets of its investors. It is odd that in intention the concept is aimed at a fair voice for all players in the market, but it can end up by unfairly disadvantaging those whose capital is essential to any business success by not transparently favouring shareholders over other stakeholders.

This view cuts across the territory of some critics of business, such as welfare theorists. Their concern for equity makes them sensitive to the misuse of public funds, a concern that might lead them to be natural allies of business were it not for competing agendas in other areas. The welfare theorist most commonly associated with the criticism of public support of business is Richard Titmuss. Titmuss argues that opposition to welfare is blinkered by ideological views that regard payments to the needy as a drain on the public purse and ignore the often hidden benefits bestowed on the better-off. Hence, Titmuss offers a redefinition of welfare to reflect the transfer of payments actually made in society. Besides the social welfare familiar to people in Canada, the United Kingdom, Australia, Germany, and New Zealand, he identifies fiscal welfare in the tax deductions allowed to wage and salary earners but denied to social welfare recipients, as well as occupational welfare in the perks offered to certain employees as part of their salary package in order to avoid tax. All of these measures and not only social welfare are part of the welfare system, argues Titmuss.[9] He has a point; opponents of social welfare are usually on unsafe ground when they base their attack on economics. The decision of society to redistribute wealth on the basis of need is no different in principle from the decision to allow certain expenditures as tax deductions. But that does not make the latter welfare. In this respect, Titmuss is guilty of the fallacy of persuasive definition: he defines his terms to suit his case rather than to make that case. The fact that welfare is a transfer payment and that tax deductions are transfer payments obviously does not make tax deductions welfare.

If incentives are offered to business to induce it to enter a particular field, this carries with it no implicit obligations. As a partner in a venture the state is no different from any other partner. But if its interest is to induce the development of a particular scheme, then whatever inducements it offers do not cover the risk to those who undertake the development. Usually the incentives simply make the scheme viable against the competition of rival opportunities for investment, and to that extent, a government might see social or economic advantages in supporting one scheme over another. Ultimately, the wisdom of such policies is something that the voters will decide, but such incentives and the provision of infrastructure and other assistance do not of themselves give government or society a stake in particular ventures. They are environmental policies to encourage private equity to flow in a particular direction, not investment opportunities to bring a direct return to the public purse. Again, the stakeholder theory blurs the kind of interest the public has in business.

The Usefulness of the Concept of Stakeholder

Despite these reservations, there are virtues in the use of the term "stakeholder" in business ethics. The point of our criticisms is to show that awareness of, and reference to, stakeholders is not the instant solution to moral problems that some writers suppose it to be. Freeman, for example, recommended the mapping of stakeholders in business decision-making as an aid to strategic management, and such mapping might have similar value in identifying the ethical dimensions of decisions. But a stakeholder map does not replace moral reasoning; it can only be a convenient starting point. The virtue of the stakeholder concept is to remind managers, investors, and others with a large vested interest in business organizations that a market economy is not an unrestricted one—that a free society makes demands on its citizens not only in a personal sense but in the sense of their being members of social institutions. In this sense, the concept of stakeholder reminds us of the principle of business outlined in chapter 2: business operates on behalf of society, and the free market economy is deemed to provide the most successful way of producing public benefits through the private sector. The concept, then, can be used as a useful corrective to the mentality that sees the market as the solution to all of life's problems.

The following cases and examples consider some of the stakeholder groups that are among the most vulnerable to corporate decisions—lessees, employees, and customers—and even some who would be thought to be rather safe—corporate directors. The cases are not all about ethical malpractice: the General Motors story illustrates cooperation between a company and a union that benefited all stakeholders (a cooperation that has become more common in the years following this case). The Burns Meats case is offered as a contrasting situation. Some of these cases—the Bond lessees, for example—are classic instances of evasion, but recent cases show that some tactics of corporate leaders remain almost timeless.

CASE 3.1: Smaller Stakes, Fewer Rights?

Among the many colourful stories in Paul Barry's book *The Rise and Fall of Alan Bond* there is the sad saga of the dispossessed pub owners. In 1985 lessees of pubs in Australia tied to the Tooheys brewing firm began receiving "notices to quit." Tooheys had recently been taken over by the Australian millionaire Alan Bond. Over the years the lessees had developed a tacit understanding with Tooheys about the value of the goodwill in their pubs. Bond declined to recognize this understanding, so when he did not renew the leases, he felt no obligation to pay for the goodwill that the pub owners had themselves paid for in the purchase of their leases. About 130

continued . . .

publicans were affected. Bond claimed that he was not party to any arrangement about goodwill and was not legally bound to make compensation. It was a matter for the leaseholders that they had decided to pay so much for the leases of their pubs. It had nothing to do with Tooheys and nothing to do with him. He regarded neither the original value of the goodwill nor the investment in maintaining it as placing any obligations on him.[10]

Tooheys had never evicted pub owners, and the lessees had (reasonably) assumed that they were making a sound investment in their pubs, although they were aware that the sale of goodwill was a matter of custom recognized by Tooheys. Bond formed a company called Austotel to buy the hotels, and this insulated Bond Brewing and Bond personally from the hostility that followed the eviction orders. According to Barry, during attempts to negotiate compensation, two representatives of the pub owners were told by Bond executive John Booth, "You want to know what Alan Bond's message is to you blokes? Well, I'll tell you: Alan says burn the bastards."[11] Bond's view was that the lessees had made a commercial decision to buy into the pubs, that they should have been aware of the basis of their entry into them, and that consequently nothing was owed to them. They were not entitled to compensation because there was no contract to that effect and the law did not require it. If such conduct was not illegal in business, it was not immoral.

This point might be rephrased to reveal more of its meaning: it really seems to mean that whatever is not explicitly forbidden is permitted; whatever is not *legally* forbidden is *ethically* permitted.

Case Questions

1. Is it possible to sustain the position "Whatever is not legally forbidden is ethically permitted" in business? What collateral damage to a conglomerate might flow from indifference to the moral claims of particular stakeholders such as the publicans?
2. Precedent is an important concept in law. If a pattern of behaviour develops that can be considered precedent setting, does this not establish a reasonable expectation for future behaviour? Does the establishment of precedent carry a moral obligation to comply with that precedent? Does the establishment of precedent make it morally permissible to comply with the precedent?

There are always ethical issues when capital is raised, and cases like this show them to be far from straightforward.

CASE 3.2: An Employee-Management Partnership: The Rescue of General Motors Canada[12]

In 2009 the North American automotive industry was facing a serious financial crisis with two of the big three North American automakers facing bankruptcy unless they were given access to public funding. The largest of these automakers was General Motors (GM). In Canada, the federal government offered to make funds available to General Motors, Canada, provided the automaker agreed to take significant and material cost-cutting measures. A large portion of the costs cut would necessarily have to come from employee wages and benefits.

This would require GM to engage in negotiations with the Canadian Auto Workers union (CAW), which represents workers in each of the big three North American automakers. The CAW has a long history of fighting fiercely on behalf of its members for increased wages and benefits. Because of the dire financial situation facing the company, the CAW agreed to accept a wage freeze through 2012 (approximately three years), shorter vacations, and higher employee contributions to benefit plans. These concessions were made in the hope that they would be enough to unlock billions of dollars in Canadian government funding for General Motors. The Canadian units of GM and Chrysler sought as much as C$10 billion from the Canadian and Ontario governments to help them survive the crisis facing the auto sector.

"The alternatives are much worse," CAW President Ken Lewenza told a news conference announcing the agreement, which was reached after round-the-clock negotiations with the company, which has some 10,000 workers represented by the CAW. "We've done what we can do as a union. . . . Now the Canadian government has got to step up to the plate."

Federal industry minister Tony Clement was responsible for deciding whether the tentative deal would be enough to unlock government funds. Clement commented, "My officials and I continue to work closely with GM as we continue our due diligence. We will ensure that there is a viable long-term sustainability plan involving all stakeholders in place before we commit any taxpayer dollars."

GM had already proposed a 10 per cent cut in executive salaries and reduced pay and benefits for salaried employees. CAW president Lewenza commented that "[t]ogether these changes represent a major sacrifice by our active members and retirees. They will reduce active hourly labor costs by several dollars per hour, reinforcing Canada's investment advantage relative to U.S. facilities. And they will significantly reduce the company's legacy costs associated with pension liabilities and retiree health benefits."

After several months of negotiations, GM Canada and its rival Chrysler were able to obtain concessions from the CAW adequate to satisfy the federal and provincial governments to provide funding to facilitate the continuing viability of their respective companies. The funding received from the government was sufficient to see the automakers through to recovery over the next few years.

The automotive industry in Canada has rebounded significantly since that time. At the time of writing, consolidated industry statistics for 2012 were not available, but growth in revenue is expected to be 17.7 per cent in 2012 and an additional 9.8 per cent in 2013. Pre-tax profit in 2012 is expected to reach $1.5 billion, the highest since 2002. Not surprisingly, the CAW used the round of 2012 contract negotiations with the Detroit auto manufacturers to try and recoup some of the concessions they made as a condition of the 2009 government bailout. The protracted negotiations with Ford, Chrysler, and GM came to a close late 2012, with the union successfully fighting off the employers' demands for further employee concessions and gaining modest concessions from the employers in terms of pay and benefits.

Case Question

1. Although, as it turned out, this seems like a good-news story, is there a way to balance the interests of employees as stakeholders with the interests of other stakeholders, particularly shareholders? There can certainly be competing interests between these two. Is there any systematic way that they can be legitimately and fairly balanced when they come into conflict?

The following case raises the question in general of the right to take industrial action. How far should it extend? How binding should contracts of employees to employers and vice versa be?

CASE 3.3: Labour-Management Negotiation Impasse: Union *v.* Burns Meats Ltd[13]

The early 1980s saw increasing competition in the meat-packing industry in Canada. Many meat-packing plants were aging, and profit margins were so low that the generation of additional revenues would not cover the capital expenditures required to upgrade and modernize existing plants.

In Kitchener, Ontario, Burns Meats Ltd operated a plant that was old, obsolete, and saddled with very poor labour-management relations. The plant lost $600,000 in 1982, $1.2 million in 1983, and $500,000 in the first six months of 1984. Burns paid its employees an average hourly wage of $15.11 (base wage plus incremental), which was well above the $11.14 average wage of competing meat-packing companies in the United States.

Burns asked its employees to accept a $5 per hour reduction in their base wages. Burns's regional competitors were already paying 10 to 20 per cent less than Burns employees were receiving. The employees voted overwhelmingly to reject the offer, knowing that this would certainly lead to the closure of the plant. Even with the prospect of losing their employment, the workers were unwilling to accept a 40 per cent reduction in their base pay.

The plant was closed in the latter half of 1984.

Case Questions

1. What was the employees' rationale for continuing to strike even though they knew it would mean the inevitable loss of their livelihoods?
2. Did the employer have any reasonable course of action open to it other than closing the plant?
3. If you were to analyze this case from a utilitarian perspective, what outcome do you think would have yielded the maximum utility or satisfaction?

Occupational Health and Safety

Canadian insurance programs for occupational health and safety are provincially administered. The respective provincial organizations maintain data on workplace injuries and health and safety issues in order to establish industry and company premiums for workers' compensation insurance premiums. Not surprisingly, the data and resultant premiums indicate that the mining, construction, manufacturing, transport, agricultural, and fishing industries, and electricity, gas, and water production, had higher incidences of occupational injury than the national average. Community services and retailing were lower than the average. A particularly interesting aspect of the findings was that most of the injuries in the high-risk categories were preventable. They were caused by overexertion and physical stress—for example, incorrect lifting or attempting to move too weighty an object.[14]

Random Testing of Employees

CASE 3.4: Weyco: A Healthy Policy?

In January 2005, four employees of Weyco Inc., a health benefits company acquired by Meritain Health in 2006, left the company rather than take a test that would reveal whether they smoked.[15] The tests were required in accordance with Weyco's non-smoking policy for all employees. The unusual feature of this ban was that it applied not only to the workplace but also to employees' private conduct at home. Testing was applied to ensure that employees did not cheat. Another unusual aspect of the ban was that it applied to employees' spouses if they were covered by the employee's medical insurance.[16] Though these measures against smokers are prohibited in some American states, policies like Weyco's are entirely legal in Michigan and 19 other states. Weyco has just one smoker on its staff, but he is employed in Illinois, which protects his right to smoke.[17] In Michigan and other states, employers have the legal right to fire at will as long as they don't violate discrimination laws, which do not apply to smokers.

The company's founder, Howard Weyers, justified the policy as protecting Weyco against high health care costs. "I don't want to pay for the results of smoking," he said, adding, "The biggest frustration in the workplace is the cost of healthcare. Medical plans weren't established to pay for unhealthy lifestyles."[18] Yet, Weyers admits he has not measured how much smokers have cost him and acknowledged that they might have cost him nothing at all.[19] After all, the serious effects of smoking frequently show up later in life, when many smokers would have left employment with Weyco.[20]

Since the introduction of the policy, about 20 of the company's employees have quit smoking. Weyco offered a variety of free programs, from drug therapy to acupuncture, to help smokers break their addiction. FreshStart, an organization that assists people who wish to stop smoking, has offered any Weyco employee free access to its program. FreshStart's CEO, Matt Godson, said that he was sympathetic to both parties at Weyco:

> From the employer's perspective the burden caused by lost productivity through excessive smoking breaks, not to mention smoking related illnesses, can be considerable. From the employee's perspective, smoking remains the No. 1 cause of preventable death in America. Quitting smoking can not only save your job, it can save your life.[21]

Part of the Weyco policy is to employ a fitness coach and to offer incentives packages called the Lifestyle Challenge. The coach teaches employees about issues such as stress management and leads exercise groups at lunchtime and after work. Those who take the Lifestyle Challenge can earn bonuses of $110 per month. There is a $45 bonus for exercising at a health club; a $20 bonus for keeping a log of water and food consumed and exercise undertaken; and a $45 bonus for meeting fitness standards based on age and sex. People are assessed for the bonus every six months.[22]

continued . . .

Weyco denied planning to fire employees who make lifestyle choices that it deems unhealthy. Weyers might have nurtured a desire to do so, but legal protections cover most other conditions, such as obesity.[23]

The company's smoking restriction has not quelled objections from civil liberties bodies. Their response has been to represent Weyco's policy as the thin end of the wedge. Civil libertarians ask whether Weyco could now require all employees to go on a low-fat diet to cut health care costs. Lewis Maltby, president of the National Workrights Institute, an affiliate of the American Civil Liberties Union, declared,

> The problem is lots of things increase your healthcare costs. Smoking. Drinking. Eating junk food. Not getting enough sleep. Dangerous hobbies. Skiing, scuba diving. If you allow employers to regulate private behavior because it's going to affect the company's healthcare costs, we can all kiss our private lives goodbye.[24]
>
> [It's] crazy . . . that an employer has the right to dictate to a worker what he or she does in their own home. It's none of your boss's business what you do in your own home—or at least it should not be. You can drive a motorcycle, you can read *Playboy*, you can do what you want as long as it does not affect your job performance. If it affects your job performance, then fine, fire them for their poor job performance, but don't fire them for smoking.[25]

As it happens, other companies besides Weyco have wellness programs: Quaker Oats, Johnson & Johnson, Honeywell, Motorola, and IBM have cut employee health insurance costs by introducing wellness programs.[26] By 2005, almost a third of US employers had introduced programs to encourage their employees to stop smoking.[27] It is an extra step to introduce non-smoking policies that apply beyond the workplace, but it is a step that a number of employers have taken. Alaska Airlines and Union Pacific Railroad question applicants about smoking. An Omaha transport company has stopped hiring smokers in seven states. In California and Florida, sheriffs' departments require applicants for jobs and employees to sign no-smoking agreements and even to take a lie detector test on smoking. Kalamazoo Valley Community College refuses to employ smokers.[28]

Howard Weyers was able to implement his policy because he owned the company. He had been a college football coach and brought a particularly strong set of values about health to the management of his firm. Morley Safer, investigative journalist with the popular television current affairs show *60 Minutes*, put it to Weyers that he had "a kind of intolerant attitude to the habits, foibles, eccentricities of other people." "Right," replied Weyers, "I would say I'm intolerable." "Intolerable and intolerant," suggested Safer. "I am. But I just can't be flexible on the policy," Weyers declared.

Clearly health insurance costs are a consideration for corporations that provide employees with coverage, but Weyers was extreme by prevailing standards. He did fitness training five times a week and wanted his employees to follow his example. "I set the policy and I'm not going to bend from the policy," he said.[29]

The question arises, where does this kind of intrusion stop? What of the case of Ross Hopkins, who worked for an Anheuser-Busch/Budweiser beer distributor? He went out with his girlfriend, ordered a beer, and the waitress mistakenly brought him a Coors (another brand of beer). He didn't want to make a fuss, so he took the beer. Unfortunately, his boss's son was at the same bar. He offered Hopkins a Budweiser, Hopkins said no thanks, and the next day he found himself fired for drinking the opposition's brew. The matter was resolved, but the terms were not revealed.[30]

Consider the issues at stake in these examples: the employer's right to foster and maintain a healthy work environment and the right to present a public image that accords with management values and objectives;

the rights of employees to privacy; the intrusiveness of breath and blood tests on workers; the adoption of inflexible policies; and the reputational cost of such policies. At the margins it is relatively easy to identify unacceptable behaviour—Mr Weyers's wish to test the spouses of employees seems to be a clear instance; the firing of Mr Hopkins seems to be another—but the ethics of testing and behaviour regulation are not black and white matters.

Case Questions

1. Was respect shown to stakeholder staff at Weyco? Were they regarded as stakeholders or merely as servants of the company and its boss?
2. Is the Weyco no-smoking-anywhere requirement justifiable?
3. Is the Weyco requirement that spouses not smoke justifiable?
4. Is there a difference, ethically speaking, between requiring something in the name of anti-smoking or anti–drug taking and requiring something in the name of anti-obesity?
5. Can you articulate a principle for demarcating areas where an employer can justifiably formally interfere with employees' personal habits/lifestyles?
6. Could Weyco have used different methods to achieve the same ends? Many firms promote employee behaviour modification through the use of persuasion rather than command. Promotional campaigns and voluntary support and wellness programs are used to promote behavioural changes that promote healthier lifestyles. What are the ethical ramifications of engaging in this type of behaviour modification versus adopting Weyco's methods?

The testing of employees for drug or alcohol intoxication at their place of work has long been discussed as an option for employers, especially those in industries and services where safety is paramount. In some industries, such as the airline industry, there are already stringent restrictions on the consumption of intoxicating substances. Ferry masters and train drivers, it has been argued, should be subject to the same random testing for intoxication as truck and taxi drivers. Opponents of such measures see this as an invasion of privacy that cannot be justified as a preventive measure. If a person is clearly intoxicated at work, then action should be taken; employers should not go looking for drug and alcohol abuse.

The problem for employers is that they are required to ensure that minimum safety measures are met. A failure in this respect could leave them and their companies vulnerable to a successful suit. Random testing could also be seen as being in the interests of employees, for it could protect them from the unsafe work of intoxicated colleagues.

The other side of the issue is that random drug testing could detect drug use by employees during non-working hours. This is an invasion of privacy that could be used as an excuse for retrenching employees, compiling damaging records on them that have nothing to do with their work efficiency, or setting a precedent for discriminatory employment policies, such as the hiring of non-smokers only. In short, once this type of intrusion begins, it is difficult to know where it should stop or to what use it will be put. When does private behaviour become of concern to employers? Victimization and discrimination could infect a workplace under the guise of occupational health and safety. Where do you stop? If some employees are tested, should this not apply to all employees from the board of directors down? And should testing just be a company-by-company matter, or should there be a rule for all in order to avoid indirect discrimination?

In any case, it is not clear that testing for substance abuse works. Lewis Maltby, speaking this time as vice-president of American manufacturer Drexelbrook rather than as president of the National Workrights Institute, said that one-third of American companies using drug testing believe it is unhelpful. According to Maltby, testing is bad management because it is aimed at drug use rather than poor workplace practice; it is looking at the wrong thing. Moreover, it establishes a climate of distrust between employees and employers.[31]

Employee Drug and Alcohol Testing

The Canadian work environment is rather different from that of the United States, but there are some parallels with it with respect to workplace testing for consumption of drugs and alcohol. The Canadian Human Rights Commission allows for random alcohol testing only in safety-sensitive positions. Alcohol testing indicates both the presence of alcohol and the level of impairment. Random drug testing is not allowed in these cases; because of technical limitations, drug testing can only indicate the presence of a drug in the blood but not the level of impairment.[32]

Corporate Surveillance

Privacy has become an increasingly important issue, as technology allows it to be invaded in novel ways. Employer surveillance of employees through hidden cameras, computer and phone monitoring, and other means has been seen as particularly objectionable.

In a 2002 case, management at Zesta Engineering Ltd accessed an employee's work computer. The court ruled that regardless of the employee's belief in his right to privacy, a computer provided to an employee at work was the legal property of the employer. Consequently, the employer had the legal right to access the computer at any time.[33]

In another case, Canada Safeway Ltd, a major supermarket chain, introduced a hand recognition system in order to reduce time card fraud. In 2003 the union representing Safeway's hourly employees, United Food and Commercial Workers (UFCW), Local 401, argued that requiring employees to submit this biometric information was a direct invasion of their privacy. The union argued that less invasive methods could be used to control time card fraud. The court ruled that the business justification for hand recognition outweighed concerns over employee privacy and ruled in Safeway's favour.[34]

Clearly a responsible corporation should develop clear IT (information technology) policies to protect its valuable resources and to guard against liability for employee misuse. Such a policy should also protect employees from passing temptations, such as the urge to fire off an irate message to a politician, another business, or a lover using corporate equipment. Banks already employ video surveillance of tellers to protect their money and the tellers themselves; such surveillance allows mistakes to be distinguished from theft and supports honesty in a potentially tempting environment. If a corporation provides access to email, mobile phones, and the web, it can be implicated in criminal and civil matters, from harassment and bullying to fraud. According to an article in *Forbes*, monitoring occurs because "[p]ress leaks, theft of trade secrets and time wasting are big concerns. But the main reason is fear of lawsuits . . . Almost 25% of companies have had employee emails subpoenaed because of a workplace lawsuit, usually involving harassment or discrimination."[35]

Here is how one company, SpectorSoft, promotes an employee-monitoring product:

> **Spector 360—Company-Wide Employee Monitoring**
> Don't have time to look at every web page each employee views, every email they send, every instant message or every keystroke they type? Let Spector 360 do the work for you by analyzing the data and showing you the worst offenders, so you know which employees to zero in on with Spector 360's detailed investigative features.[36]

If a corporation avails itself of such a product to implement its policy, how is that different from applying policies about other matters, such as rules about leave or health and safety? How is such a policy in particular a breach of privacy?

CASE 3.5: The Hewlett-Packard Case[37]

Through 2005 and into 2006, there was a series of serious leaks from the Hewlett-Packard (HP) boardroom. Sensitive information appeared in the *Wall Street Journal* and on CNET. The source of the leak might have been an HP employee or a member of the board. HP chairwoman Patricia Dunn initiated an investigation to find it. Leaks from the boardroom are an especially serious matter for a corporation of HP's size and value, and Dunn's concern was understandable: she would have been failing in her duty if she had not taken action. Clearly it was not only a matter of sensitive information about strategic matters being made public that was at issue, but also the very functioning of a board seemingly tainted by a breach of trust. The methods employed to find the culprit and Dunn's part in the investigation eventually became bigger stories than the leaks. She approved recruitment of private detectives through a series of "cutouts" designed to insulate HP executives from too much knowledge of investigative procedures. The man chosen to drive the investigation was Kevin Hunsaker, a senior attorney in charge of corporate compliance—and ethics.

continued . . .

From emails tabled later before a congressional subcommittee, it is clear that Hunsaker took to his task with relish.[38] He quickly drafted plans to spy on a journalist's email traffic; floated the idea of intercepting text messages from HP directors' mobile phones; authorized private detectives to keep surveillance on reporters, HP employees, and the suspected leaker, board member George Keyworth; and organized extensive "pretexting."[39] Hunsaker's team was at arm's length from Silicon Valley headquarters. Anthony Gentilucci, head of HP's global security unit in Boston, contracted Ronald DeLia of Security Outsourcing Solutions, who then subcontracted another firm in Florida, which outsourced surveillance and telephone records acquisitions to investigators in Florida, Georgia, Colorado, and Nebraska. This elaborate track covering seems to have been at least partly designed to keep HP and its executives in a position of "plausible deniability."

The most publicized tactics used by investigators involved pretexting and monitoring a journalist's computer messages. Pretexting is a grey area legally,[40] but it is clearly dubious. It involves pretending to be a phone subscriber in order to gain access to phone records, which could then be used to check whether HP employees or board members had been phoning journalists. Spyware was used to monitor the email traffic of CNET News.com journalist Dawn Kawamoto by creating a bogus employee called "Jacob" to gain her confidence. Jacob, under the pretext of providing information, sent Kawamoto an (undisclosed) HTML-based email that would permit HP investigators to monitor any recipients to whom this message was forwarded. Kawamoto would have thought that the email was a usual text message, not an HTML-based communication, traceable to any further recipients.

Hunsaker's emails clearly show he was aware of the need for top-level authorization to spy, but Chairwoman Dunn denied knowing the operational details of the investigation. Hunsaker knew that such spying was questionable: "Of course, I'm not sure we want this directly traceable back to HP . . . , " he said to Gentilucci.[41] Was this ethical scruple? No, it was a fear of more bad publicity for HP if CNET found out. When Hunsaker asked Anthony Gentilucci, "How does Ron [DeLia] get cell and home phone records?" Gentilucci told him that investigators call phone operators "under some ruse" to convince the operators to disclose confidential information. Gentilucci said that such tactics are "on the edge, but above board," to which Hunsaker replied, "I shouldn't have asked."[42] Vincent Nye, an internal HP investigator, recognized that pretexting was a "don't ask, don't tell" practice. "Speaking for myself, I won't use this particular tactic on those cases I have been assigned to lead," he wrote in a memo.[43]

When Hunsaker's team discovered telephone contact between board member Keyworth and Kawamoto, Nye was not excited. "I have serious reservations about what we are doing," he emailed Hunsaker. "It is very unethical at the least and probably illegal. If [it] is not totally illegal, then it is leaving HP in a position [that] could damage our reputation or worse." Nye requested that pretexting stop and that information gathered from it be discarded.[44]

The surveillance of journalists and board members was the undoing of Dunn and her confederates. Journalists can be unfriendly if cornered, and very rich board members—former director billionaire Tom Perkins and Dunn had a falling-out—can create adverse publicity about investigative methods of which they did not approve. Perkins reported Dunn's activities to the Securities and Exchange Commission, the Federal Trade Commission, the Justice Department, and the California attorney-general. The HP investigation rather than the leak became the story. As one journalist observed, "Sometimes efforts at damage control do more harm than good. HP should be winning plaudits for its recent stock price highs. Instead, the high-tech giant is in the news for the lengths it went to hunt down a board member with loose lips."[45]

Another asked this fundamental question: "How did a lawyer responsible for overseeing HP's business conduct find himself at the center of a company ethics scandal?"[46] The answer was complex. First, Hunsaker was assigned conflicting roles as a professional lawyer, as an employee answerable to his superiors, and as a source of independent compliance advice to HP. Then his enthusiasm for the investigation seems to have made him ready to believe the assurances of his associates about the legality of their methods, itself an indication of his role confusion: he was supposed to be the compliance officer. Finally, perhaps he believed that if an action is legal, it's ethical. At least this is what his lawyer said.[47]

At the conclusion of the investigation, Keyworth was alleged to have been the source of the media leaks and Hunsaker was promoted to the position of director of HP's standards of business conduct—that is, HP's chief ethics officer. Alas, he enjoyed this status for less than six months. When the scandal was exposed and a congressional inquiry set up, he left the company.[48] He was not the only one to do so. In September 2006 several HP officers and private investigators appeared before a congressional hearing into the investigation. Most, including Hunsaker, Gentilucci, and the private investigators, invoked their right against self-incrimination. Hunsaker's boss, General Counsel Ann Baskins, resigned her position only hours before she was due to testify and, like most of her colleagues, invoked the Fifth Amendment. Dunn did appear before the congressional subcommittee to claim that she believed the investigation had used legal means. Then she left HP.

That was not the end of the matter. HP have had to pay $14.5 million to settle a civil complaint filed by the California attorney-general. Dunn, Hunsaker, Ron DeLia, and two of his hired investigators were charged under Californian law with identity theft and conspiracy. These charges were later downgraded, and the judge dismissed the case against Dunn altogether. The judge ruled that the other defendants, who pleaded no contest to the misdemeanour of wire fraud, would have charges against them dismissed if they performed 96 hours of community service and paid restitution to victims. Lawyers claimed complete vindication for the defendants.[49] Legally, this might have been so, but ethically? Lesley Stahl, an investigative journalist, asked this question of Dunn on the current affairs television show *60 Minutes*: "Isn't it just wrong—isn't it just ethically wrong, forget whether it's legal or not, to go in and get people's phone records?" Dunn replied, "People who sit on public company boards have a very different attitude about this than probably the general public. . . . [Y]ou give up a lot of privacy when you go onto a board. . . . Your life is a much more open book when you have this kind of a public trust." "But what about the reporters?" asked Stahl. "That was just wrong," said Dunn. "The idea that I supervised, orchestrated, approved all of the ways in which this investigation occurred is just a complete myth. It's a falsehood. It's a damaging lie."[50] According to the Sox First and *60 Minutes* websites, Dunn also made this statement in the *60 Minutes* interview:

> Every company has investigations. Investigations, by their nature, are intrusive. If you think that Hewlett-Packard is the only company that has an investigations force—which by the way, is peopled mostly with former law enforcement officers that do all kinds of private detective work, monitoring, posing as other people in order to solve problems to protect shareholder value—you're being naïve.[51]

She is undoubtedly right: Boeing has been reported as using many of HP's tactics, including computer monitoring, spying, and following, photographing, and videoing employees.[52] Boeing's investigations confirm Dunn's comment about intrusiveness, and no doubt many corporations protect themselves by spying on

continued . . .

employees. That doesn't make such conduct ethically defensible or safe legally. In 2008 the four private detectives in the HP investigation were ordered to pay a total of $600,000 in a civil suit brought by the Federal Trade Commission.[53] In 2007 one of them, Bryan Wagner, entered a guilty plea to charges of identity theft and conspiracy. The quashing of the original charges against Dunn needs to be viewed in this light: the courts found improper conduct at the hands of people brought into HP on her authority, and she cannot disavow moral responsibility for what ensued. Public reaction might differ from boardroom reactions, but if so, it's time for boards to take a reality check. It might be board members like Dunn who are naive if they arrogantly believe that they can continue business as usual. Here is a reality check for legislators from David Lazarus of the *San Francisco Chronicle*,

> Let's get this straight: You spy on board members of the largest computer company in the world. You spy on reporters who cover the company. Your actions spark outrage over privacy violations and lead to congressional hearings. And when all's said and done, your punishment is to spend a few hours picking up trash from the side of the road?[54]

Dunn's attempt at a defence has the ring of Bart Simpson about it: I didn't do it; you didn't see me do it; you can't prove a thing. She set the investigation in motion, did not get formal board approval, approved Hunsaker's plans, and then denied responsibility when her conduct was publicized. Would she have made a similar disclaimer if the whole incident had remained inside HP?

Apart from being a topical case, this story offers some lessons in ethics. The first might be transparency: Dunn should have been open with the board. Keyworth is reported as admitting to a board meeting that he had talked to CNET. According to *Newsweek*, he said to the board, "I would have told you all about this. Why didn't you just ask?"[55] Dunn claims that she and the CEO tried to get Keyworth to admit that he was the leaker two months earlier but Keyworth had declined to do so.[56] The adoption of a more transparent investigation would have averted some of the fallout. Dunn and the board could have called in the police. The chances of keeping the investigation in proportion with the offence would have been greater with full board involvement. Reliance on legal advice, some of it second-hand, to take care of ethical matters was a mistake. This was the kind of case that lent itself to discussion through an ethical decision-making model, but when ethical objections were raised, they were buried. Only one set of stakeholders was identified by Dunn—shareholders—and others affected by the activities she initiated seem to have been unfortunate collateral damage. Finally, those in charge of the investigation tried to deflect responsibility for its damaging consequences.

Case Questions

1. Did Dunn *really* do anything that was so bad?
2. If Dunn should not have done what she did—gone to such lengths—what could she have done? After all, corporate leaks of sensitive information (not "whistleblowing" [see chapter 7]) are a very serious, potentially extremely harmful matter for a company.
3. Where should the line be drawn between corporate transparency and confidentiality?

The issue of employee monitoring goes beyond corporate protection. Terrorism—including cyber terrorism—is now a concern of governments, and they wish to combat it by using surveillance of electronic communications. Pursuant to the terrorist attacks in September 2001, several countries enacted legislation that would permit more extensive monitoring of electronic and voice communications and access to personal information held by Internet service providers. The Canadian government has been struggling to balance the need to provide law enforcement and security agencies with the tools they need to accomplish their mandates with the privacy rights and civil liberties of its citizens.

In the United States, under the Communications Assistance for Law Enforcement Act, all phone calls and broadband Internet traffic (emails, web traffic, instant messaging, and so on) are legally required to be available for unimpeded real-time monitoring by federal law enforcement and intelligence agencies. Likewise, all telephone and VOIP communications are to be available for real-time wiretapping by those same agencies. In 2001 the Bush administration authorized the use of warrantless domestic wiretaps by the National Security Agency. The NSA's authority was extended through the Protect America Act of 2007 and the FISA Amendments Act of 2008.[57]

These concerns regarding surveillance of personal communications are widely shared. The argument for security and corporate protection is strong, but not decisive. Privacy and free communication are very large considerations in a democratic society, and civil liberties place side constraints on what corporations and governments can do, even for the best of reasons. HP's Dunn seemed to dismiss this in the same way as the commandant in *A Few Good Men*.

It is reasonable to expect that corporations will try all appropriate measures to eliminate or manage risk. If the technology is available, then why not use it? Measures to minimize and manage risk will inevitably compromise discretion. Discretion involves trust, and that is a risk. That element of risk can be eliminated but at the cost of discretion and trust. In other words, an organization that tries to secure itself from liability by risk minimization will be caught in an apparent paradox: it runs another kind of risk—the risk of becoming risk averse. Without autonomy, responsibility, and trust, individual ethics withers and, with it, creativity, initiative, and the willingness to take risks that increase wealth. Judgment is risky; it is required in any healthy organization. Occasionally it can fail but a healthy organization should be prepared for that failure. Risk management that will not accept this will seek to eliminate the discretion necessary for the exercise of judgment.

Consumer Protection and Product Safety

In the United States there are many famous cases of component and product failure that raise legal and ethical questions. The Ford Pinto, *Challenger* space shuttle, Bay Area Rapid Transit System, and Ford Explorer/Firestone Tire cases are among the most famous of manufacturer neglect. To those may be added more recent cases, such as drug company Merck's foot-dragging in warning consumers about potentially lethal side effects of its pain-relief drug Vioxx; the sale of milk products adulterated with melamine by Chinese dairy firm Sanlu; and the sale of toys painted with lead-based paint by Mattel and other toy manufacturers contracting production to Chinese manufacturers.

At one time, Merck was a shining example of corporate social responsibility, indeed benevolence, for its development of the cure for the Third World disease known as river blindness. There was no profitable market for this cure, a drug called Mectizan, because the disease it treated affected people too poor to pay for it. So Merck donated the drug to prevent human suffering. Yet, in the Vioxx case, the firm was prepared to risk its corporate halo to protect a big-selling product. After a number of studies linked Vioxx to increased risk of heart attack and stroke, Merck withdrew the drug from sale in 2004.[58] Ever since, it has been fighting legal battles. It settled a class action in the United States for $714 billion without admitting liability. In Australia, a class action reached the courts in 2009. Documents made available in the Australian action show that Merck was aggressive in pursuit of critics of Vioxx and drew up a hit list of doctors whom it had to "neutralize" or "discredit."[59] Why would a drug company with a reputation to protect engage in risky behaviour? Why would such a visible corporation think it could get away with conduct that could harm the public, its shareholders, and its own success?

In the Sanlu case, 300,000 children were made sick by contaminated milk and milk products and six children died. The person primarily responsible, Zhang Yujun, was sentenced to death, along with two accomplices, for selling 550 tonnes of protein powder bulked out with melamine. The former chairwoman of Sanlu, Tina Wenhua, was sentenced to life in prison for continuing to sell contaminated dairy products after she learned that they were laced with melamine. Given the stringency of Chinese law, it is strange that the perpetrators were prepared to take these risks.[60]

The question that defenders of the minimally regulated market must answer is this: why would manufacturers with a great deal to lose risk their market by supplying dangerous goods? Undoubtedly they must in some very important respect think it is worth the risk. Still, a product that puts the lives or health of consumers at risk places a great ethical responsibility on all concerned with its manufacture, approval, and supply.

Amid the many cases of failure there are examples of good corporate conduct that mitigate the doctrine of *caveat emptor* (buyer beware). In 2000 Bridgestone/Firestone recalled 6.5 million tires installed on Ford Explorers because of an increased incidence of rollovers with this vehicle and tire combination. Although Ford and Bridgestone/Firestone were unable to agree on where the design flaw originated, Bridgestone/Firestone issued the recall as a precautionary measure.[61]

The Mistral fan case provides a good example of problems associated with the responsibilities of all the parties concerned, as well as good material for stakeholder analysis.

CASE 3.6: The Mistral Fan Case[62]

In Melbourne in January 1988 two children died in a house fire. The fire started with a Mistral fan, and the subsequent coronial inquiry exposed a sorry history of indifference and poor regulatory control.

The Mistral Gyro Aire was introduced in 1968 and soon accumulated a number of design awards. In 1976 the fans caught fire twice during quality-control testing at the Mistral factory. The following year the fans caused severe damage to a Singapore Mistral showroom. By 1977–8 the fans were the subject of a product recall notice in New South Wales, Queensland, and Asia that did not mention the fire risk; comparatively few fans were returned. In 1977 Royal Melbourne Hospital was supplied with 40 fans assembled from parts of obsolete units; two of these fans caught fire. Mistral again won a design award in 1980, and it expanded business to the United States. A further fire in the Melbourne factory in 1982 did not prevent the fan winning another award, but 19 fires were reported in 1984. In 1984 Mistral's CEO, John Hasker, resigned. In a report to the board quoted by the coroner, he stated, "The problem at Mistral had developed from poor leadership and bad management. . . . Evidence of ineffective management style was seen in excessive stocks, debtors out of control, [and] inferior quality of products, both from a design and manufactured aspect."

By 1985 the manufacturer had before it evidence of 52 fan-related fires. Mistral's product development manager, Kevin Cummins, sent a memorandum to his superiors and the firm's solicitor in which he stated, "I strongly believe there is nothing Mistral can do about these units, short of a product recall."

The deaths in 1988 of two children in a fan-related fire prompted a public warning about the faulty models by the Coroner's Court, and Mistral, which had been acquired by new owners the previous year, began a systematic recall. Following another change of ownership, Mistral issued public warnings to "destroy the old fans." This warning was echoed by the State Electricity Commission of Victoria in a full-page advertisement in *Electricity Supply Magazine*, June 1992.

The coronial inquiry revealed just how extensive were the problems with the fan and its manufacturer. The fan contained faulty or inappropriately specified electrical components that Mistral's own engineers identified in reports. The manufacturing processes were not of high quality. And the plastic case surrounding the fan was combustible. In short, the Mistral was a time bomb. The coroner put it in these terms:

> The central problem . . . is that at some point in the life of the fan . . . failure is likely and the casing is not made of flame-retardant plastic. If the failure results in sparking or overheating, ignition of the casing is a strong possibility. The fan motor will continue to operate during failure and with the fan blades turning, the fire . . . is fuelled by oxygen and the plastic body provides the combustible material.

In his report the coroner detailed a series of missed opportunities, irresponsible management decisions, and professional failures. Most of the minutes of Mistral management meetings, having gone missing, were unavailable to the coroner, and only one director, who claimed ignorance of the fire risk, gave evidence to the inquiry. Despite these handicaps, the coroner concluded, "By 1976 it should have been clear to the designers and engineers . . . that measures aimed at reducing the risk of fire should have been part of the design brief." He also criticized the manufacturers, who, "once the problem [was] identified, as a matter of expediency [chose] to supply and accept recognized underrated components with an inadequate safety factor." He found that Mistral tried to protect its corporate image at the expense of public safety and failed to seek assistance from the appropriate

continued . . .

authorities. The coroner attributed this "sheer incompetence" in management to three senior executives whose indifference to public safety in the face of known risk "contributed . . . to the deaths of the Stott children." The only risk considered by management was financial; there was no recall during 1984–5 and "nothing was done to warn the public." He concluded, "Perhaps the financial corporate ethic of the 1980s was an influence in placing public safety lower on the scale of priorities than it should have been, and the Mistral Fan fire saga is only an apparent example of where financial expediency and eventually corporate survival came first."

What of the regulatory authorities and insurance companies? The inquiry found that Mistral was evasive and sometimes outright deceptive. Management gave misleading figures about the number of fans that caught fire, although it was aware of the truth. Mistral's insurers were not told the truth about the fire risk of the Gyro Aire fans for many years, but the coroner found that by 1986 they had enough information "to take action in the public interest," as well as their own.

The State Electricity Commission of Victoria Approvals Board was criticized for failing to collate information on fan fires and for keeping inadequate records on its dealings with Mistral. One aspect of the commission's oversight of the Mistral affair was the presence on its Approvals Board of L. Milton, the inventor of the fan. Although Milton was no longer with Mistral, his presence led the coroner to make these comments: "The position of Milton on the Approvals Board is a matter of considerable concern and it is difficult to escape the conclusion that the decision not to take the matter further may have been affected by his involvement."

The technical context in which the Mistral incidents took place should have triggered a timely and complete recall. In 1977 Underwriters Laboratories in the United States evaluated the Gyro Aire and found that the plastic housing did not meet American flammability standards. Ironically, only a few years earlier a committee of Standards Australia was established to examine flammability testing for electrical products. A Mistral representative was a member of the committee. An Australian standard was not available until 1978, four years after the review began and six years after the appearance of a standard developed by the International Electrotechnical Commission. Before July 1979 the approval of electrical fans was voluntary. Electric shock was seen as the main danger, not fire risk. The coroner observed that "[t]here was a considerable delay in the introduction of an obvious safety standard."

Case Questions

1. Who were the stakeholders that Mistral noticed? Who were those it ignored?
2. Which other parties were indifferent to stakeholder interests in this case?
3. In what ways would stakeholder awareness have changed the ethics of the major parties?

The notion of stakeholder is not conceptually trouble-free, and this has practical limitations; but the notion does immediately offer a way of calling attention to the interests of others affected by a business decision. And it does enrich the business vocabulary ethically without having the appearance of unwelcome moralizing. It provides a way to take into account two very simple but universal assumptions in our society: people should be informed about things done to them and risks presented to them, and where possible, people should be asked for their consent before things are done to them, whether they are directly concerned in a business decision or are third parties.

Review Questions

1. Why would it seem important to widen business's appropriate concerns from shareholders to stakeholders?
2. Do you think that business has a duty to take account of stakeholders' interests—interests beyond those of its shareholders? Why?
3. Do you think there is a way to determine whose interests a business should take into account beyond what is legally required or required by some appropriate regulatory body—that is, who should be regarded as stakeholders in any particular business's activities?
4. Is it clear what it means to say that a stakeholder analysis is not "strategic"?
5. Sometimes looking after stakeholder interests is a matter of paternalism, and sometimes it is a matter of other things—for example, stakeholders' wishes. These are different types of considerations. Can you itemize the different kinds of considerations that can enter into an attempt to take account of stakeholders' interests?
6. We mentioned that in the United States there are many famous cases of component and product failure that raise legal and ethical questions about appropriate regard for stakeholders: Ford Pinto, *Challenger* space shuttle, Bay Area Rapid Transit System, and Ford Explorer/Firestone Tire. If you are not familiar with some or all of these, you might want to learn about them. They are easily discoverable through a search on the Internet.

Suggested Readings

Cohen, S. "Who are the stakeholders? What difference does it make?" *Business & Professional Ethics Journal*, 15 (2) Summer, 1996, pp. 3–18

Freeman, R.E. *Strategic Management: A Stakeholder Approach.* Boston: Pitman, 1984.

Suggested Website

Canadian Human Rights Commission's Policy on Alcohol and Drug Testing, 2009:

http://www.chrc-ccdp.ca/eng/content/policy-alcohol-and-drug-testing

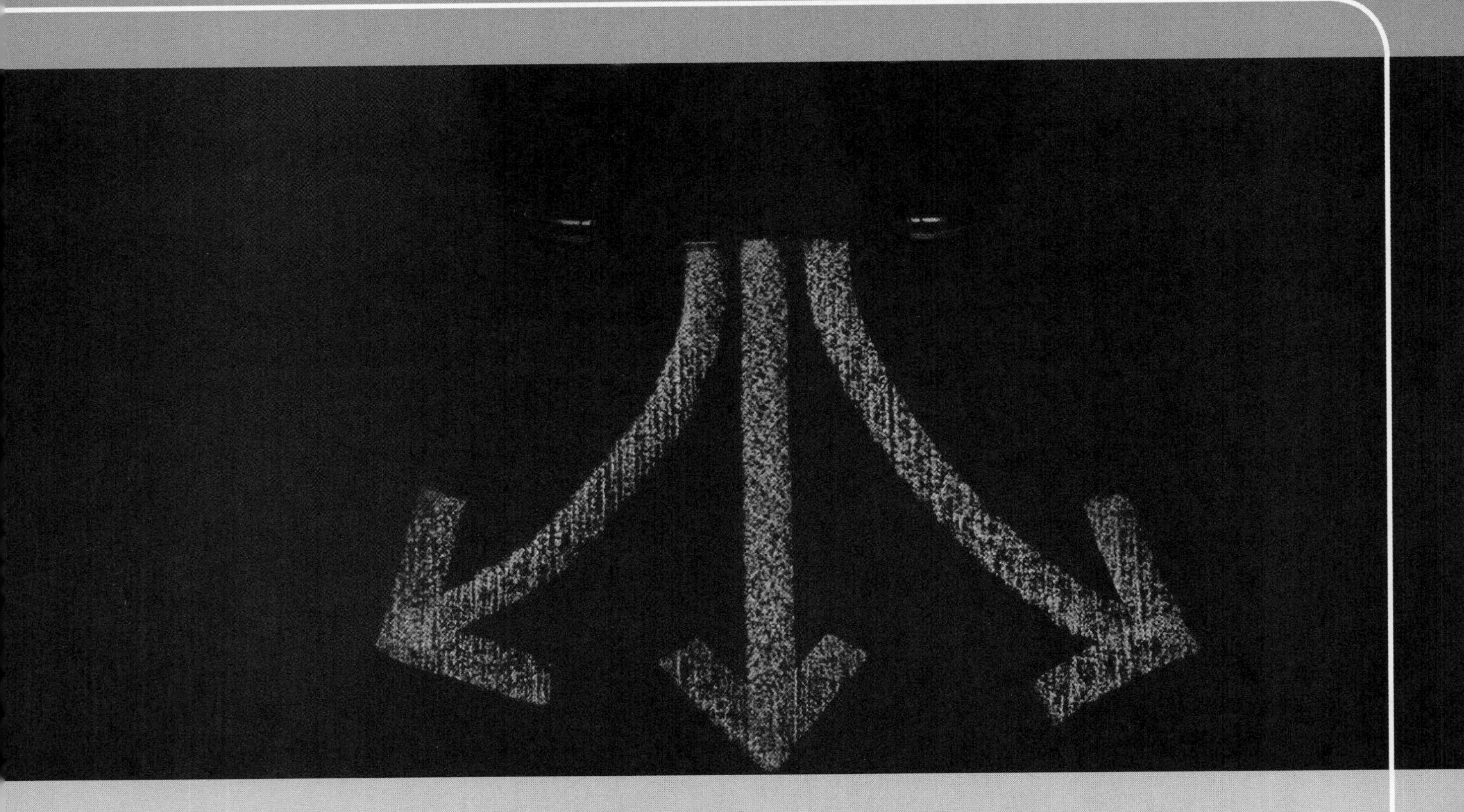

4

Ethics in the Marketplace: Generosity, Competition, and Fairness

Chapter Outline

It is not surprising that some writers, such as Albert Carr and Milton Friedman, should have applied the notion of rules and laws to business and exempted it from the moral considerations that apply to natural persons.[1] Most of contemporary business is built upon law. Businesses are commonly what might be called "enterprise associations," collectivities of people working for the purposes of the business who might not share much beyond those purposes. These enterprise associations can be distinguished from social or community ones, where conviviality or even a loose set of objectives provides the rationale for the association.[2]

The relationships in enterprise organizations serve the purposes of the organization rather than personal or social ones. We can see, then, why corporate obligations have been cast in legal terms. Corporations are legal creatures, artificial persons. They do not give up their seats in buses to the infirm; they do not argue with parking police; they do not console a colleague who has lost a parent; they do not lose their temper when the supermarket cart veers to one side. The obligations of corporations appear to be only the things that they have contracted to do or for which they are liable under law. Increasingly, however, this view of obligation has failed to meet either public expectations or legal judgments. The argument that business operates under laws, rules, and assumptions peculiar to itself, while ethics regulates the relations of real persons of flesh and blood, does not carry the conviction it once did.

If ethics is about human excellence, it is also about setting minimum standards for any agent, whether natural or artificial. Natural persons are people, human beings. Artificial persons are corporations or collectivities that can exercise powers of agency. When corporations like WorldCom or Enron fail, the ethics of the managers and directors occupy the public spotlight. Figures of the moment, such as Bernard Ebbers, Jeffrey Skilling, Conrad Black, and Bernard Madoff, have their lifestyles covered on the evening news. Ethics in such cases means personal morality. Business ethics also refers to minimum standards of organizational conduct. The nature of corporate personality has been debated, with some philosophers claiming that a corporation can have a decision-making capacity that gives it attributes of natural persons, such as a conscience. We shall not enter into that debate here. Indeed, some writers believe that the law has overtaken the philosophers and that the courts now view corporations in similar terms to natural persons.[3] This is particularly the case in the United States, where *Federal Sentencing Guidelines for Organizations* have been in force since 1991.[4] The guidelines basically penalize companies that come before the courts without having made any effort to take ethics seriously. What the guidelines seem to require, as a minimum, is the introduction of ethics programs into the workplace.

It is hardly surprising that organizational ethics should be supported legally, given the powers that corporations possess and the powers that flow to those who run them. As Lord Denning put it over 50 years ago,

> A company may in many ways be likened to a human body. It has a brain and nerve centre which controls what it does. It also has hands which hold the tools and act in accordance with directions from the centre. Some of the people in the company are mere

> servants and agents who are nothing more than hands to do the work and cannot be said to represent the mind or will. Others are directors and managers who represent the directing mind and will of the company, and control what it does. The state of mind of these managers is the state of mind of the company and is treated by the law as such.[5]

Personal ethics is a matter of virtues and character. Organizational ethics is a matter of systems of compliance, accountability, and culture. It is not usually possible to make ethically weak people moral gladiators through organizational means, but it is possible to require all members of an organization to meet minimum obligations and standards set by their employer. There might not be much personal credit in observing a minimum, but compliance can go a long way in sustaining a corporation's integrity.

Enron's Ethics Policy

The Enron Corporation collapsed in a major accounting scandal in 2001, culminating in what was, at the time, the biggest corporate bankruptcy in history. It is interesting to note that, during its preceding period of rapid growth, Enron had developed an extensive and comprehensive ethics policy that was no less than 60 pages in length, the first paragraph of which reads, "As officers and employees of Enron Corp., its subsidiaries, and its affiliated companies, we are responsible for conducting the business affairs of the companies in accordance with all applicable laws and in a moral and honest manner."[6]

An extensive and comprehensive corporate ethics policy will not save a corporation from a major scandal if the company executives fail to adhere to it in spirit and in action. Jeffrey Skilling, the former CEO (chief executive officer) and COO (chief operating officer) of Enron, was sentenced in 2006 to almost 25 years in prison for his part in the scandal. Kenneth Lay, the former chairman and CEO of Enron, was convicted of six counts of securities and wire fraud and sentenced to up to 45 years in prison; he died of an aneurysm before he could serve any of his sentence.

Ethics and the Law

Although ethics sets a higher standard than the law, the legal standard is not to be despised. Law sets the publicly promulgated, enforceable minimum standards upon which business can build. Some would say that legal standards are the only ones that should apply and that ethics is a matter for people, not corporations.[7] This is not the position of the law, especially as courts look increasingly for institutionalized ethics and corporate integrity in their deliberations and sentencing. Moreover, a reliance on law over ethics in setting standards sends a dangerous message to business. This message comes in two forms: the first states that if conduct is legal, then it is ethical; and the second states that if conduct is not illegal, then it is ethical. In other words, if ethical issues have any real substance to them, then they ought to be covered by law. This message suggests that the only effective controls on business behaviour are external. This suggestion is not only inaccurate, but also risky.[8] Demands for more regulation, increased surveillance, and harsher penalties will not produce a more successful business environment. Such demands are reminiscent of the unfortunate fashion of the 1970s, when bars and restaurants, not content with carpet on their floors, ran the stuff up the walls as well. Carpeting business with regulations is no more attractive or functional than this bygone fashion.

Consider this image of the relation of law to ethics. Imagine that you are in the Sistine Chapel. Where is your gaze directed?—to the ceiling. That is the reason you are there. What do you stand upon to observe that ceiling?—the floor. Without the floor, there is no platform from which to view the ceiling. Without the ceiling, there is no point to standing on the floor. Each has its function. So it is with law and ethics. Law is in the floor, along with directives and other limits to discretion. Ethics is in the ceiling. It is what we aspire to above the law. The Sistine Chapel would not be enhanced by having either more ceiling or more floor. So it is with laws, rules, and regulations in society. Maybe "there ought to be a law against it," but maybe the creation of new laws, more policing, and new penalties is the architectural equivalent of driving the floor of the Sistine Chapel up the walls. It is not a matter of reaching for legal measures to shore up ethics. In chapter 9, we will return to this point and, in particular, to the error of trying to create ethical behaviour and the exercise of good judgment through the creation of rules and regulations.

Corporate Gifts and Benevolence

Although gift-giving has long been an accepted part of corporate life, the practice is coming under increasing scrutiny. The rationale for external corporate benevolence is that it builds relationships with clients or that it gives a corporation public profile. Hospitality offered to staff of a corporation is justified as rewarding performance, showing appreciation, or boosting morale. Whatever the justification, corporate giving involves the expenditure of funds, which was once regarded by many as discretionary. Also discretionary within limits was the receiving of gifts. Whereas in the public sector all but token gifts, such as ballpoint pens or mugs, have been prohibited by codes of ethics, in the private sector attitudes have been more flexible. That seems to be changing. For example, the Purchasing Management Association of Canada states within its published code of ethics that members are prohibited from accepting anything more than a token gift on ethical grounds. If a company is involved in tendering, then its members are counselled not to accept even tokens as gifts. The reason for rejecting even minor gifts is to retain a sense of independence and both the appearance and reality of probity. Moreover, there will be no danger of an incremental creep: a small gift one day, a bigger one the next, and so on until the receiver is compromised. Of course, the size of some kinds of gifts may be a disincentive to accepting them. A ride in a jet trainer, for example, can cost over $1,600 for a short flight, and this can place an obligation on the receiver to reciprocate with a favourable business decision.[9]

A Guide to Giving and Receiving Corporate Gifts

Influence	There must be no influence, or expectation of influence, attached to the giving or receiving of a gift.
Reciprocity	There must be no expectation of reciprocity attached to the giving or receiving of a gift.
Awareness	Investigate cultural norms and traditions with respect to gift-giving when conducting business in another culture.
Cultural norms	The size and value of a gift must fall within the cultural norms of the society within which it is given.
Appearances	The size and value of the gift should be such that there exists no appearance of influence, either within the culture within which the gift is given or within the home culture of the giver or receiver.
Policy	The giving or receiving of a gift must not violate any existing gift-giving/receiving policies established by either the giver's or the receiver's company.
Conservatism	Where any doubt exists with respect to the motives of the giver or receiver of a gift, err on the side of conservatism and graciously decline to participate.
Integrity	Where any discomfort exists with respect to engaging in the giving or receiving of a gift, or if any doubt exists with respect to the appearances of the gift-giving, graciously decline to participate.
Sensitivity	Be prepared to explain cultural norms and gift-giving traditions and restrictions within your home culture so as to circumnavigate any possible offence that may be taken.
Permission	If there exists any doubt with respect to the appropriateness in the giving or receiving of a gift, check with superiors. Companies may recognize that the offer of a gift should be politely refused except in cultures where to do so would be seen as offensive. In such cases the employee should be able to seek permission or guidance.

Gifts that can influence a decision are corrupting and harmful. They are akin to bribes and do the same kind of damage to trust in the market system. If they influence business decisions, then products will not be bought and sold on merit but on grounds that could not be justified in the cold light of day. However, this view is not accepted universally. Some believe that if the recipient is not involved in a decision about the giver, then a large gift may be accepted, or that a gift may be given after a deal has been closed.[10] It is difficult to reconcile these views with ethical appearances. There are no free lunches, let alone free laptop computers, extreme adventures, or tropical cruises.

Although corporate gift-giving for business purposes has attracted public criticism, benevolence to charities and community projects—the kinds of giving Friedmanites would question—has not. On the contrary, it seems to be expected. This, no doubt, is because corporate persons are often held to the standards that apply to natural persons.

In the *1999 Millennium Poll on Corporate Social Responsibility*, sponsored by PricewaterhouseCoopers, more than 25,000 consumers were interviewed about the role of business in society. The poll found that "[t]wo in three citizens want companies to go beyond their historical role of making a profit, paying taxes, employing people and obeying laws; they want companies to contribute to broader societal goals as well."[11]

Two Types of Corporate Gifts

Corporate gifts come in two quite distinctive forms. The first and most common is the giving of a gift to an individual who is clearly connected to the giver in a business relationship. Corporations often provide gifts to their suppliers or to major customers. These gifts are generally relatively small and are given out of respect and in order to smooth the transaction of business. These can include business lunches, a token bottle of wine for the holiday season, or an invitation to a social or sporting event. Most companies strive to keep these gifts small to avoid any accusation of unfairly influencing business transactions.

The second form of corporate gift is that given to an organization such as a charity or foundation that is not engaged in business dealings with the giving corporation. This type of gift is philanthropic in nature and is often quite significant in terms of its monetary value. While many corporations regularly engage in philanthropic activities in the name of corporate citizenship or corporate social responsibility, this type of corporate giving is not completely selfless, for it can have positive ramifications in terms of reputation and recognition by the receiving organization. It is not uncommon, for example, for sports organizations and arts foundations to attach the name of a large corporate donor to a stadium or a concert hall.

As an example of arguing for the benefits of corporate giving in the name of good citizenship, take celebrated neurosurgeon Jeffrey Rosenfeld, who has been frustrated about inadequate funds for research and development. Rosenfeld asks, "Why can't we encourage our major companies to put major dollars into healthcare? The Government can only do so much. I'm not critical of the Government. I'm critical of the corporations."[12] Among the corporations that attract his criticism are drug companies that will not devote their resources to diseases that plague the Third World. Profits are difficult to generate in such environments, so remedies for these diseases are not researched. Rosenfeld argues that these companies have a responsibility to spend some of their profits on Third World disease. It would be good if medical science were to fight exotic diseases, but science is expensive and investors take a risk with their money in funding it. But that is not the main point. Many people—Rosenfeld included—have the tendency to treat private and corporate wealth as though they were equivalent. And corporate responsibility is taken to equate with the responsibilities assumed by generous individuals. The problem with this way of thinking is that it can lead executives to treat the corporation's money as their own as long as they believe a cause is worthy of support, and it can excuse improper uses of executive discretion. (This, by the way, was one of Milton Friedman's concerns.)

The best-known instance of this in recent times is found in the generosity of HIH Insurance founder Ray Williams.

CASE 4.1: HIH—A Worthy Cause?

Prior to its collapse in 2001, HIH Insurance was Australia's second-largest insurance company. Ray Williams, founder of HIH, was a quiet but generous donor to medical research and other worthy causes.[13] Indeed, he added HIH money to his own contributions. He gave the Reverend Dave Smith of Dulwich Hill, in Sydney, $15,000 for his work rehabilitating drug addicts and another $10,000 from HIH after reading about the difficulties facing Smith's foundation. After the collapse of HIH, Williams received more publicity than he had been accustomed to, and just about all of it was bad. Smith did not forget his friend in such difficult times. His response to criticisms of HIH's donations to charity reveals some of the confusion that surrounds this issue: "I still find it preposterous to think that the media should have acted so self-righteously, so indignant, about the fact that the poor shareholders were losing potential income because it had gone to the children's hospital. It is just ridiculous. And it is appalling the number of people who have turned their back on Ray."[14]

Another who has praised Williams's generosity is Harold Sharp, chief executive officer of the North Shore Heart Research Foundation. "If I had to stand up in court and give a character reference under oath, I would have to say he is one of the finest people I have ever met," said Sharp. The problem, according to those who worked with Williams, is that there was often confusion about whether Williams or HIH was the donor. HIH royal commissioner Justice Owen found that Williams did not keep his shareholders and directors adequately informed about company donations. While Williams's personal generosity was unquestioned, his largesse with company funds—estimated to have been worth $20 million—earned him criticism. Moreover, Williams sat on the boards of several charities that benefited from HIH donations. This conflict of interest was a point of criticism by senior counsel Wayne Martin during the royal commission hearings, but it is a problem that does not seem to have occurred to Williams.[15]

Williams is not alone in his views, and considering the value of reputation, perhaps corporate benevolence is more justifiable than Friedman and his followers have recognized. This is an area not sufficiently recognized as grey. Indeed, some who subscribe to Friedman's view wish to go further than the master. Elaine Sternberg accuses him of being "too polite" in describing the use of a corporation's funds for benevolent purposes as "socialism" and covert "taxation." She calls it theft:

teleopathy *becoming fixated on goals far from the original mission or outside the original mandate*

> Business managers who use business funds for non-business purposes are guilty not just of the legal crime of theft, but of the logical offence of **teleopathy**: in diverting funds from strictly business objectives to other purposes, they are pursuing the wrong ends. And teleopathy is a serious offence, the generic form of prostitution. Just as prostitution occurs when sex is proffered for money rather than love, so it exists when business pursues love—or "social responsibility"—rather than money.[16]

Sternberg is mistaken, of course, in calling teleopathy a logical offence. It might be a moral offence to aim at the wrong goals in corporate life, but it is hardly illogical to be immoral. It would be a nice argument with a prostitute to inform her that her trade defied logic. But Sternberg makes the same mistake as Friedman in taking profit maximizing to be the *only* goal of business and the *only* goal of the owners—by which she means shareholders. The activism of shareholders across environmental and ethical investing fronts gives the lie to this.[17] And she also seems to assume that it is possible to draw a clear distinction between business and non-business purposes. This overlooks the importance of reputation and customer perception. If the ethical use of corporate funds amounts to justifying their use in terms of business purposes, then that need not exclude benevolence. It should exclude, however, managers using their discretion unaccountably and without respect for investors. That would really be to substitute stakeholder theory for traditional concepts of ownership.

Fair Dealing and Care

The requirements of fair dealing and care in business relations are difficult to observe in the face of the competitive nature of business and its regard for self-interest, on the one hand, and for the moral and fiduciary requirement to take advantage of opportunities to improve profits for shareholders, on the other.

The ethical basis of a market economy is that it places a great deal of emphasis on respect for individual autonomy and choice. This implies strong limitations on the role of government and an anti-paternalistic bias. According to this view, if individuals are to be free to make genuine choices and to create the kind of demand that will sustain an economy, then government should not have too strong a presence. This limitation on government respects the rights of individuals to choose to consume alcohol or smoke or view pornography—as well as to invest, sell, and purchase—as they choose. This also means that governments should not fund the choices of individuals or be expected to pay for their consequences. Such an emphatically liberal view of the market has been held by prominent economists (one thinks again of Friedman),[18] but like any model, it works perfectly only in theory. We do restrict the buying and selling of certain goods, such as tobacco and alcohol, because we believe that the harm done from an unrestricted market in such goods outweighs the social benefit. In cases of hardship resulting from individual choice, the government either intervenes as the agent of society or abstains and allows the development of social conditions that make life in that society unpalatable. It is true that government interventions reduce the incentive of people to exercise their own control (as indeed insurance coverage can make people less cautious).[19] Yet it is implausible to suggest that the market could be a perfect instrument for meeting human needs and desires if it were only allowed to operate freely. Markets are social constructions; they do not arise if individuals are left to their own devices, but rather rely on a social context and, concomitantly, on government to provide order, security, and continuity.

Between government regulation and utter licence lies ethical responsibility; that is, it is possible to have a relatively unregulated society when its members preserve core ethical values—hence the importance of ethics to a market economy and to the society that benefits from it. Individuals are worthy of respect. We can take a positive ethical view of market economies and see them as being, if not perfect, at least a good way of accommodating and respecting the autonomy of buyers and sellers.

What are these core ethical values? Here are some important ones: honesty, trustworthiness, compassion, fairness, and justice.

honesty *accountability to provide the truth to certain individuals based on context and relationship*

- **Honesty** is a kind of accountability; it means being accountable for the truth to certain individuals. If a friend asks if you like his new tie, an honest answer will help him decide or perhaps save him from embarrassment. If your host at a dinner party asks you to admire her new painting, it would be insulting, not honest, to tell her she has poor taste. People's relationship to each other dictates the nature of what honesty requires. This is not a value carried around like a pocket calculator to assess situations or find universal answers; it is a way of addressing a variety of situations with very different demands and responsibilities attached to them. While one should care for the truth, not all information belongs to everybody who asks for it. An honest person will find it repellent to deceive, and especially so to deceive those who have placed trust in them—family and friends, or shareholders, employees, and customers.

trustworthiness *the ability to receive a truth or responsibility and sustain the confidence of others that you will not use it lightly or inappropriately*

- **Trustworthiness** is the other side of honesty; it is being able to receive a truth or a responsibility and sustain the confidence of others that you will not use it lightly or in an inappropriate way. A person who keeps their word is such an individual.

compassion *respect for the humanity of others*

- **Compassion** means that one respects the full humanity of others. It is a spirit of generosity that can soften the rigours of justice. It would give a sucker an even break.

fairness *the part of justice that relates to equity; giving each individual their due*

- **Fairness** does not mean being unstrategic or stupid in doing business. It means avoiding dirty tricks and underhanded tactics to get your way. Fairness is part of justice, the part that relates to equity: treat everyone with respect, and treat equals (or like cases) equally and unequal persons (or dissimilar cases) unequally. Give each and every person their due. Do not let self-interest overwhelm decision-making. Follow procedure. Beyond these prescriptions, fairness is often a matter of law and is determined in the courts. The same is true of justice, but legal justice is not identical to moral justice (what positive law calls justice can only be part of what any society means by the term).

justice *the inclusion and consideration of concepts such as equity, need, contributions, merits, social values, risks, and compassion in reaching an outcome*

- **Justice** takes into account things that many definitions of fairness leave out: need, contributions, merits, social value, and risks are seldom present in the same theory.[20] Compassion and caring could also be added to the list, and then justice becomes the inclusive virtue of ethics, the principle that orders all others and is their best expression.

There is another ethical aspect of markets that should incline us to a positive view of them. The strength of a market economy should be to provide the most efficient allocation of scarce resources to meet demand. Competition is essential to the market, for without it there is no incentive to minimize waste and maximize productivity. Without competition, resources would be allocated inefficiently and prices would be higher than they should be. From this line of thinking, it follows that businesses and customers must be relatively unconstrained. Each seeks to gain from a transaction: the customer wants the lowest price, and the seller wants the maximum profit. They meet at an equilibrium point on price. In a kind of premonition of chaos theory, Adam Smith showed how these free and competitive transactions were guided by an "invisible hand" to bring about the maximum economic benefit to society.

Smith's insight has been used to argue against government intervention in the market and to justify liberties that Smith would never have countenanced. The self-interest that he believed motivated people to be productive was not an unfettered right to pursue profit. Gain should only be sought within the confines of justice and social morality. It is these moral restrictions that are usually forgotten when Smith's theory is mentioned. Business is not, as Carr imagines, run according to its own rules, but must work within the rules and conventions of the social system.[21]

Business, then, should function in a market economy in accordance with, or constrained by, the principles of justice and morality that prevail in society. There is a constant temptation, however, to minimize competition and the access of customers to alternative sources of goods and services. Marx believed that a movement to **oligopoly** and **monopoly** was characteristic of late capitalism,[22] but this is a latent tendency of business and can be as strongly supported by labour (in order to preserve jobs) as by management and owners. Although the law attempts to deal stringently with this area of business, the pressures of competition, especially during a recession or when a business is in decline,[23] can be difficult to resist. Hence, there is a common problem in business-to-business relations of dealing fairly not only with one's stakeholders, but also with one's competitors.

oligopoly *a state of limited competition in which the market is shared by a few dominant producers or sellers*

monopoly *a situation in which a single company or entity owns all or almost all of the market for a given type of product, commodity, or service*

The following cases illustrate some of these issues. They serve to discredit the belief that market systems are self-rectifying and need no externally imposed ethical and legal constraints. They are cases not only of personal moral failure, but also of the failure of business ethics. Nowhere is this difficulty more apparent than on the issue of fairness. The three cases below illustrate some ways in which justice as fairness can be harmed.

CASE 4.2: Michael Milken[24]

The saga of the rise and fall of the investment banker who came to be known as the "Junk Bond King," Michael Milken, illustrates Adam Smith's often overlooked point that market transactions must respect fairness and common morality. Some cases give rise to ethical perplexities; this one doesn't. There is not a great deal to consider ethically, but this is an important case for illustrating ethical disengagement, which is far too common in business.

In the 1980s, Michael Milken, senior vice-president of Drexel Burnham Lambert, an investment banking firm, saw an opportunity to move into what he saw as an untapped market for commercial bonds. He found that there existed many medium-sized companies with $25 million or more in annual revenue that desperately needed capital to finance continued growth and capital investment. Because these companies did not meet the requirements for "investment grade" commercial paper status, they were previously unable to access capital

continued . . .

through banks or through the traditional bond market. Milken devised what he referred to as high-yield bonds. These bonds could be issued by companies that exhibited risk profiles that were higher than those of the traditional issuers of investment grade bonds. To offset that risk, these bonds paid a much higher yield than more traditional bonds. These bonds came to be known as "junk bonds."

In what became one of Wall Street's biggest scandals, Milken and Drexel Burnham Lambert sold billions of dollars worth of these junk bonds, which fuelled much of the corporate takeover mania of the 1980s. While Milken and several of his colleagues were eventually found guilty of a number of transgressions by the US Securities and Exchange Commission and the US Attorney's Office, much of the real pain generated by the eventual collapse of the junk bond market was borne by the investing public. When given the choice between an investment-grade bond and a high-yield bond, many unsophisticated investors jumped at the higher return offered by the high-yield or junk bond without understanding the ramifications of the associated increase in risk.

There is nothing illegal in selling high-risk investments, provided that the risk is disclosed to the purchaser. But why then can some instances of selling junk bonds be deemed unethical? Even with the risk disclosed in the purchase documents, many investors lacked the sophistication to comprehend them adequately. There were many instances of family savings being wiped out because of the failures and bankruptcies of the companies issuing these high-yield (high-risk) bonds.

Ironically, many financial institutions suffered significant losses in their portfolios containing junk bonds owing to the collapse of the junk bond market. The difference here is that these financial institutions were in a position to understand the risks involved in holding these investments.

Perhaps in the past more people in business would have excused Milken's conduct on the principle that if an activity is legal, then it is not unethical. Nowadays, that kind of rationale is no longer convincing. Talk of free markets, the free exchange of property, and the like does not excuse conduct like Milken's: such conduct is naked opportunism that violates the core values nominated as essential for the conduct of business—honesty, trustworthiness, compassion, justice, and fairness.

The case of Milken illustrates many things about the ethics of business:

- that market justifications for ethically repugnant conduct are morally irrelevant
- that law alone is insufficient to support good business, as Adam Smith recognized
- that not much can be expected ethically of persons unable to empathize with (care about) those with whom they deal
- that those without scruple can exploit trust within the law (the fragility of trust)
- that unscrupulous persons will evade legal restrictions if they are sufficiently determined.

On 4 June 1993, after his release from incarceration, Milken gave an interview to Barbara Walters on the show *20/20* in which he made clear his belief that he had been unfairly treated: "I was involved with over 3 million transactions in my career. Did we have an oversight in bookkeeping in one or two transactions? Yes. No one thought it was criminal. I am not perfect, and I've never met a person who was."

A classic case of obviously unfair competition was revealed in the legal action taken by Virgin Atlantic against British Airways.[25]

CASE 4.3: Virgin Atlantic and British Airways

In December 1991 Richard Branson, founder of Virgin Atlantic airlines, wrote an open letter to non-executive directors of the board of British Airways alleging a dirty tricks campaign by British Airways staff against Virgin Atlantic. British Airways' chairman, Lord King of Wartnaby, alleged in turn that Branson was simply trying to generate publicity for his airline. Branson replied with a libel suit, and British Airways cross-sued over his initial allegations.

In January 1993 the claims were settled in the High Court with Lord King and British Airways agreeing to pay Branson £500,000 and Virgin Atlantic £110,000 (a total of C$1.1 million) and costs of £3 million. Lord King also offered Branson an unreserved apology for the dirty tricks practised against Virgin Atlantic. Counsel for Lord King and British Airways accepted that their employees had been guilty of "regrettable" conduct, but stated that British Airways directors "were not party to any concerted campaign against Richard Branson and Virgin Atlantic."

The man directly responsible for the campaign against Branson's airline, public relations adviser Brian Basham, claimed otherwise. In an affidavit he asserted, "At no time did I act without the knowledge or approval of the British Airways board." A letter from Basham's lawyer declared:

> Lord King, Sir Colin Marshall (British Airways' chief executive) and Robert Ayling (director of marketing and operations) well know they and the company gave full authority to his actions and it was Brian himself who played a major role in exercising restraint in what was allowed to appear in the press about Branson.

The dirty tricks included computer hacking, poaching passengers, impersonation of Virgin staff, document shredding, and press smears.

Each of the preceding cases—HIH, Michael Milken and Drexel Burnham Lambert, and British Airlines and Virgin Air—involved protagonists who believed that they were operating within the confines of the law, even if they may have engaged in ethically questionable behaviour. The Bre-X case, which is presented in the next box, however, resulted from a deliberate fraud that was clearly illegal. The truly fascinating ethical elements to this case reside not with the fraud itself, but with the fact that so many people turned a blind eye to the suspicious nature of the find because it offered them an opportunity for profit.

CASE 4.4: Bre-X Minerals Ltd

In March 1993 a penny-stock mining company based in Calgary called Bre-X purchased a mining site in Busang, Borneo. In October 1995 Bre-X announced the discovery of significant gold deposits in the area. Each new sample core drilled seemed to increase the size of the potential gold deposit. Kilborn Engineering, Bre-X's

continued . . .

independent consulting firm and a division of SNC-Lavalin, a major Canadian engineering firm based in Montreal, estimated the size of the gold deposit at 70 million troy ounces. Chief geologist John Felderhof said in an interview with *Fortune* magazine that the deposit could be as high as 200 million ounces.[26]

Immediately after the gold discovery was announced, the stock went from pennies to a high of $286.50 (adjusted for stock splits). In May 1996 Bre-X had a market capitalization of $6 billion. The Indonesian government was determined to gain control of the site and have it developed by an established gold firm. Major gold producers were lobbying the government and jockeying for position. Among the most aggressive players was Peter Munk of Toronto's Barrick Gold, the world's second-largest gold producer.

In March 1997 Michael de Guzman, the head field geologist at Bre-X and the person responsible for the gold find, fell to his death from a helicopter while over the jungle near the Busang site. Whether he jumped or was pushed is a matter for speculation. Within a few days, Freeport-McMoRan, an American firm and prospective partner in the development of the mine site, conducted its own core sampling as part of its due diligence and found there to be insignificant quantities of gold. Strathcona Minerals, a third party, was brought in to make an independent analysis and found that the original core samples had been "salted"; traces of gold had been added to the samples to make it appear that they contained gold. The stock price disintegrated, investors lost billions, and stock analysts and stock exchange administrators suffered career-ending damage to their reputations. The portfolios of major Canadian public sector organizations were severely damaged by the collapse of Bre-X: the Ontario Teachers' Pension Plan lost $100 million, the Ontario Municipal Employees Retirement Board lost $45 million, and the Quebec Public Sector Pension Fund lost $70 million. Steve Maich, financial commentator with *Maclean's* noted that "some of the world's most sophisticated analysts and executives had been sucked in by a deception so simple, a child could have conceived it."[27]

Charges were never laid and the perpetrator of the scandal was never unearthed. David Walsh, president, CEO, and founder of Bre-X, moved to the Bahamas in 1998. He continued to profess his innocence until he died of a brain aneurysm that same year. Felderhof moved to the Cayman Islands and subsequently the Philippines, where he now runs a convenience store and a restaurant. The Royal Canadian Mounted Police (RCMP) concluded its investigations in 1999 without laying charges. The Ontario Securities Commission charged Felderhof with insider trading, but after several years of legal wrangling he was found not guilty in 2007.

The mystery surrounding the origin of the scandal remains unsolved. A more intriguing mystery exists with respect to the question of how this relatively simple deception remained uncovered and undetected for so long. How were so many people fooled? Duping unsophisticated investors is one thing, but pulling the wool over the eyes of the vast majority of industry experts and seasoned analysts and executives is yet another. One theory is that the underlying greed that existed within all of the players in this scandal blinded them to any negative indicators. People who want to be wealthy are positively predisposed to believe in scenarios that will allow them to achieve that wealth. Because the stake of all the involved players depended on the existence of the gold deposit, the deception (including self-deception) was propagated by all involved, albeit subconsciously in most cases.

Case Questions

1. Does the reliance on expert opinion relieve an obligation on the buyer to beware?
2. Did the securities analysts have a duty to conduct their own due diligence before supporting Bre-X's claims?

3. Other than the obvious deception around the salting of core samples with gold particles, what are the ethical issues involved in this case?
4. What was the role of Bre-X's board of directors in this case?

The following case served as the precursor for one of the biggest financial crises in history. Some notable similarities exist between the Lehman Brothers case presented in the next box and the above Drexel Burnham Lambert and Bre-X Mineral Ltd cases. Each case culminated in extensive negative consequences that were exacerbated by the reluctance of the financial industry to assess critically the somewhat obvious problems that lay at the root of each of the respective crises. In the Drexel Burnham Lambert case, many of the financial professionals involved in the buyout frenzy of the 1990s profited enormously from the rise of the junk bond. Likewise, in the Bre-X mining case, the frenzy of excitement around the gold find, however suspicious, generated significant profits for financial professionals such as brokers and underwriters and for investors savvy enough to sell their shares before the ultimate collapse of the share price. The financial industry exhibited the same type of behaviour in the Lehman Brothers case through its enthusiastic adoption of mortgage-backed securities despite the fact that the validity of the underlying assets was clearly suspect.

In each of these cases, the frenzied activity generated by the opportunity to generate profits from flawed assumptions seems to drive a moral blindness. The psychology behind this blindness is similar each time an economic "bubble" occurs. The rush to profit from the run-up in prices of shares, real estate, or any other specific class of asset before the bubble bursts and the market corrects overrides common sense and ethical sensibilities. The sale of risky junk bonds or overvalued mining shares to unsuspecting and unsophisticated investors, while legal, is clearly ethically questionable. Likewise, the issuance of subprime mortgages to people who are clearly unable to repay them and the subsequent issuance of securities backed by these unsound mortgages, while not illegal, clearly represent unsound ethical practices.

The people engaged in these practices are not without moral conscience or valid ethical frameworks. The type of herd mentality that develops during these bubbles seems to override these ethical sensibilities. "If everyone else is profiting, why shouldn't I? It must be OK!"

CASE 4.5: Lehman Brothers and the Subprime Mortgage Crisis

Before it went bankrupt in 2008, Lehman Brothers was the fourth-largest investment banking firm in the United States. Only Goldman Sachs, Merrill Lynch, and Morgan Stanley were larger. Its bankruptcy in 2008 was the largest in US history and was a precursor to the global financial crisis of 2008. Lehman Brothers' declaration of bankruptcy had been immediately preceded by a mass exodus of its clients, a downgrade of its credit worthiness by credit-rating agencies, and a drastic decline in its share price. In short, the firm was hit by a massive crisis of confidence. But what caused this crisis of confidence?

continued . . .

Accusations of aggressive short-selling and accounting malfeasance aside, Lehman Brothers was one of the many victims of the subprime mortgage crisis. Lehman Brothers was holding large positions in lower-rated financial instruments (or mortgage-backed securities) secured by subprime mortgages. "Subprime mortgages" refer to mortgages issued by aggressive lenders who use lower-than-market, short-term, flexible "teaser" interest rates to entice consumers to take out mortgages to buy homes. The teaser rate usually lasts for a period of six months, when the interest rate reverts to market levels (or higher!). These subprime mortgages were then pooled together and "securitized," or split up, into financial instruments and then sold on the market. This securitization of subprime mortgages theoretically spreads the risk of mortgage default across a large number of investors, and such risk, in diversified portfolios, would presumably be more than offset by the returns from the mortgages that did not go into default.

Several factors combined to ignite the subprime mortgage crisis:

- Aggressive lenders offered subprime mortgages to consumers with poor credit or low incomes who would not be able to afford the market mortgage rates that would kick in once the teaser rates expired.
- The aggressive mortgage lending increased the demand for residential mortgages, driving house prices to unprecedented highs.
- Once the teaser rates began to expire, mortgage defaults in the United States skyrocketed and the value of the bonds and financial instruments secured by these subprime mortgages fell.
- The housing market went into free fall, reducing the value of the property used to secure these subprime mortgages and, by extension, the mortgage-backed bonds secured by those very mortgages.
- Financial institutions that held mortgage-backed securities suffered massive losses in the value of their portfolios. Where mortgage-backed securities were held as collateral for loans, the value of the collateral began to shrink dramatically, increasing the risks from default and leading to the renegotiation, or calling, of loans.

The aggressive marketing of subprime mortgages and their subsequent securitization created a level of risk that became systemic throughout the financial system. The web of financial interrelationships among the financial institutions meant that no single institution was spared from this systemic risk.

In hindsight, it seems obvious that lending money in the form of subprime mortgages to people who can ill afford to pay them back will only lead to pain. So why do it? The people marketing the mortgages were being paid salaries or commissions and did not have to accept the risks or consequences of a default. The institutions offering these subprime mortgages were passing along their risk by securitizing the mortgages and selling them to investors.

Lehman Brothers were holding large amounts of mortgage-backed securities secured by subprime mortgages when the system began to unravel. The huge losses the firm incurred as a result were largely responsible for its bankruptcy.

Case Questions

1. Is it fair to offer a teaser rate to entice a consumer with a low income to enter into a mortgage agreement when they have little chance of being able to make the payments once the teaser rate expires?
2. When securitizing subprime mortgages in order to diversify risk, is the issuing firm not responsible for evaluating and disclosing the inherent risk levels in the underlying mortgages?

The preceding cases clearly illustrate a number of situations where companies and the individuals who lead them engage in ethical transgressions in the pursuit of profits. In each of these cases, most of those involved did not believe that they were doing anything wrong, because they were not, at least initially, breaking the law. Wherein lies the basis of this loss of moral compass in the conducting of business? Even in the case of Bre-X, where the underlying fraud in the form of falsified core samples was clearly illegal, the parties that contributed to the massive scale in the run-up in share value did so by turning a blind eye to the clearly suspicious nature of the find.

Take the case of the Lehman Brothers' sale of subprime mortgages, their subsequent securitization and sale as mortgage-backed securities, the firm's collapse, and the ensuing financial crisis. While it was not illegal to provide subprime mortgages to people who clearly lacked the capacity to repay them, it was clearly unethical and, from a business perspective, an unsustainable practice. Similarly, in the case of Michael Milken and Drexel Bunham Lambert, selling high-yield, high-risk junk bonds was not illegal, but it most certainly led to significant harm to unsophisticated investors. The ability to generate profits by any means within the law becomes a game that ignores any ethical implications beyond simply obeying the law. Clearly, from a utilitarian perspective, the damage caused to the financial system and the losses to the investing public far exceed the benefits from the profits generated for the individual firms and their shareholders.

Codes of ethics are discussed at some length in chapter 10, but suffice it to say here that many organizations do respond appropriately to a series of chastening experiences by reviewing their values and stating their commitment to ethical business. This contrasts with other enterprises whose only clear values are competitive advantage and the profits this brings. Though often obscured by the demands of competition, fairness and justice remain integral to the practice of business. Sometimes businesses are reminded of this only by the emergence of a crisis.

Review Questions

1. "We do restrict the buying and selling of certain goods . . . because we believe that the harm done from an unrestricted market in such goods outweighs the social benefit." What are the competing interests alluded to here?
2. Explain the statement "Between government regulation and utter licence lies ethical responsibility."
3. Are the demands of competition and the drive for profits so strong that they cloud the exercise of ethical judgment? To what extent should we expect this to happen?

Suggested Readings

Bailey, F. *Fall from Grace: The Untold Story of Michael Milken*. New York: Carol Publishing, 1992.

Goold, D., and A. Willis. *The Bre-X Fraud*. Toronto: McClelland and Stewart, 1997.

Gregory, M. *Dirty Tricks: British Airways' Secret War against Virgin Atlantic*. London: Virgin, 2000.

Hutchinson, B. *Fool's Gold: The Making of a Global Market Fraud*. New York: Alfred A. Knopf, 1998.

McDonald, L.G., and P. Robinson. *A Colossal Failure of Common Sense: The Inside Story of the Collapse of Lehman Brothers*. New York: Crown Business, 2009.

Purchasing Management Association of Canada; Code of Ethics, at http://www.pmac.ca/join-pmac/code-of-ethics.

Sorkin, A.R. *Too Big to Fail: The Inside Story of How Wall Street and Washington Fought to Save the Financial System—and Themselves*. New York: Viking Penguin, 2009.

Stein, B. *A License to Steal: The Untold Story of Michael Milken and the Conspiracy to Bilk the Nation*. New York: Simon and Schuster, 1992.

Stewart, J.B. *Den of Thieves*. New York: Simon and Schuster, 1991.

Stone, D.G. *April Fools: An Insider's Account of the Rise and Collapse of Drexel Burnham*. New York: Donald I. Fine, 1990.

Tsing, A. *Friction*. Princeton: Princeton University Press, 2005.

Wells, J. *Fever: The Dark Mystery of the Bre-X Gold Rush*. New York: Viking, 1998.

Williams, M.T. *Uncontrolled Risk: The Lessons of Lehman Brothers and How Systemic Risk Can Still Bring Down the World Financial System*. New York: McGraw-Hill, 2010.

Suggested Website

1999 Millennium Poll on Corporate Social Responsibility:

http://www-dev.iblf.org/resources/general.jsp?id=85.

5

Marketing and Advertising Ethics

Chapter Outline

In discussing advertising ethics, two questions come to mind at the outset. First, what scope is there for ethical concern, apart from a legal concern about the practice of advertising and the particular content of individual advertisements? (For example, fraud is illegal; what additional room is there for ethical concerns? If it is legal to sell a product, then should it not be legal to advertise that product?) Second, is there anything morally peculiar to the situation of advertising, and should any special considerations be taken into account here that might be absent from the moral arena in other situations? The short answer to both these questions is that there is plenty of room for moral concern, and that because of the nature of advertising and its audience, legal concern itself is not (and should not be) limited to fraud and the like. That is, there is an expanded set of legal interests when it comes to advertising—beyond the range of those present in other public arenas.

Moral concerns about advertising are present on three levels. At the macro-level we could discuss the moral justification of the practice of advertising per se and its place or overall justification within society. At the micro-level we could consider particular advertisements and evaluate them morally. Some writers have suggested that in order to consider the micro-level, reference must be made to the macro-level, because it is only by considering the social justification for advertising as a practice that criteria for the evaluation of particular advertisements can emerge.[1] Between these two perspectives there is another that is not related to the entire practice of advertising or to individual advertisements, but rather to concerns about advertising different types of products. The Ministry of Industry, Trade and Commerce and Advertising Standards Canada, for instance, both recognize that special considerations should apply to advertisements pertaining to alcoholic beverages, cigarettes, slimming products, and therapeutic products.

Advertisements can be "objectionable" in different ways and according to different criteria. It is possible that an advertisement offends you or that you find it objectionable, but that, nevertheless, you do not believe that it is morally objectionable or that it should be subject to legal sanctions. You may believe that it is ugly; you may find the product itself or the depiction of it unappealing; you may also find the advertisement to be in bad taste. The advertisement for Stayfree Maxipads, for example (the blood of a murder victim is mopped up with the pad), or the advertisement for Ajax multipurpose cleanser (worshipped by the housewife in the bathroom), or the ad for WILD-FM (featuring amputees who cannot dance to the great music played on the radio station) may fall into one or more of these categories.

In thinking about the ways in which advertisements, and advertising in general, can go wrong, it can be helpful to try to separate the objections into three groups: moral, legal, and other. In using "legal" here, we are not referring to present laws, but suggesting that legal sanctions should be present: "There ought to be law." Surely it is possible that some advertisement is objectionable in some sense, but nevertheless should be morally and legally tolerated—that is, there should be no legal or moral sanctions against it or legal or moral criticism of it. There is a significant question as to whether (and to what extent) it is possible to believe that an advertisement is morally objectionable and yet, at the same time, that there should be no legal sanctions against it.

One commentator on batteries for laptops put the matter with admirable clarity: "Lately we've had many people complaining about the length of time their laptops last when running on batteries. While there are many reasons for this, as a public service, I have decided to reveal the main reason: manufacturers and salespeople lie. I know, it is hard to believe they would deliberately mislead, but they do."[2]

Advertisements can deceive by means other than simply telling lies. They can deceive by means of half-truths and by implying something that is not the truth without actually lying. Esso once advertised its gasoline with the claim that cars run better on an additive present in Esso. The advertisement did not mention that all brands of gasoline—not merely Esso—had the additive. Duracell advertised that its batteries outperform Eveready batteries. The television ads showed the Duracell bunny powering ahead of Eveready in a race. In 2001, Energizer took legal action over these ads, pointing out that the ads actually compared Duracell's alkaline (top-end) battery with Energizer's second-tier Eveready carbon zinc battery, rather than with Energizer's alkaline battery, and that this was misleading to consumers. Initially, Energizer won its claim, basically on the grounds that Duracell had neglected to mention that Energizer also stocked a comparable alkaline battery, and so it appeared that the advertisement's claim was simply that Duracell's batteries outperform Energizer's comparable batteries, when, in fact, the advertisement was not comparing like with like. On appeal, however, the judges ruled in Duracell's favour, but required modification to the script so as to make clear that it was alkaline batteries that were being compared with carbon zinc-batteries. The advertisement was allowed to be aired with the script, "Duracell alkaline beats Eveready Super Heavy Duty." It would seem, however, that normal viewers would still believe that they were hearing a claim about a comparison of apples and apples, rather than apples and oranges. There is something of a technicality here that makes the story more interesting—and perhaps more difficult. Energizer batteries used to be *Eveready Energizer*. A company restructuring in 2000 and a difference of branding resulted in dropping "Eveready" from the name. So, "Energizer" is now the name of the top-tier alkaline batteries made by this company, the Eveready Battery Company. "Eveready" now refers primarily to a group of batteries that are not alkaline batteries, one type of which is "super heavy duty," that have, in fact, been around for a long time, and also to "Eveready Gold," a lesser-quality alkaline battery. So, strictly speaking, it is true to say that Duracell alkaline batteries outperform Eveready batteries—because, these days, "Eveready" refers only to non-alkaline and admittedly lower-quality alkaline batteries. It is nevertheless the case that the *meaningful* comparison would be between Duracell alkaline batteries and Energizer (alkaline) batteries. The context of the advertisements—including the history of the ad campaigns about these batteries, our out-of-date "knowledge" about "Eveready Energizer," which, in fact, no longer exists, and our expectation that the advertisement really is comparing apples with apples—leads us to believe that the claim is about two comparable (alkaline) batteries, which, of course, it is not. It is not the actual claim that would lead us to buy Duracell over Energizer or over Eveready, but our reasonable understanding (which is actually a misunderstanding) of the claim being made. Despite the fact that Duracell states the "facts" correctly, this is a readily predictable misunderstanding, one that one might well believe is being counted on in making the claim about Duracell's outperforming Eveready. After all, how effective an ad would it be if it said, "Duracell alkaline batteries outperform all non-alkaline, carbon zinc, lower-quality, less-expensive batteries, including Eveready—and, by the way, we're not talking about Energizer here"?

Advertisements can coerce and manipulate. The extreme of manipulation is subliminal advertising. The message need not be subliminal in order for it to be manipulative, however. Related to this point is the fact that it is possible for advertisements to fail to treat people as persons and fail to respect their autonomy, their role as decision-makers. They can fail to allow people to enter the transaction as autonomous agents making their own decisions through informed choice.[3] The extent to which an advertisement is coercive or manipulative depends not only on the construction of the advertisement itself (as in the case of subliminal advertising or blatant lying), but also on the audience for the advertisement. For example, advertisements that are aimed at children, that are slotted into children's television timeslots, or that have other particularly vulnerable target audiences are well positioned to manipulate either intentionally or unintentionally.

CASE 5.1: Motherhood and Spin

In October 2008, Coca-Cola ran advertisements in the press and on television featuring Australian actress Kerry Armstrong. These ads were unusual: they broke from the classic Coke techniques that celebrate youth, sports, and good times, casting Ms Armstrong in the role of myth-busting mum. They followed other motherhood types of advertisement that push an informative rather than a persuasive line, but caused ire in the dental and medical communities and, well, were not very convincing. They were soon gone.

Here is part of Kerry Armstrong's message: "When I was asked to speak out in favour of one of the world's largest brands, 'Coca-Cola,' it became clear that it was surrounded by all kinds of myths and conjecture." What myths were Coke and Armstrong busting? What about the claim that Coke makes you fat? The ad states that "[n]o one single product makes you fat." This must have been welcome news to chocolate addicts. But, if you get fat, that's your fault. Coke is about helping "people make informed choices about what's right for them depending on their individual needs." But what about all that sugar in Coke that your body burns instead of metabolizing fats and complex carbohydrates? Well, there is always sugarless Coke "Zero" and Diet Coke. What were the other myths that Coke needed to "bust" in order to burnish its image? How about that Coke was once green? That's a myth that needed fixing in a hurry, particularly for the health conscious. This "myth" has no currency and is mentioned only to enhance the informative appearance of the ad. And what about the myth that Coke "contained cocaine once upon a time"? Perhaps, "once upon a time" was meant to suggest a fairy story, but whether Coke once contained cocaine or not is hardly an issue now. Nobody with the powers of reason, let alone one who has consumed Coke, believes that a mass-produced soft drink contains a prohibited drug. So, it doesn't contain preservatives: how many know that it contains phosphoric acid (it's on the label)? The ad did not address this point, but it did state that Coke's caffeine content was basically no worse than that of other soft drinks. As for the most familiar charge, that Coke rots your teeth, the ad claims to bust this, too. It does not deny that Coke is acidic, but no more so than "many other food [*sic*] and drinks." In any case, saliva removes the soft drink from the mouth. So, it's back to you, the consumer: "Make sure you look after your teeth by brushing regularly and visiting your dentist."

No sources are given for these alleged myths, although dental advertisements warning of the dangers of fizzy, sugary soft drinks had been running on television for some time before Coke's campaign. The dental ads, however, were hardly myths: they were scientifically based and clearly in the public interest. It might seem, then, that Coke was targeting a straw man. There are no great myths about Coke that required clarification by the company, especially as its sales were healthy. The take-away message from this information campaign is that Coke does not rot your teeth—if you are sensible. Well, that is hardly news.

So, this advertisement seemed to put a spin on a product to allay health concerns and it was this spin that brought a reaction from dentists who took exception to the claim that the advertisement busted the "myth" that Coke rots teeth. Dr John Matthews, president of the Australian Dental Association, said, "We shouldn't rely upon Coca-Cola for giving us dental health advice. They have underestimated the problem and put a spin on it. Most people know Coke is bad for them but they continue to do it so I don't know why Coca-Cola feels the need to do this."[4] A number of complaints were received regarding the advertisement, but using the image of good mother to promote consumption of Coke was deemed acceptable because it did not encourage "excessive consumption." Objections to the ad's denial of the effect of soft drinks on dental health were dismissed because the ad "stressed the importance of good dental hygiene."[5] Coca-Cola stood by its ads. A spokeswoman said, "We wanted to bust the myth that you can't consume Coca-Cola and have healthy teeth. This is simply not true."[6]

In Canada, Coca-Cola makes extensive use of lifestyle advertising. Its website, interestingly found under livepositively.ca, describes the company's contributions to the community, to the environment, its transparency in highlighting nutritional information, and its promotion of healthy, active lifestyles by providing educational information on healthy diet, exercise, and weight control. In 2009, in an effort to further contribute to its positive lifestyle messaging, Coca-Cola partnered with the American Academy of Family Physicians, contributing $500,000 for the promotion of health and wellness education. Both Coca-Cola and the Academy were subjected to intense criticism over this alliance on the grounds that the damaging health effects of consumption of sugary soft drinks are at odds with the healthy lifestyle message.

Case Questions

1. Many foods and beverages can have damaging or negative health effects if not consumed in moderation. Is Coke being unfairly singled out for criticism?
2. Has Coke, in fact, done anything wrong?

There is another side to concern for autonomy. On the one hand, a concern for respecting people's autonomy is a reason to consider the imposition of formal legal limits on advertising. On the other hand, however, a concern for people's autonomy can offer reasons for refraining from imposing limits. The imposition of legal limits amounts to taking a paternalistic role with regard to the people who are exposed to advertising. It amounts to formally—legally—assuming the role of looking after their welfare and making decisions about what they should and what they should not be exposed to and what they should and what they should not be allowed to expose themselves to. The other side of the concern for protecting people from entering into unfair, manipulative transactions is the possibility of not allowing people to enter into transactions into which they would otherwise choose to enter. This question about how paternalistic it is desirable to be in this area has been briefly considered by Richard De George, who suggests that this is a political question rather than a particularly moral one; that is, in this area, "the proper paternal role of government should be decided by the people through their representatives, and with a majority rule, limited by the rights of individuals and minority groups."[7] According to this view, there is nothing morally compelling about paternalistic concern in the area of advertising, but neither is there anything morally repugnant about it. Like a number of other important matters within society, this one is properly left to society's preferences about what it would like to do—whether it wishes to be more or less paternal in its conduct in this area, whether it wishes to have more or less paternalistically oriented legislation about advertising. This is a very important point. Not every significant decision that we make about what to do or what kind of society or person to be must be a moral decision. Many very important decisions are rightly matters of preference or "politics"—that is, decisions about which it is appropriate to take a vote.

Labelling of Genetically Modified Foods[8]

In an effort to improve agricultural productivity, scientists look for ways to create plants that resist disease and pests. Likewise, plants with desirable characteristics, such as faster growth, brighter colours, more consistent or hardier textures, and increased nutritional value, are formulated through genetic modifications. These genetic modifications are achieved by removing a gene from one organism and splicing it into another.

In Canada, rules governing the identification of genetically modified (GM) foods are difficult to formulate and even harder to enforce. Canadian farmers produce many varieties of corn and wheat, some genetically modified and others not. Where these crops grow in close proximity, it is all but impossible to ensure that seeds from GM crops do not stray into non-GM crops. There are genetically modified elements in a broad variety of Canadian foods. The difficulty in ensuring that any food is completely free of genetic modifications makes labelling very difficult. Does the label say "May contain genetically modified products"? It is virtually impossible to certify that food is completely GM free.

The Canadian Federation of Agriculture is concerned that labelling genetically modified foods in Canada as such could be seen as a warning to consumers, leading to a reluctance on their part to purchase GM foods and a movement by the food industry away from the production of foods that have been genetically modified. Increased labelling requirements will also increase the costs of food products in Canada. Food must be labelled in Canada if it is pasteurized, is irradiated, or contains possible allergens such as peanuts, but there are currently no labelling conventions for GM foods.

While Greenpeace and other environmental advocates contend that GM foods are dangerous, Health Canada takes the position that GM foods are just as safe as conventional foods. The truth is that there have been no long-term studies that either support or refute either of these positions.[9]

In appraising whether or not an advertisement or an advertising practice should have moral and, in particular, legal sanctions imposed on it, we must consider not merely whether the advertisement or practice is morally offensive or is in some other respect morally objectionable. Having decided that it is objectionable should not settle the question of whether the advertisement should have sanctions imposed on it or whether those who judge it to be objectionable should tolerate it. Toleration is recognized as an important principle in other areas of interpersonal activity, and the principle should carry some currency in this area as well. Having said that, however, we offer no suggestion about exactly how much weight should be accorded to this principle.

Some things that we might want to consider as unethical advertising are actually scams and not advertising at all. Sometimes there are no actual products on the other end of these "advertisements," just someone to take your money. The Internet has certainly given rise to lots of these and has also provided lots of examples of unethical advertising (probably, in fact, far more unethical and/or illegal advertising than legal).[10]

Here is an interesting type of misleading advertisement. Different people react to this case in different ways: some are outraged and completely misled by it, while others seem not to be misled at all.

CASE 5.2: Free Sunglasses

An email arrives with the subject line "Free sunglasses for j. brown [the name of the email addressee]—pick them up today!" The body of the email then says "Overstock sunglasses. Sunglasses for free." And then, "WHAT'S THE GIMMICK? How are you giving away sunglasses for free?"

The answer, we are told, is this:

> Sunglass Manufacturers produce millions of dollars in excess inventory each year. Overstocked Sunglasses has built a relationship with select, leading manufacturers, and retailers to move this inventory and make room for new merchandise. *While these manufacturers will accept a loss on these products, they would rather give them away and opt for a Tax Write-off than sell them for near cost and reap no benefit.
>
> **click here to view entire selection of Free Sunglasses or to order** [hotlink]
>
> The Sunglasses featured here are First Quality Sunglasses you will find in the store that sell for anywhere between $19.95 & $49.95 and compare to designers like Armani, Maui, Ray-Ban, and Killer Loops!
>
> **click here to view entire selection of Free Sunglasses or to order** [hotlink]
>
> The only catch is that most of our products come in limited quantities—so if you see something you like, choose it now, because when they're gone, they're gone!

continued . . .

click here to view entire selection of Free Sunglasses or to order [hotlink]

If we go to the website, we see a list of brands of sunglasses. We can click on any of them and we get a better look at and description of those glasses—and all the rest are shown under them. We then discover that the particular ones we are interested in cost either $1 or are free, and the postage and handling to anywhere in the United States is, roughly, US$5. This still seems like a tremendous deal for good-quality sunglasses. If we look carefully, we might notice that above the list of brands of sunglasses, the heading is "Inspired Styles." Then, we might also happen to scroll clear to the bottom of the screen and happen to notice this, in very small print:

> Disclaimer: *We have no association or relationship with the above-named sunglass companies, stores, products, or trademarks whatsoever. The reference is to simply compare our prices and products to the above. Our products are unique and different than the above-mentioned products. We do not represent our sunglasses to be the originals nor are they copies of the above.

So, an "inspired style" might be Christian Dior, Nike, or Bollé, but those are "inspired styles" only. And while it is true that the disclaimer does appear on the website, it would be very difficult to argue that the website is not designed to appear to provide sunglasses that are the real McCoy, particularly when one goes to it by means of the direction that is included in the personalized email. If we reread the second paragraph of the email, after having noticed the disclaimer on the website, then *maybe* we can get an inkling that the sunglasses are not really name brands at all. But even here, it is still *maybe*; and it is a certainty that the enticement for the sunglasses is a claim that the sunglasses on offer are the real thing.

Formal Regulation in Canada

In Canada, advertising is scrutinized and subject to formal regulation and legislation from a number of sources, particularly the Competitions Act (1985), the Consumer Packaging and Labelling Act (1985), the Textile Labelling Act (1985), and the Precious Metals Marking Act (1985).

The Canadian advertising industry has a long history of self-regulation. This self-regulation is carried out by a number of industry bodies, including Advertising Standards Canada (ASC), the Canadian Radio-television and Telecommunications Commission (CRTC), the Canadian Broadcasting Corporation (CBC), and the Canadian Marketing Association (CMA). ASC is the industry organization that administers the Canadian Code of Advertising Standards and the more specific Gender Portrayal Guidelines. The CRTC is responsible for maintaining the Broadcast Code for Advertising to Children and the Code for Broadcast Advertising of Alcoholic Beverages, while the CBC adheres to its own specific advertising standards. Finally, the Canadian Marketing Association (CMA) has published the Protection of Personal Privacy Code and the Code of Ethics and Standards of Practice.

Advertising Standards Canada was originally founded under the name "the Canadian Advertising Advisory Board" in 1957 by the Canadian advertising industry to "foster the ethical practice of advertising." The first Canadian Code of Advertising Standards was published in 1963. In 1972 the ASC was asked by the Canadian Radio-television and Telecommunications Commission to review practices in the broadcasting of advertising to children. In the 1990s, ASC actively investigated the role of ethnicity and race in advertising and published its first *Ad Complaints Report*, which includes actual case reports. ASC has become increasingly involved in public and consumer awareness campaigns around advertising standards and truth in advertising.[11]

The Canadian Code of Advertising Standards (Code) is administered by ASC and sets the criteria for acceptable advertising in Canada. Originally introduced in 1963, the Code is kept relevant and current through regular reviews and updates. Currently the Code contains 14 clauses that inform the review of consumer complaints and concerns expressed by special interest groups. It is the foundation document for advertising industry self-regulation in Canada. The Code can be viewed online at http://www.adstandards.com/en/standards/canCodeOfAdStandards.pdf.

ASC does not preview, or function as a clearance body, for advertisements. Its role is to respond to complaints from members of the public concerning advertising that they had seen or heard. In order to impose any sanction on an advertisement (such as requiring that the advertisement be altered or that it be removed altogether), ASC would have to find that the advertisement breached one or more clauses in the Code.

The CRTC is an independent public organization that regulates and supervises the Canadian broadcasting and telecommunications systems. It regulates in excess of 2,000 radio and television broadcasters and reports to the Canadian Parliament through the minister of Canadian heritage. Using the Broadcasting Act and the Telecommunications Act as a basis for its policy decisions, the CRTC acts to ensure that the broadcasting and telecommunications industries serve the Canadian public.

The CRTC's mission is as follows:

> to ensure that Canadians have access to a variety of Canadian programming and to high-quality telecommunications services, while protecting Canadians from unsolicited communications and contributing to a more secure online environment for consumers and businesses.[12]

While its primary role in broadcasting is to ensure that Canadians have access to a variety of quality domestic programming that fosters Canadian content and talent, the use of both official languages, Canadian multiculturalism, and the role of aboriginal cultures, the CRTC is responsible for maintaining the Broadcast Code for Advertising to Children and the Code for Broadcast Advertising of Alcoholic Beverages.

The CBC is Canada's national public broadcaster. Its mandate, as set out in the 1991 Broadcasting Act, is as follows:

> to provide radio and television services incorporating a wide range of programming that informs, enlightens and entertains;

> . . . the programming provided by the Corporation should:
>
> i. be predominantly and distinctively Canadian, reflect Canada and its regions to national and regional audiences, while serving the special needs of those regions,
>
> ii. actively contribute to the flow and exchange of cultural expression,
>
> iii. be in English and in French, reflecting the different needs and circumstances of each official language community, including the particular needs and circumstances of English and French linguistic minorities,
>
> iv. strive to be of equivalent quality in English and French,
>
> v. contribute to shared national consciousness and identity,
>
> vi. be made available throughout Canada by the most appropriate and efficient means and as resources become available for the purpose, and
>
> vii. reflect the multicultural and multiracial nature of Canada.[13]

In order to facilitate its mandate, the CBC has developed its own set of advertising standards as part of its published policies and guidelines. These advertising standards are broken down along the following categories:

- Objectives and Values
- Truth in Advertising
- Standards of Taste and Fair Representation
- Advertiser Identification
- Endorsement
- Program Integrity
- Language of Broadcast
- Advertising Directed to Children under 12 Years of Age
- Advocacy Advertising
- Political Advertising
- Unacceptable Advertising
- Contests and Games of Chance
- Alcoholic Beverage Advertising
- Access to Advertiser Property
- Advertising Limits
- Provincial Regulations[14]

The full text of the CBC advertising standards can be found online at http://cbc.radio-canada.ca/en/reporting-to-canadians/acts-and-policies/programming/advertising-standards/.

The Canadian Marketing Association is a national non-profit corporation established in 1967. The CMA is the marketing community's advocate on public policy issues affecting both business-to-consumer and business-to-business marketers. The CMA also develops self-regulatory policies and marketing best practices on issues in marketing and advertising.[15] The CMA has issued an extensive Code of Ethics[16] and Standards of Practice, the full text of which can be found online at http://www.the-cma.org/regulatory/code-of-ethics. Adherence to this code is compulsory for all members of the association.

The Story of Advertising

Here is how advertising advertises itself:

> **Without Advertising, the Price of a Jar of Honey Could Really Sting You**
>
> It's basic economics. The more people who know about a product, the more people are likely to buy it. Advertising is the medium that brings the message to millions. It helps increase the volume of sales and decrease the cost. So whether it's a jar of honey or a jar of pickles, advertising helps keep a lid on the price.[17]

The basic function of advertising is to inform buyers about what is available in the market. It allows sellers to attract customers by praising the virtues of their goods and services. Advertising, then, may reasonably be seen as a fundamental part of the operation of markets. It informs, allows comparisons of products and prices, and is essential to competition. As these basic functions also support newspapers and other media outlets, advertising thus performs a public service beyond its role in marketing.

These basic functions, however, have become more complicated in the world of modern technology. Advertising is more than just the transmission of essential information. True, most advertising is still placed in the classified columns, but most of the national advertising budget is spent on mass campaigns through direct mail, glossy magazines, posters, radio, television, and film. Most of the services and products advertised are consumer goods that depend on volume sales for their success. So advertising must persuade as well as inform. This is where modern technology comes in and where most ethical objections arise.

Persuasion has always been a part of selling. Socrates had a good deal of sport at the expense of the universal persuaders of ancient Athens, the Sophists. In turn, the Roman satirist Lucian made fun of the extravagant claims of philosophers to give instruction in what today we would call lifestyles. But modern techniques of persuasion, together with the ability of modern media to use information on demographics, allow for more pervasive, intrusive, and subtle forms of persuasion than were previously available. The excessive boosting of products, the use of subliminal and other psychoactive techniques, product placements and endorsements, and the use of sexual or violent images all give rise to ethical concerns about advertising. The question is whether such concerns are justified.

Perhaps the central ethical issue in advertising is deception in a variety of hues. It is questionable, however, how far this issue extends. Medieval philosophers distinguished between officious, jocose, and mischievous lies. The last kind, outright lying, say for the sake of fraud, is not ethically contentious: it is just plain wrong. Real questions arise, however, about the first two cases in which the truth is distorted or exaggerated. St Thomas Aquinas was prepared to countenance the first two types—lies that have a good purpose—as not seriously wrong. The law, as well, tolerates a fair amount of **puffery**—untruths or exaggerations that are assumed to be recognized as such by people who are exposed to them.

puffery *untruths or exaggerations that are assumed to be recognized as such by people who are exposed to them*

In Canada, an extreme case of deceptive advertising arose involving the promotion of a product that does not exist. As part of an advertising campaign to promote War Child Canada, a charity dedicated to addressing the use of child soldiers in conflict areas, the charity put up large posters for a non-existent children's camp called Camp Okutta. The posters depicted ordinary-looking children between the ages of 8 and 12 attending an adventure camp where they received instruction on a variety of activities, including grenade throwing, the use of assault weapons, and minefield management. The posters made reference to a website that showed an illustration of the camp and its various activity stations. It is not until the user clicks on one of the activities that they are redirected to the War Child Canada website. A number of citizens who were unaware that the advertisement was a hoax were so offended that they attempted to remove the posters from public view by ripping them down. War Child's marketing director, James Topham, stated that the website was to be so outrageous that it would be obvious that the camp was fake. The intent of War Child Canada, which operates humanitarian programs for children in 10 countries, was to draw attention to the plight of more than 250,000 child soldiers and to convince the Canadian public to help them. Topham contends that "[t]he message of the advertising is that we would never stand for it over here, so we should not stand for it over there either."[18] This is the kind of story more commonly associated with improbable fiction than fact. It is amusing, but those who were taken in by the hoax advertisement were not favourably impressed and many were quite upset. The point about the case is that it illustrates the enormous power of advertising in the creation of a market, as well as the opportunities to deceive consumers with that power.

It is generally accepted that advertising does exaggerate, but it is not always clear that this is wrong, for if everyone is in on the act, it hardly becomes a matter of deception.[19] For quite some time, the law has recognized puffery as acceptable, for exactly this reason. In the film *Crazy People,* Dudley Moore plays an advertising man who is tired of lying. He suggests to his employer that it would be novel to tell the truth about the products he is promoting: Volvo is boxy but good; Metamucil keeps you regular and lessens the risk of death from colonic cancer; "Sony—because Caucasians are too tall" (to work accurately on integrated circuits). The humour only works because these are precisely the concealed messages of conventional hyperbolic advertising. The low-voltage irony of this film is that the only people capable of telling the truth are psychiatric patients; when the Madison Avenue executives realize that truth works, they try to write truthful campaigns themselves—and fail. They have become so used to lying that they can no longer talk straight, no matter how hard they try. This irony is underlined by a role reversal in which the patients become more like the men on Madison Avenue the more advertisement writing they do.

The point is that most of the time exaggerated advertising is obvious. Is this a moral problem? To insist that it is would ally us with a venerable but mistaken line of moral theorizing. Tertullian, a father of the Christian Church, wrote against stage plays because the players took the parts of various characters. Tertullian held that such pretense was a species of lying and therefore forbidden to Christians. What he seems to have ignored is that such impersonations were not designed to deceive the audience into believing that dramatic roles were anything but roles. Therefore no deception was intended and indeed could only arise for a few exceptional people not familiar with the conventions of the theatre.

The same is true of advertising. Anyone unfamiliar with its idioms is likely to make poor judgments about the moral problems involved. This is not to deny that product boosting often crosses the line between praising real or imputed virtues and making claims that are insupportable. Just as dubious is what is left unsaid, or merely suggested. Lying and deception take their character from the contexts in which they are practised and are difficult to define in simple generalizations.

It might be thought that saying something false is lying, but people can often mislead others by saying something that they believe to be true but that is nonetheless false. A resident of Alaska, for example, when asked by his daughter about the capital of Canada, might tell her that it is Toronto. Or we might honestly but falsely believe that Labrador is part of the island of Newfoundland. On the other hand, we might tell an ailing relative that they will get better soon, believing their death is inevitable when in fact a misdiagnosis has been made, and the relative will recover. The fact that we believed that death would come makes well-intended words a lie even though they turned out to be true. So we can lie even if we are not telling a falsehood. Even a relatively straightforward definition of lying, then, turns out to be difficult to construct. If it were simply about intention to mislead, then fairy tales told to children would be lies, and so would many a compliment around a barbecue and dinner table. If it were simply about deception for personal gain, then do untruths designed to protect other people cease to be lies?

Not only is the definition of lying difficult, then, but also, more importantly, the significance of lying is context dependent—that is, it depends on what the liar is trying to do in a particular context. A person who intentionally and deliberately misleads you so that your surprise party will not be spoiled should be judged after the party, not at the point of telling the lie. And what of the lie that is so blatantly outlandish that no one would be expected to believe it? Advertisements for Axe deodorant purport to make men instantly irresistible to women, causing them to completely lose control once they catch a scent of the man wearing the product. This lie is told for comedic effect, but still gets the message across that the product smells good.

Advertising that makes false statements that the public is expected to take at face value is patently wrong and that is the end of the story. The real issues reside in advertising that does not make false claims, but which may nonetheless be misleading. The important point has to do with misleading, not with lying. People can mislead by telling the truth. Remember the example of Esso noted earlier. The line between what is permissible boosting of a product's merits and misleading exaggeration is a matter of pitch, context, and the assumptions of the reader.

1. Should advertisers and marketers avoid exaggerated, offensive, or tasteless campaigns altogether?
2. Should there be legal prohibitions on them?
3. Are there any principles that can be employed to determine whether or not a particular advertisement is unethical?
4. Are there any principles that can be employed to determine whether or not a particular advertisement should be legally prohibited?

It is clear that many vocal groups in society would answer "yes" to questions 1 and 2. Not long ago, a brand of beer advertised itself in a poster featuring a smiling African man with an elongated neck adorned with rings and the caption "Didn't even touch the sides." A number of people found this advertisement racist. Similar complaints of tastelessness and sexism have been made in the case of a Canadian used car dealer's advertisement depicting an attractive woman in a provocative pose with the caption "You know you're not the first, but do you really care?"[20] Likewise, an ad by Fortnight Lingerie depicting two attractive women in their underwear demonstrating CPR (cardio pulmonary resuscitation) in a provocative manner also received numerous complaints of sexism.[21] Sometimes it is the slogans that seriously offend. An advertisement for Thermos hot and cold containers proclaimed, "It takes more than big chests and nice jugs to attract customers." Many years ago, an advertisement for Speedo women's swimwear featured an attractive woman in a brief (for then) swimsuit, with the caption "Gentlemen, start your engines."

One of the most controversial advertising campaigns of recent times was run by Benetton with eye-catching posters of a burning car, poverty, an AIDS sufferer, and a naked Signor Benetton himself. These advertisements attracted much comment and some outrage from people who thought they exploited human suffering for commercial advantage. Perhaps the most controversial advertisement of 1993 was a one-day newspaper poster by Saatchi and Saatchi for the Toyota wide-body Camry, a description of which follows.

CASE 5.3: The Toyota Case

The advertisement for the Toyota wide-body Camry attracted a great deal of public attention, for it featured not a picture of a car but the naked torso of a pregnant woman together with the caption "There's Nowhere More Comfortable Than Inside a Wide Body." The advertisement parodied a Ford campaign that featured a man jumping into his Falcon and travelling at high speed in wet conditions. At the end of that advertisement, we see that he has been driving his very pregnant wife to hospital. The advertisement also suggested the controversial cover of *Vanity Fair* featuring a pregnant Demi Moore posing naked. The Toyota advertisement certainly attracted much public attention and created debate about whether it demeaned or exploited women. Many feminists found it offensive and exploitative. And, at least as far as the media reported the reaction, only a few women commended the advertisement or were neutral towards it. As those who found the use of the pregnant woman objectionable had not been asked about the cover of *Vanity Fair*, it is not possible to state whether they also found that objectionable. What is clearer is that the controversy surrounding the Moore photograph was of a different kind, more about seeing a celebrity disclosing her pregnant nakedness than about her appearing naked per se. Yet this act was no less commercial: Moore was selling *Vanity Fair* and selling herself, too.

Increasingly, the idealized male form is appearing in various advertising media. The print campaign by clothier Abercrombie and Fitch features what some would refer to as the flagrant flaunting of young male flesh—well-muscled, shaved, and oiled torsos used as a vehicle to sell apparel. In an even more blatant objectification of the male form, an advertisement for Voodoo winter hose features an attractive woman dressed in a skirt and a pair of brightly coloured opaque hose (the product being advertised) and holding a pair of leashes attached to two naked, well-muscled young men straining ahead of her like dogs on all fours. Some advertisers see this type of advertising as a positive representation of the evolution of men and a sign of greater equality between the sexes. After all, women have endured this type of objectification for decades. Others see the objectification of men in advertising as being just as psychologically damaging to men as it has historically been to women. Setting up unachievable ideals of physical beauty creates insecurities among the majority of individuals incapable of achieving these ideals.

The questions that arise in the Toyota case are many.

Case Questions

1. Why is it objectionable to use a naked pregnant woman in an advertisement to sell cars, but less controversial to use one to sell magazines, or for that matter, Demi Moore herself?
2. What precisely is objectionable in the Toyota advertisement: the use of a torso without a head, the use of pregnancy to sell cars, the caption across the photograph, the calculated and dramatic use of an ordinary but very precious human condition to capture public attention, or the sexist nature of the advertisement (using naked women yet again as objects to sell other objects)?

These questions apply to many advertisements today and are perplexing in a liberal society. The same kinds of displays can be acceptable or objectionable depending on who is publishing them, the purpose for which they are being published, and who is viewing them. The feminist journal *Refractory Girl* published a photograph of a naked pregnant woman holding a melon in front of her head in its August 1993 issue. Fairfax and Roberts jewellers ran advertisements for Paul Picot watches featuring a Helmut Newton photograph of a woman sitting on a chair with one hand on her lap and the other holding a book, which she is reading. She is wearing a satin evening gown, one strap falling off her shoulder. Standing behind her chair is a man with his hand down the front of her dress, holding her breast. The following are two quotes from the copy: “If you’re searching for satisfactions . . ." and "When you see this model in the flesh, you'll express your desire for it on sight. After all we never told you to look but not touch."[22] As with the Toyota advertisement, regulators received a great number of complaints. Typical of the complaints were these: "[The advertisement] conveys the dangerously misleading message that women condone and enjoy being molested by men and that this behaviour is completely normal. It objectifies women, demeans women and advocates sexual harassment and abuse, which is absolutely unacceptable"; and "I am amazed that an advertisement which is blatant soft pornography is tolerated in what I would consider a family newspaper."[23] As with the Toyota advertisement, this advertisement was withdrawn from publication. Notwithstanding this sanction, and perhaps owing in some measure precisely to the storm of protest that they generated, the advertisements were surely effective as one-shot exposures.

The line between sexy and sexist may not be clear. The term "sexist" implies that women are being demeaned or dominated for the purposes of men. The use of women in sexual advertising is held by some feminists to be objectifying. Suppose this is true: why is it unethical? Other feminists, however, believe that there is a puritanical strain in feminism that wants to deny that the sexual element in women is as strong as it is in men. If this were so, it would explain the tendency to blur the distinction between sexual and sexist.[24] A market-oriented view would take the position that if advertisements are sexist, offensive, or inane, they will not work and will be killed off by others in a kind of Darwinian struggle to survive. This libertarian view could be applied to all the ethical questions about advertising. It would hold that if a product or service is legally available, then its advertising should not be restricted.[25] The market will decide what kinds of advertisements will work. Obviously, advertisements that offend most people will be ineffective, as will misleading or exaggerated or deceptive advertisements. But is this so?

The Moral Problem in Advertising

It is often said that the only kind of advertising that is objectionable is that which does not work. Advertisers often strive to shock people through controversy, arguing that an advertisement that outrages or offends is more likely to be remembered. If a portion of the target market is offended to the point where they refuse to purchase the advertised product, another portion of the target market will remember the product because of the controversial nature of the advertisement, increasing the likelihood that they will purchase it. It is not the fact that a controversial advertisement may lose some people that is the issue. It is, rather, the increase in customers created by the fact that the advertisement is memorable. The worst thing that can happen to an advertisement is that it is not memorable or easily forgotten. Toyota's wide-body advertisement might not be as successful as the company had hoped. It seems sensible that when selling to a mass market, the advertiser should be aware of consumer values. Still, this is a liberal pluralist society, and if firms with services and products to sell wish to use unorthodox, even outrageous, means to do so, should they not be permitted the liberty to fail or succeed? This is an ethical question. So, too, is the issue of stereotyping women, people with disabilities, or ethnic groups. It is simply incorrect to say that the market will exclude bad advertising, unless "bad" is used in the sense of "unsuccessful," in which case it is trivially true that bad advertising will be excluded. Advertisements that sell may still be offensive.

Some people believe, simply, that free speech will ensure that advertisers are self-regulating and that advertisers will not run advertisements that alienate customers. However, to opt for political correctness, to deny free expression even of offensive views, is contrary to the kind of democracy that the West has long stood for. It may seem a small cost initially to ban advertising that offends anyone, but the long-term costs—political and social rather than economic—will be much greater. Balancing the important democratic principle of toleration and an advertising code of ethics that provides any sort of meaningful guidance is very difficult indeed.

Advertising Placements and Endorsements

Concern has been expressed in the United States about the ethics of product placement, and we see the same trend in Canada. Product placement involves buying a place for a product in a film or television show. Clearly identifiable products, such as cars, will be commonplace fixtures of film and video entertainments, but product placement can enhance the prominence of, say, a soft drink or evade restrictions on tobacco advertising. Some years ago, Paramount Pictures produced a television series called *Viper* after the name of its central "character," a Dodge Viper sports car. A *New York Times* report commented on the marketing-entertainment symbiosis:

> Not only would Viper double as a program-length commercial for the Chrysler model but plans call for merchandising the series with tie-in products such as toy cars and apparel. That, of course, offers the potential to deliver still more advertising messages, over and above those that the viewers of Viper would watch in the form of commercials appearing in each episode.[26]

Similar concerns would apply to some game shows. Some companies are virtually acting as sponsors for game shows by donating prizes in return for publicity. Is this not product placement? And what if it is? What is wrong with product placement?

Product placement is an ethical problem because consumers are exposed to a form of subliminal advertising. The placing of subliminal messages in films was banned in the 1950s, but product placement is a camouflaged variation on the practice. The camouflage used is in a sense obvious: the Coke signs are obvious when Sally Field walks into James Garner's drugstore in *Murphy's Romance* (1985). And that is the whole point. Depending on the context, the reference to a product might or might not be an endorsement. In the film *Rain Man* (1988), two large corporations are mentioned favourably and unfavourably. In the most famous piece of (apparently) free advertising it has ever received, Qantas is endorsed by Raymond, the autistic prodigy, who refuses to travel by any other airline because they have had crashes. However, K-Mart does not fare so well. Originally an exclusive K-Mart shopper, Raymond changes during the course of the film and says at its conclusion, "K-Mart sucks!" Of course, if this is product placement, not endorsement, then mere mention of a retailer is more important than endorsement, and K-Mart's unfavourable mention counts for as much as the implicit endorsement of Qantas.

Clearly the fortunes of K-Mart or Qantas will not stand or fall by these few remarks, but it is also clear that it would be unethical to pay for such lines to be inserted into a script. Why? Is it important that we know that an advertisement is an advertisement? Is this an element in the objectionability of product placement? Brand names are part of our lives and our culture (some, like Band-Aid, Kleenex, Thermos, and Skidoo, become generic names), and it would be artificial—and silly—for cinema and video to refrain from mentioning them. (Was Andy Warhol's painting of Campbell's soup tins an endorsement, a subtle product placement?) But this is precisely why it would be unethical to seek favourable treatment or to belittle a competitor by paying for product placement or displacement. Like subliminal advertising, it would be an abuse of freedom of speech and artistic licence. When endorsements are made by prominent people or organizations, it should be clear that the endorsement is not posing as something else—say, information, entertainment, or even news.

Endorsements

It is not always necessary or desirable that endorsements be paid for. Some public interest organizations make recommendations for the public good. The Heart and Stroke Foundation counsels people about diet in terms that are not helpful to the dairy industry. Alberta singer K.D. Lang's endorsement of vegetarianism has been met with scorn by the Alberta Beef Producers. Ontario Hydro openly endorses the low-energy, long-life light tube to replace the conventional incandescent light bulb. It sees this product as furthering its interests in energy conservation, pollution reduction, and so on. The danger with paid and unpaid endorsements is that the credibility of the public figures and public interest organizations can be brought into question.

CASE 5.4: The Heart and Stroke Foundation's Health Check Program

In January 2008, *Marketplace*, the Canadian Broadcasting Corporation's investigative consumer television show, aired a segment on the Heart and Stroke Foundation's Health Check initiative.[27] Under this initiative, producers of consumer food products could apply to have their products endorsed by the Heart and Stroke Foundation. The endorsement appeared in the form of a check mark together with the Heart and Stroke Foundation's logo prominently displayed on the package. The foundation's Health Check website claims that

> [a]ll Health Check grocery products and menu items are evaluated by the Heart and Stroke Foundation's registered dietitians! To earn the Health Check symbol, every food or menu item in the program must meet nutrient criteria, established by Health Check, based on the recommendations in Canada's Food Guide.[28]

The controversy regarding the Health Check program arose when Wendy Mesley of *Marketplace* revealed that the Heart and Stroke Foundation charged a fee for these endorsements. She then went on to examine some of the recipients of the foundation's Health Check endorsements, only to find several of them were of questionable nutritional value.

While no sanctions were ever issued, the question that the *Marketplace* exposé posed was whether the intent of the Heart and Stroke Foundation was truly to inform consumers regarding their grocery choices or to raise funds by allowing grocery producers to purchase its endorsement for use as a marketing tool. Many argue that as soon as an endorsement is paid for, its integrity and reliability are compromised because the motivations of the authority providing the endorsement are suspect.

Because the Health Check appeared on products such as french fries, which are seen to be of negligible nutritional value compared to other food choices, *Marketplace* raised the question of the reliability of the endorsement. The counter-argument was that, of course, people know that french fries are not as healthy a food choice as broccoli, but if you are going to eat french fries, you should be able to choose the healthiest brand of french fries.

While the Health Check program stirred up considerable controversy, it continues to run, offering endorsements and providing guidance and advice on strategies for healthy eating and active living.

Bait Advertising and the Bait-and-Switch

bait advertising *advertising a very limited number of items at a very low price as a means of attracting customers*

bait-and-switch advertising *advertising a product that is either unavailable or that seems to be a bargain, with the intention of substituting a more expensive item*

Bait advertising is the use of selected items to attract customer interest when the advertiser knows full well that there is sufficient stock for only a few customers. The practice is for sellers to harness the interest of the potential buyer in the unavailable item and use it to sell another product. In other words, it falls under the head of false pretenses. The **bait-and-switch** is even worse. The ploy here is to advertise something that you plan not to sell: either you do not have it and you then try to convince the prospective buyer that something else (more expensive or with a higher markup) is available, or you have it but have planned to try to convince the prospective buyer that it is not the thing to buy, whereas something else that you stock is. The idea is that you use something that sounds very attractive as bait, planning all the while to switch the prospective buyer's interest to something else. Here is an interesting example of bait (perhaps bait-and-switch).[29]

CASE 5.5: Le Winter's Radio Stores

In New York in 1938, Le Winter's Radio Stores displayed a refrigerator attached to which was a sign. On the sign was printed—in large letters—"1938 Norge $119.50." In smaller letters, the word "from" was placed in front of the price. Le Winter's was taken to court over this matter. In *People v. Le Winter's Radio Stores, Inc.*, it was argued that Le Winter's was not ready to sell the refrigerator at the price printed on the sign, but rather was ready to sell only a smaller refrigerator.[30]

Case Questions

1. Apart from the legality of the matter, the sign was clearly misleading. Still, it is worth asking, given that a prospective buyer does not have to buy, what is so terrible about bait advertising?
2. What about bait-and-switch advertising?

Some situations are not so clear-cut.

CASE 5.6: Grace Brothers

It is common practice for department stores to hold post-Christmas sales. In 1992 the Grace Brothers store had advertised remarkable bargains on selected household appliances, typically refrigerators. The store stated in its advertisements that only a certain number of such items would be available. Crowds gathered in such numbers for the bargains that people were hurt in the crush to reach the few heavily discounted items first. People knew that bargains on household appliances were few, so this form of merchandising does not seem at face value to be bait advertising. Yet the offer, even of a few items at extraordinary discounts, raises an interesting ethical question. The fact that people have been hurt in the rush for such discounts indicates that they are substantial crowd-pullers. And the selected appliances themselves would surely not have been regarded by Grace Brothers as warranting such massive advertising.

A change of heart ensued in the face of poor publicity. Grace Brothers no longer massively discounts a few appliances, and security procedures have been improved for the post-Christmas sales. Moreover, the store has also improved the atmosphere among the bargain-hunters who gather outside its doors in the early morning. Both the publicity for the sale and Grace Brothers' image has improved.

Case Questions

1. Were the Grace Brothers' post-Christmas discounts a form of bait advertising?
2. Grace Brothers' initial response was to deny responsibility for the harm caused to customers by this "first-come, first-served" form of marketing. Was this defensible?

The online travel industry is an area that has been hard hit by accusations of bait-and-switch tactics.

CASE 5.7: Bait-and-Switch in the Travel Industry

The online travel industry has suffered mounting bad publicity around accusations of bait-and-switch behaviour. Internet consumer advocacy websites such as pissedconsumer.com and scambook.com and travel websites such as traveladvisor.com are rife with complaints from consumers who have purchased a flight at one price only to be billed at a significantly higher rate. While bait-and-switch behaviour is illegal, industry spokespeople contend that the rapid adjustments in prices are the result of the dynamic pricing environment that exists within the travel industry.[31]

An equally frustrating form of bait-and-switch occurs when a consumer purchases a flight that he or she is later informed has been cancelled. While the price remains the same, the substitute arrangements often include much less desirable or convenient times with multiple layovers or the departure and/or arrival at more remote or less convenient airports. Similarly, bait-and-switch accusations apply increasingly to the purchase of hotel stays. Regardless of whether or not these accusations are justified, the high volume of complaints and the associated negative publicity have damaged public consumer perceptions and the reputation of the online travel industry. The consumer rankings for online travel web services continue to languish while online purchases in other areas continue to grow.[32]

Morals and Marketing

Rogers Cable Inc. is Canada's largest provider of cable television services. In early 1995, Rogers and a number of other cable companies added several new cable channels under a negative-option billing program. **Negative-option billing** is a practice in which a good or service is automatically provided to the customer without the customer having requested it. The onus is then on the customer to cancel the service or return the good within a specific timeframe after which they will be deemed to have accepted the good or service and billed accordingly.

negative-option billing *the practice of automatically providing a good or service to the customer without the customer having requested it, placing the onus on the customer to cancel the good or service or be billed accordingly*

Rogers subscribers who opted out of paying for the new channels stood to lose much of their existing specialty programming. The implementation of the negative-option billing program by the cable companies was greeted with both a regulatory and public opinion backlash. The cable companies were ultimately forced to split the specialty channels included in the negative-option plan into two separately purchasable product blocks, a move Rogers had initially opposed as administratively and technically cumbersome.

Negative-option billing was outlawed by the Ontario government in July 2005 in an amendment to the Ontario Consumer Protection Act (2002) to protect consumers from being liable for paying for goods or services that they had never requested.

1. If Rogers provided full disclosure with respect to its negative-option billing plan, why was it considered to be an unethical practice?
2. Can you think of any instances where negative-option billing would be a valid strategy?

It will not always be possible to monitor the ethics of marketing, but this does not relieve marketers of their responsibility to have a strong regard for core ethical principles. Sometimes they do not even seem to perceive the presence of an ethical question. The following case illustrates this situation.

CASE 5.8: School Sample Bag Company

In June 1993 a school-based marketing scheme was the subject of some controversy. Children in the Australian state of New South Wales who attended primary schools were given sample bags to take home by the School Sample Bag Company, and the schools received cash payments of up to $500. The practice attracted the ire of Carl Vagg, a parent at Falconbridge Primary, whose six-year-old daughter brought home a bag labelled "dedicated to learning" and containing product samples and a survey with a Gold Coast holiday as an incentive to return it. Also in the bag to which Vagg objected was a copy of *Who Weekly*, which contained a photograph of a woman showing scars from the removal of breast implants.

The Department of School Education's policy was to let individual principals decide whether to distribute the bags. Vagg, however, found the practice objectionable: "It is a deceptive Trojan horse invasion into the home posing itself as an educational product, whereas it's really a slick marketing exercise." Of course, there is nothing intrinsically wrong with slick marketing, but the president of the Federation of Parents' and Citizens' Associations, Dr Graham Aplin, said he was "dumb-founded" at this use of children.[33]

Case Questions

1. Can an arrangement that benefits schools, parents, marketers, and producers be unethical? Why?
2. If the contents of the bags were uncontroversial, would the ethical difficulties disappear?

The moral issues in marketing are an extension of those in advertising.

1. Is it wrong to market foundation and skin-nourishing creams to women knowing that claims about skin rejuvenation are false? Cosmetics manufacturers say that they are making women feel better about themselves. Marketers know that some kinds of packaging are more appealing than others.
2. Is it wrong to sell products in large-volume containers that suggest a larger product or which give a better image or a higher profile to perfume or breakfast cereal?

Some of these questions are clearer if we take as a case a range of children's bath-time products from Johnson & Johnson.

CASE 5.9: Johnson & Johnson

Johnson & Johnson's children's bath-time products come in the shape of animal characters from A.A. Milne's stories of Winnie the Pooh. The first question that arises, then, is the marketing of such products in packaging that will appeal to children (and perhaps their parents) because they have the appearance of toys. These products could be harmful to children if their contents were consumed from the container or came into contact with their eyes. Hence there is a warning on the label, in rather small type, "This is not a toy." Might such a warning not be rather beside the point when the product presents as a toy, is modelled on a storybook character, is cast in soft plastic, and belongs to a range of similar items that distinguish themselves from other shampoos and bubble-bath soaps by their shape and colour? Such denials are known in philosophy as pragmatic contradictions, and Johnson & Johnson would do well either to acknowledge that their product differentiator is in fact a toy and take appropriate safety measures or to repackage their products and find some other marketing strategy for selling children's bath soaps.

A second question arises in relation to these products, however, from a report made public by the ABC Television program *The Investigators*.[34] The program found that Johnson & Johnson had imported bottles of bubble bath from the United States in the shape of the Pooh character Tigger the tiger. The American label with a warning about safety had been covered by an Australian label with no warning at all. Australian labelling laws are less strict than their American counterparts and do not require the safety warning that the soap could sting a child's eyes. Johnson & Johnson's new label covered this warning on Tigger, the only one of the five characters whose contents are not "no more tears." This action was legal. But was it ethical? This behaviour might seem all the more peculiar, given the particular position of Johnson & Johnson, which apparently has taken to heart and seriously tried to put into practice its credo, which includes the following:

> We believe our first responsibility is to the doctors, nurses, and patients, to mothers, and all others who use our products and services. In meeting their needs everything we do must be of high quality . . .
>
> We are responsible to our employees . . .
>
> We are responsible to the communities in which we live and work and to the world community as well. We must be good citizens . . .

In a series of "Credo Challenge Meetings," the company's CEO held frank and open discussions with employees around the world about how to implement the philosophy and provisions of the credo, allowing that the document could be changed. Commitment to the credo was truly put to the test in the late 1980s. Over a short period there were instances of intentional contamination of some containers of Tylenol, one of the company's products. A very expensive decision was made (not even by the top management, so well was the credo instilled throughout the company) to remove all Tylenol from the retail shelves in the interest of customer safety. In the company's view this was the right decision. The public's welfare was seen to be paramount, and this ethos was evident throughout the company. Of course, the possible damage that could be caused by the Tigger bubble bath cannot be compared with the damage that could have been caused by the spiking of Tylenol. There is, nevertheless, a generic question about looking out for the welfare of the consumers of the product.

Consider the marketing of the Saturn automobile in the United States compared with the marketing of other new lines of automobiles.

CASE 5.10: Saturn Cars

Honda marketed the Acura in separate showrooms and under a separate badge from the rest of its range of automobiles. Honda distanced (not to say, "concealed") its association with the Acura. Nissan did the same thing with the Infiniti. Toyota has the Lexus. In each case, the manufacturer was trying to enter a market with which it had not been associated, and it believed it could best move up in class by, as it were, introducing a new player rather than by introducing a new product by an old player with a reputation in a lower-class market. On one level, the situation in the United States with Saturn automobiles could be regarded as analogous. The Saturn is a General Motors car, marketed, manufactured, and sold under its own badge. It is, in fact, produced by the Saturn Corporation. In this case, however, the car itself is quite mediocre. Unlike the story of the Acura, the Infiniti, and the Lexus, the story here is not one of moving into a more expensive market, where the quality of the car is higher. Its new class is one of ethics and customer care. The Saturn distances itself from General Motors by breaking new ground in these areas. There are basically two fundamental tenets underlying the marketing of the Saturn that mark its move to a higher class:

1. Absolutely hassle-free car buying

Saturn's prices are transparent and non-negotiable. They even have a website where you can click on the various options (there are not many) and the model and colour you are interested in (there are not many) and see the price. And it shows you what you will pay. Salespeople are not pushy. They have escaped the mould of "car salesman." Apparently, the car has become particularly popular with women car buyers, who statistically are more put off or intimidated by the typical car sales techniques.

2. Fair, above-board dealing in selling cars and an ethical approach to manufacturing them

Throughout the company, the employees are recognized as part of the management team. Throughout the organization, the notion of "team" figures prominently. The Saturn "Shared Values" statement promises that "[w]e, at Saturn, are committed to being one of the world's most successful car companies by adhering to the following values: commitment to customer enthusiasm, commitment to excel, teamwork, trust and respect for the individual, continuous improvement." Saturn boasts that at its factory in Spring Hill, Tennessee, "the air leaving the plant is cleaner than the air going in, and when we built the plant, two hundred trees were moved to a nursery and later replanted on site, rather than being killed."

The company's approach is very much as stated in its "Shared Values": it is out to do the right thing by its customers. It is this, rather than any particular qualities of the cars themselves, that Saturn is trading on. And it is apparently doing so with considerable success. Saturn reports that it leads the automotive industry in customer and sales satisfaction. Saturn captured the No. 1 position in the J.D. Power and Associates Customer Service Index and Sales Satisfaction Index—the first non-luxury brand to capture the top position for both in the same year.[35]

Review Questions

1. Do you think there is anything ethically objectionable about the advertisement for sunglasses that was described in the chapter?
2. We mentioned one view according to which the only kind of objectionable advertising is that which doesn't work. What do you think about this point of view?
3. Not everything that is objectionable—even morally objectionable—should be sanctioned (that is, have laws or formal regulations against it). Toleration is the appropriate regard for some such things. Could you give an account of what makes any particular objectionable advertisement sanctionable rather than tolerable? What role, if any, does "awareness of community standards" play in your thinking?
4. Do you think there are "special" moral considerations about advertising of some types of products, such as alcohol, tobacco, firearms, prescription drugs, breakfast cereals, toys, health food, or anything else? If you do, why?
5. Do you think that, legitimately, there is anything left to "let the buyer beware," when it comes to listening to an advertisement?
6. What are the responsibilities of the consumer to remain informed and vigilant when it comes to consumer issues and advertising?

Suggested Readings

Marchant, G.E., G.A. Cardineau, and T.P. Redick. *Thwarting Consumer Choice: The Case against Mandatory Labeling for Genetically Modified Foods.* Lanham, MD: Rowman & Littlefield, 2010.

Pardun, C.J. *Advertising and Society: Controversies and Consequences.* Chichester, UK: Wiley-Blackwell, 2008.

Weasel, L.H. *Food Fray, Inside the Controversy over Genetically Modified Food.* New York: AMACOM, 2009.

Suggested Websites

Advertising Standards Canada:
http://www.adstandards.com.

Canadian Broadcasting Corporation (CBC) Policy and Guidelines for Advertising Standards:
http://www.cbc.radio-canada.ca/docs/policies/ads/.

Canadian Federation of Agriculture:
http://www.cfa-fca.ca/policy/biotechnology.

Canadian Marketing Association:
http://www.the-cma.org.

Canadian Marketing Association, Code of Ethics and Standards of Practice:
http://www.the-cma.org/regulatory/code-of-ethics.

Canadian Radio-television and Telecommunications Commission:
http://www.crtc.gc.ca.

6

Equal Opportunity, Discrimination, and Affirmative Action

Chapter Outline

- Employment Discrimination
- Sexual Harassment
- Disability
- Review Questions
- Suggested Reading
- Suggested Websites

Perhaps one of the earliest lessons in life is that outcomes are not equal. This is clear from games, school, and business. The very existence of difference seems to breed inequality. Yet one of the most familiar democratic ideals is equality. As a society we identify injustices and seek policies to remedy them. The notions of "one vote, one value," of "the equality of franchise," and of "equality before the law" are the normal expectations of citizens in a democracy.

For all that, there is constant confusion between the political and moral senses of equality on the one hand and people's physical and psychological qualities and abilities on the other. Most people do not believe that we are all equally endowed with talents or that the talents of each person are merely different in kind rather than in degree. Some people are very gifted and some are relatively deprived. This confusion becomes more clearly an issue when the moral ideal of equality is transposed into corporate life. How can business be expected to compensate for the missed life chances of individuals, and why is it the responsibility of business to do so?

Identifying the responsibilities of business in these respects is first a matter of looking at the law. Equal opportunity, anti-discrimination legislation, and affirmative action programs all regulate business to some degree. Beyond these requirements, the old questions about equality arise.

A voiced concern is that disadvantaged groups lack the power to rectify the legacy of discrimination and that injustices will be remedied much too slowly if radical measures are not employed. If a lack of power has prevented some members of society from enjoying equality of opportunity, then power should be used to redress this. While this view may have had some sway with governments and the requirements they impose on business, what moral obligations are there on business itself to pay regard to equality?

If people differ in ability, what is it that business should pay attention to? When we talk of people being equal, it is obvious that we do not mean that they are the same height or weight. Nor do we mean that they have the same talents or the same potentials. What we mean is that their differences should not be used as a reason for treating them less fairly than others. For example, in the past, women were paid less for doing the same work as men. Such distinctions are unfair and inappropriate, inasmuch as they have nothing to do with criteria of reward, such as merit and contribution.

But what if a person has a disability or becomes pregnant? Why should they not be less well favoured than a person able to fit more easily into a company's system? A caution is necessary here: we should not assume that a disability or pregnancy is a barrier to high performance. It is easy to find examples—Stephen Hawking, for instance, who is a first-rate mathematical physicist despite suffering motor-neuron disease for virtually all of his adult life, or Canada's minister of state Steven Fletcher (appointed in 2008), who has been a quadriplegic since 1996 as the result of an accident . Too much can be made of disability or pregnancy and not enough of a person's abilities.

Still, there is a legitimate question here. A company might not be set up to employ people who use wheelchairs. Most do not have child-care facilities. Over the past two decades, changes to the law have required more of business, and doubtless more changes in the name of equality will follow. But what is the moral basis of this?

The idea of equality behind anti-discrimination, equal opportunity, and affirmative action is that of fairness. If people are worthy of equal respect, then there is an obligation to place them in a position to give their best, just as the state provides public education to allow all people to develop their abilities and potential. Hence, those who have suffered some disadvantage must be treated "unequally" in some circumstances in order to satisfy the demands of fairness. Those in need or denied opportunity might receive more resources than people without disadvantages so that they might attain some social norm, such as a certain level of education or employment. Likewise, appropriate arrangements must be made for those with disabilities. Not long ago, ignoring the needs of the disabled, even for everyday amenities such as access to shopping centres or public transport, would not have caused a second thought. Today, it is regarded as a form of negligence. The courts will decide the legalities, but the central ethical idea behind such decisions is fairness.

Employment Discrimination

Employment is considered almost to be a right in advanced industrial societies. People depend on employment, unemployment is regarded as a personal and social problem, and governments institute programs to enable people to find work. The denial of work on irrelevant grounds to those who are capable of performing it is unfair. It can cause personal harm by denying a host of life opportunities—independence, personal development, family, education, and a full social life—as well as various social and economic losses—lost wealth generation, welfare dependency, health expenditures, and taxes forgone. Thus employment is an area that is subject to criteria of individual and social justice.

The same is true of the work environment. Issues such as wages and conditions have long been subject to regulation, but stronger measures to protect the health and safety of workers and others in the workplace have increased the regulated responsibilities of employers. So have anti-discrimination measures. In line with a theme that runs through this book, if the responsibilities of employers are restricted to observing the letter of the law, they will not achieve fair hiring and promotion policies, a safe workplace, or a confident and fully productive workforce.

Comments about Discrimination in General

Discrimination can be a virtue—as in "Exercise discrimination in choosing your career, your friends, and your wardrobe"—or a vice—as in "The firm's failure to promote him was discrimination." "Discrimination" is often used in the latter sense as a kind of shorthand for "unjust discrimination" or "unfair discrimination." But it is important to keep in mind that "discrimination" per se is not a dirty word. Some instances of discrimination are matters of legitimate preference. What is the difference between unjust discrimination and a legitimate preference?

Let's think for a moment about discrimination in general, not solely within the context of business. Let's consider three types:

- commendable or benign discrimination
- invidious discrimination
- formally intolerable discrimination.

As we have just indicated, discrimination can be benign, so it may be nothing to worry about, and in some cases it may even be something to applaud. In other cases, discrimination is objectionable; let us call that "invidious discrimination." This is discrimination in areas where one should not engage in such conduct. In these areas, the behaviour is offensive and obnoxious. To say that some behaviour is invidiously discriminatory, however, is not, by itself to say that there ought to be a law (formal regulation) against it. Assume, for instance, that a person, Bob, wants to associate only with people of his own race and would never invite someone of another race to his house or even engage in any social interaction with other races. Perhaps he does this merely (merely!) because of his personal preference and comfort level, and perhaps he does this because of some morally obnoxious beliefs about either his race or other races. Bob's behaviour is not only discriminatory, but also invidiously discriminatory. Still, most of us believe that there should not be any law against Bob's behaviour in this regard. Rather, we believe that our society should, in fact, formally tolerate Bob's behaviour. We believe that Bob should be allowed to act on his preferences or beliefs, even though those preferences or beliefs might be obnoxious. We certainly do not condone the behaviour or the beliefs, and we probably regard them as morally condemnable; it is simply that we do not believe that the behaviour or beliefs should be made illegal. We do not think there should be a law—or other formal regulation—against it. This is a separate matter: whether or not we (society) should tolerate it.

In the world of thinking about discrimination, these are important distinctions. In the context of business and the professions, it is reasonable to ask whether (and where) the distinctions between the second and third types of discrimination (invidious discrimination and formally intolerable discrimination) have applicability: Is it an important distinction when thinking about someone in their private business? A corporation? A profession? The public service? Employees' personal behaviour in all aspects when at work? We will not go further with these distinctions here, but we do regard them as important and believe that discussion about discrimination in general should bear them in mind. Simply, not all discrimination is bad, and not all bad discrimination should have formal prohibitions and/or sanctions attached to it.

Here are three cases, all of which involve discrimination. Do you think that they are different from one another? Do you think that it would be appropriate to have formal rules or regulations in the workplace that prohibit any or all of them? Do you think that informally (without rules or regulations) any or all of them should be frowned upon or discouraged?

1. A group of employees eat lunch together. They would rather not have Ahmad, a Muslim, eat with them, and so they don't allow him at their table.
2. A Christian reading group gets together at lunchtime twice a week to discuss issues of Christianity. They do not want people of other faiths to come along and have made this known by publicizing their meetings as for Christians only.

3. A women's issues discussion group gets together at lunchtime twice a week. They do not want men to attend, as they regard such attendance as inhibitory to frank and open discussion of the issues that are important to them, and have made it known that men are not welcome to attend.

Discrimination can be direct or indirect. It can be overt or concealed. It can be intended or unconscious. It can be singular or systematic. It can be an effect of history or result from a current prejudice. In each case it is an example of unfairness and injustice, and that means that it requires rectification. That rectification is not always in the form of compensation for individuals. When people are discriminated against because they are members of a group or class, then provision for that class might be necessary. The following discussion deals with these issues.

indirect discrimination *the result of some activity without being the aim of that activity*

direct discrimination *the intent to discriminate*

Discrimination does not result only from an intention to discriminate. Discrimination can be the result of some activity without being the aim of that activity. Sometimes this is referred to as **indirect discrimination**, in contrast to **direct discrimination**, which is the intention to discriminate. Suppose a business advertises for "men to load trucks" and then hires accordingly. This is direct discrimination against women. Suppose that a business, concerned that its employees be strong enough and able to negotiate over tailgates, stacked-up cartons, and so on, advertises for "truck-loaders, must be at least 175 cm tall." Hiring according to this criterion would result in a (statistically) disproportionate number of male employees, as a much higher percentage of men than women would meet the height requirement. As such, this amounts to indirect discrimination against women. It is, of course, direct discrimination against everyone shorter than 175 cm. Of course, any conditions or criteria of employment—for example, the ability to type at least 55 words per minute—would, strictly speaking, amount to direct discrimination against those who do not satisfy the conditions. But not just any employment criterion is fair, relevant, or appropriate. A height requirement for truck loaders may or may not be irrelevant. Thus, ethically speaking, notions of fairness, relevance, and appropriateness make all the difference in an analysis of justified or permissible discrimination and impermissible discrimination. Equality is a remedy against unjustifiable discrimination. It remains a relevant principle in measuring injustice, and for that reason it is an important concept, not only in political ethics, but in business as well. The importance of the effect of discrimination is illustrated in the cases that follow.

CASE 6.1: *Walmart v. Dukes*

In California in 2000, 54-year-old Betty Dukes filed a sex-discrimination claim against Walmart, her employer. Dukes claimed that she was unfairly denied advancement opportunities to a higher-salaried position, despite six years of hard work and positive performance reviews. Walmart claimed that Dukes had a dysfunctional relationship with her supervisor and was disciplined for consistently being late returning to work from her lunch breaks.

Dukes became lead plaintiff in a class action lawsuit launched in 2001 in which the plaintiffs sought to represent 1.6 million women who were either working for or had previously worked for a Walmart store subsequent to late December 1998. A federal district judge ruled in favour of class certification in 2004. Walmart appealed the decision, and a series of rulings and appeals ensued over the course of a protracted and frustrating 10-year odyssey through the US system of lower courts.

On 20 June 2011, the Roberts Supreme Court reversed the class certification in *Dukes v. Walmart*, the largest class action in US history. The rationale for disallowing the class certification of the more than 1.5 million women Walmart employees who had alleged gender discrimination in promotions and pay was that the individual parties to the class action suit and their individual circumstances differ to such an extent that they fail to constitute a class.[1]

The ruling denying class certification effectively means that each woman wishing to take legal action against Walmart for discriminatory practices must do so either individually or as part of a smaller local or regional group of women with similar experiences. Several regional class actions have since been filed against Walmart.[2]

The irony here is that a decade has been wasted on a technical determination of whether or not the approximately 1.5 million women constitute a class. The primary issue of whether or not Walmart has been guilty of engaging in large-scale systemic gender discrimination has thus far been virtually ignored by the legal system.

Conservative commentators criticized the lawsuit as abusing the class action mechanism, while proponents of the lawsuit suggested that the requirements of discovery in determining what constitutes a class are so onerous that corporations can use the legal system to effectively dodge class actions. This raises the question of whether or not anti-discrimination legislation designed to ensure equality in the treatment of employees actually does so if those seeking redress do not have equal access to the resources required to take fair advantage of the legal system.

The following case provides another example of gender-based employment discrimination with a somewhat different outcome.

CASE 6.2: BHP Co. Ltd and Employment Opportunities for Women

In a classic case of victory over employer discrimination, 743 women won compensation from Australian resources giant BHP Co. Ltd for their exclusion from the workforce in the early 1980s. BHP had maintained two waiting lists for employment at its Port Kembla steelworks, one for men and one for women. The women's list had more than 2,000 names and up to seven years' waiting time for employment. Those on the men's list usually had work within a month. Women constituted only a small part of BHP's workforce. After complaints to the Anti-Discrimination Board in the late 1970s, women were hired at Port Kembla, but within three years most of these women had been retrenched in line with the company's "last-on, first-off policy." Thirty-five of the women alleging discriminatory employment practices took their case to the New South Wales Equal Opportunity Tribunal, which

continued . . .

awarded them more than $1 million. This determination was overturned by the New South Wales Court of Appeal, and the women then took their case to the High Court. In 1989, the court, following Canadian and American precedents, found that eight of the women had been indirectly discriminated against, and confirmed a $1.4-million compensatory damages payment.[3] Then 709 women, mainly of non-English-speaking backgrounds, took legal action on the same grounds, and this matter was settled out of court in February 1994. The compensation agreed to by BHP is confidential but is believed to have been about $9 million.

Michael Hogan, director of Sydney's Public Interest Advocacy Centre, which assisted in the women's case, said,

> This historic case has resulted in jobs being available to women in a host of areas, not just the steelworks, based on merit and capacity rather than on stereotypes and prejudice. . . . The case drew attention to the unfairness of and inefficiency of traditional approaches to the employment of women.

This case had positive results in other areas. Quite apart from changing attitudes towards women workers, it brought reforms to old safety procedures and regulations and led to the adoption of improved codes of practice.

Workplace Discrimination

What is workplace discrimination? Employers are responsible for providing a safe but also a non-threatening working environment. That means that harassment or bullying in the workplace is an employer responsibility, not merely a matter of personal relations. What happens in the workplace is a matter for employers, managers, and colleagues. An illustration of this point is the case of Marion Shaub and the Federal Express Corporation. As the result of a lawsuit filed in 2002, Ms Shaub was awarded a multi-million-dollar settlement by a federal jury in a harassment case against Federal Express and its employees.

CASE 6.3: Marion Shaub and the Federal Express Corporation

In October 2000, Marion Shaub of Wrightstown, Pennsylvania, was terminated from her employment at the Federal Express Corporation. At the time, Ms Shaub was the only female tractor-trailer driver at her particular FedEx facility. In the lawsuit she filed against FedEx in February 2002, she alleged that, based on her gender, she was subjected to a hostile work environment. She claimed that she was subjected to threats and anti-female remarks by her male co-workers. When she complained to management about this treatment, she faced retaliation in the form of her co-workers' refusal to assist her in the loading of her truck and, more alarmingly, the sabotage of her truck brakes.

A federal jury returned a multi-million-dollar verdict in favour of Ms Shaub and the US Equal Employment Opportunity Commission. The jury found that FedEx had intentionally inflicted significant emotional distress upon Ms Shaub and had violated Title VII of the Civil Rights Act of 1964. Title VII requires that each employee be provided by their employer with a safe working environment without any harassment or adverse discrimination based on their gender, race, colour, religion, or nationality. Title VII also prohibits employers from taking retaliatory action against an employee for exercising their right to lodge a complaint with the employer regarding behaviour that is reasonably believed to violate Title VII.

The US Equal Employment Opportunity Commission regional attorney stated in a press release,

> This verdict sends employers a loud and clear message that sex discrimination and retaliation are simply unacceptable. The EEOC, as well as the US Supreme Court, have consistently pointed out to employers the benefits of adopting and enforcing an effective policy opposing harassment in the workplace. It is the employer's responsibility to demonstrate that such conduct is inappropriate and will not be tolerated.[4]

While most people would agree with the decision of the jury, some would find it to be purely for the sake of political correctness, paternalistic, and even undemocratic. They would ask these questions:

Case Questions

1. Why should one woman be able to dictate to a facility full of men what they can say? Why should the union take a special interest in the moral and gender position of a single member against the wishes of the overwhelming majority of its members?
2. Why should the employer support one woman who has a choice between working under prevailing conditions or resigning?
3. Why should minorities be able to arrange things as they please and have their private choices backed up by public authorities?

These questions are not uncommon, and in answering them, we can provide a model for case analysis in business ethics.

First, what is the nature of the offence? This case offers a clear example of the violation of the ethical principle of respect for persons. The woman was respected neither by her fellow workers and union nor by her employer. This is ethical failure at the personal, group, and institutional levels. When a dispute affecting individuals and their access to work cannot be resolved by employers, unions, and employees, it becomes a matter for independent arbitration. As the charges of harassment affect legally protected rights, the US Equal Employment Opportunity Commission had a proper role in this case. The legal protection of rights can hardly be considered undemocratic because it safeguards a minority from the majority.

To suggest that one woman wished to dictate to the overwhelming male majority misrepresents the situation; the threats and anti-female remarks were anything but innocent. The female worker was bullied because she was different. This difference happened to be one of sex. It might as easily have been one of religion. How would a Muslim have greeted such behaviour? The fact that the harassed employee was a woman is in one sense not significant, for bullying tactics against anyone is morally reprehensible. In another sense, the harassment is a particularly nasty display of sexism: the woman was attacked as a woman. There was a clear assumption that women did not qualify for esteem equal with that accorded men (let alone equal employment opportunity and conditions), that they were powerless, and that they could be degraded through ridicule of their sex. None of this is acceptable in society at large, and it has been proscribed in the workplace. Yet the union turned a blind eye to the plight of the woman, whom it seemed to regard as insignificant and expendable in the face of a hostile majority and their threat to strike. This reveals moral cowardice in an organization that, one would expect, has a role to defend the powerless against the arbitrary exercise of power. To suggest that the victim of harassment should accept such treatment or resign is to abandon the notion of justice in the workplace.

It is the employer's responsibility to ensure that the workplace is a safe and suitable environment for employees. This means that an employer should know if overt harassment is being practised and should treat complaints from employees seriously. The failure of the employer in this case illustrates the dangers of ignoring this. Quite apart from considerations of justice, the penalties attached to discrimination and negligence in protecting employee rights can be heavy. Many Canadian and American laws give protection to moral rights, not only to the benefit of the individuals directly concerned, but also to the community of stakeholders with an indirect interest in such exemplary cases.

A modification of the facts in this case could give rise to some other serious questions, such as,

1. Should the presence of material that could be deemed either misogynistic or offensive on religious grounds be regarded as harassment and be prohibited? The transmission of off-colour jokes and images in the workplace via email has met with increasingly tougher penalties from employers.[5]
2. What if there were no objections to the verbal abuse raised by the woman? Should some types of objectionable behaviour be tolerated? As a matter of fact, commitment to a principle of toleration is itself an important moral commitment.
3. At what point, in the matter of morally objectionable conduct, does toleration become less important than some other moral value?

These issues are the foci in the following cases.

Pregnancy Discrimination

When Lesley Mutsch was dismissed from her position as a record keeper at Beaurepaires Tyres, her employer claimed that the dismissal was part of a retrenchment scheme following the introduction of a computerized accounting system. The authorities found, however, that Mutsch's pregnancy was a factor in her dismissal, and awarded her $12,000 compensation.[6]

Mutsch's case is an old one, but even today it not unusual to find pregnancy discrimination. The existence of such discrimination despite legislation and huge shifts in attitude over the past couple of decades is strange. In 2009 the *New York Times* reported that subtle forms of pregnancy discrimination persist despite laws against it dating from 1964. Discriminatory dismissals, for example, can be disguised by restructuring and downsizing, making legal appeals difficult.[7] In Canada, employment law prohibits the inclusion of questions on plans for children and contraceptives in application forms and interviews. Other forms of discrimination identified include dismissal, demotion, denial of promotion, loss of employment benefits and training, and workplace harassment.

CASE 6.4: Pregnancy Discrimination in New Brunswick[8]

Patricia Donnelly had worked for eight years as the marketing director for Kings Landing, an outdoor living-history museum in New Brunswick. In late 2009, when she was on maternity leave after giving birth to twins, she received a letter informing her that her job had been eliminated and she need not return to work at the end of her maternity leave. She was offered one month's pay.

Donnelly decided to take legal action against her employer, and after a two-year battle, the court ruled in her favour and she was awarded eight months of severance pay. The court ruled that if a woman was on maternity leave, she must be treated in exactly the same way as she would be if she were still on the job.

The New Brunswick Human Rights Act was amended in 1992 to explicitly prohibit discrimination on the basis of pregnancy, the possibility of pregnancy, or circumstances related to pregnancy.[9] The Human Rights Act defines pregnancy as running from conception to the post-delivery period and encompassing medical complications, fertility treatments, breastfeeding, miscarriages, abortion, and family planning.[10]

Case Questions

1. Maternity leave and benefits vary significantly in developed countries; legislated leave can be anywhere from a few weeks to several years. How do policy-makers decide what is fair while taking into consideration the interests of parents, children, and employers? What do you think is fair?
2. Some employers will admit (albeit behind closed doors) that they feel an element of concern when hiring women who may be in circumstances where they may want to start a family. How can this concern best be either eliminated or allayed? What should policy-makers do to ensure this concern does not unfairly disadvantage women seeking employment?

Pregnant women were being denied access to sick-leave related to their pregnancies, and confusion about entitlements to annual and long-service leave during pregnancy and maternity was widespread. Discrimination against pregnant women has been worst in areas of employment that have been traditionally male and in small business.[11]

Glass Ceilings, Glass Walls

When Patsy Peacock, partner and director at McCarthy Watson and Spencer, resigned from the advertising agency, she reflected on the difficulties of a woman making it to the top. She had become frustrated over the years with the struggles faced by women in reaching senior-level management positions in the advertising industry. At the time of her resignation she was one of the last female executives left in advertising. Peacock believes that agencies have not adequately recognized the merit and contributions of women:

> Definitely the talent is there, all you have to do is look in middle management in agencies. [Women] seem to be held at that level. . . . Advertising is a combination of a lot of commonsense and emotion and traits that women generally have a greater percentage of than men. In my almost 19 years in the business I've only ever had one client that had a problem working with a female in the agency side.[12]

Patsy Peacock had hit her head on the "glass ceiling."

glass ceiling *an invisible barrier that prevents qualified people from rising above a certain level of rank or salary in business organizations*

The **glass ceiling** refers to an invisible barrier that prevents qualified people from rising above a certain level of rank or salary in business organizations. Although the term came into widespread usage in the 1980s to label one kind of discrimination against women, it also applies to minorities such as particular ethnic and religious groups and to people with disabilities. It is an institutionalized form of bias that prevents the promotion of qualified individuals to higher levels of management on the basis of characteristics such as sex, religion, or ethnicity. This is different from discrimination in employment; equal opportunity and affirmative action programs are aimed at minimum requirements, but strategies to remove transparent barriers to executive positions demand a lot more of a company.[13]

In the 1990s, the United States Department of Labor investigated the problem. It was not seeking to advance women and minorities in some token way, but to remove "artificial" barriers to fair competition on merit. The promotion of women, say, on gender grounds alone does neither the women nor the organization any good. It can breed hostility from men who are evaluated on merit and from women who have to try harder to prove that they hold their positions because of their abilities. And, of course, it raises ethical problems: is it fair to advance individuals from under-represented groups at the expense of individuals from over-represented groups in order to correct systematic biases? The crucial aspect was not necessarily to change corporate culture but to change corporate behaviour so that women and minorities were included rather than excluded from career development on demonstrated merit.[14] In Canada in 2010, the average woman made 68.1 per cent of the income earned by the average man. This statistic, although an increase from 58.4 per cent in 1990 and 61.7 per cent in 2000, shows that Canadian women, for whatever reason, make on average significantly less money than men.[15] The figure below shows the annual average income of Canadian men and women between 1990 and 2010 in adjusted 2010 Canadian dollars.

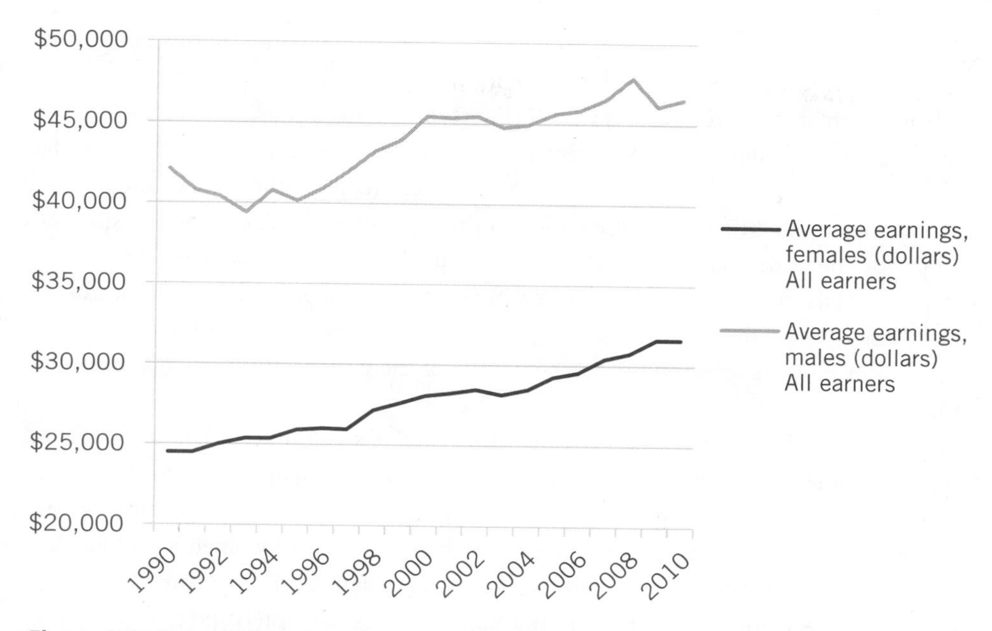

Figure 6.1 Average income of Canadian men and women (2010 dollars)

Source: Statistics Canada, Table 202-0102 – Average female and male earnings, and female-to-male earnings ratio, by work activity, 2010 constant dollars, annual (accessed 3 Sept. 2012).

There is often a tendency to look at the raw data on earnings and attribute the disparity between the sexes to gender-based discrimination when, in fact, there may be other factors at play such as career choice, time off for child rearing, lifestyle choices, and so on. Nevertheless, the disparity exists and it is safe to say that a significant portion of it can be attributed to gender-based discrimination.

One female manager of human resources at a manufacturing company believed she had hit a glass wall rather than a ceiling. Although her firm was paying her way through a management school, she felt she had few future prospects because she headed a service, not an operational division. "I'm seen as the soft option," she said. "I am often excluded from general manager meetings because they don't think I have anything to offer. A lot of stuff gets done on the golf course and I don't play golf."

This view encapsulates the subtlety of "glass" barriers. They allow a clear view to the top and suggest that corporations have transparent promotion and performance evaluations. Thus bias is not apparent, and because the culture of organizations can be invisible, men are quite likely to be unaware of it. They would deny overt prejudice, but if business culture is organized around male interests, gatherings, and social occasions such as golf, then some adjustments beyond the more obvious structures are required for women to be accepted at the top. The glass ceiling can be a nasty shock for women. It can also confirm the secret belief of some men that women cannot really succeed at the highest levels of business.

Not all women, however, accept that the glass ceiling is a barrier of this kind. Some say that the very concept is disempowering for those whom such awareness is supposed to help. There may be truth in this view (Leonie Still points out that some barriers attributed to the glass ceiling have been erected by women themselves),[16] but it cannot go far in explaining the kind of pattern that betrays the existence of the glass ceiling. While statistics do not tell the whole story, they can reveal patterns that cannot be explained simply by the particular circumstances of individuals. Women who should have every prospect of advancing to the highest levels of organizations stop well short of the goal in sight, resign, and typically go off to work in smaller ventures, often ones they start themselves. Still suggests a reason why: "The culture of the current business organization is not comfortable for women."[17]

The trend, then, over the past two decades in both Canada and the United States has been for women to respond to corporate frustrations by setting up their own small businesses. It could be that women are choosing not to pursue executive positions in the same numbers as men. In a small survey (138 responses) of Yale women for a *New York Times* article, Louise Story found many women contemplating full-time parenthood after a period in the workforce.[18] They did not mind short careers interrupted to have children and resumed on a part-time basis. Story commented, "For many feminists, it may come as a shock to hear how unbothered many young women at the nation's top schools are by the strictures of traditional roles."[19] More significant than such anecdotal findings is the change of mood in reporting them. The representation of women as victims of structural injustice seems to have softened, and this is reflected as well in other studies. Without discounting sex discrimination altogether, Susan Pinker has argued that if women are as talented as men and have had decades of affirmative action and equal opportunity but still do not populate the board rooms of the corporate world, then it must have something to do with their choices. Pinker gives a large weighting in these choices to women's differences from men, and part of this difference is their choice to find significance in their lives outside that epitome of male achievement—the corporation. Pinker does not believe that the glass ceiling explains the relatively small number of women climbing the corporate ladder. She argues that women, "on average, are more motivated by intrinsic rewards at work. An interest and an ability to contribute to a field, and a capacity to have an impact in the real world are more powerful drivers for women . . . than higher salaries, job security and benefits."[20] The glass ceiling explanation assumes that women would desire the same things as men; that if employment conditions were fairer, women would succeed on the same model as men. Pinker questions this.[21] She believes that women have choices that are discounted and that women who have exercised their choices against standard (male) models of success are unfairly branded as victims of discrimination.

These theories notwithstanding, the number of women in leadership roles in Canadian business is low by international standards. The 2009 Catalyst Census found that only 5.6 per cent of CEOs of Canadian companies listed in the Fortune 500 were women, only 3.2 per cent of board chairs were women, and just 14 per cent of board directors were women.[22] Clearly there is something to be explained here. While the theories of difference between women and men make an interesting story and could be relevant to workplace issues, the story about discrimination does not change. The low participation of women at senior levels of management is a question of equity for corporations. Whatever women's choices and the influences upon them, there is an ethical obligation upon corporations and employers to ensure that merit is recognized, prejudice is eliminated, and opportunities are open to all. This is a matter of justice to employees and shareholders alike.

Sexual Harassment

Sexual **harassment** has been mainly, but not exclusively, an issue of discrimination against women. It is surprising that it should still be considered acceptable in some quarters. **Sexual harassment** is like any other form of bullying or abuse of power. Its distinctive element is the making of sexual comments, suggestions, jokes, remarks, or gestures that are objectionable to the person to whom they are directed. Showing an interest in someone is not sexual harassment. Pestering them with sexual innuendo or touches is.

harassment *continual pestering or bullying*

sexual harassment *continual pestering, bullying, or unwanted attention of a sexual nature, often associated with an abuse of power*

Although a great deal of publicity has been given to the problem of workplace sexual harassment, it still occurs. This is not surprising: the workplace provides many opportunities for the development of personal relationships as well as harassment. The important thing is to recognize the difference between showing an interest in a co-worker and making their work life difficult, if not miserable. Suppose, however, that a manager is engaging in sexual banter and is not seriously pursuing a staff member. Is this harassment?

CASE 6.5: Sexual Harassment as Discrimination[23]

In a landmark case in 1989, the Supreme Court of Canada ruled that sexual harassment constituted a prohibited form of discrimination under Canadian human rights legislation. Shortly after Diana Janzen accepted a position in a restaurant, she began to experience unwanted sexual advances from the cook, Tommy Gammas. He would make suggestive comments and touch Ms Janzen inappropriately. After repeated and forceful objections by Ms Janzen over a month-long period to Mr Gammas regarding his continued unwanted and inappropriate behaviour, the cook finally desisted. Mr Gammas, however, then began a campaign of obtrusive and threatening behaviour, continually criticizing Ms Janzen's work and refusing to cooperate with her in the fulfillment of their mutual responsibilities with respect to the operation of the restaurant. The manager of the restaurant refused to intervene and insinuated that Ms Janzen was herself responsible for the cook's conduct.

Two weeks before Ms Janzen quit her job at the restaurant, another woman, Tracy Govereau, was hired. Within a week, she experienced the same type of sexual harassment as Ms Janzen. Ms Govereau strenuously objected to the cook's behaviour and complained to the manager. She was subsequently fired. Both women

continued . . .

testified that they were unable to find alternative employment for several months and had suffered a significant degree of mental anguish following their treatment by the restaurant cook and manager.

The Supreme Court of Canada ruled that sexual harassment also constituted discrimination under human rights legislation. While those engaging in sexual harassment may not realize that they are unfairly discriminating on the basis of gender, they are creating a work environment that leads to adverse work-related consequences for their victims.

Case Questions

1. What are the ethical issues in this case? Would those issues be clearer if the employee had been paying unwanted attention of a sexual nature to the employer?
2. What if, instead of making sexual innuendos in front of staff, a boss had celebrated an employee's birthday by hiring a stripper to deliver greetings?
3. What, ethically speaking, should employers and employees be aware of in cases of sexual harassment

Disability

It is common now to talk of "people with disabilities" rather than talk of "handicapped" or "disabled" people. This is not just pedantic language. The idea is to stop the identification of the whole person with the particular disability she or he has. Some disabilities, of course, make it difficult for a person to participate fully in the workforce, but too much is made of this. With appropriate assistance many people with disabilities make a valuable contribution in the workplace.

As the demographic breakdown of Canadians with disabilities shown in the table below illustrates, 14.3 per cent of the Canadian population has some sort of disability that limits their activity and/or ability to participate. If we exclude children under the age of 15 and adults 65 years of age and older in order to establish the proportion of working-age people with disabilities, we can see that 11.5 per cent of working-age Canadians have a disability that limits their activity or ability to participate. This is a significant segment of the working population.

Two obstacles to fuller participation in the workforce for those with disabilities have been the lack of access to services such as transport and attendant care and a lack of sympathy.

What are the rights and responsibilities of business with respect to people with disabilities? Employers have a right to expect that a person appointed to a position will be able to assume its duties fully and productively. In turn, employers should know something about disabilities so that they may give fair consideration to a person's capacity to do a job, rather than prejudging that their disability automatically precludes them from doing it.

Table 6.1 Demographic breakdown of Canadians with disabilities

Canadians with disabilities (2006)	Number			% of age group
Total – all ages	**4,417,870**			**14.3**
Total – less than 15 years		**202,350**		**3.7**
0 to 4 years			27,540	1.7
5 to 14 years			174,810	4.6
Total – 15 years and over	**4,215,530**			**16.6**
15 to 64 years		2,457,940		11.5
15 to 24 years			195,500	4.7
25 to 44 years			696,530	8
45 to 64 years			1,565,910	18.3
65 years and over		1,757,590		43.4
65 to 74 years			739,500	33
75 years and over			1,018,090	56.3

Source: Statistics Canada, Participation and Activity Limitation Survey, 2006, Catalogue no. 89-628-x.

These social responsibilities are supported by legislation. Canada has a robust federal legislative framework that guarantees equal rights for people with disabilities. This framework consists of the Canadian Charter of Rights and Freedoms, the Canadian Human Rights Act, and the Employment Equity Act. The Employment Equity Act requires employers to modify the workplace in order to allow a person with a disability to perform a job properly if they are the best person for that job—for example, by building ramps or providing a large computer screen or by giving mentoring support. Employers can gain advice on these matters either from the employee or from a qualified agency or expert. The Employment Equity Act does contain an unjustifiable hardship provision that exempts an employer from making these modifications if the costs are unreasonable. This does not let employers off the hook. A claim of hardship has to be backed up with evidence. A range of measures has been introduced to protect the employment rights of people with disabilities and to encourage their participation in the labour market. In 2010 the Accessibility for Ontarians with Disabilities Act (AODA) required that a set of standards for customer service apply to all public sector organizations. These same standards were to be applied to most private sector organizations in 2012. Additionally, accessibility training is mandatory for all managers and employees dealing with individuals with accessibility issues.[24] None of this government-sponsored support can address the demands of fairness by itself; it is necessary but not sufficient. It is important that employers should not see the hiring of staff as a private matter for which they might not be held accountable by an external body. On the contrary, it would be in the best interests of all stakeholders for employers to be proactive in the cause of fairness, if not for ethical reasons then for prudential ones.

CASE 6.6: The HIV-Positive Employee[25]

In the United States, the Transportation Security Administration (TSA) turned down Michael Lamarre for a position as a baggage screener because he was HIV positive. Prior to his interview in 2009, Mr Lamarre had passed an aptitude test and undergone a comprehensive security clearance. At the interview he was told that he would have to undergo a physical examination, at which time he disclosed that he was HIV positive. He was asked to submit his most recent test results and a form from his doctor stating that his condition would not interfere with his ability to perform the duties required by the position.

Mr Lamarre had been diagnosed with HIV 19 years previously. His condition was controlled through medication, and he had never exhibited any of the symptoms generally associated with HIV or AIDS. He pursued a healthy, physically active lifestyle. After submitting the requested information, Mr Lamarre received a letter from the contractor who administered the physical, saying that his HIV status disqualified him from consideration for the job. He was later told by the contractor that he was rejected because his medical condition increased his susceptibility to virus and infections, despite the fact that medical experts and his own doctor contended that he was no more likely to catch a cold or virus than anyone else.

The American Civil Liberties Union filed a complaint on behalf of Mr Lamarre with the TSA charging that the TSA was in violation of its own policy prohibiting discrimination against people with disabilities. In a settlement reached between the American Civil Liberties Union and the TSA, the TSA agreed to review and amend its employment policies for applicants with HIV or otherwise compromised immune systems.

Case Questions

1. What was the ethical responsibility of the Transportation Security Administration in this case?
2. Was Mr Lamarre being discriminated against?
3. What are the ethical issues relevant to this case?

Perhaps the most obvious aspect of equal opportunity programs to business is their cost. Such a focus ignores the benefits of such programs not only to individuals but also to commerce, industry, and the community. Equal employment and anti-discrimination programs might also be viewed as prejudice-removal programs. When prejudice obscures respect for persons and limits the capacity to make a fair assessment of their abilities, then all parties lose. Business needs the best people. Prejudice against women, people with disabilities, or any other group is not only morally objectionable, it is also bad business.

Canada is a country with a culture based on diversity and acceptance. Canada also prides itself on equal treatment with regard to gender, sexual orientation, and ability/disability, as well as religion, race, ethnicity, language, and culture. To illustrate this diversity, Table 6.2 provides a breakdown of the population of Canada who identify themselves as members of a visible minority. In the 2006 census, 16.2 per cent of Canadians identified themselves as members of a visible minority, and 14.3 per cent of Canadians were recognized as having a disability. These two statistics, together with the ongoing movement towards equal rights for women and other possibly disaffected groups, show how vital equal opportunity is to business and society as a whole.

Table 6.2 Visible minority population in Canada (2006)

	Number	% Population
Total population	31,241,030	100.0
Total visible minority population	5,068,095	16.2
South Asian	1,262,865	4.0
Chinese	1,216,565	3.9
Black	783,795	2.5
Filipino	410,700	1.3
Latin American	304,245	1.0
Arab	265,550	0.9
Southeast Asian	239,935	0.8
West Asian	156,695	0.5
Korean	141,890	0.5
Multiple visible minority	133,120	0.4
Japanese	81,300	0.3
Visible minority, not included elsewhere	71,420	0.2

Source: Data from Statistics Canada, 2006 Census of Population (accessed 3 Sept. 2012).

Review Questions

1. Much of the concern about anti-discrimination is over the provision of "equal treatment." Yet much of the concern seems to require "special allowances." Do you think these two notions can be reconciled?
2. Many people have discriminatory biases that they themselves seem to be unaware of. In the role of employer, these biases may result in differences in the way an interview for employment is conducted. The tone or body language may differ, and questions of differing levels of difficulty may be asked depending on the characteristics of the interviewee. How should employers ensure that their personal biases do not colour their decision-making when they attempt to assess the best possible candidate for the position?
3. Describe the relationship between employment equity, anti-discrimination, and human rights. Do these concepts overlap, and if so, how significant is the overlap?
4. The term "political correctness" has increasingly developed a negative connotation based on its perceived effect of inhibiting natural human interaction in the workplace and indeed within greater society. Is this justified, and if so, what should people do to mitigate any perceived negative effects of political correctness while continuing to support equality and respect in the workplace and in society?

Suggested Reading

Pinker, Susan. *The Sexual Paradox*. London: Atlantic Books, 2008.

Suggested Websites

Access for Ontarians with Disabilities Act:

http://www.e-laws.gov.on.ca/html/source/regs/english/2011/elaws_src_regs_r11191_e.htm.

AccessAbility Advantage:

http://www.aodatraining.org/.

Canadian Human Rights Commission:

http://www.chrc-ccdp.ca/.

Ontario Human Rights Commission:

http://www.ohrc.on.ca/.

Statistics Canada:

http://www.statcan.gc.ca/.

7

Whistleblowing

Chapter Outline

- Internal and External
- The Evolving Situation
- Review Questions
- Suggested Readings
- Suggested Websites

"If ye cannot bring good news, then don't bring any."
– Bob Dylan, "The Wicked Messenger," *John Wesley Harding*, Columbia, 1967

whistleblowing *making public matters that organizations have ignored or wish to keep hidden but which constitute a significant wrong or an immediate danger*

Whistleblowing is making public matters that organizations have ignored or wish to keep hidden but which constitute a significant wrong or an immediate danger. It might be done in response to an endangerment of the public or it might be done to protect employees or others affected by the organization's disregard for their safety or well-being.

Historically, protection in Canada for whistleblowers has been notoriously poor. Even within government, employees or civil servants could be summarily dismissed for speaking out about internal abuses. In the private sector, Canada's libel laws act as a deterrent to the raising of corporate issues construed to be detrimental to the public interest because of the very real possibility of legal action.

In 2007, the Canadian Parliament instituted the Public Sector Integrity Office as part of the Federal Accountability Act[1] to protect whistleblowers speaking out against ethical transgressions within government. Few protections exist for whistleblowers in the private sector.

The important thing to note about whistleblowing is that it is a matter of judgment. There are no rules for blowing the whistle, although some conditions for its permissibility are stated below. Some professional bodies and some writers believe that there are some circumstances in which it is mandatory to blow the whistle, but given the personal losses of those who do so, it seems clear that this is a matter that calls for moral judgment rather than clear requirements.

Remember Frankena's four basic requirements of ethics: avoid evil, prevent evil, remove evil, and do good. Concern for others seems to extend our minimum ethical obligations beyond not participating in evil to preventing harm. Whistleblowing is an attempt to avoid, prevent, and perhaps remove evil. The question then arises, why should I be the one to blow the whistle? About 40 years ago a woman was assaulted and killed in New York in full view of a large number of bystanders (see case 7.2). The assailant was convicted of the crime, but the judge was most scornful of the so-called innocent bystanders who might at least have called the police or even gotten together to stop the attack, but who did nothing but watch. While you are not required to intervene in such a situation if your vital interests are likely to be endangered, you are morally required to intervene to the extent that such interests are not threatened. So if you were not a large person and had no one to assist you, then you might not intervene personally but would call the police. If you had an infant in your care, then you might call for help from others rather than risking the infant. The point is that you should do something in such cases if you can, and if so doing poses no serious risk to your vital interests.. Bowie and Duska argue that personal responsibility is commensurate with

- the extent of the need
- one's proximity to the person(s) in need
- one's capacity to assist
- the availability of others likely to render assistance.[2]

These grounds for acting are relevant to the evaluation and justification of whistleblowing.

Consider the following cases from this point of view.

CASE 7.1: Dan Applegate and Convair

In 1972, Dan Applegate, a senior engineer with Convair, wrote to his vice-president detailing design faults in the fuselage of the DC-10. Convair was a subcontractor on the project for McDonnell-Douglas, and Applegate was director of the project. Applegate's concerns focused on the design of the cargo doors, which he believed could open during flight. This would depressurize the cargo bay, causing the floor of the passenger cabin above to buckle. As the floor housed the plane's control lines, the risk of a crash was very high unless design modifications were made to doors and floor.

Convair's response was a financial rather than a technical one. Management argued that informing McDonnell-Douglas of the problems would place Convair at a competitive disadvantage because the costs of delays and rectifications would be very high. In 1974, a fully loaded DC-10 crashed on the outskirts of Paris; 346 people lost their lives.[3]

CASE 7.2: Murder Unseen?

In 1964, the *New York Times* reported on the murder of a young woman named Kitty Genovese in the Kew Gardens area of Queens, New York. Apparently this murder took place in full view of 38 people. Although Ms Genovese called for help as she was being stabbed, and although the attack lasted some time, most of the witnesses—the so-called innocent bystanders—declined to get involved by, for example, calling the police. At the subsequent investigation their conduct was condemned as morally inexcusable.[4] This case is often cited in psychological textbooks in discussions about what restrains people from intervening to stop wrongdoing or to minimize harm. Here it may stand for the inaction of people who are aware of corruption and unethical practice in their workplace but do nothing to stop it because it is "none of my business." They, too, are "innocent bystanders." They, too, refuse to take responsibility.

Whistleblowing is reporting on misconduct or potential harm or failure from within an organization or after separation from it. Investigative reporting is not whistleblowing, nor is the work of private investigators. Dissent is not in itself whistleblowing, but public dissent in order to prevent harm or injustice may be. Whistleblowers are insiders in the organizations where the reported misconduct occurs, and therefore in some sense they are party to the harm caused by the organization. Usually it is moral revulsion that leads them to speak out. Typically this is at some cost to themselves. In this they are somewhat like civilly disobedient protesters: although they do not challenge the law, they do challenge established practices. And, like civil disobedience protesters, whistleblowers are usually prepared to take the consequences of their acts.

Common mythology notwithstanding, an ethical stand does not confer "good guy" protection from the adverse consequences of whistleblowing. With the exception of the province of New Brunswick, there are currently no explicit protections in Canada for whistleblowers in the private sector. Section 28 of the New Brunswick Employment Standards Act states, in part,

> Notwithstanding anything in this Act an employer shall not dismiss, suspend, lay off, penalize, discipline or discriminate against an employee if the reason therefore is related in any way to
>
> . . .
>
> (b) the making of a complaint or the giving of information or evidence by the employee against the employer with respect to any matter covered by this Act; or
> (c) the giving of information or evidence by the employee against the employer with respect to the alleged violation of any Provincial or federal Act or regulation by the employer while carrying on the employer's business;
>
> or if the dismissal, suspension, layoff, penalty, discipline or discrimination constitutes in any way an attempt by the employer to evade any responsibility imposed upon him under this Act or any other Provincial or federal Act or regulation or to prevent or inhibit an employee from taking advantage of any right or benefit granted to him under this Act.[5]

In other parts of the country, going to the media might invite an injunction against publication or even a defamation suit. The wise course is to see a lawyer before a reporter.

Whistleblowers commonly suffer for their actions. Most lose their jobs or are demoted. Many are subjected to psychological testing by their companies. Some are prosecuted. Many of them face lives marred by marriage failure, alcohol abuse, and bankruptcy. Consider the case of Sean Bruyea.

CASE 7.3: Sean Bruyea and Veterans Affairs

In 2005, Sean Bruyea, a former Canadian intelligence officer, objected to new legislation that would replace the lifelong benefits traditionally provided to injured veterans with a one-time lump-sum payment of much less value. The Veterans Affairs bureaucrats who were attempting to pass this legislation quietly without media or public scrutiny objected to Mr Bruyea's tactics and set about trying to undermine his credibility. To accomplish this, they suggested that Mr Bruyea was mentally unstable and they released information from his medical files outlining physical and psychological injuries, including post-traumatic stress disorder, received during his posting in the 1991 Gulf War. In blatant violation of Canadian privacy legislation, this information was shared with in excess of 800 people within the government.[6]

Being subjected to attacks on personal credibility should not be a necessary consequence for the conscientious and honest employee. John McMillan has put the principle succinctly:

> Telling the truth should be neither difficult nor costly. Employment in an organization should not require that a person accept complicity in all activities which the employer has decided to pursue or to conceal. To accept that employees can be persecuted for honesty, loyalty, or upholding the public trust undermines some of the legal and moral principles on which a society is necessarily based.[7]

While McMillan is undoubtedly correct from a moral point of view, in practice we live in an imperfect world and organizations develop lives of their own that defy the rational expectations of justice. Whistleblowing tells an organization that something is gravely wrong with it, and the organization reacts to this threat.

Internal and External

Whistleblowing usually begins internally—that is, information on the conduct is reported to superiors in the organization—as happened, for example, in the cases of the DC-10 and the space shuttle *Challenger*, which was launched despite clear indications of a significantly high probability of a disaster.[8] If reporting to your superiors through the established channels of authority fails, you might pursue the matter **internally**, but outside the normal channels of authority. Here, you would report to someone else (usually higher up) within the organization. If neither sort of internal reporting succeeds in preventing potential harms from becoming actual ones, then the next stage is often the riskier option of seeking external intervention to overcome the problem. This might mean informing a senior public authority or seeking to elicit public interest through the media. Such actions are examples of whistleblowing.

internal whistleblowing *blowing the whistle inside the organization—reporting the concern outside the normal channels of authority, but still not going public (not reporting outside the organization)*

Although some writers distinguish between internal and external whistleblowing, we believe that only the latter is genuine whistleblowing. Take as an example *Time* magazine's nomination of its "Persons of the Year" for 2002, Cynthia Cooper, Coleen Rowley, and Sherron Watkins.[9] There is no doubt that these are unusually courageous and principled women, but should their actions properly be called whistleblowing (see Case 7.4)? If a matter can be dealt with by an organization's internal procedures, then reporting it internally hardly fits the category.

CASE 7.4: Is This "Whistleblowing"?

Cynthia Cooper, vice-president of internal audit at WorldCom, discovered inaccurate accounting and pursued it. Hunting down a $400-million anomaly, she found that WorldCom's auditors, Arthur Andersen, seemed not to have noticed. So Cooper brought it to their attention—without success. Then she informed the CFO (chief

continued . . .

financial officer), Scott Sullivan, who told her to mind her own business. Cooper used her internal audit team to review Andersen's audit and discovered the extent of misreporting—a $662-million loss had been accounted as a $2.4 billion profit by calling operating expenses capital expenditures. Cooper informed Sullivan, the audit committee of WorldCom's board, and the corporation's comptroller, David Myers, of her findings. The audit committee fired Sullivan and told Myers to resign. Unusually, Cooper kept her job. At no stage did Cooper resort to publicity. Her pivotal part in the exposure of sharp practice was made known to the press by a congressman who released her audit memos to the press. She and former FBI agent Coleen Rowley reject the term "whistleblower."[10]

Coleen Rowley's "whistleblowing" was to testify at congressional hearings into FBI shortcomings after the 9/11 tragedy. Rowley believed that the agency had information—if not the systems—that would have enabled it to track the terrorists who committed the atrocity, but she sent her concerns in a memo to FBI chief Robert Mueller and members of the Senate Intelligence Committee. She did not solicit media attention and came to the notice of the press only after her memo was leaked.

Sherron Watkins's whistleblowing was to respond to an invitation to employees from Enron chairman Kenneth Lay to voice any concerns they had about the company. Watkins's reply was an anonymous memo expressing concern that Enron might collapse because of the accounting scandals she had lately uncovered. She had been unable to make sense of accounts that basically hid debt in off-the-books partnerships. When her memo had no effect, Watkins arranged a time to see Lay in person, and she laid out before him the crooked deals that had brought Enron to the brink. Lay told her he would get the firm's lawyers to look into her allegations, but shortly afterwards Enron filed for bankruptcy. Watkins did not go to the media and only became known to the public after the bankruptcy action.

In each of these cases, the term "whistleblower" is appropriate in the context of the gravity of the issue and the courage needed to bring it to the attention of appropriate authorities. Nevertheless, it is better to reserve the term for last-resort measures to rectify grave injustices. Internal reporting should be part of the normal feedback channels of an organization, and if these channels work, there is no need to go outside. Even if they do not work, internal whistleblowing—for example, going straight to the CEO—does not violate the authority of the organization per se, nor does testifying before a parliamentary or congressional hearing.

Whistleblowers are not merely up against petty superiors or incompetent colleagues, but against corporate closure—the mutual protection that can seize members of an organization and cause it to intimidate, scapegoat, or expel dissidents who disturb its unspoken rules of survival. Whistleblowers have in a sense already moved outside an organization when they take it on, so only external whistleblowing will be treated as the definition of the term in our discussion.

"Whistleblowing" appears to be a term denoting accomplishment; that is, it is not the mere communication of information to a superior, but the achievement of some exposure through doing so. Whistleblowers often have to persist in the face of substantial obstacles in order to achieve an effect. Although persistence is not necessarily part of whistleblowing, it is one of the challenges that many whistleblowers have to overcome in order to act effectively. One can think of cases in which important information has been communicated without result. Whistleblowing is not mere communication of the nature of the wrong; it is the pursuit of changes that avert a public harm in the face of indifference or opposition. Imagine that when the mysterious "Deep Throat" in the Watergate affair told Woodward and Bernstein that Nixon's "plumbers" were resorting to dirty tricks to have the president re-elected, these journalists had thought the story too far-fetched to print. That would not have been whistleblowing. It was the persuasiveness of the information that marked Deep Throat as a source and the publication of a story that made him a whistleblower. The view that whistleblowing is an accomplishment restricts the concept in a useful way, but also seems to suggest that the focus of the discussion should be on the heroes who perform this public service. Most studies of whistleblowing have this focus, not unreasonably considering the human drama involved and the fact that case studies of whistleblowing are also the case histories of brave individuals. As Quentin Dempster remarks, "Without the courage of the whistleblowers we would not be informed about what really goes on in our sometimes very uncivilized world."[11] The danger with this focus, however, is that it can mistake the conscientious dissenter for the whistleblower and genuine organizational disciplining of the dissenter for intimidation and retribution.[12] The key question is whether there are adequate systems of reporting, accountability, and control within the organization, rather than whether individual rights to dissent are recognized. As we note below, not all wrongs call for a principled disclosure. A person who took an officious interest in smoking in the toilets or in colleagues who conducted an extramarital affair out of working hours might be a principled nuisance rather than a whistleblower. We regard this point as important: it is one of the reasons we advocate a restricted definition of whistleblowing.

What count as genuine and morally justifiable cases of whistleblowing? First, the matter has to be serious, and the informant should have good evidence of the alleged misconduct. Sissela Bok suggests that the threat from the misconduct should be imminent and specific: grapeshot disclosures with no immediate effect might make good gossip, but they are not whistleblowing.[13] Second, the information has to be of public benefit, and the public must have a right to know (the public might benefit from many things that it does not have a right to know, such as the secret recipe of Coca-Cola). The information should not be mischievous or malicious. This would exclude from public disclosure personal details of a political, religious, or sexual kind. Third, less damaging ways of rectifying the problem, such as internal procedures, must not be available to the whistleblower. Fourth, if other avenues for rectifying the problem were available, they should have been tried. Fifth, blowing the whistle is likely to remedy the problem.

Two considerations run through these criteria. The first is that the public interest is threatened by some policy or procedure of the organization, and the second is that employees of the organization have tried to rectify matters through normal lines of responsibility and management. Where the first is present and the second fails, whistleblowing is a legitimate option.

Richard De George goes further and says that if these conditions are met and the whistleblower has documented evidence that would convince an impartial person of an organization's potential to harm the public interest, and if the probability is good that going public will bring about change for the better, then the employee not only has a right to blow the whistle, but an obligation to do so.[14] Others have argued that, at most, employees can have a right to blow the whistle, but because of the real possibility of resultant hardship to themselves, they never (or only in exceptional circumstances) have a duty to blow the whistle.[15] Whether an employee looks to the right or the duty, it is important to stress that the means used should be proportional to the end to be achieved, or, more simply, do not use a sledgehammer to crack a walnut.

Whistleblowing is, on the whole, a grey area. It is important to be aware of the conditions of its justification, but it is equally important not to be beguiled into believing that the term names a clear, identifiable type of conduct that can be used as a template for resolving moral conflicts in the workplace. Whistleblowing is simply a shorthand way of referring to classes of information disclosure.

Ross Webber echoes some cautions about whistleblowing first made by Alan Westin:

1. Verify your evidence. Is it sufficient?
2. Are you objecting to illegal or immoral conduct? If the conduct is morally objectionable but legal, you might not have a future in your industry. Illegal conduct is not as likely to damage your career.
3. Discuss your proposed action with close stakeholders; namely, your family. They will be affected by what you do.
4. Exhaust organizational procedures for dealing with complaints and objections.
5. Consider whether it is better to act publicly or anonymously.
6. Document every action you take.
7. Don't spread your heat: keep the objection confined to those who need to deal with it, and be civil to those handling it.
8. If you are fired you may resort to publicity, but recognize that your right of free public discussion might be limited.
9. Consider a lawsuit.
10. Appreciate that your hands will get dirty whatever you do about unethical conduct.[16]

This last point is worth emphasizing. Whistleblowing exemplifies the problem of dirty hands. It does seem to involve betrayal of friends, stress on one's family, and hurt to the good as well as to the bad. Apart from the personal risks involved, it amounts to placing an individual judgment above that of the organization and forsaking the duty (sometimes a fiduciary duty) that an employee owes to the organization. Consider the following objections to whistleblowing. First, it is informing, perhaps on peers or mates. Informing was characteristic of the worst excesses of Nazi Germany and the Soviet system. It is sneaky, underhanded, and destroys trust in the workplace. Second, it involves disclosure of information that is owned by the organization, not by individuals. It is theft to disclose that information without authorization. This might lead competitors to gain an advantage and destroy an organization as effectively as leaking damaging information might do. Hence, the third objection: taking on the responsibility of looking after the public interest is arrogant and might destroy the organization and the jobs of colleagues. How can this kind of conduct be distinguished from leaking? Fourth, a person does not necessarily have the full picture in going public with potentially damaging information and hence might not be in a good position to judge if the public interest will be served by disclosure. In this respect (like the arrogance to which the third objection calls attention), whistleblowers place their own judgment above that of the organization. Fifth, the act breaks an employee's contract with the employer. Sixth, an employee has a duty only to report concerns to superiors, not to rectify the problem personally.

These objections will vary in strength depending on the particular circumstances a potential whistleblower is facing. A whistleblower might be a hero, someone who is not a sneak but puts his or her neck on the line for honesty, probity, and the public interest. If other avenues existed for bringing harms to public notice or correcting the harms in some in-house way, who but an idiot or a misdirected hero would risk discovery, loss of job and career opportunity, and perhaps professional censure?

It is also conceivable that a whistleblower might be a sneak or someone with an illegitimate interest, a grudge, or a cockeyed perspective on an organization's activities. We disagree with Bowie and Duska that whistleblowers necessarily act from an "appropriate moral motive."[17] A whistleblower might act in the public interest because he or she seeks revenge after being sacked. It is still whistleblowing. Awareness of a whistleblower's ignoble motives might affect his or her credibility (as a practical matter), but it does not mean that they have not blown the whistle.

As for loyalty, moral obligations to colleagues or to an organization cannot bind someone to immoral conduct—at least not to seriously immoral conduct. Given the damage usually done to them, the question is not whether whistleblowers are morally justified, but whether the silence of others can be excused. This may seem unrealistic or heartless, but perhaps it is better to talk of loyalty in emotional rather than moral terms in relation to major issues. When the DC-10 went ahead, there were people in a position to know but who did nothing. The same is true of other disasters, such as the *Challenger*: people who knew of the unacceptably high risks did nothing.

What could excuse such inaction? Usually it is a reluctance to report colleagues or a fear of retribution. The reporting excuse really does not hold water any more. A University of Chicago study revealed that whistleblowers are widely considered the best tool for fighting corporate fraud. The same study, however, found that in cases in which the identity of the whistleblower(s) was revealed, 82 per cent resulted in the whistleblower either being forced from their position or resigning their position under duress.[18] This may, however, be too simple. Research suggests that organizations with cultures that encourage consultation and participation in decision-making view loyalty in terms of people voicing their views. Conversely, silence is likely to be taken as disloyalty. On the other hand, organizations with strong hierarchical cultures are likely to perceive loyalty in terms of silent compliance and disloyalty in terms of overt criticism.[19] Such organizations are more likely to encourage internal critics to leave than to voice their criticisms. They are also more likely to create the conditions that give rise to whistleblowing.

In all of this there is an important distinction to be made between petty informing and bringing matters of public interest to the public's attention. A criterion of proportionality should help in deciding on borderline cases, but we hold that there is no duty to inform on others where the matter is not serious or the damage caused by informing is not justified by the benefits to be secured. This qualification should not be seen as minimizing the issue of rights; we are not arguing that one person's rights may be sacrificed for the good of an organization and its stakeholders, but that the good to be achieved by whistleblowing should be in proportion to the gravity of the act.

Retribution is a large issue and is likely to remain so, even where whistleblower protection is present. Until recently there were no such protections for whistleblowers in the public or private sectors in Canada, and whistleblowers have had to take heroic measures to bring matters of urgency to public attention. Ideally, there should be procedures and mechanisms for dealing with genuine concerns inside an organization so as to minimize the need for heroism with its attendant risks and disincentives. Criticism should be taken seriously, and the reporting of transgressions could be made mandatory, thus removing the discretion from the individual and avoiding the opprobrium that can sour relations between a whistleblower and even colleagues of goodwill.[20] Such measures would need to be internally enforceable, but could be complemented with external safeguards in law.[21] Yet even with better organizational procedures and protective legislation in place, there will still be some instances where whistleblowing is appropriate as the only means of rectifying a serious problem or danger. It will remain an extremely courageous act.

In the United States, the National Society of Professional Engineers (NSPE) has recognized that there are situations where there can be a conflict of responsibility for the professional and where the professional's chief responsibility is not to the organization but to the public. The first fundamental canon of the NSPE Code of Ethics says, "Engineers, in the fulfillment of their professional duties, shall hold paramount the safety, health, and welfare of the public."[22] This tenet amounts to a declaration of commitment on behalf of the professional organization, as well as to a requirement that professionals take responsibility for acting in the public interest, specifically when the public interest comes into conflict with other responsibilities they have by virtue of being professionals and employees. This would seem to be a commitment to blowing the whistle when that would best serve the public interest. This tenet of the code appears to do significantly more than affirm and inspire institutional ethics among engineers. It is a deterring and disciplining statement: the NSPE can suspend or expel members for breaches.

A great deal of work has been done to take the heroism out of whistleblowing—indeed, to make the act unnecessary by instituting procedures to deal with ethical difficulties and to make it unnecessary to go outside the normal chain of authority. Nevertheless, the fact remains that there will always be some circumstances that procedures will not remedy. And personal courage will always be necessary for ethical decisions. Procedures cannot be a substitute for integrity.

The Evolving Situation

Whistleblower protection legislation now exists across Canada for employees in the public sector and private citizens in some jurisdictions (for example, the New Brunswick Employment Standards Act). Public sector whistleblowing protection only came about after a significant number of fairly embarrassing public sector cases came to light. An organization called FAIR was established by Joanna Gualtieri, herself a whistleblower who exposed lavishly excessive spending by staff in the Department of Foreign Affairs and had her career sidelined as a result. The purpose of FAIR is to expose cases of public sector malfeasance and to protect whistleblowers from retaliation by government officials.[23] The same protection is not clearly extended to whistleblowers in corporations or other private businesses, and prosecutions are difficult to obtain. Extending the legal protection of whistleblowers in the private sector is even more difficult and, in an open society, might never be satisfactory.

No contemporary discussion of whistleblowing can now be complete without reference to WikiLeaks and its founder Julian Assange.

CASE 7.5: Julian Assange and WikiLeaks

In 2006, Julian Assange, an Australian Internet activist, established WikiLeaks, a not-for-profit online repository that published submissions of classified, private, or secret documents and other media received through anonymous individuals wishing to make this material public.

Since 2010, WikiLeaks has published, either on its own or in collaboration with major commercial media organizations, in excess of 76,900 classified documents pertaining to the war in Afghanistan, almost 400,000 classified documents relating to the Iraq War, and 776 documents relating to the prisoners in the Guantánamo Bay detention facility in Cuba. WikiLeaks has also been involved in the release of United States State Department diplomatic cables and internal documents from several significant financial institutions and corporations.[24]

While WikiLeaks' activities have raised the ire of numerous government and corporate entities, Assange claims that real democracies can only function in an environment characterized by a free flow of information. It is this availability of information that allows the general public to make truly informed decisions with respect to the election of its leaders.

WikiLeaks ultimately constitutes a facility for anonymous whistleblowing through the leaking of incriminating documentary evidence. WikiLeaks allows whistleblowing by proxy. Assange claims that he has no axe to grind with the institutions or organizations whose documents are released; his organization is merely facilitating the free flow of information to the greater public.

Assange is, at the time of writing, being provided asylum in the Ecuadorean Embassy in London, England, where he is fighting a European arrest warrant for extradition to Sweden to assist in investigations of sexual assault. Assange claims that the allegations against him are baseless. While it is unproven, many view the sexual assault charges against Assange as an effort to attack his character and credibility in an extreme form of negative advocacy.

The following case of Rudolf Elmer and a major international financial institution illustrates some of the difficulties whistleblowers face.

CASE 7.6: Rudolf Elmer and the Bank

Early in 2007, Rudolf Elmer, a Swiss bank executive with Julius Baer, handed across account details of 2,000 prominent wealthy individuals and corporations to the WikiLeaks organization. Elmer claims that this material provides evidence of enormous potential tax evasion. After working for Julius Baer for two decades, Elmer was dismissed in 2002. He went public as a whistleblower in 2008 by releasing information to WikiLeaks detailing activities allegedly engaged in by Julius Baer and its clients in the Cayman Islands.[25]

Elmer had worked his way up through the banking system, gaining increasingly responsible international management experience. He was formerly the chief operating officer in the Cayman Islands for Julius Baer, during which time he brought to the bank's attention what he perceived to be abuses by clients of a system that allowed them to evade taxation. He contends that when his warnings went unheeded by the bank, he went to the Swiss banking authorities with his observations and was again ignored. It was only then that he decided to make his concerns public by releasing information to WikiLeaks. Julius Baer has accused him of stealing this client information.

Elmer's stated belief is that the release of this information will inform society with respect to the significant abuses of banks and their privacy regulations that allow their clients to conceal massive amounts of wealth for the purpose of evading legitimate taxation. His stated intention was not to point the finger at any specific institution or individual, but to illustrate systemic failures and abuses within the financial system. He contends that senior officials in powerful financial institutions and governments turn a blind eye to these behaviours in the interest of maintaining profitable business relations. The information he provided to WikiLeaks includes incriminating data on individuals, multinational corporations and conglomerates, financial institutions, and hedge funds. These parties hail from the Americas, Asia, Europe, and across the globe. The individuals named (many are recognized pillars of the community) include people who have made their fortunes in business and the arts, as well as a significant number of politicians.

Elmer was charged and convicted in 2011 with breaking a number of Switzerland's bank secrecy laws, forging documents, and sending threatening communications to Julius Baer officials. He was convicted and given a choice of serving 240 days in jail or paying a fine of 7,200 Swiss francs, but the sentence was suspended in favour of two years' probation. Two days after the trial, he was arrested for releasing information to WikiLeaks. A judge ruled this to be a contempt of court on the part of the authorities, and Elmer was subsequently released. The original sentence is being appealed.

As a result of the hounding he has received from Swiss officials since he stepped forth as a whistleblower, his health has been adversely affected and his career has suffered irreparable damage. He has been portrayed in the Swiss media as a paranoid and mentally disturbed person, prompting him to live in exile on the island of Mauritius. Elmer's lawyer, Jack Blum, one of the premier American experts on tracking offshore assets, made this statement:

> Elmer is being tried for violating Swiss banking secrecy law even though the data is from the Cayman Islands. This is bold extraterritorial nonsense. Swiss secrecy law should apply to Swiss banks in Switzerland, not a Swiss subsidiary in the Cayman Islands.

Elmer's case illustrates that protections for whistleblowers are inherently difficult to devise, and thus changes in public policy will never remove the need for personal courage, sometimes of a high order, in bringing to light institutional failures that prejudice the public interest. The case fits the typical profile of whistleblowers in most respects. In general, publicity can offer some protection because it increases the whistleblower's visibility. It also lends credibility to the whistleblower's claims and puts a face to them. In Elmer's case, his mistake was in his belief that exposing abuses internally would make him more acceptable to the bank he worked for and to the society it served. In the end, his public challenge threatened an entrenched and powerful system that could rally significant financial, media, and judicial resources to discredit and disgrace him.

Case Questions

1. What else could Elmer have done? Could he have fought for banking reform internally without going public?
2. Would you base your view about Elmer's conduct on a consideration of his responsibilities as an executive of the bank or on the fate that befell him?
3. What would have happened to Elmer and his complaint had he not had the option of having his data publicly posted on WikiLeaks?
4. Elmer said that he did not intend to point the finger at any specific institution or individual. However, he did, in fact, name a specific institution and a number of specific individuals. Isn't his claim hollow? So what?

"Aberrant behaviour" has long been used to explain away whistleblowing in Canada. As noted in Case 7.3, when Sean Bruyea publicly protested against the enactment of legislation detrimental to injured veterans, his credibility was attacked when the authorities released personal medical records that referred to his post-traumatic stress disorder and implied that he was mentally unstable. Bob Stenhouse, an RCMP officer with almost two decades of experience, was accused of "discreditable conduct" and forced to resign for releasing details of a media campaign describing RCMP strategies for addressing gang activities; he felt the campaign provided an inaccurate description of police activities and was simply a public relations exercise.[26] Lesley Anthony has been accused by the authorities of professional misconduct for her role in releasing a videotape showing the abuse of an elderly woman in a long-term care facility.[27]

Engaging in **negative advocacy** by focusing on attacking the credibility of the whistleblower as a solution to public interest issues is still common. Negative advocacy is part of the general strategy that organizations adopt in response to whistleblowing because it takes the spotlight off the problem and puts it on the whistleblower. It is a way to avoid dealing with the problem and at the same time make the whistleblower the problem.[28] Of course, if a psychologist or psychiatrist assesses the whistleblower as "having a personality disorder," then it is possible not only to discredit the complaint and the person making it, but also to shake the person's self-confidence and perhaps control damage. Consider the case of Dr John O'Connor:

negative advocacy *focusing on attacking the credibility of the whistleblower in an attempt to divert attention from the problem issue being exposed by the whistleblower*

CASE 7.7: Dr John O'Connor's Environmental Warnings

Beginning in 2003, Dr John O'Connor, an Alberta doctor who regularly visited patients in the northern community of Fort Chipewyan, suspected a possible connection between an unusually high incidence of rare human cancers and carcinogens released into the environment by the oil sands development located upriver from the community.[29] In addition to gleaning evidence when diagnosing patients, he began to review the health histories of the town's residents, finding an unusually high occurrence of colorectal cancers and cholangiocarcinoma, a rare cancer of the bile duct.

Shortly after Dr O'Connor's warning was widely publicized in 2006, he was shocked to find that Health Canada had accused him of raising undue alarm in the community, engendering mistrust, performing billing irregularities, and unduly restricting access to files. Each of these represents serious charges that could have led to the suspension or withdrawal of Dr O'Connor's licence to practise medicine.

Dr O'Connor's findings were subsequently supported by scientist ecologist Kevin Timoney in his reported conclusions of a water study conducted in and around Fort Chipewyan. Timoney, who has studied the Athabasca River for 14 years, found contaminants that "are significantly high enough to raise the risk of cancer."[30] Timoney described the government's claims against Dr O'Connor as an unwarranted attempt to silence someone with legitimate concerns. Dr O'Connor's case has raised the concern of the Canadian medical profession that they risk possible persecution and prosecution for speaking out as advocates for public health. One of Dr O'Connor's colleagues, Dr Michel Sauvé, has called for whistleblower legislation in order to protect health professionals from repressive government censorship of legitimate public health concerns.

Late in 2007 and early in 2008, Dr O'Connor was cleared of the charges brought against him by Health Canada, but not before the legal actions taken against him had adversely affected his health and caused him to leave Alberta for a quieter life in the Maritime provinces.

Without doubt the stress caused to whistleblowers can damage their health. Furthermore, the sheer struggle to have the truth recognized and accepted in the face of official denials can make them obsessive or appear to be so. Nevertheless, it is disturbing that the first reaction of those who are accused or who stand to lose is often to call in psychiatrists and psychologists in an attempt to discredit the accuser. The matter raises ethical questions for these professions, as well as for those who turn to them in cases like these.

Although we have argued that external protections will never make whistleblowing safe, we believe that they should go some way towards changing a culture of reporting. Whistleblowers may always be necessary, but they should not be seen as deviant. The fact that whistleblowing is now taken seriously by authorities marks a considerable change in attitude and should soften the instinct for retaliation, even in the absence of legislative protection. The environment for public interest disclosures has changed. Transparency is demanded of government, the public sector, and business. The dire consequences that inevitably flow from whistleblowing are likely to be less severe today than a decade or so ago. After being subjected to punitive measures designed to deter them from their continuing investigation of fraudulent dealings within the Royal Canadian Mounted Police pension fund, five current and former members of the force, known as the RCMP Five, belatedly received commendations from the force.[31] While Rudolf Elmer faced legal action and was branded a troublemaker, that tag does not automatically affix itself to people who try to do the right thing. That still does not nullify the costs of whistleblowing—costs that can be imposed from unexpected quarters. Consider the well-publicized case of Jane Akre and Steve Wilson.

CASE 7.8: Jane Akre, Steve Wilson, and the Prosilac Story

In 1997, Jane Akre and Steve Wilson, two investigative reporters with an affiliate television station of Fox News, presented a story on a synthetic hormone marketed under the name Prosilac by pharmaceutical giant Monsanto. Prosilac was designed to increase milk production in cows, but it produced a number of serious side effects in the cows to which it was given. One of these side effects was mastitis, a serious infection of the udder that required treatment with antibiotics. These antibiotics were then passed into the milk that was ultimately consumed by the public, and as a result, the consumers would potentially suffer from a reduction in their resistance to disease.[32]

When Akre and Wilson refused Fox News' demand that they rewrite their story prior to airing to minimize any negative publicity for Monsanto, a major source of advertising revenue for Fox, they ultimately lost their jobs with the network. The reporters sued Fox under the whistleblower statute that exists in the state of Florida. Akre was awarded $425,000 after proving to a jury that the amendments to the story demanded by Fox would have been false and misleading. Fox appealed and the case verdict was overturned on a technicality. Fox ultimately won the case based on the fact that Akre and Wilson did not have whistleblower status under the Florida statute. Were Akre and Wilson, in fact, whistleblowers? In the course of exercising their duties as investigative journalists, they uncovered and attempted to report on a story that was damaging to the subject company, Monsanto. This is not in itself whistleblowing because the reporters are not exposing a breach of ethics that they were privy to as part of Monsanto. The fact that Fox News, Akre and Wilson's employer, attempted to disguise the story and mislead the public in order to protect its advertising revenue, however, may well be a breach of ethical behaviour that the reporters could and should expose as whistleblowers. Strangely enough, the reason that the reporters failed to meet eligibility requirements as whistleblowers was because it is not in fact against the law to report false news.

At one point in all of this legal wrangling, the investigative reporters were found to be liable for Fox's legal and court costs of $1.8 million. This was subsequently reduced to $200,000, still a significant amount.

Because of the courage typically involved in whistleblowing and the damage that it often does to career, family, and social life, whistleblowers are rightly viewed as noble and self-sacrificing. They are defenders of the public interest. We do not usually see them as public nuisances. But there is another side to all of this. Because of its claim to special status, there is the potential to abuse whistleblowing.

Consider the following case of Orlando Helicopter Airways as related by its founder, Fred P. Clark.

CASE 7.9: Orlando Helicopter Airways

In 1986, Orlando Helicopter Airways (OHA) won a contract with United States Army Missile Command to produce special helicopters—basically imitations of the Soviet Hind attack helicopter—for training purposes. It supplied 15 aircraft over a three-year period for around US$7 million. Large defence contractors had quoted $20 million and a much longer completion time. The army commended the OHA aircraft and support service as "outstanding." In November 1989, however, an office employee of six months' standing at OHA, wrote a memo to the Defense Criminal Investigation Service (DCIS) alleging engineering safety breaches in the construction of the helicopters. This person was not a pilot, an aeronautical engineer, or even a mechanic. He did, however, owe $500,000 in back taxes, and in the United States whistleblowers are promised up to 30 per cent of the money the government recovers from successful prosecutions resulting from their evidence. The army's own investigation found no fraud or other wrongdoing at OHA. An ambitious investigator at the DCIS, however, was determined to make a case against OHA and encouraged past and present employees to remove company documents. Although nine separate investigations had found no evidence of any corruption at Orlando, this investigator pursued his quarry by digging into OHA's certification compliance procedures back to the 1960s. Some people in the DCIS were determined to prosecute OHA.

During the two years of investigations, the company was the victim of slander and innuendo, its reputation suffered, business fell off as contracts went elsewhere, and it eventually closed its doors, throwing 40 employees out of work. No findings were made against OHA.[33] It was the victim of zealotry and officiousness and perhaps defence industry politics.

So, while whistleblowing is usually depicted as the heroic stand of a principled individual against some system, this is not the only aspect that should be considered. The fate of organizations and those who depend on them, together with the dangers of encouraging malicious reporting, should be kept in mind when protection and support for whistleblowing are being determined.

Some writers are concerned about danger from a different quarter: namely, ethical support itself.[34] The argument is that ethical support for whistleblowing will actually harm whistleblowers. It holds that once an organization adopts ethics strategies, it will claim that evil has been eliminated from the workplace. If this occurs, then the whistleblower will, by definition, be excluded. By thus excluding the dissenter, the supposedly ethical organization is able to use ethics strategically to protect itself. This is an argument reminiscent of Marxist analyses of reform in capitalist economies: the union movement, welfare, and state sponsorship of sport and the arts all contribute to keeping "the revolution" at bay. Popular discontent is abated by such measures, so any view that governments under capitalism can act in the interests of justice is naive: governments act to protect their capitalist masters. On the other hand, if governments do not redistribute wealth or support social activities, then this is proof that capitalism controls the state in the interests of the ruling class. In brief, the Marxist can never be satisfied: governments in market economies are damned if they support social institutions and damned if they do not. The negative analysis of whistleblower support described above comes off the same template as the Marxist analysis of the state. An organization that acts to minimize the necessity for the practice is enhancing social control in the workplace; an organization that does not address the problem colludes in exposing the whistleblower to all the penalties of acting according to conscience.

People have to be cautious about informing on illegal, harmful, or unethical conduct, not only because they will have to bear the consequences, but also because others will have to live with them, too, and there is in any case no easy way of dealing with dissent in the public interest. The best of protective procedures and policies will be limited and can probably be used for corrupt purposes. This is not an argument for doing nothing, but a caution against believing that laws and procedures can accomplish everything we should desire for whistleblower protection.

Review Questions

1. Do you think that there is good reason for limiting the term "whistleblowing" to cases of "external whistleblowing"?
2. Do you think it is ever the case that a person "ought" to blow the whistle—that if they fail to blow the whistle, then they will have done something wrong? Or, do you believe that any case of justifiable whistleblowing will be a case of heroic action—that is, action above and beyond what is morally required?
3. Employees in the private sector have a contract with their employer. What moral justification can supersede a commitment already made to be loyal to this employer? Is it not morally discreditable to inform on a corporation to a regulator? What about leaking information to shareholders via the media?

Suggested Readings

Bakan, Joel. *The Corporation: The Pathological Pursuit of Profit and Power*. New York: Free Press, 2004.

Leigh, David, Luke Harding, and the *Guardian*. *WikiLeaks: Inside Julian Assange's War on Secrecy*. New York: Guardian Books, 2011.

Westin, Allen, ed. *Whistleblowing: Loyalty and Dissent in the Corporation*. New York: McGraw-Hill, 1981.

Suggested Websites

WikiLeaks:
http://wikileaks.org/.

Federal Accountability Act:
http://laws-lois.justice.gc.ca/eng/acts/F-5.5/index.html.

FAIR:
http://fairwhistleblower.ca/.

Rudolf Elmer:
http://www.rudolfelmer.com/home/.

8
Corporate Governance

Chapter Outline

- The Principal-Agent Problem
- Control and Monitoring
- Weaknesses in the Board of Directors Model
- Corporate Citizenship and Corporate Governance
- Review Questions
- Suggested Readings
- Suggested Websites

In June 2011, a little known short-seller, Muddy Watters LLC, made accusations that Canadian forestry firm Sino-Forest Corp. had overstated the size and value of its forestry assets held in mainland China. Carson Block, president of Muddy Watters LLC, described Sino-Forest as a giant "Ponzi scheme." Sino-Forest Corp., Canada's largest forestry company, has raised in excess of $3 billion from investors through equity and debt markets in recent years to fund the expansion of its operations.[1]

By the end of August 2011, Sino-Forest Corp.'s share price had dropped 72 per cent to $1.38 even though the company continued to insist that the accusations were unfounded.[2] If these accusations were indeed unfounded, why did Sino-Forest Corp. not simply disprove them? Surely assets such as forests should be relatively easy to validate; ownership title and/or logging rights would have to have supporting documentation. Sino-Forest Corp., however, was unable to validate these assets on a timely basis. Herein lies an example of a serious failure in corporate governance. A company with strong governance mechanisms could have validated the assets and transactions in question, disproved the short-seller's accusations, and continued on with business as usual. In the case of Sino-Forest Corp., the company found it necessary to launch its own internal investigation to satisfy itself that its Chinese forestry assets were indeed accurately stated. This, of course, raised red flags with the Royal Canadian Mounted Police (RCMP) and the Ontario Securities Commission (OSC), which subsequently launched their own investigations. A committee of Sino-Forest directors, assisted by a major auditing firm, spent in excess of five months and $35 million investigating Sino-Forest's business practices, producing a 111-page report that was at best inconclusive.[3] The report actually raised more questions than it answered with respect to how the company's business model functioned and the way in which Sino-Forest Corp. generated revenues.

At the time this chapter was written, no charges had been laid against Sino-Forest Corp. or its management and no criminal proceedings had been launched. Sino-Forest's lack of transparency and inability to easily disclose the complex web of relationships between its suppliers, its intermediaries, Chinese governmental organizations, and offshore entities are examples of a colossal failure in governance.[4] The management at Sino-Forest claims that the unique and distinct characteristics of Chinese business practices are largely responsible for the lack of transparency in many of their informal business relationships and resultant transactions. These informal business structures make the verification of the ownership of the forestry resources virtually impossible. Professor Paul Gillis of Beijing University asks the obvious question of whether "it's appropriate for a company that operates in this manner to be listed on the Toronto Stock Exchange."[5]

Corporate governance refers to the controls put in place that ensure that a corporation acts in an ethical, legal, and transparent manner in the best interests of its shareholders and, to an increasing extent, involves the consideration of the interests of all of its stakeholders. Effective corporate governance greatly reduces the chances of ethical transgressions or the negative ethical consequences that may arise from a laxity of oversight and control. Corporate governance can also be defined as a relationship among stakeholders that is used to determine and control the strategic direction and performance of organizations. Governance is also concerned with identifying

corporate governance *the controls put in place to ensure that a corporation acts in an ethical, legal, and transparent manner in the best interests of its shareholders*

ways to ensure that strategic decisions are made effectively. It is used in corporations to establish order between the firm's owners and its top-level managers.

The need for strong corporate governance is the result of the requirement to address the problems created by the separation of ownership and control that is characteristic of the corporation as a model for business ownership. While there are numerous forms of business ownership, the three most commonly occurring ones are the sole proprietorship, the partnership, and the corporation. The sole proprietorship is wholly owned by a single person, quite often the founder; a partnership is shared ownership among two or more individuals; and a corporation is a form of multi-party ownership by many shareholders. The corporation as a form of business ownership has several advantages over other forms:

- It offers its owners limited liability (to the maximum of the amount invested).
- It allows greater access to capital markets.
- It facilitates liquidity in corporate ownership.
- It is an independent entity with an ongoing lifespan (unless bankrupted or merged with, or acquired by, another company).

For these reasons, with very few exceptions the corporation has become the de facto form of business ownership for business entities of any significant size. The corporation as a form of business ownership is not without its challenges. Because of the inherent complexity of a corporation, the cost structure involved in the running of it is greater, and because of the corporation's status as an independent entity, its shareholders may face double taxation; corporations are taxed on their profits, and the shareholders as owners are taxed as individuals on the dividends they receive from the corporations as well as on any capital gains upon disposition of their shares. Most importantly, however, are the potentially serious governance issues that corporations face because of the separation of ownership and control. These challenges are discussed in greater detail later in the chapter.

CASE 8.1: Two Examples of the Separation of Ownership and Control

Hewlett-Packard's Takeover of Compaq

In 2001, Hewlett-Packard announced that it would acquire the Compaq Corporation for $25.5 billion. There was an almost unanimous negative reaction from the investment community, stock markets, industry experts, and the business media. Stock prices for both Hewlett-Packard and Compaq plunged—down 18 per cent for Hewlett-Packard and 10 per cent for Compaq. While it is not unusual for the stock price of an acquiring company firm to dip, the stock price of the target firm usually increases.

The founders of Hewlett-Packard, David W. Packard and Walter Hewlett (beneficial holders of 18 per cent of Hewlett-Packard stock) were strongly opposed to the transaction and engaged in an active campaign to persuade shareholders to reject the proposed takeover of Compaq. They went as far as purchasing newspaper advertisements in US national publications.

The CEO of Hewlett-Packard, Carly Fiorina, decided to proceed with the acquisition despite the opposition to the transaction from the founders, the markets, the experts, and the media. At the shareholders' meeting where the proposed acquisition was to face a vote, the majority of shareholders voted in favour of the transaction. Even with opposition from influential shareholders with significant holdings, the majority of the shareholders voted with management, reinforcing the idea that management does indeed control the firm. This control is informal in nature and has as its basis the notion that management preferences and directives have traditionally carried extraordinary weight with shareholders.

Apple Computer and Steve Jobs

Steve Jobs cofounded Apple Computer and became the company's first CEO as well as its largest shareholder when it went public. Apple was going through a period of rapid expansion when the board of directors began to question whether Jobs was experienced enough to lead the firm through its tumultuous development. In 1983, the board of directors hired John Sculley as CEO. A struggle for control of the firm ensued between Jobs and Sculley, with the board of directors backing Sculley. Jobs was removed from all operational decision-making and forced out of the company despite being its largest shareholder.

In this case, as with the Hewlett-Packard acquisition of Compaq, management ultimately exercised control over and above the desires of influential company founders with significant shareholdings. It must be noted that in neither of these cases did founders exercise majority control. It is also interesting to note in the case of Apple that once the company began to experience difficulties in the latter part of the 1990s, the board of directors made the decision to bring back Steve Jobs as CEO.

The Principal-Agent Problem

The thousands or more of investors who own public corporations do not have the ability to collectively make the daily decisions needed to operate a business. A management team of executives is required to direct the operations of the business in the interests of the owner/shareholders. To facilitate this, the shareholders, as **principals**, elect a **board of directors** to act as their **agents** in supervising the firm. The directors then appoint the executives to actually run the firm on a day-to-day basis.

The separation of ownership and control leads to a situation known as the **principal-agent problem**. The principal-agent problem represents the conflict of interest between the principal (owner/shareholders) and the agent (management or executives). The primary principal-agent problem occurring in corporations arises when shareholders lack the ability to effectively monitor management's behaviour. Management executives may be enticed to use a firm's assets in ways inconsistent with the best interests of the shareholders. Management executives may be tempted to use a firm's assets in their own best interests, but they may also face a conflict between the interests of shareholders and the interests of the firm as an entity. This may occur in situations where the short term interests of the shareholders conflict with the interests of the firm and its long term survival as an independent business entity. This conflict occurs often when the sale of a firm generates benefits for the shareholders but leads to the effective demise of the firm being sold.

principal *a person or entity first in rank of importance or level of ownership*

Board of Directors *elected by shareholders to represent them in overseeing the executive level of management to ensure that management does indeed act in the shareholders' best interests*

agent *a person or entity that represents the interests of another party*

principal-agent problem *represents the conflict of interest between the principal and the agent*

This conflict of interest that arises between managers and owners can manifest itself in many different ways. Managers have the temptation to engage in one or more of the following practices:

- shirking (that is, not working hard)
- nepotism (hiring friends and/or family)
- exhibiting favouritism in compensation or promotion practices
- self-dealing and/or engaging in non-arm's-length transactions
- consuming excessive perks
- building empires
- taking no risks or chances in order to avoid being fired
- taking excessive risk to earn large bonuses
- having a short-run horizon if the manager is near retirement.

CASE 8.2: Dennis Kozlowski and Tyco Corporation

Dennis Kozlowski, former CEO of Tyco International, was convicted in 2005 of crimes relating to a number of excesses committed during his tenure as CEO. Kozlowski was found guilty of accepting $81 million in unauthorized bonuses. Among other things, he had Tyco pay for his $30-million New York apartment, which included a $6,000 shower curtain and $15,000 umbrella stands. He also expensed half of his wife's $2-million birthday party, held on the Italian island of Sardinia, under the guise that it was in fact a shareholder meeting.

In his defence, Kozlowski argued that under his leadership Tyco International had expanded significantly and continued to be profitable. While his compensation scheme was very large and complex, he argued that he was compensated for his performance and that this compensation was sanctioned by the board of directors.[6]

Dennis Kozlowski's excesses were a manifestation of self-interested behaviour unchecked by corporate governance mechanisms. The board of directors approved outrageous compensation packages for Kozlowski and his inner circle (Kozlowski had a salary in excess of $100 million) and failed to call him to task on his abuse of his power and privileges. It is clear that these abuses were not in the best interests of the shareholders of the corporation and that both internal and external governance mechanisms were either ineffectual or not implemented.

Control and Monitoring

There are a number of possible solutions to the principle-agent problem. These fall into two main categories: controls and monitoring. Many of the controls take the form of incentives that are intended to align the interests of executive management with those of the shareholders, while monitoring includes various methods of policing and oversight that ensure that executive management is indeed acting in the best interests of the shareholders.

Incentives that align the interests of executive management with shareholders can be either internal or external. Internal incentives generally revolve around executive compensation in the form of pay-for-performance bonus strategies or executive stock options. External, or market-driven, incentives include the external market for executive employment or the spectre of corporate merger or acquisition. Performance by an executive seen to be contrary to the best interests of shareholders would reflect badly on that executive, thus harming his or her prospects for future executive employment. Likewise, poor performance by an executive can have an adverse effect on share price, which can make the price of acquisition by another firm increasingly attractive. A merger or acquisition enabled by the decreasing share price of the target firm usually results in the removal of the target firm's executive management. These scenarios all create incentives for management to align their interests with shareholders in terms of maintaining or increasing share value and profitability.

An effective governance model requires transparent and comprehensive flows of information to ensure that stakeholders have the ability to rapidly assess the current state of the corporation. In order to achieve this transparent flow of information, effective monitoring systems need to be in place. Monitoring involves the setting up of mechanisms to oversee the behaviours and evaluate the performance of managers. Internally to the corporation, monitoring is the role of the Board of Directors, its associated committees, and, to a lesser extent, activist shareholders. Externally, monitoring is accomplished by a number of monitors—auditors, bankers, credit agencies, analysts, attorneys, and government regulators such as security commissions and stock exchanges. Table 8.1 summarizes the major control and monitoring mechanisms that corporations have in place, both internally and externally, to ensure that management acts in the best interest of the shareholders. The control and monitoring mechanisms noted in the table are presented in further detail in the following sections.

Table 8.1 Corporate governance control and monitoring control mechanisms

Internal	External
Board of Directors	The market for executive employment
Incentive-based executive compensation	Mergers and acquisitions (the market for capital control)
Shareholder activism	Government oversight and regulation

Board of Directors

The original intended purpose of the Board of Directors was to represent the shareholders in overseeing the executive level of management to ensure that management was indeed acting in the shareholders' best interests. The Board of Directors is elected by the shareholders for this very purpose. The role of a Board of Directors is summarized as follows:

- to act as the shareholders' agent with fiduciary responsibility
- to hire and evaluate management

- to approve major operating proposals
- to approve major financial decisions
- to offer expert advice to management
- to ensure that the firm's activities and financial condition are accurately reported to its stakeholders.

Reporting to the Board of Directors is a group of standing and ad hoc board subcommittees made up of board members. These subcommittees are set up to address specific tasks or functions that fall under the jurisdiction of the greater board. *Standing* subcommittees are committees set up to monitor specific ongoing board functions, while *ad hoc* subcommittees are more task oriented and are often disbanded once the specific task at hand is completed. Table 8.2 illustrates some examples of standing and ad hoc board subcommittees. Not all companies will have all of these subcommittees, and some companies may initiate subcommittees not listed below to address issues specific to their company or industry.

Table 8.2 Examples of board subcommittees

Committee	Function
Executive	Oversees the operations of the board and its processes. Usually made up of the board chair and the committee chairs. May act on behalf of the board for activities occurring between meetings that are later ratified at the board meeting. Conducts the performance evaluation of the CEO.
Development	Oversees board planning and development, including orientation and training of new board members, evaluating the effectiveness of the board and its subcommittees, and ongoing professional development for board members.
Finance	Often chaired by the board treasurer. Oversees the budget process and ensures adequate financial controls provide accurate monitoring and accountability of financial assets and transactions.
Personnel	Oversees design, development, authorization, and implementation of policies and procedures governing compensation and other personnel issues. May assist CEO in executive leadership and compensation issues.
Public relations	Oversees the management of the company's reputational capital. Oversees communications to the public, the press, and sometimes the shareholders.
Ethics	Ensures guidelines, policies, and procedures are in place for promoting and ensuring ethical conduct and corporate social responsibility and for effectively resolving ethical conflicts.

Incentive-Based Executive Compensation

incentive-based executive compensation *the use of salary, bonuses, and long-term incentives to align managers' interests with shareholders' interests*

Incentive-based executive compensation involves the use of salary, bonuses, and long-term incentives to align managers' interests with shareholders' interests. Incentive-based executive compensation is used primarily to mitigate the risks associated with the principal-agent problem. By aligning executives' interests with shareholders' interests, the self-interest of the employee no longer competes with shareholders' interests. The removal of this conflict of interest results in self-interested executives working to exactly the same ends as executives with the best interests of the shareholders at heart, regardless of their internal motivations.

Examples of incentive-based executive compensation include performance bonuses, stock options, profit-sharing plans, and stock purchase plans. It has been found, however, that many of these vehicles do not necessarily create a seamless alignment of executive and shareholder interests. Stock options, for instance, may provide incentives for executives to artificially inflate share prices in the short term in order to maximize their payout upon exercise of their options. Likewise, performance bonuses may be incentives for management executives to focus on performance during the period in which their performance is evaluated to the detriment of overall longer-term corporate performance. There have been numerous of examples of outgoing presidents or senior executives engaging in this practice. Consider the case of the Nortel Corporation:

CASE 8.3: The Rise and Fall of Nortel

At its peak, Nortel was a giant diversified corporation focused primarily on telecommunications. In July 2000, Nortel's market capitalization peaked at more than $350 billion. Ranking among the largest companies in the world, Nortel accounted for just over 37 per cent of the total value of the Toronto Stock Exchange Composite Index.[7]

Nortel's expertise in wireless and broadband communications allowed it to achieve unparalleled revenue gains in the rapidly growing telecommunications sector. Nortel was intent on exploiting this rapid growth based on the international trend towards deregulation in the telecommunications industry.[8] Using an aggressive acquisition strategy, Nortel quickly established itself as a global corporation. Its share price tripled in four years, reaching a peak of just over $200 per share by the middle of 2000.

Nortel's CEO compensation strategy was heavily based on option compensation. The fixed salary awarded to the CEO each year amounted to slightly less than $1 million, while short-term bonuses reached $1.3 million in 1998, $4.2 million in 1999, and $5.6 million in 2000. Nortel's 2000 and 2001 proxy statements indicate that the most heavily weighted driver for bonus compensation was revenue, followed by operating earnings per share. As such, there was significant incentive for Nortel's CEO to pursue an aggressive strategy of growth through acquisitions.

Although John Roth, CEO of Nortel between 1996 and 2001, was well compensated in terms of salary and bonus, this compensation appeared meagre relative to the value of options awarded to him: $5 million in 1998, $18 million in 1999, and $33 million in 2000. It was shortly after the last that the bottom fell out.

Nortel's decline was rapid and multi-faceted. The apparently accelerating levels of growth and earnings were largely informed by massive accounting and financial irregularities that supported the manipulation of earnings over a multi-year period. Nortel was forced to restate its financial statements several times, one of these restatements involving the largest changes in a restatement in Canadian history. Further investigation showed that many of Nortel's aggressively pursued acquisitions were overvalued and ill-advised. Nortel's stock went into a free fall—from a share price of more than $200 down to $0.67.[9] Two-thirds of Nortel's workforce were let go, and the CEO and several other high-level corporate executives resigned. Shareholders and institutional investors complained that these executives continued to receive bonuses even as the company slid towards insolvency.

There has been much speculation that the excessively generous incentive-based executive compensation led to the culture of unbridled risk-taking, aggressive and unsustainable growth strategies, and the fraudulent manipulation of financial information that ultimately led to the collapse of Canada's largest corporation.[10]

Case Questions

1. A former employee of Nortel made the statement that, for the most part, the Nortel executives consisted of a group of "good people" caught up in a "bad culture." Do you think there is any merit to this statement, particularly concerning employees knowingly engaged in misstating financial performance?
2. Should stakeholders such as employees and pensioners have any recourse against management in leadership positions who play a significant role in the decision-making that ultimately leads to the collapse of an organization?
3. Would a different executive compensation strategy have minimized the probability of excessive management risk-taking? What role should the Board of Directors have played in managing compensation strategies?

Shareholder Activism

The usual *modus operandi* of corporations results in the hiring of professional managers by the principals or shareholders through their representatives, the Board of Directors. This situation does not necessarily confer an abdication of power or influence by shareholders to the executive management team or to the Board of Directors. Shareholders retain the democratic right to vote on critical matters, their right to be heard and to propose shareholder resolutions for consideration at public shareholder meetings, and their right to organize and challenge the management of the corporation they have invested in. Shareholders with significant levels of shareholdings have even greater power and influence over the executive management team because of their proportionally higher voting power. Ownership concentration in terms of the relative amounts of stock owned by individual shareholders and institutional investors acts as an internal governance control mechanism influencing the behaviour of the executive managers in ways that allow them to satisfy the interests of these influential shareholders and ultimately to retain their own positions. In instances where corporate shareholdings are widely dispersed, an individual, institution, or dissident group with a relatively small percentage of the aggregate shareholdings may exert significant influence when voting is required. To be successful, this type of shareholder activism often requires a significant level of shareholder dissatisfaction with current management to overcome the high level of informal control traditionally held by management over shareholder decisions. The dissident group must also be credible, be respected, and offer up an extremely convincing alternative in order to sway shareholders away from their traditional support of incumbent management.

The case of Sherritt International Corp. presented below illustrates just how powerful and effective shareholder activism can be when shareholders perceive their interests are being neglected or mismanaged by an incumbent Board of Directors and/or executive management team.

CASE 8.4: Shareholder Activism and Sherritt International Corp.

In 1990, led by former securities trader Ian Delaney, a dissident group of shareholders of the Canadian firm Sherritt International Corp. launched a proxy battle against the incumbent management team and Board of Directors. With control of just slightly over 5 per cent of the corporation's voting shares, Mr Delaney and his small group of dissident shareholders argued that Sherritt's incumbent board and management team were mismanaging the company and that the corporation's ability to maintain itself as a viable ongoing entity was in jeopardy. The dissident proxy and supporting material for this argument were sent to the shareholders of Sherritt in the hope that they would be persuaded to vote in favour of the removal of the incumbent board and the instatement of an alternative Board of Directors recommended by the dissident group.

Delaney and his group were successful in wresting control away from the incumbent Board of Directors and installing the board put forth by the dissident group. An ensuing shakeup of management left Mr Delaney as President and CEO of the company. Sherritt went from being a nearly bankrupt nickel miner and fertilizer producer to being a large diversified corporation with annual revenues of $1.8 billion and international operations in mining, oil and gas, resorts, and hotels. Mr. Delaney continued at the helm of Sherritt as President and CEO until his retirement in early 2012.[11] He remains with the company as Chairman of the Board of Directors.

The Market for Executive Employment

The **market for executive employment** is an external control that naturally gives corporate executives the incentive to act in the best interests of the shareholders in order to maintain or increase their own desirability in the external job market. An executive with a track record of increasing corporate profitability and shareholder value will ultimately command a higher salary if he or she moves to, or is courted by, another company. Conversely, a management executive who is perceived to have failed to act in the best interests of the shareholders will see a lowering of his or her career prospects and potential earning power.

market for executive employment *an external control that naturally motivates corporate executives to act in the best interests of the shareholders in order to maintain or increase their desirability in the external job market*

The Market for Capital Control

The **market for capital control** is an external control that involves the purchase of a firm that is underperforming relative to industry rivals in order to improve its strategic competitiveness. As an example, executives who fail to act in the best interests of the company for which they work are susceptible to the market for capital control. The failure to drive corporate interests first often results in a reduction in profitability and a subsequent loss of share value. A reduced share value can make a firm a target for a takeover or acquisition by another firm because of the favourable price tag afforded by its reduced market capitalization. Struggling firms are often bought out by their competition or by other groups (private equity firms, employee buyouts, or other corporate entities looking to either diversify their holdings, pursue greater economies of scale, or take

market for capital control *the purchase of a firm that is underperforming relative to industry rivals in order to improve its strategic competitiveness*

advantage of either vertical or horizontal integration) that believe that better management can salvage the struggling firm's fortunes. When a struggling firm is acquired, the first casualties of employment are usually the executives of the target firm.

The Sherritt International Corp. example shown in Case 8.4 is an example of the market for capital control, albeit one that was driven by shareholder activism. The takeover of Sherritt by a dissident group of shareholders effectively transferred the control of the corporation from an underperforming group of managers and directors to a new group that promised a higher level of performance. These underperforming managers, executives, and directors were very quickly released by the new management team.

Government Oversight and Regulation

The most obvious form of external control is government oversight and regulation. Governments have significant influence over corporate activities. Canada Revenue Agency and the provincial securities commissions and exchanges dictate corporate reporting requirements for the purposes of taxation and public disclosure, respectively. Competition bureaus monitor business corporate practices in order to facilitate fair and free competition and the effective functioning of markets. Multiple layers of legislation influence everything from employee rights and responsibilities to corporate environmental performance. Much of this government oversight and regulation requires the measuring, monitoring, and reporting by the corporation to the various levels of government on a myriad of corporate activities.

Sarbanes-Oxley Act of 2002

In July 2002, in response to a number of high-profile accounting scandals—for example, Enron Corporation and WorldCom and the subsequent collapse of the public accounting firm Arthur Andersen—US president George W. Bush signed into law the Public Company Accounting Reform and Investor Protection Act, more commonly known as the Sarbanes-Oxley Act. The Act established an oversight body to regulate public accounting firms and legislation pertaining to corporate responsibility and institute increased punishments for corporate fraud and white-collar crime. The following is a brief summary of the sections of the Act.

Public Accounting Oversight Board

The Public Accounting Oversight Board operates under the auspices of the Securities and Exchange Commission (SEC) independently of the public accounting firms. The board's function is to provide oversight to the auditing of publicly traded companies to improve the quality and accuracy of the audit reports.

Auditor independence

Auditors play a key role in monitoring the financial position and performance of a corporation. The Sarbanes-Oxley Act ensures the independence of the auditors by disallowing the retention of the same public accounting firm for audit and consulting, by requiring that corporations change auditors at least every five years, and by preventing public accounting firms from auditing corporations if any of the corporations' senior executives were employed by the accounting firm within the previous year.

Corporate responsibility
Sarbanes-Oxley increases the responsibilities and the monitoring capabilities of corporate Boards of Directors by making them more independent from management and by restricting trading activities by executives and board members during blackout periods.

Financial disclosure
The Act strives to enhance financial disclosure by improving the transparency of executive activities to shareholders. This is achieved by requiring the reporting of "off balance sheet transactions," increasing internal controls, mandating financial expertise on the Board of Directors' audit committee, and restricting non-arm's-length loan transactions between the corporation and its executives.

Securities analysts and conflicts of interest
The Sarbanes-Oxley Act requires the SEC to demand the independence of securities analysts from investment banking activities and to facilitate the full disclosure of any conflicts of interest that securities analysts may have.

SEC resources and authority
The Act increases both the authority of the SEC and the amount of resources available to the SEC so that it may more effectively regulate its industry.

Corporate fraud, accountability, and penalties
The Act tightens the definitions of activities that constitute corporate fraud and white-collar crime. The Act also establishes increased penalties in terms of fines and incarceration for those engaging in these fraudulent activities.[12]

Weaknesses in the Board of Directors Model

The size of corporations and the disparate nature of their shareholders have led to practices that deviate from the original intended role of the corporate director. Many corporations have tens or even hundreds of thousands of shareholders, ranging from small individual investors to large institutional investors such as pension plans or mutual funds. Many individual investors lack the knowledge or sophistication to be able to provide an informed opinion on who should be elected as a director to a corporate board. Many institutional investors are interested only in the returns or dividends provided by the corporation. A significant number of shareholders are traders who are looking for short-term gains and have little interest in the corporation's long-term governance.

Management generally has much greater insight than the average shareholder into who would make an effective corporate director for their company. As such, management provides its recommendation for a slate of director candidates on the shareholder proxy. The voting shareholders, not having adequate knowledge or the experience necessary to make an informed nomination for director candidates, ultimately rubber-stamp their approval of management's recommended slate of directors by signing and returning the proxy. Since these directors are selected by the management executives that they are subsequently elected to oversee, a certain conflict of interest is created. The power to select a Board of Directors has fundamentally shifted from the shareholders to executive management even though the shareholders continue to vote in the board. Conflicts of interest arise when the board member is forced to choose between the interests of the shareholder whom he is elected to represent or the interests of management, who have put him forward as a candidate for director and who have the ability to continue to do so in the future. If it is in the director's best interest to remain a director, there is a temptation to act in the best interest of management even though this conflicts with their elected duty to shareholders. This is another example of the extraordinary level of informal decision-making control that management possesses relative to shareholders. Table 8.3 illustrates how current practice differs from the manner in which corporate Boards of Directors are theoretically supposed to be selected.

Table 8.3 Comparison of theory and practice in the selection of corporate Boards of Directors

Theory	Practice
• Shareholders own the corporation	• Shareholders own the corporation
• Shareholders elect a Board of Directors	• CEO/corporate officers select Board of Directors
• Board of Directors selects corporate officers	• Shareholders rubber-stamp the Board of Directors proposed by management

Directorships are often given to senior people with strong, well-established links to industry and government. Members of Boards of Directors are selected on the basis that their aggregate experience can assist and inform the CEO on governance and high-level management issues. Having a Board of Directors composed of high-profile and successful executives and public figures is seen to be a testament both to the credibility of the board and to the prestige of the corporation. While in many instances this may be true, senior executives often lead busy lives, running their own companies, serving on multiple boards, and engaging in community-based or philanthropic activities. This raises the question of whether these individuals have the time or resources to discharge their duties effectively as corporate directors. Much criticism has been levelled at the effectiveness of the Board of Directors in several high-profile corporate scandals.

One notable example of the failure of the directors to exercise their expertise in the governance of a corporation is the dramatic collapse of the Enron Corporation, recognized at the time as the largest accounting scandal in history. One of Enron's directors and the chair of its audit committee was a chartered public accountant, a former executive of a major public accounting firm, and a professor of accounting at one of North America's most prestigious business schools. While this director clearly had the expertise to have recognized some of the accounting problems at Enron, he was clearly not engaged enough to apply that expertise.[13]

This is not to say that the blame for failures in corporate governance should lie solely with the corporate directors. Board members have significant responsibilities and need to be provided with the tools and resources that allow them to execute these responsibilities effectively—namely, administrative support, legal support, information technology, support and information access, as well as sufficient remuneration to justify and enable the time for them to discharge these responsibilities. One suggestion is that a maximum limit be placed on the number of corporate directorships that any one individual can hold. Another is that some, or all, corporate directorships should be either full- or half-time. Of course, there are costs associated with increasing the resources provided to corporate boards, and thus there is inevitably a trade-off between the costs of providing these resources and the added effectiveness that doing so adds to the board's effectiveness.

CASE 8.5: WorldCom and a Failure of Governance

In 2002, the WorldCom Group filed for Chapter 11 bankruptcy protection under the US Bankruptcy Act. At the time WorldCom, a telecommunications company, had 60,000 employees, $104 billion in assets, and $30 billion in revenues. Effectively, WorldCom was the result of the acquisition and consolidation of numerous regional telecommunications companies in the United States throughout the 1980s and 1990s and the acquisition of larger competitors such as MFS Communications and MCI in 1996 and 1997, respectively.

WorldCom's spectacular growth coincided with significant changes in the telecommunications industry. Significant build-outs of fibre-optic networks and infrastructure to accommodate the rapidly increasing demand for the transmission of data and video drove significant growth throughout the telecommunications sector. WorldCom's growth through acquisition resulted in a conglomerate of enterprises with differing operating models, information systems, and corporate cultures. The speed with which these acquisitions were undertaken meant that little attention was paid to their integration within the larger company. This situation made the collection and monitoring of information a significant challenge. The WorldCom Board of Directors was left with little choice but to rely on the information provided to it by management.

With the slowdown of the technology and telecommunications sectors in the late 1990s, WorldCom's management was under great pressure to maintain share price and to continue to drive profitability and revenue growth. To achieve these targets, the CFO engaged in such practices as overstating revenues and inflating the balance sheet by recording operating expenses as assets. Both of these practices were in contravention of generally accepted accounting principles and ultimately resulted in the misstatement of WorldCom's income and financial position. Between 1999 and 2002, WorldCom had overstated its pre-tax income by more than $7 billion and its assets by $82 billion (more than 75 per cent of its total assets reported).

The SEC investigation found the WorldCom Board of Directors to be disengaged and distant from the operations of the company. A company as large and complex as WorldCom would require the Board of Directors to

continued . . .

apply a significant amount of expertise and energy in order to discharge their governance duties effectively. They were provided false information by management and did not engage to the extent necessary for them to fully comprehend the culture, direction, and strategy of the company. The board tended to ratify recommendations by management with respect to executive compensation and employee loan agreements without question.[14]

To compound matters, WorldCom's auditor, Arthur Andersen, continued to audit WorldCom as a "moderate risk" client even though it recognized the company as being "maximum risk." Arthur Andersen was never made to account for its failure to audit WorldCom effectively, owing to its effective dissolution as a result of its document-shredding activities in connection with its role in the collapse of the Enron Corporation.[15]

The WorldCom case illustrates the consequences of the failure of a Board of Directors to engage adequately in the affairs of a company. In hindsight, it seems absurd that the WorldCom Board of Directors could fail to observe the company's overstatement of its corporate assets by approximately 300 per cent and allow such flagrant accounting abuses to go undetected. Even analysts and industry insiders were at a loss as to how WorldCom could continue to be profitable as the rest of the sector went into decline. A functional board would have tasked the corporation to provide the information and resources necessary to effectively understand the complexities of the organization whose shareholders they were supposed to be representing.

Corporate Citizenship and Corporate Governance

Many of the difficulties presented in the discussion of corporate governance emerge from the separation of ownership and control and the conflicts of interest that arise between management and owner/shareholders. Governance mechanisms are designed to reduce these conflicts of interest by aligning the interests of management with those of shareholders. Where conflicts of interest do exist, these governance mechanism are designed to facilitate transparency, keeping conflicts in view so that any untoward effects are readily detectable. This transparency and openness acts as a deterrent to the temptation to act in any way that conflicts with the interests of the owner/shareholders. The success of these mechanisms is traditionally evaluated by measuring the company's performance in monetary terms. This is seen by many as a limited or narrow view of corporate governance because it largely ignores the interests of other stakeholders, such as employees, the natural environment, and the community or society. Designing governance mechanisms to monitor the interests of these other stakeholders is often difficult because the extent to which the interests of these stakeholders are addressed in many cases cannot be measured in monetary terms.

Additionally, the interests of these stakeholders are often seen to be in conflict with the interests of management and the owner/shareholders. Provision of expanded compensation and benefits and improved working environments for employees are often viewed by management and shareholders alike as costs that eat into profits. Likewise, investing in the improvement of a corporation's environmental performance above and beyond minimum levels of legislated compliance may also be viewed by management and shareholders as a drag on profitability. While improvements in employee satisfaction and environmental performance yield benefits in terms of productivity and reputation, it is often difficult to measure and quantify these benefits in monetary terms.

The discussion of stakeholder theory presented in chapter 3 illustrates the growing complexity that exists with respect to issues relating to corporate governance. The simple idea that Milton Friedman so eloquently presented in a 1970 article[16]—that the only moral obligation that a corporation was subject to is the obligation to maximize profits for the owners—has been significantly complicated by the emergence of stakeholder theory. Upon reflection, however, the differences between Friedman's view that a corporation's sole duty is the maximization of profits for its shareholders and the view of the proponents of stakeholder theory that consideration of all stakeholders needs to occur in order to maximize long-term organizational wealth are not insurmountable and are more a matter of scope and time frame. Both points of view purport to maximize benefits. Friedman supports the maximization of profit for shareholders. Taking care of key groups of stakeholders, even at a net monetary cost to the organization, supports the growth of organizational wealth, which would presumably have positive effects with respect to intangibles such as reputation, morale, retention, talent acquisition, and so on, which, over the longer term, can benefit shareholder return. In the case of stakeholder theory, the longer-term investor would be more likely to reap the benefits, whereas in Friedman's vision the benefits would accrue to investors in the more immediate term.

The prevailing direction in corporate governance development is the adoption of the longer-term view with a stakeholder focus. With a greater number of stakeholders interacting in increasingly complex networks, the formulation of governance infrastructures becomes ever more challenging. Add to this the idea that organizational wealth does not necessarily lend itself to measurement in strictly monetary terms and the waters within which governance issues must be addressed become even muddier.

From an international perspective, while North American countries continue to focus on bottom-line economic performance, other jurisdictions have taken conscious steps to integrate stakeholder interests into their governance structures. In Germany, for instance, employee representation on corporate boards is mandated. In the United Kingdom corporate directors are required to take the interests of employees into consideration in their decision-making processes. The European Union permits companies to consider the interests of employees, customers, creditors, and potential future investors.

Some of the precedents for including the interests of a broader cross-section of stakeholders and corporate citizenship in the governance of companies date back several decades. After the Second World War, it was the Japanese corporate sector that was tasked with rebuilding Japan's infrastructure and its economy. Similarly, after the Korean War, it was the South Korean corporate sector that was expected and encouraged by the government to attract capital for economic development through export incentives.

In a Conference Board survey conducted in 2002, CEOs in over 700 companies across North America, Europe, and the Asia-Pacific were asked what they thought their company's role should be in shaping good business and good societies. In North

America, the predominant position taken by CEOs who responded to the survey was that corporations should adopt a leadership position in focusing on benefiting society. In Europe and the Asia-Pacific, respondent CEOs felt that their role was one of partnership with governments in addressing society's needs. This seems at odds with the observation in the preceding paragraphs that North American companies are less likely to have stakeholder interests built into their governance structures, at least until one considers the respondent bias that inevitably exists within a survey of this type; only CEOs with a focus on corporate citizenship are likely to respond to such surveys, while those who place little value or importance on corporate citizenship will probably ignore the survey.

In the same survey, CEOs were asked how effective their firms were in developing and implementing governance mechanisms that would enable them to achieve their desired outcomes in the area of corporate citizenship. While the great majority of respondents expressed that there was room for improvement in this area, the respondent firms in the Asia-Pacific overwhelmingly felt that their governance mechanisms supporting corporate citizenship were either not very effective, not effective at all, or simply did not exist. North American and European firms, however, responded that their governance mechanisms were either very effective or somewhat effective in supporting their corporate citizenship goals.

Proponents of stakeholder theory argue that the recognition and consideration of all stakeholders in the process of corporate decision-making lead to the long-term sustainable creation of corporate wealth. Consideration of all stakeholder groups does not mean that the needs, wants, and desires of each of these groups needs to be met. Nor does it require that each of these stakeholder groups carry equal weight. Clearly some stakeholder groups carry more importance than others. Likewise, some stakeholder groups hold a larger stake in the activities of the firm. In considering a broader group of stakeholders the firm then makes judgments as to which stakeholders it is in the best position to help in ways that will ultimately benefit both the stakeholder and the firm. In an effort to quantify the monitoring of corporate performance as it relates to this broader group of stakeholders, concepts such as the "triple bottom line" have been developed, and relative indices such as the Dow Jones STOXX Sustainability Index have been established. The triple bottom line relates to the measurement and disclosure of corporate performance in social and environmental terms as well as economic. The Dow Jones STOXX Sustainability Index measures corporate competence in a broad range of areas, including corporate strategy, economic performance, customer relations, employee satisfaction, stakeholder engagement, and governance standards.[17]

While the concept of corporate governance was originally designed to compensate for the principal-agent problem that resulted from the separation of ownership and management control, the role of corporate governance is evolving and expanding to include a much broader spectrum of stakeholders and issues. It is hoped that corporate performance, by aligning the goals of management with the interests of other stakeholders in addition to the company's shareholders, provides an increased level of benefit to society as a whole while continuing to provide economic benefit to investors.

Review Questions

1. Significant criticism has been levelled in recent years about the effectiveness of boards of directors in corporate governance. Explain how current practice within corporate boards differs from the theoretical role the board is designed to play in corporate governance and the effect this has on the board's effectiveness.
2. Which do you believe are more effective in responding to the principal-agent problem—internal or external governance controls? Please explain why.
3. In what ways does the inclusion of the interests of stakeholders rather than just those of shareholders complicate corporate governance models?
4. Assume that it is possible for corporations to be good citizens. How can corporate citizenship be measured? How can it be enforced?

Suggested Readings

Eichenwald, K. *Conspiracy of Fools: A True Story*. New York: Broadway Books, 2005.

Hunter, D. *The Bubble and the Bear: How Nortel Burst the Canadian Dream*. Toronto: Doubleday, Canada, 2003.

Jeter, L.W. *Disconnected: Deceit and Betrayal at WorldCom*. Hoboken, NJ: John Wiley and Sons, 2003.

Kim, K.A., and J.R. Nofsinger. *Corporate Governance*. 2nd edn. Upper Saddle River, NJ: Pearson Prentice Hall, 2007.

Toffler, B.L. *Final Accounting: Ambition, Greed and the Fall of Arthur Andersen*. New York: Doubleday, 2003.

Suggested Websites

The Canadian Coalition for Good Governance:

http://www.ccgg.ca/.

Emes, A.S. "Corporate Governance and Directors' Duties 2011." Practical Law Company, Toronto, 2011:

http://www.torys.com/Publications/Documents/Publication%20PDFs/AR2011-21.pdf.

The Sarbanes-Oxley Act 2002; A Guide to the Sarbanes-Oxley Act:

http://www.soxlaw.com/.

9

The Ethics of Accounting: The Case of a Profession in Business

Chapter Outline

- Overview of the Accounting Profession
- Professional Codes of Practice
- Conflicts of Interest
- Harms That Arise from Conflicts of Interest
- Constitutive and Regulative Rules
- Litigation and Auditing
- Review Questions
- Suggested Readings
- Suggested Websites

Professional ethics is sometimes thought to involve no more than observing the norms and regulations of the professions. Nothing could be further from the truth. Good professional practice calls for judgment because the principles of a profession need to be interpreted and applied in ways that are just and compassionate. This is true whether the practitioner is self-employed or works in an organization. While being a salaried professional—a lawyer, architect, engineer, or accountant, for instance—does not exempt one from judgments and ethical responsibilities, it can put a twist on common problems. This is well illustrated in the decisions facing accountants and auditors. Many of these problems relate to the issue of autonomy. The ethics of being a loyal servant of the organization while at the same time exercising professional judgment gives rise to a host of potential ethical conflicts. On the one hand, organizations have a right to expect that directions will be followed. On the other, professional status is often defined in terms of independence. Professionals take on ethical responsibilities additional to those that apply to people generally. Richard De George makes this point: "Any profession . . . is appropriately given respect and autonomy only if it lives up to a higher moral code than is applicable to all."[1]

Overview of the Accounting Profession

The practice of accounting is centuries old, but the profession of accounting grew out of the Industrial Revolution and the use of the limited liability company as the engine of economic growth. The need to give a clear accounting of the performance of companies necessitated the development of management accountants to advise senior management of the options open to them in decision-making, and of financial accountants to prepare accurate reports on the financial health of companies. External auditors were needed to assess the fairness and accuracy of financial statements, and accountants in public practice progressively grew in importance, offering a range of financial services, from personal taxation to superannuation.

Traditionally, accountants have enjoyed good public regard for honesty and trustworthiness. In the wake of Enron—and other corporate disasters during the first decade of the twenty-first century—the reputation of accounting has taken its share of knocks. One 2002 poll showed that after the Enron collapse, accountants achieved a score of zero for image. A Canada Speaks survey released in 2007 by Sympatico/MSN rated them better, with a trustworthiness score of 54, well behind nurses, teachers, and police, but ahead of religious institutions (37), lawyers (25), and chief executive officers (CEOs) (21).[2] Their public esteem has continued to improve,[3] although there seems to be an established order of merit in the ranking of the professions, with nursing consistently at the top and other helping professions occupying the next highest places. According to the 2008 Gallup Poll, which unsurprisingly saw public confidence in bankers take a plunge, accountants held their position. Most Americans do not perceive accountants to be "highly ethical," but the profession is "much more likely to be viewed positively than negatively."[4] One small research project indicated that ethics might not be the only concern for the US accounting profession. It showed that although accountants outranked financial analysts, lawyers, and CEOs in ethics, they were well behind these other professions in terms of power and agency. "Although they are seen as being very trustworthy, competent, and honest, . . . [accountants] do not appear to have as much impact . . . [as] CEOs and attorneys. They are good but not powerful or engaged."[5] Perhaps it is not surprising, then, that according to Harris Polling, American accounting does not enjoy strong perceptions of prestige compared with doctors, teachers, and lawyers. Similar findings have been made in the United Kingdom.[6] According to a large Australian survey conducted in the 1990s, accountants themselves had misgivings about the standards of their colleagues and the ethical standing of their profession. Over 37 per cent of accountants surveyed believed that ethical standards had declined in the preceding decade, and a further 18.5 per cent were uncertain.[7] The family was rated as the strongest source of values (94.2 per cent), then the conduct of peers (88.2 per cent), accounting practices (87.5 per cent), prevailing societal norms (76.9 per cent), then the professional code of ethics (68.1 per cent) and religious formation (61.5 per cent). This relative weighting can mask the still high impact of the profession on members' ethical perceptions. Yet only 49 per cent of members believed that their colleagues had any degree of familiarity with the professional code.[8] Perhaps, in the light of subsequent failures, these accountants were prescient; perhaps their ethical perceptions were better tuned than they realized.

The ethical issues they identified as most important were the following:

1. client proposals for tax evasion (83.3 per cent)
2. client proposals to manipulate financial statements (80.2 per cent)
3. conflicts of interest (79.3 per cent)
4. presenting financial information so as not to deceive users (76.3 per cent)
5. failure to maintain technical competence in professional practice (71.3 per cent)
6. coping with instructions from a superior to behave unethically (70.7 per cent)
7. integrity in admitting one's mistakes (66.7 per cent)
8. using insider information for personal gain (63.8 per cent)
9. maintaining confidentiality (63.6 per cent).

The respondents also ranked favours and gifts and the solicitation of work as significant ethical issues.[9]

Some of these items apply to accountants in public practice, some to salaried accountants, and some to both. The strongest theme running through these results is professional independence and the proper exercise of professional judgment. Of the most important ethical issues identified by respondents, the first, second, third, sixth, and ninth all relate to independence and the pressure applied by clients or employers to achieve a certain result.

A strong sense of independence is characteristic of most professions. Some observers make it a necessary condition of professional status: "[S]o long as the individual is looked upon as an employee rather than a free artisan, to that extent there is no professional status."[10] According to this view, only accountants in public practice would be true professionals. The concern informing this view is that employees are unable to make serious commitments to ethics and the public good on the basis of their own independent assessment because an employer can issue contrary directives that must be obeyed, even if an individual disagrees with them. Even if such directives are not made, the professional judgment of the employee is circumscribed in a way that does not apply to a self-employed practitioner. This view, extreme though it is, stems from a very commonly held belief that professional status derives at least partly from the fact that those practising within a profession must regard the public interest as their first priority.

A contrasting view holds that it is precisely in serving their clients and employers that professionals attain their status. According to this view, "it is essential that professionals should serve" those employing their services rather than "filtering their everyday work through a sieve of ethical sensitivity." Personal judgments are alien to this concept of professionalism: the professional is not an expert on the public good and should not be called upon to make judgments about it. Regulation and law, not personal morality, are the appropriate constraints upon that which a professional may do for a client.[11]

The view that internal accountants are restricted in their professional judgment by the power and authority of the employer is correct in certain cases (though it must be remembered that their role is not that of a watchdog in the manner of an external auditor). But even external accountants in the best accounting firms can have difficulties. Consider the following case based on an actual incident.

CASE 9.1: Bruce's Dilemma

Bruce was 26 years old when he joined a large accounting firm after graduating with a good degree in commerce. He was assigned to a team of auditors at Transition Technologies, which had just been acquired by Paradox Corp. Bruce's firm had been the auditors at Transition before the takeover and had offered to continue at around half the going rate. Shortcuts in auditing resulted. Proper auditing procedures were not adhered to, and Bruce was frequently left to make decisions by himself, although he was not experienced. Bruce was aware that he was in a competitive environment and that he was, in a sense, on trial. He did not agree with the shortcuts and felt that it was unfair to Transition and himself that he was sometimes left to deal with matters beyond his experience. But he also remembered being asked at his job interview if he was a team player who could carry other members of the team when circumstances required it.

Case Question

1. What should Bruce do?

Whatever you decide in the case of Bruce, one aspect should be noted: it is not the fact that he is a salaried professional per se that limits Bruce's professional judgment; it is that his firm is not behaving ethically, that he is a new and junior member of the audit team, and that he should have been under close supervision until he had developed the expertise—including independent judgment—that comes with experience. None of these conditions need exist for a salaried accountant.

According to the second view of professionalism, Bruce is in the clear until he breaks a law. This view, however, is far too restrictive of the role that professionals play in organizations as diverse as schools and hospitals. The notion that true professionals should serve their employers as far as the law extends confuses servility with service. The old maxim that it is stupid to buy a dog and bark yourself applies here: when a salaried professional is hired, that person is expected to exercise independent judgment within the limits of her or his expertise. Working to direction is part of working in an organization, and having to do so in some areas does not imply a lack of independence in all of them.

In any case, independence, for all its importance, must take its place beside other values in professional settings. According to the British Statement on the Ethical Responsibilities of Members in Business, "the concept of independence . . . has no direct relevance to the employed member. . . . Even for the practicing accountant independence is not an end in itself: it is essentially a means of securing a more important end, namely an objective approach to work."[12] This objective is also secured by other key professional values: honesty, trust and good faith, fidelity and loyalty, justice and fairness, care and compassion, responsibility and accountability, and the pursuit of professional excellence all contribute to the ethics of a professional. So, too, does regard for the public good, but this value usually differs significantly from the global suggestion that a professional accountant, lawyer, or teacher should act in the public interest as the first principle of practice. Regard for the public good means something more important: taking a principled position on issues of public importance that come within the area of one's professional expertise.

Independence is important to accountants in two ways. The first might be peculiar to their technical expertise, and the second is generic to professions in general. First, independence is especially important to accountants who are providing external certification of a company's financial position. It goes to the heart of the profession's role that the declarations that an accountant makes in, say, a financial report are not prejudiced by the power and influence of those who stand to gain by a particular result. It is equally important that the accountant have no interest at all in the company and should not stand to gain or lose by any outcome of financial scrutiny. This aspect of independence is at the very basis of the profession of accounting, for upon it rests the trust of the public in the most inclusive sense. Threats to this independence typically come in the following forms:

- undue dependence on an audit client
- loans to or from a client, guarantees, or overdue fees
- hospitality or other benefits
- actual or threatened litigation
- mutual business interests
- beneficial interests in shares or other investments
- trusteeships
- voting on audit appointments
- provision of other services—such as valuations—to audit clients
- acting for a client over a prolonged period of time.[13]

The central importance of independence to accountants is clear from even a cursory look at the profession's code of ethics, but independence clearly serves a professional purpose and harmonizes with the other values enshrined in the code. This brings us to the second sense of independence. Many of the classic injunctions of professional practice have a strong personal direction. "Do no harm" is a principle directed not so much at a profession (though it might be) as to its practitioners. The same applies to other precepts and principles about competence, confidentiality, trustworthiness, and honesty. In turn, each of these principles assumes a high degree of professional autonomy and occupational discretion on the part of individual practitioners. These are often the very qualities that organizations try to restrict. Organizations are not peculiar in this; individuals, too, often compromise their ethics when it suits them. Professional people who act with integrity retain sufficient independence to allow them to act ethically, but accountants must do this in a very special way in order to do their job at all. One of the issues raised by the collapse of Enron and other US corporations was whether the auditor was too enmeshed in their affairs. Consider the case of Arthur Andersen and Enron.

CASE 9.2: The Fall of Arthur Andersen

In June 2002, after 10 days of deliberating and a difficult time sifting through the evidence, a federal jury in Houston convicted the accounting firm Arthur Andersen of obstruction of justice in the Enron case. Arthur Andersen then announced that it would cease auditing publicly listed companies from the end of August. Thus fell one of the giants of modern accounting. With revenues in 2001 of over $9 billion and 85,000 employees in 84 countries, the fall of Arthur Andersen caused shock waves around the world. Founded in 1913 by Arthur Andersen, the firm had become a byword for integrity until its pursuit of profits led to its entanglement in the adventurism of the "new economy." Enron was not the only dubious client for whom Arthur Andersen provided services. Others included WorldCom, Sunbeam, and Waste Management. The fallout from such clients cost Arthur Andersen its reputation and money. The Securities and Exchange Commission (SEC) fined the firm $7 million for overstating the earnings of Waste Management Corporation by $1.4 billion. Shareholders sued Arthur Andersen when Sunbeam admitted inflating its earnings, and Arthur Andersen settled out of court for US$110 million.[14]

What could have led a firm founded on integrity to abandon its basic values? Barbara Toffler describes Arthur Andersen as rotting from within, a victim of its own demand for conformity from employees.[15] According to Toffler, it lost its independence when it placed its lucrative consulting services before its auditing role and became less inclined to risk the anger of clients. That might account for its failure to caution Enron and clients like WorldCom about their revenue statements. The fundamental value of accounting—independence—had been compromised. Arthur Andersen was Enron's auditor for 16 years. In 2002 alone, Enron paid Arthur Andersen US$25 million in audit fees and $27 million for consulting services.

Enron's accounts were notoriously difficult to understand and for a very good reason. Its chief financial officer (CFO), Andrew Fastow, had created a number of "off the books" partnerships—that is, related but separate entities in which Enron could place debt or assets that it did not wish to appear on its balance sheets. Such partnerships are not of themselves improper, but the uses to which Enron and its executives put them were. Fastow, for example, made millions of dollars in secret transactions at the expense of Enron.[16] And, investments in the partnerships were reported by Enron as revenue.

Generally Accepted Accounting Principles (GAAP) *The common set of accounting principles, standards, and procedures that companies use to compile their financial statements. GAAP are a combination of authoritative standards (set by policy boards) and represent the commonly accepted ways of recording and reporting accounting information.*

There was an issue here for Arthur Andersen because the **Generally Accepted Accounting Principles** (GAAP) required partnerships with more than a 3 per cent investment from Enron to appear with the consolidated accounts. Enron's investments in its partnerships exceeded this minimum. Arthur Andersen should have presented balance sheets that accounted for the partnerships, but according to its CEO, Joe Berardino, it did so only in 2001. Arthur Andersen's alleged departure from GAAP standards has been investigated by the Securities and Exchange Commission.[17] Beyond the requirements of the law, there was the propriety of using related entities as Enron did. The wisdom on this is well established. Clarke and Dean note that similar arrangements have served improper purposes in the Australian context, where

> the corporate group emerges as a corporate oddity. Parent companies and the entities they control are selectively considered to comprise a single entity, more or less according to how the circumstances suit. Selectively, because changed circumstances usually dictate whether management regards it financially beneficial to present the companies comprising a group as separate companies, or lumps some or all of them together and treats them as a composite unit.[18]

Clarke and Dean identify typical signs of stressed corporations in Australia, and perhaps not surprisingly, they are similar to those at Enron and WorldCom in the United States and to Polly Peck and Canary Wharf in the United Kingdom. Complex corporate structures with many related-party transactions, overvalued assets, understated liabilities and bad debts, reckless borrowing, and the use of accounting "fictions," such as Future Income Tax Benefits, can camouflage the precarious position of corporations at risk.[19]

Arthur Andersen's problems compounded when it was disclosed that a Houston partner, David Duncan, had ordered the deletion of emails and the shredding of Enron documents relating to Enron after the SEC had commenced its investigation. Andersen informed the authorities of Duncan's actions, but the firm was indicted and found guilty of obstruction of justice.

A clutch of Enron executives were indicted. In January 2004, Andrew Fastow, CFO at Enron, pleaded guilty to charges of fraud in a bargain that saved him years in jail in exchange for assisting in the investigation of other Enron executives. In 2006, Fastow was sentenced to six years in prison. The indictment of Enron accounting and financial services executive Richard Causey quickly followed that of Fastow. The SEC alleged that Causey, Fastow, and others manipulated "expenses, revenue, debt levels, cash flow and asset values . . . through means including fraudulent valuations, misuse of off-the-books partnerships . . . and intentional mistreatment of accounting reserves."[20] Causey also pleaded guilty and was sentenced to five and a half years in jail and fined.[21] It has emerged that Enron exploited California's deregulated energy market to hike prices and "extort" US$30 billion from that state.[22]

Enron's operations were riddled with deception and sharp practice. There are questions of law about this and questions of ethics. While the law takes its course, the ethical questions hang in the air.

1. What should have been the role of the auditor with clients like this? Arthur Andersen seemed content to take the view that the data it was given could be interpreted according to prevailing accounting standards.
2. Should Arthur Andersen have noted that the thicket of Enron accounts was a classic indicator of corporate risk? (The chair of Enron's audit committee was a professor of accounting at Stanford, and he claimed he didn't understand the corporation's audits.) Enron could not have got into a mess without its auditors having some idea of what was going on.
3. Did Arthur Andersen's duty of confidentiality to the client override its obligation to the SEC and various stakeholders from investors to taxpayers?
4. Did not Arthur Andersen have a duty to investors to prepare reports that more accurately reflected Enron's level of risk?
5. Should Arthur Andersen have warned that it would not continue to act as Enron's auditor unless the conglomerate changed its conduct?
6. Did Arthur Andersen compromise professional independence by becoming too dependent on contracts with Enron?
7. Should it have been an internal auditor, external auditor, and provider of management consulting services to Enron simultaneously?
8. How could shredding Enron documents be called a normal part of document retention policy when Arthur Andersen knew that its client was under investigation by the SEC?

There is a bigger question to be answered as well:

9. Would a closer adherence to accounting standards have prevented the Enron debacle? Would more rigorous standards and policing of them have prevented the rash of corporate collapses that occurred at the same time?

One answer to this has already been delivered by American legislators. Another quite different answer is given by Clarke and Dean.

The huge losses of Enron, WorldCom, and other corporations proved too much for Congress and the American public. The response was the typical one of tightening regulations, although the SEC's powers were already considerable. Nonetheless, Congress passed the Sarbanes-Oxley Corporate Reform Act of 2002. That Act and the SEC regulations under it seek to strengthen the independence of external auditors. Auditors may no longer be appointed by senior management but only by the audit committee of the board, and auditors must report to that committee, not to management. All members of the audit committee must be independent directors. The reforms prescribe the structure of boards and specify the duties of directors and some employees. The same firm cannot offer auditing and consulting services. Transparency is enhanced and off-balance-sheet transactions must be disclosed. Audit records must be retained. Companies must disclose whether they have a code of ethics for their CEOs, CFOs, and senior accountants.[23] This is the kind of reaction to large-scale ethical failure that enshrines ethical basics in law and, as we noted in chapter 4, that will not be sufficient to do the job. The profession itself has been sensitive to issues of independence and professional integrity. The International Federation of Accountants (IFAC) has proposed amendments to its code because of the risk that auditors might be captured by their clients. The amendments for auditors require the leading partner on the contract to be rotated at least every seven years, and they prohibit that partner from participating in assurance for a further period, normally two years.[24]

The Sarbanes-Oxley Act has been much criticized in the United States, but there are similar criticisms of ever more regulations and their effect on professional judgment. The argument of Clarke and Dean has been that "shackling" auditors' independence to accounting standards will do no more good in the future than it has in the past.[25] In other words, it might not matter where the shackles are anchored—whether to corporations and their fees or to regulations and standards—if the independence of auditors to draw upon their experience and practice wisdom is curbed. Moreover, Clarke and Dean argue that standardization of input has obscured the importance of the usefulness of output in financial statements. If the notion of "true and fair" is equivalent to "meeting the defined standards" then, despite the best of intentions, the published financial statements of a firm might not meet the criterion of serviceability. They conclude: "Unquestionably, compulsory compliance by accountants and auditors with prescribed Accounting and Auditing Standards provides them with a safe harbour."[26]

Accounting practices referred to as "aggressive" at Enron challenged the spirit of the law and of professional probity. Individuals intended to evade ethical obligations by concocting schemes that boosted the price of Enron stock and hid debt and poor performance. Years before the courts decided upon the culpability of those who devised Enron's schemes, the legal verdict on Arthur Andersen in Houston in 2002 was enough to bring down the whole enterprise. This was a case, if ever there was one, where the higher standard of ethics was also the prudential one.

Professional Codes of Practice

In Canada, there are three distinct professional accounting bodies, each with its own professional designation: the "certified management accountant" (CMA), the "certified general accountant" (CGA), and the "chartered accountant" (CA). CAs are currently the only professional body with the authority to issue audit opinions on corporate financial statements. At the time of writing, an initiative was being undertaken to consolidate the three bodies under the designation of "chartered professional accountant" (CPA). This consolidation, should it come to fruition, would take several years to implement and operationalize.

Each of the three professional accounting bodies in Canada has its own code of ethics. It should not be assumed that any of these codes provides a comprehensive and exhaustive list of what is and is not permissible, although they are all specific about some points. The codes, in fact, leave room for judgment in a number of areas. However, leaving room for judgment does not amount to countenancing or allowing just anything. Judgment can indeed be shown to be bad or outside the limits of what is allowable under the values identified in the codes.

While each of the three codes of conduct subscribed to by the respective Canadian professional accounting bodies is distinct, there are some values that are appropriate to them all:

- the public interest
- integrity
- objectivity
- independence
- confidentiality
- technical and professional standards
- competence and due care
- professional behaviour.

It is appropriate to consider technical and professional standards and competence and due care together, even though they are speaking about different concerns: "technical and professional standards" concerns a requirement to maintain an up-to-date knowledge base, whereas "competence and due care" concerns the standard at which one is required to exercise that knowledge base. It would be impossible to perform competently and with due care if one did not possess the requisite skills and knowledge, but possession of those skills and knowledge on its own is a different matter from applying them competently and with due care.

"Professional behaviour" is considered synonymous with "ethical behaviour." After all, it is a code of ethics, and as such, it would seem somewhat odd to have as a principle "ethics," given that the principles themselves are identifying the areas of particular ethical concern. It is in the area of professional behaviour that there is concern about not merely behaving in a professional manner, but also avoiding behaving in ways that bring the profession into disrepute.

With respect to the concept of "independence," it is critical not only that independence not be compromised but that the appearance of independence be respected and maintained.

The central professional values expressed in the codes of Canadian accountants are similar to those that apply internationally[27] and mirror the generic values of professional ethics discussed above. Basically, these codes address the relations of practitioners to various stakeholders and the standards of professional and personal integrity expected of accountants. There is a high degree of linkage and overlap between the principles that can be summed up under six headings:

1. *The public interest.* Accountants are expected to act in the best interests of clients except when those interests conflict with obligations to *society*, the law, and social and political institutions.
2. *Integrity.* Accountants should be honest and sincere in their work. They should do nothing to bring their profession into disrepute.
3. *Objectivity.* Accountants must act fairly and be free from conflicts of interest.
4. *Independence.* Accountants should not do anything, either real or apparent, that could suggest that their independence might be compromised.
5. *Diligence.* Accountants should exercise diligence and due care in the performance of their duties. They should exhibit competence and ensure that they are competent to perform the work assigned by clients, and they should maintain their competence through appropriate measures. They should adhere to accounting and auditing standards and to standards issued by their professional association.
6. *Confidentiality.* Accountants must maintain confidentiality, which means not only that they may not disclose information provided by clients to unauthorized third parties, but also that they should not use information gained in the course of their duties for personal or third-party gain.

As we have noted, there is much in these principles that applies generally to the professions. In this respect, accountancy represents an example as much as it represents a special instance, but the responsibilities of accountants in the business world, and hence in society at large, mean that ethical failure can have huge ramifications.

Recognizing conflicts of interest is very important. It is also important that the professional not even appear to be in a position in which there could be a conflict of interest. This is important in all professions, but it is especially important in accountancy, which frequently identifies independence as the cornerstone of the profession. Consider, for instance, what the purpose of an audit is and what it is that an auditor attests to. The requirement of independence is closely related to what the profession has come to recognize as a central ethical issue in accountancy: whistleblowing (see chapter 7).

Professions almost always recognize both a duty to the public interest and a duty to the maintenance of the profession itself. These duties are often expressed in terms of, on the one hand, making the public interest a first priority and, on the other, doing nothing that brings the profession into disrepute. These are very important duties, but they can sit uneasily next to each other. For example, it might be in the public interest to criticize some aspect of the profession. Such situations—and they are not uncommon—can easily bring these two duties into conflict with each other.

As with other professions, issues accompanying the position of the professional as salaried employee are prevalent and often difficult to resolve. Professionals carry the ethical responsibilities of the profession with them into their positions as paid employees—positions that have their own ethical requirements. Put simply, you owe something to your employer (call it "loyalty" to a greater or lesser degree) and you also owe something to your profession as a professional. You carry this obligation with you into your employment.

Conflicts of Interest

Much of the domain of independence concerns avoidance or management of conflicts of interest. Conflicts of interest are among the most pervasive concerns in organizational ethics. They are the cause of controversy in corporate governance, and they merit protection in recruitment, in tendering, in business-to-business relations, and in a host of other operational areas. Most businesses and professions have mechanisms for dealing with conflicts of interest and potential conflicts of interest. The mechanisms are usually good. But there are often misfires. These occur most frequently at the individual level, not the organizational level. Many—probably most—difficulties encountered with respect to conflicts of interest arise through a reasonably simple misunderstanding about what a conflict of interest is.

Conflict of interest ≠ being adversely affected by a conflict.

A person's *having* a conflict of interest is not the same thing as a person's *being affected by* a conflict of interest.

Most commonly, difficulties over conflicts of interest arise because a person (or an organization as a whole) confuses "having a conflict of interest" with "being affected by a conflict of interest." If the person (honestly) believes that their judgment or behaviour is not affected by conflicting interests, then they believe that therefore they do not have a conflict of interest. This is not correct! Having a conflict of interest is being in a situation where there are conflicting interests that impinge on the person concerned, regardless of whether or not that conflict has any effect at all on that person. It is the interests that are in conflict. And whenever you are in a situation in which you have to act or form a judgment or deliver an opinion in the presence of interests that conflict with each other, then you have a conflict of interest.

Let's go a bit further with this. We often deal with matters in which *competing* interests exist, interests that conflict with each other. That alone is not enough to produce a conflict of interest. For instance, in the context of a business wanting to function more efficiently, you might be asked to give advice about whether or not to reduce the size of staff. In such a situation, the overall interest of the business and the interest of the staff of the business (particularly those whose jobs are at risk) conflict with each other. But *you* do not have a conflict of interest in your role in offering advice. The situation would be different, however, if, say, one of the employees in that business—one whose job is at risk—is your spouse. Here the interest of the business (efficiency only) and the interest of your spouse (and hence you) are in conflict, and you have a conflict of interest.

You have a conflict of interest if you have competing (conflicting) professional, personal, and/or business interests. If you are forming a judgment, offering an opinion, or engaging in any action in the context of these competing interests, then you are acting in the context of a conflict of interest. It is *your* interests (professional, personal, and/or business) that are in conflict. And you have this conflict of interest whether or not you are affected by the conflicting interests involved. We will explain this further below.

conflict of interest *the presence in a person of competing (conflicting) professional, personal, and/or business interest*

Sometimes, **conflict of interest** is characterized in terms of interests that pose a threat to impartiality. Although it can be helpful to think of "conflict of interest" in this way, it is not entirely accurate, for two reasons:

1. It puts emphasis on the effect or possible effect of the conflict, rather than on the conflict itself. While this is clearly a central part of the rationale for paying attention to conflicts of interest, potential conflicts of interest, and apparent conflicts of interest, it need not be the defining feature of the conflicts themselves.
2. There are many occasions in which your role is not that of being impartial: you might be asked precisely for an opinion supporting a particular course of action. You are asked to muster the best arguments you can in support of that particular view. The (unobjectionable) goal here is quite expressly partial, but it does not involve a conflict of interest simply by virtue of that fact.

Personal and business matters are not the only interests that can come into conflict, though it must be said that this is by far the most common form. Even when the precepts of a code of ethics are clear, the exercise of good judgment is indispensable in managing such conflicts. The key word here is "managing." Not all cases of interest-holding or even conflict of interest need be fatal to the involvement of the interested party in a decision. Everything resides in the way that the interest and the involvement of the interested party are managed. "Transparency" is important in this regard. Transparency is the enemy of improper conduct and nowhere more so than in conflicts of interest.

Above all, it must be realized that the real damage done to an organization by the confusion of interests lies in the bad example given to others. Staff must not treat professional entitlements as personal ones or corporate assets as their own. Managers who do this effectively license those below them to take similar liberties. This is an area where hypocrisy goes well beyond being a personal fault and is an organizational danger.

A person with a conflict of interest must be in a position to affect a decision within an organization either directly as the decision-maker or indirectly through the exercise of influence or power on others.

When in doubt about whether you have an interest in a matter affecting a client, *declare* it. The declaration of an interest does not mean that you believe your judgment is compromised or that you could not be fair or impartial. And it need not always involve removing yourself from that matter. What it does mean is that since all dealings with clients and groups will be transparent, if you remain involved in the matter, the presence of the conflicting interests will be known by the appropriate parties.

Very often the focus of conflict of interest analysis is on the individual rather than on the interest. Yet the question is not primarily one of objective judgment or an individual's capacity to distance him- or herself from personal interests in making professional decisions. These are important questions, but the first question is about whether the *interests* involved in a decision are in conflict. Does your role, say, as an accountant conflict with your role as a private citizen or with your personal goals? Does your role as an accountant conflict with your role as a business person or as an employee?

One should manage conflicts of interest by being as transparent as confidentiality and prudence allow, by reporting interests to superiors and seeking their advice, and by documenting decisions fully. Because conflicts of interest are the source of so much trouble, concern, and misunderstanding in business and the professions, we want to expand on the discussion and explore in some detail why we have characterized "conflict of interest" in the way we have.

In discussing the problems of living without a government in a state of nature, the seventeenth-century philosopher John Locke famously declared,

> In the state of nature there wants a known and indifferent judge, with authority to determine all differences according to the established law: . . . men being partial to themselves, passion and revenge is very apt to carry them too far . . . in their own cases . . . (and) to make them too remiss in other men's. (*Second Treatise*, §125)

The legal remedy for people being judges in their own cases is impartial judicial officers, but the law is only one domain in which judgment is called for. Business and the professions constantly demand the exercise of judgment and dedication to fiduciary duties. Self-interest or partiality to the interests of others—loved ones, comrades in sport or business, members of one's community—can prejudice fiduciary duty and bias one's judgment. That is why impartiality of judgment is so central to the management of conflicts of interest. This concern is expressed in what we call the standard account of conflict of interest. The following paragraph is a good statement of the standard account.

A conflict of interest is a situation in which some person P (whether an individual or corporate body) stands in a certain relation to one or more decisions. On the standard view, P has a conflict of interest if, and only if, (1) P is in a relationship with another, requiring P to exercise judgment in the other's behalf; and (2) P has a special interest tending to interfere with the proper exercise of judgment in that relationship. The crucial terms in the standard view are "relationship," "judgment," "interest," and "proper exercise."[28]

Any number of definitions will agree in one way or another with the standard account. At its heart is a major issue: if a large part of ethics is about the exercise of sound judgment, then anything that endangers that judgment, such as self-interest or competing interests, must be identified. Good judgment bespeaks independence and fairness, an absence of bias and emotion, and skill and competence in decision-making. It is obvious how good judgment can be compromised by conflicts of interest.

Still, bias is not the only issue, and perhaps it is not even the main issue in coming to terms with such conflicts. One can imagine a dispassionate person protesting that her judgment would never be compromised by private interests, family connections, or other affiliations. We can imagine indignant responses from prominent people when conflicts of interest are alleged, such as "Are you impugning my integrity?" Such responses have a point. If impartial judgment is all that is at stake, it's not so difficult just to ask, "How would an impartial judge see this situation?" If a reasonable answer to this question lines up with the judgment of the person with a conflict of interest, then it is clear that she has remained impartial.

Unfortunately, conflicts of interest are not as simple as this. In the first place, judgments do and perhaps should vary—that is, people can arrive at different justifiable conclusions about the same issue and all of them be right. The fact that there are wrong decisions does not mean that there is only one right decision. Different judgments can be defensible. The existence of a "God's-eye view" of every issue is a myth. Some issues are clear and often do not require judgment or discretion. Other issues are not resolvable without judgment, and that means that there is unlikely to be just one right view to be taken. In other words, testing for impartiality—testing for whether or not one's judgment is impaired—is not at all simple even where it is possible.

Second, and more importantly, meeting charges of conflict of interest with this response—"My judgment hasn't been compromised: how dare you impugn my integrity!"—misses the point about conflict of interest. Yes, judgment *is* an issue, but it is not *the* issue. Even if it were possible, demonstrating impartiality of judgment would not make the issue of conflict of interest disappear. Impartial judgment is not necessarily evidence for the absence of a conflict of interest because *having a conflict of interest is not the same as being affected by a conflict of interest.* We call this emphasis on the interests in conflict rather than on the person in conflict "the revised account" to contrast it with the standard version of conflict of interest.

Thus, claims that one is unaffected by a conflict of interest do not change an objective state of affairs in which interests are at odds. Managing the conflict might require the restoration of objective judgment, the removal of the conflict, or the removal of oneself from the position of being the one to make the judgment or take some other course of action. What will not suffice is a simple declaration that one's judgment is unaffected—that because the integrity of the person holding the interests has remained (or will remain) intact, therefore there is no conflict of interest.

Of course, a conflict only arises because an individual has two sets of interests to serve, but that doesn't make the problem (only) a psychological one. If that were the case, then, as we argued above, all one would have to do to avoid a conflict of interest is show sound and unbiased judgment and a lack of cognitive dissonance. And one would be perfectly entitled to demand from those accusing one of having a conflict that they show biased or unsound judgment. Showing a biased judgment in business decisions can be as difficult as showing that judgment is sound.

As it happens, regulators and courts do not depend on the standard account of conflict of interest. They look at the interests in question, and if an individual has not declared private interests that conflict with professional or public duties, then there can be a case to answer.

A second reason to prefer the revised over the standard account is that it simplifies the relation of conflict of interest to "potential conflicts of interest" and "perceived conflicts of interest." According to the revised account, either interests conflict or they do not.

That interests might appear to conflict presents us with a problem akin to having to clarify any perception. If I say that there appears to be a camel on the road, we can take a closer look and discover that it is in fact a rock. It is not an "apparent camel." So, too, with interests: an apparent conflict is either a conflict or it is not, and if it is a conflict, then identifying it as such is the beginning of managing it, not some kind of final judgment about an improper state of affairs. If there is potential for a conflict, then this is something for the person in the situation to consider: some types of conflict just have to be avoided, and in many instances avoidance is preferable to management of the conflict.

Conflicts of interest turn out to be like bacteria: they are everywhere. Some are benign or relatively harmless or can be controlled. Others are toxic and need to be treated before they fester. There is a perception, however, that all conflicts of interest (like all germs in some home-cleanser advertisements) are signs of ethical failure and that they need to be eliminated from business, the professions, and political life. This misconception is dangerous: if people with a conflict of interest believe that, just because of that fact, they have somehow been enmeshed in wrongdoing, they might very well be tempted to conceal their interests instead of declaring them. Media dramatization of conflicts of interest as ethical failures can discourage disclosures of small matters whose importance is then magnified by cover-up.

Conflicts of interest do not necessarily arise from failures of ethics or good judgment. That they require management and good judgment is indisputable, but the big problem with conflicts of interest is denial. That is what gets individuals and corporations into hot water and leads to neglect of the problem. When conflicts of interest are acknowledged as an issue, they can be managed appropriately. A member of a Canada Scouts council who happens to work in the timber industry could use his scouting connections to the advantage of his corporation.[29] Or an executive in a food conglomerate who serves on her children's Parent-Teacher Association (PTA) committee could be in a position to favour her corporation when decisions are taken about what products will be available in the school canteen. It seems unlikely in either of these examples that the business interests of the executives would constitute a large conflict of interest with their private commitments: these would be minor conflicts. Small though these conflicts are likely to be, the important thing is to declare them, not because the Scouts councillor or the food executive is likely to have their judgment impaired, but because transparency is the first step to managing conflicts—large and small—and preventing damage to either interest. Transparency is to conflicts of interest what antibodies are to bacteria.

Harms That Arise from Conflicts of Interest

Conflicts of interest can harm trust in a variety of ways. First, they can damage the notion of fiduciary duty in a professional relationship. Such a relationship requires the professional person, in acting for the client, to put the client's interest first. Analogous duties apply to directors of corporations in relation to shareholders. Second, trust in a particular profession or business can be damaged by conflicts of interest among its practitioners. Third, conflicts of interest can engender wider distrust in a society. When conflicts are found in both high and low places, self-interest seems to be the only motivator that can be relied on. Other values in business and the professions, such as loyalty, impartiality, and care, seem at best rhetorical camouflage that allows self-interest to work more effectively.

Examples of such harms abound in business (see the Merrill Lynch cases below), but they are also quite widespread in the professions. A relatively new area is academic medicine, where researchers with an entrepreneurial spirit are favoured and academic salaries can be very handsomely supplemented.

CASE 9.3: Conflicts of Interest in Academic Medicine

In 2008, a congressional inquiry led by Senator Charles Grassley uncovered widespread evidence of mismanagement of conflicts of interest in American academic medicine. Senator Grassley took conflict of interest statements from medical researchers in some of the leading universities in the United States and compared them with statements of payments from drug companies. He found widespread discrepancies. The first was Dr Melissa DelBello's statement to her employer, the University of Cincinnati, that she had been paid about $100,000 over the period 2005–7 by eight pharmaceutical makers. Grassley discovered that, during that period, just one manufacturer, AstraZeneca, had paid her $238,000. Drs Joseph Biederman and Timothy Wilens of Harvard Medical School reported earning hundreds of thousands of dollars each from drug companies in the period 2000–7. The true figure was around $1.6 million. The issue here is not mainly about money, but about what it buys from scientists and clinicians who are supposed to offer objective, trustworthy, unbiased opinions about pharmaceuticals and medical devices. Universities and medical grants bodies are supposed to ensure that conflicts of interest are declared and that transparent procedures govern the work of those they employ. What Grassley found was that self-regulation was not working: universities and the procedures they employed were failing to manage (and, in many cases, even identify) conflicts of interest adequately.[30] Clinical research is now so extensively entangled with the pharmaceutical industry that self-regulation seems out of the question. One study indicated that "about two-thirds of academic medical centers had financial stakes in companies that sponsored research within their facilities. In another study, two-thirds of medical school department chairs were found to receive departmental income, and three-fifths received personal income, from drug companies."[31]

Perhaps the most publicized of the many cases uncovered by the Grassley inquiry was that of Dr Charles Nemeroff, a research psychiatrist at Emory University in Atlanta, Georgia. Because his research was federally funded, Dr Nemeroff was subject to external as well as university rules and appears to have violated both in failing to report earnings from drug companies of at least $1.2 million.

As it turns out, Dr Nemeroff had a history of not declaring interests. Over a period of four years while he was principal investigator on a National Institute of Mental Health grant, he assured Emory that he did not receive income from GlaxoSmithKline of more than $10,000: "[M]y consulting fees from GSK will be less than $10,000 per year throughout the period of this N.I.H. grant," he declared, having already earned $98,000 that year. Fees at this level breached rules about conflict of interest, because GlaxoSmithKline, as provider of drugs for the project, was an interested party.[32] Yet, in each of the years that Nemeroff worked on this grant, his fees from the drug company exceeded the allowable amount. In 2004 alone, he received $170,000. From 2000 to 2006, a period that covers the work done on the NIH grant, Nemeroff earned more than $960,000 from GlaxoSmithKline, but declared only $35,000. Even when Emory investigated Nemeroff and found other anomalies—for example, failure to declare conflicts of interest in drug trials involving Merck, Eli Lilly, and Johnson & Johnson—it seemed unable to bring him into line.[33] One who tried was Associate Dean Claudia Adkinson. She demanded assurances from Nemeroff about consulting fees and took issue with him about a favourable review, published in a journal he edited, of a device made by a firm with whom he had undisclosed financial ties. Adkinson reproached Nemeroff for not disclosing a range of interests, including payments to Nemeroff and his co-authors by the device manufacturer and a grant to Nemeroff's department. Said Adkinson, "I can't believe that anyone in the public or in academia would believe anything except that this paper was a piece of paid marketing."[34]

Nemeroff's failing is not simply a matter of a person's judgment being impaired by the presence of a conflict of interest. It seems to be, in addition, a matter of outright dishonesty. It appears to be a matter not of a person trying to do the right thing or of having their judgment compromised, or inappropriately influenced, by an outside interest. It appears, rather, to be a matter of a person simply trying to get away with something.

But why would so many medical researchers feel unconstrained by conflict of interest and considerations of honesty? If Nemeroff is any guide, professional arrogance and a view that the end justifies the means might account for indifference to professional and regulatory disclosure rules. Nemeroff felt his service to the advisory boards of drug companies was of benefit to his institution and not merely to his advantage. He wrote to the dean of medicine at Emory:

> Surely you remember that Smith-Kline Beecham Pharmaceuticals donated an endowed chair to the department and that there is a reasonable likelihood that Janssen Pharmaceuticals will do so as well. In addition, Wyeth-Ayerst Pharmaceuticals has funded a Research Career Development Award program in the department and I have asked [other firms] to do the same. Part of the rationale for their funding our faculty in such a manner would be my service on these boards.[35]

If one's activities tend towards public benefit, then how is it a conflict of interest if there are private benefits also?

CASE 9.4: Merrill Lynch

In January 2009, financial services giant Merrill Lynch (acquired by Bank of America in 2009) agreed to pay a $1-million fine to settle Securities and Exchange Commission charges.[36] The SEC alleged that Merrill Lynch investment advisers failed to disclose conflicts of interest when advising clients to invest through its brokerage services. According to the SEC, "Merrill Lynch and its investment adviser representatives could and often did receive significantly higher revenue if clients chose to use Merrill Lynch directed brokerage services."[37]

continued . . .

The advice being offered to clients was not, then, impartial. Merrill Lynch did not admit to or deny the SEC's allegations, but agreed to be censured and undertook not to breach securities laws in future.

A Merrill Lynch spokesman said that the activities of one team of investment advisers based in Florida had caught the attention of the SEC, but that these advisers had now left the firm. Merrill Lynch had initiated changes, improved oversight of consulting services, and compensated clients whose interests had been affected. The spokesman noted, "The assets of our consulting services clients in Florida grew substantially during the years we provided services to them."[38]

Now compare this case with another. In May 2002, Merrill Lynch paid $100 million to short-circuit an investigation initiated by New York attorney-general Eliot Spitzer (later famous as the short-term governor of New York who resigned over a prostitution scandal in 2008). Spitzer was investigating claims that Merrill's stock analysts had promoted the stocks of certain companies in order to secure investment banking business for the firm. Allegedly, this was encouraged by links between the analysts and investment bankers at Merrill Lynch, including the evaluation of analysts' performance and the determination of their salaries by investment bankers.

Spitzer's evidence consisted of emails from former Merrill high-flier Henry Blodget that disclosed that he and other Merrill analysts privately derided stocks that they were, in fact, promoting to clients. According to Spitzer, this showed that the analysts made their recommendations not to advance the interests of clients, but in order to boost Merrill's relationships with companies whose stocks were recommended.[39]

The media gave the story wide coverage. Merrill's chairman and CEO, David H. Komansky, admitted to being embarrassed, and the firm apologized: "We sincerely regret that there were instances in which certain of our internet sector analysts expressed views that at certain points may have appeared inconsistent with Merrill Lynch's published recommendations."[40] That apology was repeated to shareholders and in the settlement with Spitzer, but these apologies stopped short of admitting that Merrill had done anything wrong. Nor was such an admission forthcoming when, as part of the settlement, the firm agreed to change the way it operated. Merrill restructured its research department to separate its analysis from the banking side of the business; it agreed to stop analysts from suggesting that the firm's corporate clients would enjoy good stock ratings or that the ratings of non-clients might fare less well; and it stopped using input from investment bankers in determining the salaries of analysts.[41] Moreover, Merrill undertook to strengthen objectivity in changes to stock ratings by instituting a Research Recommendation Committee, and it began to monitor communications between analysts and banking staff. In future, analysts would "be compensated for only those activities and services intended to benefit Merrill Lynch's investor clients" rather than businesses related to the broker.[42]

So, why would a firm that shied away from admitting any wrongdoing submit to such a large penalty and restructure its operations to avoid conflicts of interest? Merrill Lynch claimed that the investigation was harming its reputation—the value of Merrill's stock had dropped sharply after the accusations—but Spitzer saw Merrill's payment of the penalty differently: "Clearly, the world is shifting. . . . You don't pay a $100 million fine if you didn't do anything wrong."[43] He hoped that Merrill's structural changes "would serve as a model" for other Wall Street brokers, a claim reiterated by Komansky as he set about rebuilding investor trust in his firm. Shortly after the settlement was announced, Goldman Sachs followed suit by reviewing its research policies, analyst compensation, and the independence of its research.[44]

Some Wall Street observers were skeptical about such reforms, believing that in serving two masters—their clients, who sought objective investment advice, and their firms, whose profitability relies substantially on investment banking fees—analysts have a fundamental conflict.

Conflicts of interest cannot always be avoided. Where they are present, it is important to declare the interest and to refrain from voting on matters pertaining to it. Other measures to build a barrier between interests can be employed. Partners in a large accounting firm might feel better able to serve their clients and their firm by placing their assets in a blind trust, a strategy employed by politicians who need to be free to vote on bills without inadvertently favouring their personal interests.

The issue of gifts figures in a number of discussions in this text (see particularly chapter 4), but it is usually in the context of commercial relations. Consider this case, which is slightly different.

CASE 9.5: A Gift among Friends

Michael Bennett is the city manager of the rural Canadian town of Westborough. For his fiftieth birthday, his family and friends throw him a surprise party at the city golf football club. All in all, it is a typical country gathering. The guests include several of Mike's staff, city councillors, the doctor, the school principal, and local business people and contractors. After the speeches, Mike opens his gifts. Among them is a video camera. It is from one of the leading contractors for municipal works in Westborough. Mike's spouse and children are thrilled.

Case Questions

1. Does he have a problem?
2. If so, what should he do about it?
3. Would your view of the situation change if the story was varied slightly; if it was Mike's forty-eighth birthday; if the gift was, say, a nice watch? What about a boxed set of Beatles CDs or a good bottle of whisky?

Constitutive and Regulative Rules

Ethics and the law are closely associated. This is probably because both are regulative and ethics is embedded in many of our laws. Ethical and legal prohibitions against stealing property and harming persons give mutual support to each other. When ethical failures occur in business or the professions, demands for tighter regulation or stronger policing are often made as though more laws and tougher enforcement will produce better ethics. While such demands are not always misdirected, in most cases they do not address what is needed if business and the professions are to conduct themselves ethically. For one thing, if law and ethics are identified with one another, then people are apt to think that if an act is legal, then it is ethical. The slogan, "If it's legal, it's ethical" is often heard in business, and it is mistaken.

The importance of ethics in just observing the ordinary requirements of the law is obvious if one takes the example of an archer trying to hit a distant target. The archer has to aim high. If he aims straight at the target he will miss. So, too, with organizations and society more generally: just aiming to observe the law sets the sights too low. Like the archer, we have to aim higher—towards ethics—just to be minimally law-abiding.

Alan Greenspan, former chairman of the United States Federal Reserve Board, has put the matter well: ethical companies do not need rules to persuade them to act in the long-term interests of shareholders, but because some firms are unethical, these rules are necessary. The question then becomes one of balancing potentially restrictive and expensive regulation against other drivers:

> [T]here can be only one set of rules for corporate governance, and it must apply to all. Crafting the rules to provide the proper mix of regulatory and market-based incentives and penalties has never been easy. And I suspect that even after we get beyond the Enron debacle, crafting and updating such rules will continue to be a challenge.[45]

Just four months after Greenspan uttered these words, the Sarbanes-Oxley Act was passed by the US Congress.

Accounting is one of the most regulated professions. It seems that when any major infraction hits the headlines, a new rule is introduced to prevent its recurrence or there are calls for new rules and tighter standards. The rules of accounting are not primarily regulative, however, but **constitutive**[46]—that is, most of the rules in accounting are about the practice itself, not about the regulation of practitioners. These rules determine, or define, what the practice amounts to—that is, what constitutes it. They exist to promote the practice of accounting, not to restrict practitioners or catch out frauds. The whole purpose of accounting is to give an accurate and reliable—or, according to the classic phrase, "a true and fair"[47]—account of a company's business affairs, but that does not stop some practitioners from committing crimes and many more from deviating from the spirit of accounting standards. Introducing tighter regulations or new standards might not be the way to counter such deviations. Rather, ethical controls related to the personal principles of the practitioner might be a better way of assuring fairness and honesty in the duties accountants perform than imposed external regulations—rules whose aim is not constitutive but regulative. Clarke, Dean, and Oliver argue that the ethos of the accounting profession—its commonly understood and shared principles and norms—has been replaced by regulations and standards: "Contrary to the popular view, it is our proposition that compliance with the so-called spirit of many conventional practices and endorsed Standards produces grossly misleading data, without necessarily any intention to deceive on anybody's part."[48] The situation is very much compounded when a wobbly professional ethos is required to stand up to deceptive and legally risky conduct, as the case of Arthur Andersen shows.

constitutive rules *rules about what constitutes, or defines, a practice*

Accounting is not the only profession or activity to suffer from the misconception that the way to rectify ethical difficulties is to introduce more and more regulation. It is, in fact, quite a common call to arms in the face of ethical (or other) difficulties: "We need more regulation." However, not only is increased regulation not always an effective remedy; it can sometimes exacerbate the difficulty by shifting attention from the real difficulty—which is usually a matter of the exercise of bad judgment and a systemic problem with the organizational culture—onto the regulation and its technicalities.[49] There is an attractiveness about regulation as a solution to problems in that it is simple and neat, whereas doing what is necessary to improve the judgment of individuals and corporations, their ethical decision-making skills, and an organization culture is much more difficult.

This is only a slight exaggeration, and it is easy to give lots of examples, including many from accounting failures. Something has gone wrong; there has basically been an ethical failure. The profession and the community at large want to remedy the failure—they do not want it to happen again. So, from whatever external controlling body (or bodies) there is comes the pronouncement, "Clean up your act, or else!" The "or else," as a threat, usually amounts to the possibility of dramatic legislation or regulation from an external body. Under this threat, the profession knows what is being targeted and knows what needs to be improved—and it is almost always an ethical failure of one kind or another. The focus of the profession is on the ethical failure. It wants to fix it. Now, suppose the situation progresses, and regulation is introduced. The stimulus for the new regulation was the failure, by virtue of which there was the threat. Now that there is regulation, however, the focus of the practitioners—and maybe even of the profession itself—is directed towards that regulation specifically, rather than towards the stimulus and the real problem. So, the practitioners' concern now becomes doing exactly what the regulation requires or, better, doing whatever can be done to get around the new requirements.[50] Any concern for the real problem—and the concern to "clean up their act"—becomes lost in technicalities, procedures, and repairs. "It's simpler that way!"

In accounting education, ethics is sometimes discussed separately from skills and knowledge. We suggest that this view is mistaken. Rather, ethical performance is integral to the practice of accounting. The internal ethical requirements of a profession—standards, norms, expectations, competences, commitments, and procedures—both enable and govern its effective practice. If a doctor refuses to treat patients with chronic illnesses, that doctor is hardly practising medicine. If a lawyer takes only cases that can be confidently won, this is hardly the competent practice of law. If an engineer takes shortcuts that endanger lives, that person is a substandard engineer. If an accountant does whatever an employer instructs, even if the accountant believes it to be unprofessional, then that accountant is behaving not only unethically but also incompetently. In all these instances, the practitioners behave unethically because they behave in a manner contrary to the standards of their professions. These standards create the internal obligations of a profession. They do more than regulate; they constitute the competent practice of the profession. Professions have a tradition of service to the public, and in return, the public confers upon them certain rights of practice. Betrayal of this trust through shoddy, careless, negligent, or hasty professional practice is unethical. It is not only the nakedly corrupt professional who has abandoned ethics; it is the uncaring, "unprofessional," and incompetent practitioner as well. A wilfully under-skilled, ignorant, or negligent practitioner is unethical. In this internal sense, ethics is integral to professional practice, not an add-on component to the knowledge-plus-skills model.

Consider the following case.

CASE 9.6: Succession Planning?

You have been an accountant in public practice for 10 years. One day at a family picnic, an old friend and colleague asks what arrangements you have made for your clients in case you suddenly die or become incapacitated. Does this strike you as an odd question? Is it your responsibility to provide for your clients? You have provided for your family because they are your responsibility. But is not the responsibility of the professional accountant more limited? These seem to be ethical questions, but they are also professional because they have impact on your clients.

Case Question

1. What would your immediate response to these questions be?

Litigation and Auditing

There are penalties for not retaining sufficient professional independence in auditing. The two cases below illustrate just some of the litigation brought against auditors in recent years.

CASE 9.7: Bankers Trust

In a landmark Australian case, Bankers Trust and eight individual shareholders brought an action in 1992 for $60 million against the former auditors of Westmex Ltd for negligence and for misleading and deceptive conduct. The unusual action under section 52 of the Trade Practices Act 1974 was filed in the Federal Court of Australia against Richard Moffitt, Westmex's former auditor, and his partners. Westmex, Russell Goward's vehicle for buying and selling companies, went into provisional liquidation in February 1990. Just five months earlier, it had received an unqualified auditor's report from Thompson Douglass and Co., of which Moffitt was then a partner. Bankers Trust's action was directed against the firm and all of its partners.

Proceedings in the matter commenced in 1992 but received fresh impetus in January 1996, when the Companies Auditors and Liquidators Disciplinary Board (CALDB) suspended Moffitt from registration as a company auditor for five years. The suspension followed an application by the Australian Securities Commission. CALDB found that Moffitt had not adequately and properly performed the duties of an auditor during the course of the Westmex audits in 1988 and 1989.[51]

The second Australian case involves issues related to an "independent" report that turned out to be not so independent.

CASE 9.8: An "Independent" Report?

Angus Pilmer, partner in the leading Perth audit firm of Nelson Wheeler, completed an "independent" report on a takeover by Kia Ora Gold of the merchant bank Western United in September 1987. Pilmer valued Western United at between $101 and $113 million. Following the disastrous October stock market crash of the same year, its value fell to $3 million, but Kia Ora proceeded with the takeover. It later emerged that Western United and Kia Ora had common directors who were the main beneficiaries of the takeover. Even before the crash, however, Pilmer's valuation was a long way from the figure put on it by Jeff Hall of Grant Samuel: a mere $10 million. In what was to become the world's longest trial, Pilmer and his firm were sued over his report.[52]

All professions must now consider the possibility of litigation, and accountants and auditors are no different. The pursuit of remedies in suits against auditors will not solve the basic problem of greed. Moreover, litigation can have unintended and undesirable side effects. According to one commentator, "Men and women of means and competence may well decide that being an auditor or company director is just too difficult. It is a reasonable observation that ever increasing professional indemnity cover is likely to increase legal suits rather than decrease them."[53] In other words, the distinction between culpable and accidental error is in danger of being blurred, and particularly so if competency is reduced.

George Sutton suggests some strategies to protect the auditor. First, he recommends a cap on professional liability; such a cap would reduce the incentive for litigation and subsequently the costs of insurance premiums. Second, he seeks a return to the old-fashioned notion that the auditor's real clients are the shareholders by whom they should be thoughtfully elected and to whom they should be accountable by being required to present a company's accounts. The corporation that employs an auditor is, in effect, identified merely with its officers and employees:[54]

> The good auditor understands that transparency sometimes requires going beyond the scope of strict legislative disclosure requirements and after intensive discussion with the board, he must be secure enough to push for his view for the benefit of the shareholders. The auditors should read aloud their audit report as part of the formal proceedings at the annual meeting.[55]

If ethical decisions are inescapable in professional life, they are almost an occupational hazard in accounting and auditing. Clarke, Dean, and Oliver lament that "there are no good explanations within the framework of accounting and auditing rules with which accountants have to comply," so that exposure to litigation and loss of professional status are persistent occupational risks.[56] If this is true of formal standards and rules, then most of the general points about ethics will be less helpful than practitioners might expect because rules in accounting are not transparently grounded in ethical principles. An ethical accountant might well claim to know what honesty requires, but that is of little help when confronted with a case in which adhering to the letter of a set of accounting standards involves departing from their spirit. Everyday practice decisions do have ethical implications. In a sample of 108 financial reports in the first half of the 1992–3 financial year, 65 reports prompted inquiries about apparent departures from accounting standards—that is, 60 per cent of the sample raised questions about accounting practices and compliance with standards and the law. If this is so, then such practices also raise ethical questions, but this would not seem to be acknowledged, perhaps because the survey was not concerned with imputing improper conduct. If this is so, then an excessively narrow view of ethics is at work, for, as stressed above, ethics deals also with matters of competence, discretion, responsibility, and excellence. It should be noted that, of the 65 inquiries about departures from standards and regulations, 36 were regarded as matters for the professional discretion of auditors and most of the rest received satisfactory explanations. Practitioners need to be able to justify their decisions, and most can. This, too, is a matter of ethics. So when most of the auditors surveyed "accepted the need for improved presentation and disclosure and undertook to persuade their clients to make improvements in the following year's financial report,"[57] they were facing up to professional responsibilities that were both technical and ethical. Whether they recognized the ethical element of their position is another matter.

The accounting profession in Canada continues to focus on strategies to raise the ethical awareness of its members and to reinforce the importance of ethics in accounting education. Most of these initiatives are aimed at individuals rather than at the systemic problems of the profession identified by Clarke, Dean, and Oliver. Given the immensity of that task, it is more a matter for public policy than a matter for the action of professional associations.

Consider the following fictional case, one that raises some of the kinds of problems that confront accountants working in organizations.

CASE 9.9: Zanicum Metals

Zanicum Metals is a rapidly expanding producer of non-ferrous metal castings. Demand for its product is strong, and it is negotiating a large bank loan in order to increase production. As part of its regular maintenance cycle, Zanicum must decommission some of its furnaces so that they can be overhauled. This is an expensive process, and it is important to minimize the impact on the company's total operations. Management accountant Richard Ng and a team of engineers have been assigned to prepare comparative cost evaluations and recommend one of three potential contractors for the furnace overhaul. The kinds of factors they have to consider include the time the furnaces will be out of commission, the likely effect on production, and the cost and quality of the overhaul. Richard's team recommends Thermatic, but the managing director of Zanicum, Sally Richfield, is unimpressed. She seems to regard it as a matter of course that the contract will go to Fusion Furnaces, an enterprise in which her family company, MTSC, has an interest. Sally questions some of the assumptions upon which Richard's team made its recommendation. She requests Richard to reconsider his assumptions and to make appropriate changes to the cost analysis. Richard agrees that some assumptions are open to different interpretations, but asks her whether there might not be a conflict of interest in her position. Sally laughs and tells him that she has more shares and options in Zanicum than in Fusion and that her success is bound up in leading Zanicum to successful expansion. There is no conflict of interest, she declares. Richard is directed to revise his analysis and his recommendation of a furnace maintenance contractor.

Gloria Vineman, the newly appointed finance director with Zanicum, is preparing the company's annual financial statements. She knows from the previous year's audited accounts that cumulative provision of $1.5 million had been made for furnace maintenance and that a cost analysis had been prepared in the current year for the work to proceed. She asks Richard Ng for details of the cost analysis, but he merely gives her his recommendation and refers her to Sally Richfield. Sally is evasive and eventually does not present the cost analysis. She informs Gloria that the costing exercise put a figure of $1.5 million on the overhaul of furnaces, but Gloria is unhappy about this verbal advice. She has heard engineers in the firm mention a figure twice as large. Sally firmly states that if Gloria has any concerns based on such hearsay, she should keep them to herself and not upset the auditors—especially during the negotiation of a large loan from the bank.

John Ryan is the senior partner in Ryan McGrath, auditors for MTSC, Fusion, and other metalworking companies, including Zanicum. Almost all of Ryan McGrath's business comes from the metals industry. John reviews the financial statements of Zanicum prepared by Gloria and notes a significant audit risk against the refurbishment of furnaces. Despite direct requests to Gloria, John has been unable to obtain the cost analysis documents from Zanicum. Sally will not discuss the matter beyond saying that the growth of the company and sustained demand for its products are the best evidence of the financial health of Zanicum. She also makes an indirect but clear suggestion that if Ryan McGrath cannot provide a trouble-free audit before she meets with the bank to finalize the loan, then there are other auditors who are more familiar with the operations and needs of the metals industry.

John and Sally eventually reach an agreement that Zanicum should make provision of $1.75 million for furnace maintenance, and Ryan McGrath signs Zanicum's statements as presenting a true and fair view. The bank loan goes through, and the furnaces are serviced by Fusion at a cost of $2.7 million.

This case raises a number of ethical problems, but the central one concerns professional independence.

Case Questions

1. What would you have done in Richard's and Gloria's positions?
2. To whom are Richard and Gloria accountable? Is it Sally? Does she have the right to exercise her position as she has with Richard and Gloria?
3. To whom should the accountant be responsible in these cases?

continued . . .

4. What of the responsibilities of Ryan McGrath? John Ryan has placed a large part of his company's business in a narrow field: the metals industry. Has he not put himself under avoidable pressure by auditing companies with business connections and sometimes overlapping directorships?
5. Is Ryan properly cognizant of his statutory and ethical responsibilities? Sally Richfield made it clear that Ryan McGrath would be jeopardizing its own business if an unfavourable audit went forward. Is this a credible threat? What, for an auditor, constitutes a proper distance from a client?

There are also other issues here that draw upon the problem of dirty hands (see chapter 2). If one is implicated in covering up sharp practice, then later one can be caught in all kinds of difficulties that seem to result in disaster no matter what one does. This might well apply to John Ryan, but consider also the position of Richard Ng. Say he changes his cost analysis at the behest of Sally Richfield. He considers this a small thing. Then, when he is approached by Gloria Vineman for details of the cost analysis, he must evade the difficulty and refer her to Sally. If he tells John Ryan what he knows, the loan with the bank might be jeopardized and the future of the company and the benefits to its employees and other stakeholders might be adversely affected. If he conceals what he knows, he is acting against his professional integrity. This is a situation he has got himself into by initially acceding to Sally's request—that is, by initially compromising his independent professional judgment. Of course, not all cases of professional failure give rise to dire consequences or produce dirty hands later. But ethical consistency can at least reduce the chances of being confronted with such problems down the track. In this case, consistency would involve saying "No" to Sally initially and sticking with that decision. This view says nothing about personal costs, but these are often entailed in principled action in any case and there is always the possibility that one unethical act will create the conditions for much more costly ethical failures later.

The significance of professional independence is clear in the light of these reflections. Note that similar ethical issues regarding independence, responsibility and accountability arise in connection with the roles of other kinds of salaried professionals working in organizations. One has only to think of the engineers who advised against the launch of the space shuttle *Challenger*. These issues are about the nature of the professional role and about what can reasonably be demanded of people whose profession entails a good measure of autonomy.

Review Questions

1. We note the results of a survey about where accountants identify the source of their values: family, conduct of peers, accounting practices, prevailing societal norms, professional code of ethics, and religious formation. Such surveys are not uncommon. If such places are where people believe their values come from, is there any place for critical reflection or critical evaluation—making up one's own mind—or independent thought about values?
2. We discuss two senses of "independence" as the notion applies to accountants (see pages 192–3). Are you clear about what these are? Do you agree that these are different senses?
3. What do you think of the suggestion that increased regulation can exacerbate a problem rather than solve it?

Suggested Readings

Collins, D. *Behaving Badly: Ethical Lessons from Enron*. Indianapolis, IN: Dog Ear Publishing, 2006.

Fusaro, P.C., and R.M. Miller. *What Went Wrong at Enron: Everyone's Guide to the Largest Bankruptcy in US History*. Hoboken, NJ: John Wiley & Sons, 2002.

Toffler, Barbara Ley, with Jennifer Reingold. *Final Accounting: Ambition, Greed and the Fall of Arthur Andersen*. New York: Broadway Books, 2003.

Suggested Websites

CICA Code of Conduct and Intellectual Property Rights Agreement:

http://www.cica.ca/about-cica/cica-volunteer-central/item29361.pdf.

AICPA Code of Professional Conduct:

http://www.aicpa.org/Research/Standards/CodeofConduct/.

10

Codes of Ethics and Institutional Ethics

Chapter Outline

- Codes of Ethics and Codes of Conduct
- Accountability and Responsibility
- Back to Codes
- Professional and Business Codes
- Content of Codes of Ethics
- Two Brief Stories of Industry Codes
- Institutionalizing Ethics
- Review Questions
- Suggested Websites

> An employee shall not conduct himself or herself in a manner which directly or indirectly would be detrimental to the best interests of the Company or in a manner which would bring to the employee financial gain separately derived as a direct consequence of his or her employment with the Company. Moral as well as legal obligations will be fulfilled openly, promptly, and in a manner which will reflect pride on the Company's name.
>
> —Enron Code of Ethics, 2000, p. 13

Enron's code was 65 pages long and had high-sounding phrases about values, human rights, and compliance. However, when it conflicted with the goals of corporate executives, it was put in the trash. That is the handy thing about codes. Even the long ones can be dumped quickly in time of need.

Yet **codes** in one form or another have been used to regulate behaviour since antiquity. The Code of Hammurabi is one such and the Ten Commandments another. We are most familiar, of course, with legal codes, and we expect that codified principles will be clear-cut and not open to dispute and personal interpretation. Codes have various forms; there may be codes of ethics, conduct, or practice, each species being framed to meet the specific needs of the organization that produced it.[1] Their common purpose is self-regulation through peer enforcement. This is often overlooked: codes are not about external regulation but self-regulation. Too much can be made of them, and on the whole, too much is expected of them. There is too ready an acceptance of rules as "fixes" for our social problems and not enough faith in judgment. Consider this illustration of the point.

code *an established set of principles or rules of behaviour*

In 2007, the German town of Bohmte decided to remove its traffic lights and signs from its roads. This decision seemed precarious given that Bohmte lies on a main truck route to the city of Osnabrück—13,000 trucks and cars pass through the town daily. Still, Bohmte removed its signs in 2008 and traffic accidents not only declined but, in the first months after implementation, had ceased altogether. The architect of this radical experiment, traffic management expert Heiner Monheim, declared, "What's revolutionary about Bohmte is that it took off its signs on a state highway with a lot of traffic."[2] Instead of masses of rules and signs to keep vehicles from hitting cyclists and pedestrians, all users of the roads have to pay attention to each other and exercise appropriate care. Monheim's principle of "shared space" is based on a number of factors, including self-interest, responsibility, and a greater consideration for others than is required in a rule-bound environment. Well, there is one rule: give way to traffic on the right. One resident said of the new system that "[i]nstead of thinking, 'It's going to be red, I need to step on the gas,' people have to slow down, to look to the right and the left, to be considerate." This counterintuitive scheme does away with the segregation of people and traffic. It replaces rules with "negotiation" based on eye contact and other signals. Shared space apparently has social as well as aesthetic and safety benefits. According to the resident, "The whole village has become more human. We look at each other, we greet each other."[3]

The "radical" aspect of this story is the removal of rules and their replacement with judgment. This substitution carries a heavy responsibility: fail in your judgment and you might end up in an accident. As judgment is pretty much required in order to walk, let alone drive, in Bohmte, it might be expected that the townsfolk would be edgy. Not at all, according to news reports. They are more sociable. It is tempting to think that regulation, formalized directives, rules and regulations are obsolete and that we might expand the Bohmte experiment into other areas of life. Notice, however, that this example shows that judgment has to be responsible: it is emphatically not a matter of "Do as you like." The Bohmte experiment seemed to work because it called forth deep values from its citizens and visitors. They recovered sociability and respect. It should not be an unintended consequence of codes that they mask such basic human values or render them redundant. Codes should elicit good judgment and the appropriate values to inform it. Codes should be an aid to judgment, an affirmation of deep values, not a cheap substitute for them.

Codes have long been used to establish standards in the professions. Medicine came first in the early nineteenth century when physicians wished to establish their respectable credentials by distinguishing themselves from con artists and snake-oil salesmen. Pharmacists soon followed, and gradually, over the next hundred years, other professions set boundaries around their tasks and professional identities and established regulatory mechanisms to go with them. Codes came to be accepted not only as important in the ethical sense, but as necessary to a professional status. In this sense, they not only serve the public by regulating standards and behaviour, but also restrict trade, keeping certain professional territory the exclusive preserve of those approved by the profession. In this way, professional bodies serve as "credential certifiers" for practitioners under the conditions set out in their codes. A certain degree of skepticism about the self-serving nature of professional codes is justified, but a profession without a code would be impossible these days.

In business, there is altogether more skepticism. For a start, some would not like to see business called a profession because that would seem to restrict entrepreneurship. Professional constraints would limit business opportunities and the participation of people whose qualifications were enthusiasm, ideas, and a willingness to take risks rather than a business degree. The ability to develop markets, innovate, and sell is not the preserve of professional elites and those with specifiable credentials, and attempts to introduce business codes modelled on the codes of professions would be inappropriate.

The most common form of skepticism, however, is the view that business codes, values statements, and proclamations of this kind are simply so much hot air. One does not have to be unduly cynical to see that codes and statements making grandiose claims are unlikely to be realized in practice. If practice can conform to the code only with great difficulty, then the code is effectively impractical. Such self-defeating statements breed cynicism and reinforce the view that they are useless in all cases.

Another form of skepticism lies in the observation that codes can discourage excellence or even encourage unethical behaviour by stipulating what must or must not be done: where unethical conduct is not prohibited, it may be assumed that it is permitted. Similarly, by setting out the minimum requirements of ethical performance, expectations might be pitched too low and thereby discourage higher achievement. As codes can never be comprehensive and are usually general, these objections have some force.

The reply to this form of skepticism is simple. Some codes and values statements are ineffective and unrealistic, while others are vital parts of more extensive programs to promote corporate ethics. Codes can be used to escape ethical requirements but also to enforce them. Codes are not magical, but they are indispensable to the development of an ethical culture in a modern organization.

Because corporations are not natural persons, formal rules are important in establishing their moral status. Although they have their own cultures, organizations do not possess emotions, a conscience, intellect, or will. They are composed of individuals who have these things, but as Machiavelli showed so well in *The Prince*, private judgments can bring calamity on a society or organization. We do not expect individuals to act in a private capacity in performing their employment duties. The closest analogue in a corporate organization to the virtues embodied in the characters of persons is an ethos. This is where rules come in, and clear ethical rules are no less important than other formal regulations and informal habits of conduct. Ethical rules are ways of ensuring minimum standards, of offering guidance for conduct, and of stating in a concise way the main values of the culture of the organization. They are no more dispensable for organizations than virtues are for individuals.

The motivation for a company or a business to institute a **code of ethics** need not come from a commitment to morality or from, say, an altruistic concern for the public at large. No doubt a number of business and professional organizations do have such concerns, but it is clear that the history of business is not about these things. Having an altruistic concern or being interested in moral behaviour for its own sake is not the only adequate motivation for a business or a profession to find a code of ethics desirable. Self-interest can (quite properly) furnish the stimulus for a code. Put simply, good business requires the presence of a code of ethics. Perhaps the strongest motivation for creating a code of ethics is that the present climate of accountability, fair-dealing, public awareness, and governmental regulation is such that it is a situation of "Do it, or else." In many cases, it is precisely a situation of "You set particular standards for yourself, or we'll do it for you," where the "we" is some external, perhaps governmental body. Given those alternatives, any organization would prefer to play a major or perhaps exclusive role in setting its own ethical standards and enforcing them. An organization will be more sensitive to its own structure, aims, limits, operating costs, and benefits than will an external standard-setter.

code of ethics *a formal statement of an organization's ethical values and principles*

Avoiding the imposition of external regulation is only one prudential reason for business to take the initiative. If an organization does not have a code of ethics, it can suffer from a number of undesirable effects in the marketplace. Public trust and confidence are clearly commodities that can have a dollar value attached to them. They are good for business. It is interesting to note that the presence of a code of ethics itself has been used by some businesses as a form of competitive advertising, a way of promoting that business above others. For example, the Insurance Brokers Association of Ontario and Nissan have both dedicated entire advertisements to their codes of ethics.

Consumers can simply turn their backs on products and services with a poor ethical reputation. The market can be as effective on ethical matters as a regulatory body, as the damage to Nestlé over Third World infant milk formula sales in the 1970s showed. Its competitor, Abbott Laboratories, developed a code of marketing practice in response to the public reaction to the selling of infant milk formula in societies where its use might be inappropriate, but Nestlé persisted with its marketing practices and lost public support.[4]

As protection against increased external regulation, it is desirable for an organization itself to institute its own code of ethics. Shareholders, as well as the public at large, now react adversely to perceived unethical conduct, and information about such conduct is readily available and highly visible in newspapers and popular magazines. In the United States some years ago, Chrysler made a different kind of move in this direction. It established a "car buyers' bill of rights" and a mechanism to enforce it. Chrysler then claimed that it judged the success of dealerships by levels of customer service and satisfaction rather than by volume of sales. It is, of course, possible (and likely) that this was itself an indirect gauge of volume. Nevertheless, it was the service and not the volume that was targeted. Chrysler is not unique in valuing honour as a badge to place on a business. International executive-search firm pioneer Egon Zehnder believed that demonstrated integrity is as basic to the appointment of an executive as demonstrated management skills. According to Zehnder, in selecting someone "for a key job, select above all, the [person] with high integrity. Such an integrity-based selection will permeate through management making a strong management team."[5]

This is not to say that prudential, self-interested reasons for having a code should be allowed to prejudice its content or its implementation; many things in life are done for prudential reasons and are still done well. The same is true of compulsion: although attendance at school is compulsory and it is prudent to conform to this legal requirement, children nonetheless benefit, even if they would rather be elsewhere. Business, like a reluctant pupil, can read a bottom line: if trust and confidence and the profits attached to them are at stake, it pays to take ethics as seriously as other matters of competitive service. Nevertheless, attempts to extract greater public accountability from some industries, such as banking, have not met with an altogether positive response.

Not all businesses and professions are unconcerned about morality except insofar as moral behaviour is good for business. If we can indicate that even for the extreme case the business itself should see the presence of a code of ethics as desirable, then there can be no question of its general desirability. Devising a code can be part of a review process. The drafting and adoption of a code are opportunities for a firm to think through and articulate its values and objectives. The process can be as important as the result. It can reveal accepted practices that the organization would not affirm publicly and that, on reflection, it would wish to change. Once a firm has done an audit on its ethical practices, it will be in a better position to develop its organizational culture in more productive and responsible ways. So devising a code of ethics could be seen not as an end in itself but more as the beginning of a monitoring and reform process. The resultant code is a good platform for measuring the success of change and developing the strengths of an organization to meet emerging ethical challenges. The process that produces a code can be refined and modified to update the code. The production process is thus both the first stage in the renewal of an organization and the object of continuing review.

Every organization has rules about behaviour, even if these rules are not made explicit in written or oral form. Some organizations have a written code of practice and some do not. Sometimes the written code of practice of an organization is at variance with its unwritten operational code. When the two are in conflict, the unwritten code is usually the more effective. This can be very sobering. An executive of a large corporation once spoke about being the student of a famous professor of accounting. "He was a wonderful teacher," said the executive. "He had wonderful ideals, we learned a great deal from him, and he enjoyed great professional respect. But when I joined my firm I was told, 'The first thing you have to do is forget everything Professor X taught you. We do things differently here.'" The executive was referring not just to skills, but also to values. Organizations may profess one thing and practise the opposite. All have de facto codes of practice, though not all have de jure (or formal) codes of ethics.

If an organizational culture fosters sharp practice and rewards unethical behaviour, the superimposition of a formal code of ethics will merely be window dressing. A code of ethics prominently displayed can be misleading, far worse than no code at all. Yet contemporary social pressures on business almost compel the adoption of formal codes. Good intentions notwithstanding, this might at best be useless and at worst a trap for the unwary. It is also paradoxical: at the heart of written codes is self-regulation, yet implicit in the social demand is the threat that if a written code is not adopted, then government will do the regulating. This demand seems almost to see regulation, or rather codification, as an end in itself. The essential questions should be these: what are codes of ethics for, and what benefits should be expected from their adoption?

The first answer must be that a formal code of ethics states where people in an organization stand in relation to each other and to the organization itself. It also states where the organization itself or members of the organization stand in relation to entities outside the organization (most typically, members of the public, stakeholders, or other organizations). The effect of this should be to bring the **de facto** and **de jure** value systems of the organization into alignment. Then the ethical culture, or ethos, of the organization will be transparent: every stakeholder group will know where it stands.

de facto value system *a value system that exists in actual fact; it is in place and acted upon in good faith, even if not officially codified*

de jure value system *a value system that is formally codified*

The model for this view is the principle of the "rule of law" in the legal system. Rule of law is an important notion in legal theory and in the philosophy of law. It encompasses a number of aspects, one of which is particularly important in the context of codes of ethics. An environment of rule of law, and a code of ethics, allows the subjects, or clients, as well as the practitioners to know where they stand in relation to the practice. It allows people to know (and so allows them to expect and to plan accordingly) how they will be treated in certain situations. If the prices of products are announced, then people can choose either to buy them or not and can expect to pay that amount if they decide to buy. People can plan accordingly. Similarly, if people know that certain behaviour is prescribed in certain situations for practitioners, then they know what to expect and can plan accordingly. This element of consistently knowing what to expect and of being able to plan is itself valuable. To some degree it may not matter what is prescribed (although there are important limits and whole areas where this is not true); predictability and consistency are valuable in their own right.

The model of the rule of law is useful in another way. Just as the law should apply to all people equally, so a business code should apply to all people in an organization, from the chief executive officer (CEO) down. A set of rules, principles, or values for employees that excludes management, even implicitly, is sending a false message to the organization and to the public at large. When staff know where they stand in relation to each other and the organization and when they have a clear statement of moral equality, a barrier has been placed between them and unethical conduct. If a manager were to request a junior staff member to do something unethical, the junior employee could point to provisions in the code forbidding this. In other words, unethical conduct cannot be disguised as legitimate direction. This barrier should discourage managers from making unethical demands, protect individuals from being placed in difficult or compromising situations, and safeguard the integrity of the organization. It should lessen resort to whistleblowing and allow ethical employees to act with the assurance that they enjoy the support of the organization as a whole in adhering to the spirit and letter of the code.

The point of a code of ethics is to declare professional or organizational standards for all to see. It is an invitation for those outside the profession to judge it and its practitioners by the standards it declares. It announces to members of a profession that certain standards and values should be respected in practice. It sets a level playing field for all practitioners. It is an instrument for accountability and responsibility. And it is an affirmation of the identity of an organization, industry, or profession. Codes are not surrogate forms of law, but declarations that certain principles will be observed in the operations of the institutions that adopt them. These principles can be broad and general (as in the case of codes of ethics) or quite specific (as in the case of codes of conduct). It is often asserted that the development of a code is as important as the finished document because the process brings people together around a common purpose and agreed values and encourages ownership of the code. There is truth in this when codes are produced with the participation of all levels of an organization or profession, but the production of a code cannot of itself bring purposes and values into being. If the entity has no clear conception of its own identity, then a code will not give it one or substitute for one. In this respect, a code is better seen as the result of a process rather than as itself the instrument of initiation of a process.

It is hardly likely that an organization without a strong sense of what it stands for would pay more than lip service to a code of ethics. A firm sense of identity can give rise to a wish to affirm certain values, both to encourage public trust and for internal reasons, such as induction of new staff or sustaining a certain type of culture in an expanding organization. But such a strong sense of identity will not of itself ensure that a code is used or even useful. There are still many ethical organizations without codes in Canada, although it would be almost impossible for a profession to practise without one. The presence of a code of ethics is often taken to be a necessary or defining feature of professions, yet even when codes are adopted, uncodified or implicit norms can govern the ethics of corporations and professions. This is because there can be two sets of norms in organizations: the informal ones that operate on the basis of example and organizational culture, and the formal ones that are written down after deliberation and reference to best practice. The latter are sometimes seen as an imposition on an organization. If the formal code cuts across the informal one, then there will be problems about compliance. On core ethical matters in professional practice, the values of practitioners should accord with those in the code.

Let's think very generally about what a code of ethics is and how, in broad strokes, someone might go about constructing one. A code of ethics is not all there is to ethics; it does not refer to the entire range of ethical matters. It is not out to cover the ethical landscape *writ large*. Why not? Why doesn't the code of ethics have just one provision: "Be ethical"? In constructing a code of ethics, one needs to be concerned, of course, with all of ethics, but with a view to what there is about ethical considerations, directions, and constraints that have particular relevance to the organization or profession concerned. Suppose, for instance, that you believe that "respect for human life" is an important ethical value. If you are a firm of chartered accountants, while you might individually believe this to be an important value and something that you certainly would not want to breach, it has no particular relevance to your organizational activities. And so it has no place in your firm's code of ethics. The situation could well be different if, say, you were a firm of armed security guards. For this organization, it might be important to include something like this value in your code of ethics. It does have particular relevance for what you do and how you go about doing it. The point is simply that a code of ethics is not all there is to ethics; a code of ethics is not an attempt to itemize and categorize all of ethics; but a code of ethics is importantly related to ethical considerations in general in that it identifies ethical considerations and constraints that have particular relevance and application to the organization. We will continue with this point below in talking about an organization that addresses the question of what its organizational values are.

Another general feature to be kept in mind about codes of ethics is that they must be enforceable. There are two parts to this point:

1. Code of ethics statements of values must be more than motherhood statements. They must actually have content that is "breachable." For any provision in a code of ethics, it is important to be able to conceive of examples of what failure to comply with that provision would be. If you cannot imagine what a breach of a provision would amount to, then that provision is absolutely pointless.
2. An organization must provide a mechanism for evaluating purported breaches and imposing sanctions where breaches are found to have occurred.

Codes of Ethics and Codes of Conduct

It is important to distinguish between a code of ethics and a **code of conduct**. Not everyone uses the phrases in this way (although over the past few years, it has become more common to do so), but the distinction itself is important, whether or not one uses the mechanics of a code of ethics and a code of conduct to make that distinction. The codes of a number of organizations are actually an amalgamation of these two. We think, however, that it is a good idea to keep them separate.

code of conduct *an established set of specific and enforceable ethical prescriptions, which eliminate the uncertainty, variability and the necessity of judgment and discretion of a code of ethics*

Let's return for a moment to the distinction between "What should I do?" and "What kind of person should I be?" from chapter 1. In terms of the applicability of this distinction to business, it can be helpful to look at it in the way shown in Figure 10.1.

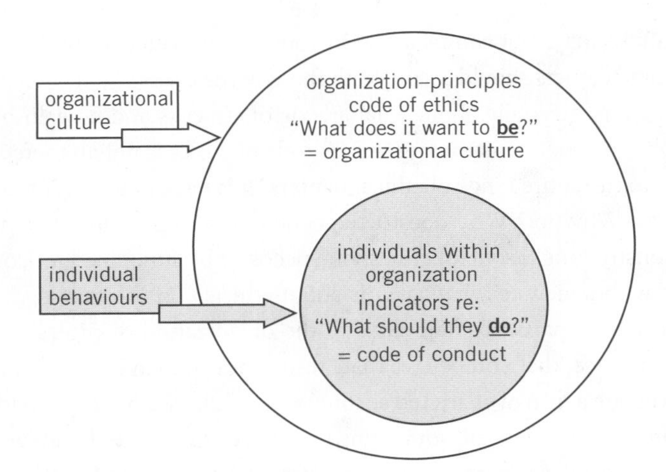

Figure 10.1 Organizational culture and individual behaviours

We can think of codes of ethics as statements about what kind of organization the organization is. They are statements of principles and values that the organization professedly subscribes to. They are statements about what kind of culture the organization has and/or aspires to have. In values terms, a code of ethics states the standards to which it holds itself and its employees to account. These are its professed "virtues."

The purpose of a code is not only to state the values of the organization, but also to provide serious guidance to people within the organization about how they should act. In the extreme, organizations are not particularly concerned about what kind of people work for them; they are concerned about the kinds of behaviours their employees exhibit. If a business holds "equal treatment for all" as a value, for example, it professes a non-discriminatory environment. In terms of any particular employee, it could well be that the business really does not care at all if that person is the most ardent racist on the face of the earth. The business does not care if an employee has very seriously objectionable racist beliefs. What the organization is saying to such a person is something like this: "Believe anything you like, but do not ever display anything here but an indication of a commitment to equal treatment for all." Statements about the organization's values or principles—its culture—speak to employees about their behaviour, not about their beliefs and attitudes. Organizations are concerned with employees' behaviours.

In this respect, then, although a code of ethics is a statement about values, or culture—"who we are"—its directive to employees is aimed at the question "What should we do?" If, say, a value identified in a code of ethics is "honesty," the directive to employees is to behave in ways that exhibit honesty. The concern is not so much that employees possess this virtue, but that they behave in ways that indicate or exhibit it.

General statements of values to which people are held accountable require the exercise of judgment on the part of any employee. This is the way it is with any statement of value whatsoever.

Table 10.1 Codes of ethics versus codes of conduct

Code of Ethics	Code of Conduct
General	Specific
Values/principles	Prescriptions/directives
Judgment	Uniformity
"Empowering"	Enforceable statements of specific behaviours
"Aspirational"	

Notice in Table 10.1 that the word "prescriptions" can be used in a more general sense or in a more specific sense:

1. Any statement with an "ought" or a "should" in it, or any statement that tells somebody to do anything at all, is a prescription. "You should be a good person" is prescriptive, but in this case, the statement is not at all specific about what particular bits of behaviour are required in order to comply. Moreover, there is most certainly no definite list of requirements that could be specified. Notice, however, that even so, in most cases it could be established that the person either is or is not complying with the prescription. Sometimes we do not need more specification in order to give clear direction and to establish either that the prescription is being complied with or that it is not.
2. Sometimes we talk about things such as regulations, laws, or directives as being prescriptive—sometimes "overly prescriptive." This is a different sense of the word. In this sense, "prescriptive" means, basically, prescribing specifically what to do. "You should never tell a lie" is prescriptive in this sense. "You should answer the questions with a number 2 lead pencil." Behaving in accordance with the prescription allows no room for manoeuvre, and no room for judgment.

Codes of ethics are prescriptive in the first sense. They not only allow for judgment; they require it. That's the way it is with a statement of any value or principle. Honesty, integrity, and safeguarding the public interest—these are values, they are prescriptions, they can be breached or complied with, and they all require the exercise of judgment on the part of whoever is expected to comply with them. And, by and large, they cannot be replaced with or comprehensively expressed in terms of something more prescriptive that does not leave room for judgment. Take the following as clear examples to illustrate this point (admittedly, one is a bit extreme):

Examples

1. A nasty fellow, who simply hates Jones's looks, wants to hurt him. Jones comes to you for some help and advice (just because he happens to know that you're an okay person). You ask him to calm down, to have a seat and a cup of coffee, and you suggest

continued . . .

that you'll help him try to figure out what to do. In the midst of this, you get buzzed to the front office, where there's a nasty fellow, smacking his fist into his hand: "Where's Jones? I thought I saw him come in here, and I want to teach the jerk a lesson." Honesty does not require that you say, "Right. You'll find him back in my office." And not only that, we would rightly think that anyone who thought of honesty this way—as simply, "Tell the truth; there's nothing more to think about"—did not really appreciate what the virtue of honesty is: telling the truth when that is the right thing to do.

2. When your lovely, somewhat forgetful Aunt Margaret asks you how you like her hat just as she is getting into the taxi, it would clearly be a misguided view of honesty to think that honesty requires telling her at that moment that you think it's ugly.

Judgment is required, and for this reason, we say that codes of ethics are "empowering." Statements of values or principles empower those to whom they are directed to use their judgment, or their discretion, and they hold people responsible for this.

A code of ethics speaks in general terms. It articulates ethical values and principles that are important to the organization. As a simple example, let's say "honesty" is one of the organization's values. Stating it and saying something about what it amounts to—in general terms—for the organization is appropriate to the organization's code of ethics. For those people operating under this code of ethics, honesty is a requirement, then. Now, exactly what honesty amounts to in any particular situation will require judgment. This is the situation for any value or principle listed in a code of ethics. Honesty is different from, say, a fanatical devotion to telling the truth. Although extreme, the situations in (1) and (2) above make it clear that (even) honesty requires judgment in particular situations. Usually the correct judgment will be to tell the truth, but judgment is necessary in order to appreciate a situation for what it is and for what honesty requires. So much for honesty. We could make the same points—and it would be much easier—with any other value or principle that finds a place in a code of ethics. To recognize that judgment is required is to recognize that different responses might be justified. This in itself can be empowering for people operating under the code. They are empowered to behave ethically. They have to make decisions, and they have to be prepared to offer justifications for those decisions. They are responsible for behaviour exhibiting the values and principles articulated in the code. And their actions with respect to each of those values or principles are to be judged by the justifications that they as individuals can offer. That's what the code requires.

aspirational *desiring and striving to improve; to be better than the current state*

Aspirational is a word that is often used in talking about codes of ethics. To appreciate the sense of aspirational in this context, it is helpful to indicate what it does *not* mean here. Again using the example of "honesty" as the value, saying that the code of ethics is aspirational does not mean something like this: "Right now we're not an honest organization—actually we're quite a dishonest organization. However, we aspire to behave honestly—one day." Rather, it means that although we don't always exhibit the value of honesty in the best way, and sometimes we might fall short, we aspire to get it exactly right every time. We realize that these things involve judgment calls, and we aspire to always exhibit excellent judgment. To say that the code of ethics is aspirational is to admit that there is room for improvement in our judgment and behaviour with respect to the values that the code articulates.

The difference between codes of ethics and codes of conduct is not that codes of conduct are enforceable and codes of ethics are not, or that codes of conduct, but not codes of ethics, are prescriptive (in the first sense, above). It is, rather, that the enforceable provisions of codes of conduct are prescriptive in the second sense, above.

A code of conduct should not introduce new values or principles beyond those present in the corresponding code of ethics. Rather, a code of conduct removes discretionary, or judgmental, elements that would otherwise apply to a code of ethics. They do this by prescribing certain behaviours specifically. They do not do this holus-bolus, but, rather, selectively.

A code of conduct does not replace a code of ethics. If there is a repeatable type of occurrence within which a value should be exemplified, a code of conduct can specify exactly what that behaviour should be. This removes any room for manoeuvre on the part of the agent. It removes any differences that could exist in deciding what one should do. Prescribing modes of behaviour can produce uniformity in the way employees deal with such situations. Consider this as an oversimplified example:

Example

Suppose you work for the mortgage-lending section of the bank. The bank has a code of ethics that includes the values "honesty," "integrity," and "transparency." There has been a bit of trouble in your section, with some clients coming away from meetings with mortgage lenders not fully aware of the bank fees associated with their mortgage. A code of conduct might specify that in dealing with a potential mortgagee, the bank officer should disclose all the fees that the bank will charge and how these will be calculated. Notice that this stipulation does a few things:

- It removes any judgment call on the part of the bank officer as to what information should be disclosed about fees. It has produced a specific prescription in this area, leaving no room for discretion.
- It has not introduced a new value. It has simply specified what the bank understands as complying with the values already present in its code of ethics in this identifiable, repeatable situation (in this case, honesty and transparency).
- It has addressed a specific problem that was solvable with the introduction of a clear and specific prescription. That is, there was a problem, and appropriate use of a code of conduct has solved it.

Provisions in codes of conduct can also send a message, both inside an organization and outside it, not necessarily that there are problems that need to be solved, but that the organization stands quite clearly for these behaviours. Whether it is a matter of reputation (as is often the case in the private sector and sometimes with professions) or a matter of the public trust (as is often the case in the public sector and sometimes with professions), prescriptions in a code of conduct can give a clear message: "Let there be no mistake about what we stand for here." These are the kinds of things that a code of conduct can do.

It is important to recognize, however, that a code of conduct cannot comprehensively spell out all that is involved in the values present in a code of ethics. And, in fact, the more provisions there are in a code of conduct, the more the code of conduct can give the impression—to employees and to anyone else who cares to look at it—that it is completely comprehensive in terms of articulating the values present in the code of ethics and all the behaviours that are required. This, by itself, is dangerous, as it gives an impression that an organization should very seriously try to avoid. Judgment simply cannot be replaced by a set of rules, no matter how comprehensive they appear to be. Not only can there be situations that happen not to be specified. There can also be situations—even somewhat predictable ones—where there can be a range of ethically acceptable ways to proceed, and so the degree of prescriptivity present in a code of conduct would be inappropriate.

Sometimes codes of ethics are described as "living documents." Probably it would be better to consider codes of conduct this way. An organization's central values really do not change very much. There can be changes over time, but these are probably neither frequent nor dramatic. What does need frequent revisiting is a code of conduct, questioning not only whether additional prescriptions are, or have become, desirable, but also whether any current prescriptions need revision or should simply be jettisoned.

Recognize that judgment is valuable and that it is not eliminable. If an organization believes that it is important to empower, or authorize, people to behave ethically, and so to encourage sound ethical judgments and ethical decision-making, then the organization must recognize that each specific prescription in a code of conduct amounts to a diminution of ethical empowerment. As we have indicated, there can, of course, be good reasons for specifying particular behaviours, but the organization should realize that these requirements come with the attendant cost to ethical empowerment. Given that this is so, careful thought should go into any curtailment of judgment in a code of conduct. For any provision contained in a code of conduct, we should be able to answer the question, "Why is this there?" Placing limits on judgment should be something that any organization is reluctant to do, and any limits should be justified.

Before going further with this account of codes, let us say a bit more about the idea of **ethical empowerment** in general.

ethical empowerment *the delegation of authority for ethical decision-making*

Ethical empowerment is a top-down notion. It involves delegation of authority for ethical decision-making. It authorizes, or empowers, members of the organization to exercise judgment in decision-making. Increasingly, organizations have recognized that they simply cannot afford to be "risk averse." They cannot afford to have their people in managerial or supervisory roles avoid making decisions in ethically charged situations. The organization recognizes that the alternatives to ethical empowerment are simply not good because

- to pass all ethically charged decisions up the line is a recipe for inefficiency
- to simply avoid making decisions in ethically charged situations is a recipe for stagnation
- to go ahead and do something, whatever you want, is cavalier. It is *very* dangerous to an organization not to invest in systems (for example, training) that equip managers to systematically exercise good judgment in such situations. It is a common error to simply trust in common sense (or something like this), rather than realizing that the matter of ethical decision-making can be approached specifically and dealt with seriously.

Rather, charging managers with responsibility to make ethically defensible decisions is a matter of authorization, or empowerment. Appropriate responsibility, or decision-making discretion, is delegated downward through the organization. Those receiving the responsibility should recognize that they must make decisions and that they must exercise demonstrably good judgment in making them. Trust goes downward. From top downward, those authorizing people below them must trust that those to whom a task is being delegated are up to the task. Of course, this should not be simply a matter of luck—the person to whom a task is being delegated must actually have the ability and skills to exercise the task. It can be a matter of the right person for the job, providing the necessary resources and training, installing appropriate systems, and so on. Whatever provisions are made, it is a matter of trusting that the person who is empowered can do the task. Now—and this is at least as important—it is necessary that those who receive the delegation actually trust that the people who gave it to them actually meant what they said. We all know people who, when they say "Exercise your discretion" actually mean something like, "You had better do this exactly as I would if I were in your position. Otherwise, I'm going to come down on you like a ton of bricks." This is not trust. This is not delegation. This is not a recipe for authorizing ethical decision-making in ethically charged situations. It is, rather, a recipe for second-guessing and looking over one's shoulder. It is not empowerment at all. It is, rather, instilling fear and distrust. So, in an environment of ethical empowerment, responsibility is delegated downward, and trust must go in both directions. By and large, this is an important notion for any organization concerned with promoting ethical performance. Codes of ethics can themselves be an important tool in this mechanism.

Accountability and Responsibility

Discussion of codes of ethics and codes of conduct and the difference between them is closely linked with discussion of the notions of **accountability** and responsibility. As we have indicated, operating according to a code of ethics necessarily requires judgment. We want to take a little time here to focus on accountability and responsibility, particularly with respect to their roles in an environment that nurtures ethical judgment and the promotion of ethical culture.[6] We suggest that focusing on accountability systems can be like focusing on rules and procedures rather than on judgment—that is, it can be more like focusing on the domain of a code of conduct than on the domain of a code of ethics.

accountability *the requirement to justify decisions in terms of the delegated powers and authority of one's role*

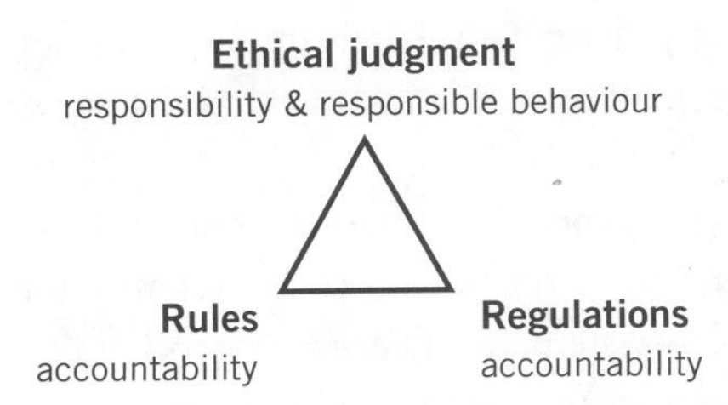

Figure 10.2 Indispensability of judgment

A first reaction to an ethical failure or breach or shortcoming is often "We need more regulations." It need not be a matter of trains literally running off the rails, as it was for Amtrak in the United States in the 1990s, where the causes of whatever ill effects had been occurring were seen to be largely ethical. Train drivers' lack of judgment and attempts to thwart some procedures resulted in more than one terrible accident. The response from the organization was to try to install new mechanical devices and tougher rules and regulations on drivers' behaviour.[7] In short, the organization's approach was to try to make the "dead man brake" foolproof. And, of course, with its focus only there, the remedy was bound to fail. The point is that rules, regulations, and mechanical fixes cannot do the job of replacing judgment. They cannot replace judgment any more successfully in matters of ethics than in matters of technical expertise and compliance. They cannot remedy all behavioural difficulties. Focusing on such things fits with a view that if we can just get the procedures, rules, equipment, and hardwiring right and get people to comply with these requirements, then we will not have these difficulties any longer.

The attraction of such a view is clear. It implies that a straightforward, often reasonably quick and certain remedy can be produced to handle a recognizable difficulty. It also fits nicely into any accountability or compliance regime. The difficulty is that in many situations that are ripe for ethical failure or in which there are ethical shortcomings or issues to be addressed, mechanical fixes very often simply do not work. And, worse than that, such fixes sometimes make matters worse. We are certainly not the first to point out that general rules cannot handle all cases. This is what Aristotle had in mind with the notion of "equity."[8] It amounts to the necessity of judgment making a correction to a rule—not because there is something wrong with the rule, but because of the generality of the rule, which will necessarily make it inappropriate to some cases that it would seem to govern. Trying to accommodate, or replace, equitable judgment with additional rules simply will not work.

Accountability is a very important notion these days. Serious concerns about accountability have developed in areas where, not all that long ago, "accountability" did not receive even a mention. People in various roles—employees, employers, directors, managers, CEOs, professionals, academics, and so on—are held accountable. It used to be that, for better or worse, people in director or managerial (or academic) positions were simply trusted to get the job done. There were serious problems. We will return to this briefly below.

Accountability systems—and, in general, a focus on accountability—signal a diminution of an environment of trust. Again, this is for better or worse. Accountability systems focus on various elements of job requirements. They identify these and keep track of performance in the various areas. In part, such systems are historical in that they keep track of who did what when. People have to sign off. This can make for clearer lines about where the buck stops and who will be liable for what.

Table 10.2 Accountability versus responsibility

Accountability	Responsibility
Historical track	Proactive
Check the box	"Take responsibility for"
Reveals liability	Discretion
Focus on process and procedure	Ethical empowerment, ethical authorization

Accountability requirements not only keep account of who does what; they also define what activities, decisions, and so on are to be kept track of. They have to do this. We are not accountable for *everything*. Accountability systems not only keep account; they also declare what is to be accounted for and what counts. They define those activities and decisions for which people are to be held accountable, and they themselves set standards: "You are expected to do this, this, this, and this, and you are to sign off after having done them." In this respect, accountability systems declare baselines. They define the problem (if there is one), and more importantly, they set the parameters for identifying the remedy or improvement and for measuring these things: "In the name of X (say, "satisfying your job requirements" or "excellence in performing your function in the organization"), it is these things that count. We are going to count them and hold you accountable accordingly."

To hold people—or institutions—accountable for things, the things must be declared, the methods of counting must be specified, and a timetable must be introduced. "Inputs," "outcomes," "milestones," "key performance indicators," "metrics," "productivity," "quality check," "schedule," and "timetable": these are some of the notions that apply. Time frames become important. For example, the people in the "materials procurement" section are accountable for ordering, paying for, and sending out to the appropriate departments the materials that those departments need. These people can keep records and can show the incomings and outgoings over a specified period, say three months. We can see not merely that there was no fraud, but also that there is efficiency in the operation in terms of what and how much they are ordering and what and how much is being distributed to the departments of the organization. We might also have in place an accounting requirement for how the people are spending their time. The idea is the same: we need to see evidence of inputs and outcomes—and perhaps the procedures followed—over a specified period of time.

Accountability systems do not sit very well with the creation and nurturing of good judgment. They keep track of and report what people are doing—they keep track of those declared items that have been specified and are now countable, the identified items that are produced, or the identified procedures that are followed. They establish and then keep track of the norm. By and large, accountability systems fail to look at, let alone pay recognition to, anything else. And it is precisely in the "anything else" basket that "excellence" will belong. If we have become preoccupied with prescribing, recording, and counting the ordinary, and with defining procedures for doing these things, then there is little opportunity for even tolerating, let along promoting, the extraordinary.

Here, an argument might extend further: in defining the norm, defining what is to be regarded and what is not, the declaration certainly *prescribes* those activities and, in effect, *proscribes* others (or, at the least, offers no encouragement or incentive to engage in them): "Your brief is to make widgets. You are to produce however many of them you can, and this will be recognized. This recognition will play a part in whatever promotions, benefits, and remuneration you are to receive in the organization." Under this regime, when you are giving an account of your achievements, as well as your job description, within the organization, this must all be referable to your widget production. The prescription to make widgets offers incentive to make them. It also offers disincentive to make anything else. If the business is simply the manufacture of widgets and the accountability regime is aimed only at those whose jobs are hands-on on the assembly line, then this is probably not a bad effect. However, let us suppose that the business is not so clearly defined or that you are considering those whose job descriptions are not as easily specifiable or have a more obviously qualitative aspect to them.

It is a well-known phrase—and the title of numerous articles in management literature—that "what gets measured gets managed." If something cannot be, or for whatever reason is not, measured, then that thing cannot be, or simply is not, managed. The easier and the clearer the measure, the easier and the clearer the management and the management strategy. By and large, other things are simply left by the wayside. They do not count. If the basis on which an evaluation is made is a set of quantifiable criteria that apply to a large range of activities, then this is very attractive. The evaluation itself can become mechanical, and there is no need, and no room, for the exercise of judgment in evaluating anything.

A serious difficulty with such evaluations is that in attempting to evaluate something, strong emphasis is placed on particular specifiable facets of that activity to the exclusion of all others. It also, like other accountability systems, focuses attention *solely* on those facets. Important questions are largely left unanswered; for example,

- Are the criteria we are measuring really relevant to measuring what we are interested in measuring? (This is a central aspect of the general issue of "concept validity.")
- Should we allow them to be the sole criteria?
- In any particular area, is it necessary—and is it possible—to have generic criteria?
- In some particular areas, is it necessary—and is it possible—to have quantifiable criteria?
- Can we legitimately do away with a judgmental element in the evaluation of these areas?

In identifying which activities or results are to count, an accountability system prescribes what activities to undertake. This, too, serves as a prescription: if some activity cannot be done in ways that have countable outcomes over a short period of time, then, inasmuch as it falls outside the accountability regime, the activity itself does not count. It is, in this respect, a waste of time and a waste of resources.

Satisfaction of accountability requirements is not all there is to achievement—and certainly not all there is to ethical performance. It is a misfit to try, as organizations typically do, to put accountability systems in the same basket as whatever is directed towards promoting excellence. These are different things.[9] And the worry is that in the respects noted here, accountability systems and promotion of excellence can come into conflict with each other. Accountability systems display excellence in reporting within their terms. They do not show excellence in accomplishment. Accountability systems not only are different from excellence-producing systems; they also can work against promotion of excellence.

Onora O'Neill discusses some of these difficulties in *A Question of Trust*.[10] For the failing trust from the era of managerialism ("Let the managers manage"), the remedy was seen to be provided by increased, and then strict, accountability regimes, with their emphasis on transparency and openness. There are serious difficulties and dangers inherent in this remedy:

- Such requirements (ironically) heighten an incentive of deceit. For example, the more likely you think it is that someone will be looking at the notes you have written, the more careful you will be that those notes reflect what you want those people to see (not at all necessarily the same thing as the thoughts and decision procedures that you actually engaged in).
- Such requirements encourage whitewashing. For example, if the minutes of the meeting are going to be open to public scrutiny, it is more likely that the minutes themselves will be written in a bland and uninformative way: "Discussions were engaged in, and decisions were taken."
- Transparency and openness themselves do not guarantee that people will be informed of what they are supposed to be informed of. For example, the fact that directors own shares in what are conflict-of-interest ways is "revealed" in small print on page 137 of the 300-page annual report in the list of shares held by each director.
- There are the worries (identified above) that go along with "what gets measured gets managed," including a failure to have a look at the big picture or what really matters, which would amount to a more holistic view.

What is called for, according to O'Neill, is something that remedies the defects in managerialism without creating an environment with the defects accompanying the new emphasis on accountability. What is needed is (1) focus on creation of an environment in which those who manage are trust*worthy* (not merely trust*ed*, as in the old managerialism days); and (2) cultivation and encouragement of a climate and wherewithal that produces an exercise of judgment that is *worth trusting*.

Back to Codes

There can be reasons for not empowering, and the reason why the specificity and particular prescriptions of a code of conduct may be desirable is that specific prescriptions may produce uniformity. Two other possible benefits of codes of conduct are these:

- A specific requirement can sometimes take the heat off an employee. Suppose the code of ethics mentions integrity and also some appropriate reference to handling conflicts of interest. Perhaps the code of conduct goes further—removing judgment in this particular situation—and prohibits employees from accepting any gift with a value greater than $20. Now, imagine a scenario where a contractor is offering a Christmas gift of Johnny Walker Black Label scotch. The employee wants to decline the gift. The contractor might say, "What do you think, mate, I'm trying to bribe you? It's a Christmas gift. That's all." Here the employee might simply point out that the code of conduct prohibits taking the gift. That's all there is to it. "It's not that I think you're trying to bribe me. It's just that I'm not permitted to accept gifts."
- A specific requirement can help the organization with respect to public trust: it can make a clear, public statement about the types of organizational values that are important to the organization. It can be a statement about what the organization allows or tolerates or, more likely, what it does not tolerate—that is, what behaviour simply cannot be done. Such a statement can be very important. It can be important throughout the organization, in an organization's interface with its stakeholders, and with the public at large. It can be a clear statement such as "This is what we stand for" or "No, no, no—we will not tolerate *that*." This is more than a public relations matter, but it can also be that as well. We mentioned that in a set-up for ethical empowerment, or authorization, trust must run in two directions. In what we are now discussing, an organization recognizes that trust runs in only one direction: the organization needs the public's trust. Sometimes the device of a clear statement, a specific prescription, can help towards that.

The following points are also important to think about with regard to an organization's creating its codes. First, what are our values? What are the moral values that have particular relevance to and resonance in the activities we engage in? For example (as discussed earlier; see page 223), suppose that we believe that "respect for human life" is an important moral value. If we are a firm of chartered accountants, then, although this remains an important moral value for us personally, it is not relevant in our practice and hence has no place in our statement of values or in our code of ethics. However, if we are a firm of armed security guards, it could be a good idea to express this value because it would be relevant to what we do in our business and would show our awareness of our responsibilities and commitments.

Beginning with the values and principles expressed in the code of ethics, the organization might then consider whether there is need to spell out some of these further and more prescriptively. This, we believe, is the best way to approach the design of a code of conduct. Remember the above example of the insurance company deciding that it is desirable to spell out in this way a particular situation involving honesty.

Professional and Business Codes

Structural differences between professions and businesses distinguish a professional from a business code of ethics.[11] A **professional code** operates throughout a whole profession and sets the standard for its practitioners. In this respect it operates on a monopoly. Furthermore, it also operates on an area of expertise that is known better by the profession itself than by those outside it. Some of the distinguishing features of what it is to be a profession are related to the area of expertise exercised by those people within it. This point is significant in that it furnishes a justification for the profession to police itself (at least partially). With the profession itself being the repository of the requisite expertise, who is in a better position to know what the profession should do? And who could be in a better position to police its activities?

professional code *an established set of principles or rules of behaviour that operates throughout a whole profession and sets the standard for its practitioners*

A **business code**, however, can operate at the level of individual businesses. One business can have one code, and another a different code or no code at all. And businesses with vastly different codes of ethics might even be in competition with each other. By the nature of what it is, however, a professional code takes in everyone who is going to perform a specified activity.[12] The same is true of **industry codes**.

business code *an established set of principles or rules of behaviour that operates at the level of an individual business*

industry code *an established set of principles or rules of behaviour that operates throughout a whole industry and sets the standard for firms and employees within that industry*

Professional and business codes express a moral dimension to the activities of professions and businesses. However, codes are not the whole moral story, even for the individuals who work within them. As already indicated, codes of ethics do not replace or embody all of morality, even for those activities for which they are written. A code of ethics is not a formal apparatus for rendering an individual's conscience unnecessary; it is not a codified conscience. It is a matter of some argument about how much of morality per se is appropriate in a code of ethics.

Content of Codes of Ethics

Beyond having the proper regard for morality per se and beyond giving due recognition to creating an environment of predictability and consistency in the behaviour of its members, what else should an organization consider in determining the content of its code of ethics? Each organization has requirements and values that are particularly appropriate to it, but codes typically contain provisions about the following:

1. a general statement of the values of the organization and its guiding principles
2. definitions of what constitutes both ethical and corrupt conduct
3. competence requirements and professional standards

4. directives on personal and professional behaviour
5. affirmations of fairness, equity, equal opportunity, and affirmative action
6. stipulations on gifts and conflicts of interest
7. restrictions on use of the company's facilities for private purposes
8. guidelines on confidentiality, public comment, whistleblowing, and post-separation use of company information
9. identification of different stakeholders and other interested parties and their rights
10. a commitment to occupational health and safety
11. a commitment to the environment and social responsibility (a broader concern than stakeholders alone)
12. a mechanism for enforcing the code, including sanctions for violations
13. advice on interpreting and implementing the code.

These provisions can be combined or expanded in various ways depending on need. Not all of them are necessary for every business organization, but the list covers the most common concerns. We shall comment only on some of them.

General Statement of Values and Guiding Principles

A general statement of values and guiding principles should commit the organization to ethical principles as foundations for the conduct of its operations and the basis for the other provisions of the code. Levi Strauss and Co. begins its Aspirations Statement thus:

> We all want a company that our people are proud of and committed to, where all employees have an opportunity to contribute, learn, grow, and advance on merit, not politics or background. We want our people to feel respected, [be] treated fairly, listened to, and involved. Above all, we want satisfaction from accomplishments and friendships, balanced personal and professional lives, and to have fun in our endeavours.

This style of values statement is unusual in a code, but it is clearly consonant with the reputation for ethical business that Levi's has built up over 150 years.[13] Values statements, vision statements, or codes express the common values of an organization, so that everybody not only knows where they stand, but knows what everybody else stands for. According to management consultant Lee Edelstein, "a good values statement constitutes the ultimate control system: When everyone agrees on values, you don't need a lot of managers."[14] This sentiment is echoed by John Oertel, president of ME International of Minneapolis:

> When you've got people sharing the same values, you've got what amounts to a built-in quality inspector. It used to be our workers picked up ME's values at the company picnic or on the bowling team. Not now. We're growing. Half our people are new. Society itself is becoming scattered.[15]

Oertel's point is that corporations operating in a morally pluralist society need a code of ethics to act as a unifying device. A code permits the declaration and dissemination of a common set of values and demands behaviour in accordance with them.

Competence and Professional Standards

Matters of standards, competence, and quality require reference to the kind of role—or better, the social rationale or justification—of an activity or business in the society as a whole. As a very rough example, suppose we are constructing a code of ethics for civil engineers as a profession. We should ask what the social rationale is for that profession. Let us suppose that the answer is to build safe bridges. The answer is not simply "to build bridges." Bridges are no good to society unless they can be crossed safely. If this is so, then something like "provision of public safety" (where this can be spelled out in enforceable terms) belongs in a code of ethics for civil engineers. The general point is that significant elements of a code of ethics do not come after the fact of the activity; they are inherent in it. A code of ethics does not come simply as a result of considering what would be good ways for the profession or the professional to behave. It does not come from asking in the abstract about what the particular profession, as a profession, should demand from its practitioners. Rather, the question can come about by consideration of the basis of the profession as an enterprise that is socially justified.

Personal and Professional Behaviour

Codes of ethics provide guidance especially in cases that present themselves as morally uncertain. A code of ethics can give a clear directive about how to behave. However, there is both a good and a not-so-good aspect to this point. The not-so-good aspect is that a code may assume for people the air of an *ersatz* conscience or may come to be viewed as dictates of morality requiring no further consideration. Another aspect of this is that a code may be seen as covering everything of moral significance that could occur in the behaviour of the organization and its members or staff. This danger, then, is that the code could be taken to replace conscience, to speak with the authority of morality, and to cover all areas of moral difficulty for the people involved. The good aspect of a code that provides guidance in morally unclear situations is related, again, to the desirability of the rule of law. Situations that are recognized as morally unclear are those where responses by individual practitioners could be expected to vary. This could result in a departure from uniform standards of conduct. However, the important point here is that this lack of moral clarity creates a reduced level of predictability for those served by the organization. They would not know what to expect in certain circumstances, and knowing what to expect is itself of considerable value.

For all their affinities with the law, codes differ because they are internally generated and self-regulating in the corporate and the personal sense. In stating organizational values explicitly, a code does not displace a conscience, but it does mean that the individual does not have to rely on conscience alone. An effective code is part of a culture that supports individuals ethically. The code itself can be conscientiously reflected upon, further developed, and modified at the organizational level. As it stands in relation to the conduct of individuals who are members of the organization, it by no means has the status of stone tablets. In this sense, also, it does not replace an individual's conscience, and it does not replace morality or encompass all of morality.

Social Responsibility and the Environment

A code of ethics can specify the social responsibilities of the business—that is, the responsibilities that are assumed towards society in general, not only towards the business's stakeholders and customers. To a great extent, business can set the parameters of those responsibilities. An organization can present a formal statement concerning its responsibility to society and can give formal recognition to the fact that it cannot do everything itself. A business has a limited amount of resources, and through a code of ethics, it can make a statement about the areas in which it is prepared to take social responsibility. For example, the organization might make a formal commitment to reducing pollution while not making any other commitment to the environment. To a point, this is a perfectly acceptable way of operating. The existence of a formal statement gives the organization direction and can also act as a shield against potential claims that the organization is not doing anything in other areas of social concern.

Interpretation, Enforcement, and Sanctions

A professional code is not merely a claim about an ethical commitment of the organization. It must have substance in two ways:

1. The code must actually prescribe or proscribe something that is identifiable. Perhaps this does not sound like much of a requirement on a code, yet it is surprising how many codes fail to meet this requirement. A code cannot merely be a claim that "we're good people, and we'll treat you right." It must say what this kind of treatment amounts to.
2. There must be some sanctions attached to the code. A structure is required so that breaches of a code can be identified and penalties can be imposed. This requires, in addition, that there is a body that has the authority and capability of enforcing sanctions. A code cannot be merely a paper tiger.[16]

It is worth articulating these two requirements further. A code that is too general or vague has virtually no value. A code must say something, and it must operate in an environment in which there is the real possibility of inflicting sanctions on offenders. As not all cases will be black or white, a body to interpret and apply the code is necessary. In this respect, the situation is analogous to a law court. The provisions of a code must be capable both of being observed and of being policed. A code must require something more than what would be illegal anyway: it is not simply a statement that "the law has our wholehearted support." Whatever the purpose of a code of ethics is, it is not simply to affirm the law. Norman Bowie (among others) has suggested that a code introduces a "higher standard" than the law.[17] Whether or not the standard is higher, it is not simply the same as the law.

Also, a code of ethics must not be like fire regulations taped to the back of a door—unread, unintelligible, and unserviceable in time of need. The idea of a code of ethics should be to prevent fires. It should not be consigned to the desk drawer after cursory perusal, but should be a document that is useful in guiding the actions of staff because it embodies the objectives of the business and the considered ways of reaching them.

The code should be of the same importance as a business or corporate plan, as well as part of a vision statement or company credo. In order for a code of ethics to function effectively, its relation to the overall structure and policy of the organization cannot have the character of an appendage. It must be integrated into the organizational structure and mode of operating throughout the organization. The presence of a code of ethics and the central features of its content must be part of the ethos of the organization. The credo of Johnson & Johnson (discussed in chapter 5) illustrates this point. So, too, does the code of Levi Strauss.

We have suggested that for "rule of law" reasons (among others) a code of ethics is desirable. Those reasons are closely related to another feature of a code of ethics—namely, that it fosters trust and confidence. The presence of a code of ethics need not foster this atmosphere merely by implying the goodwill or altruism of the profession or business it governs. A strong code of ethics, operating in the environment in which it can flourish, should have more substance than that accorded to it merely by the goodwill of the business or profession. A code of ethics can become integral to the business's infrastructure itself.

Two Brief Stories of Industry Codes

Codes have grown in importance in recent years. Canada has emulated the United States in this. In the United States, there are legislated incentives to develop ethics programs, including codes, in the revised *Federal Sentencing Guidelines for Organizations*, which have applied since 1991. The guidelines give parity to Federal Court sentencing across the United States. In the case of transgressions by organizations and their employees, they allow for lighter sentences, including drastically reduced fines, for corporations that have made concerted efforts to introduce ethics programs into the workplace. They are a "carrot and stick" approach to self-regulation by corporations, primarily in response to amazing accounting and financial failures (Enron, Lehman Brothers). Other formal reactions, in particular the American Competitiveness and Corporate Accountability Act 2002 (the Sarbanes-Oxley Act), require the corporations to which they apply to develop codes of ethics. The adoption by the United States of the Sarbanes-Oxley Act placed pressure on Canadian regulators and Canadian public companies, together with the latter's directors, officers, and advisers, to examine the adequacy of the Canadian corporate governance regime. Regulation in Canada has historically been much more principles based than that in the United States. While this principles-based regulation has led many Canadian companies to have freely developed and adopted formal codes of ethics, regulation in Canada does not require companies to do so.

On 17 September 2002, the president and chief executive officer of the Toronto Stock Exchange (TSX) wrote a letter to the chair of the Ontario Securities Commission (OSC) to the following effect:

> As you know, our Canadian approach has been to set out comprehensive governance guidelines based on the paramouncy of the underlying principles that are involved. We then require that companies disclose the extent of their compliance with the guidelines and explain publicly why they may choose not to follow certain of them. In the U.K., European and Australian markets, a similar principles-based approach is preferred.

> The effect of strong guidelines in combination with mandatory disclosure is to place in the hands of investors the information they require to punish or reward companies, by their trading and pricing choices, for their governance practices.
>
> The American approach, in contrast, has been heavily oriented toward a mandatory reliance with highly detailed legislation, regulation and stock exchange listing requirements, with a much greater emphasis on regulatory enforcement rather than voluntary compliance.
>
> The U.S. legislative and regulatory changes over the last two months seem largely consistent with their past rules-based approach. The appeal of "strong action" in the face of unprecedented problems in their markets notwithstanding, I am convinced that our approach has been the more effective.[18]

As already indicated, codes that are embraced by those they regulate will be more effective than those imposed by governmental direction.[19] As if to give proof to the letter from the OSC president, a significant number of Canadian corporations have indeed implemented organizational codes of ethics not because they have been legislated to do so, but because of pressure from internal and external stakeholders.

The Banking Industry Code of Practice

voluntary code of conduct *a set of non-legislated commitments made by a company or organization to influence or control behaviour in the interest of protecting the industry, its customers, and other stakeholders*

Over the past 15 years, the Canadian Bankers Association (CBA) has adopted several voluntary codes of conduct. A **voluntary code of conduct** is a set of non-legislated commitments made by a company or organization to influence or control behaviour in the interest of protecting the industry, its customers, and other stakeholders. The following voluntary codes of conduct are listed on the CBA's website:

- Code of Conduct for the Credit and Debit Card Industry in Canada (2010): Code of conduct that sets principles for business practices related to the issuance and acceptance of payment cards and operation of payment card networks.
- Cheque Holds (2007): Voluntary commitment—Reduced cheque hold periods.
- Online Payments (2005): Consumer and industry responsibilities related to the use of online payments systems in Canada.
- Canadian Code of Practice for Consumer Debit Card Services (1992, revised 2004): Industry practices and consumer and industry responsibilities related to debit cards.
- Guidelines for Transfers of Registered Plans (1992): What to expect and where to get help when transferring a registered savings plan (RSP) between financial institutions.
- CBA Code of Conduct for Authorized Insurance Activities (2003): Outlines the banks' standards for branch employees offering credit, travel and personal accident insurance with respect to training, disclosure, promotion practices, customer privacy protection and customer redress.
- Principles of Consumer Protection for Electronic Commerce: A Canadian Framework (1999): A guide to protecting customers in online transactions, developed with input from industry, government and consumer groups.

- Model Code of Conduct for Bank Relations with Small- and Medium-Sized Businesses (1994): Model code of conduct for bank dealings with small- and medium-sized businesses. The key elements of the model code are incorporated into individual bank codes.
- Plain Language Mortgage Documents—CBA Commitment (2000): A commitment by Canada's banks to improve readability of residential mortgage documents.
- Undertaking on Unsolicited Services (2002): Six Canadian banks provide consumers with assurances related to the marketing and provision of new unsolicited services and the provision of modified or replacement services.[20]

As noted previously, these voluntary codes of conduct are not legislated and not a mandatory requirement for membership in the Canadian Bankers Association. Member banks have the ability to choose to comply with these codes by signing on them or to adopt different organization-specific codes. Most Canadian banks have their own internally generated codes of conduct in addition to those supported by the CBA.

The importance of these measures in contributing to the robustness of the Canadian banking system should not be underestimated. During the global financial crisis of 2008–9, that robustness served Canada well. The role of codes in building strong institutions is sometimes overlooked. It is easy to do this when times are good, but when the fundamentals of business are put under pressure, the cry goes out for better codes and regulatory frameworks.

These provisions are typical of professional and industry codes. They protect the banking industry as well as its customers and other stakeholders. It is clear that one of the motivators for the development of industry-specific codes of conduct is to pre-empt government legislation, which has the potential to be much more stringent and much less flexible; if business does not self-regulate, government will intervene. Enlightened self-interest in this matter can benefit stakeholders. If, however, there is a real divergence between the actual values of the industry (its de facto code) and the values embodied in a formal code, the imposition of the latter will fail to provide the ethos in which it has practical effect. In such circumstances, it is better for the law to set operating conditions that will ensure compliance.

Clearly, what is needed is a proactive response to the spur of government regulation. The usefulness to business of embracing codes has to be promoted if their effectiveness is to be maximized. This is not a plea for ethical propaganda. In surveying 145 British companies with codes, Walter Manley found that senior management identified 18 major benefits conferred by the adoption of codes of ethics.[21] His research supports the case we have made regarding the benefits of codes for business.

Institutionalizing Ethics

Codes of ethics are not a stand-alone treatment for the problems of organizational ethics. Together with training programs, mentoring, exemplary leadership, and structural incentives for ethical behaviour and disincentives for unethical behaviour, codes form part of the mutually supporting structures of an ethical organization. As we have suggested, they can also be an excellent starting point in the process of reviewing the values of a business and devising other structures necessary for the development of an ethical climate.

There will always be temptations for people to do the wrong thing. Sometimes these temptations can be removed or made less attractive by a system of incentives and disincentives. Such organizational strategies are ways of institutionalizing ethics. This involves focusing on the ethics of the organization and what its members perceive its values to be, rather than on individual moral probity. As James Waters puts it, "Rather than ask 'What was going on with those people to make them act that way?' we ask, 'What was going on in that organization that made people act that way?'"[22] This is the question that needs to be answered in order to see why people who are morally decent in their private lives behave in unacceptable ways at work.[23] It is a question that organizations need to answer in order to create an ethical climate in which staff can develop professional excellence and shun improper conduct.

This is not to suggest that there are just two types of organizational culture: an ethical one, which produces good employees, and an unethical one, which produces bad ones. There is no blueprint for an ethical organization, and Waters's point is that the normal operations and structures of an organization can unintentionally give rise to unethical behaviour. For example, while role modelling and mentoring are important means for initiating new employees into an organization, they can also be used to induct people into unethical practices. Similarly, a strict hierarchy that allows an employee to report only to an immediate superior can prevent adequate feedback about the growth of unethical practices. A corporation that has successfully implemented many of these mechanisms for developing and sustaining an ethical culture is Honeywell.

CASE 10.1: Honeywell—An Ethical Culture

As a corporation based in the United States, Honeywell falls under the *Federal Sentencing Guidelines*, but its practice nevertheless exemplifies how organizations can take ethics seriously. Honeywell clearly states its values; takes ethical leadership seriously; makes knowledge of ethics part of the normal expectations of all employees; audits this knowledge as well as the practice of ethics; requires reporting of code violations and provides support and feedback for those reporting; and imposes penalties for violations.

Honeywell's Code of Business Conduct comes with a "Message from the Chairman of the Board and Chief Executive Officer." It explains that while observance of the code is mandatory, it cannot be comprehensive and does not replace common sense or conscience. It also warns that unethical conduct can sometimes arise from good but mistaken intentions. It stresses that "[i]n the conduct of Honeywell business, observance of the law and strict adherence to company policies and practices are requirements without exception. We clearly want to succeed, but never at the expense of our integrity. In everything we do, our ethics and our values must be the first consideration in our minds." In other words, there is no room here for mixed messages from management. The code comes with a card that employees are required to sign to indicate their commitment to observance of its principles.

Because of the *Federal Sentencing Guidelines*, it is now common for US corporations to include ethics compliance in management auditing, and this is the case at Honeywell. In the last quarter of each year, the external auditors obtain from managers at each level of the organization a certificate that "confirms that they and their key employees understand and comply with [ethics] policies."[24] Managers are held accountable for ethical leadership.

The code contains a set of "Honeywell Behaviors" along with a summary of how these behaviours should be applied to major stakeholder groups. This effectively serves as a statement of Honeywell's values. It is divided into sections that are clearly labelled for quick accessibility, and it includes anecdotal examples of employee behaviours referred to as "Integrity in Action". It should be difficult for an employee to plead ignorance of Honeywell's ethics policies.

Within the code, options for reporting violations are given. Employees may report to a manager or supervisor, a Human Resource representative, Integrity and Compliance Representatives or Business Conduct Leaders, a member of the Legal Department or Global Security, a member of the Integrity and Compliance Office, the Local Honeywell formal complaint, grievance processes, or through the Integrity and Compliance Helpline or email address. These options make reporting of ethical failure less like snooping and more the routine expectation of a good employer, which Honeywell insists it is. It goes some way to removing the problem of whistleblowing while building employee confidence in the support of the organization if the employee acts conscientiously.

Discipline for breaches of the code includes cautions, suspensions, and dismissal. Such discipline applies not only to direct breaches of the code, but also to situations in which "circumstances reflect a lack of supervision or diligence by a violator's superiors in enforcing Honeywell's policies"; in which a supervisor has directly or indirectly retaliated against an employee who suspects a violation of the code; and in which employees deliberately fail to report violations or withhold information.

Ethics evaluation of managers by subordinates and peers as well as superiors is part of the strategy for entrenching ethics into corporate life.

Honeywell exemplifies support of an ethical culture that goes beyond the minimum. The *Federal Sentencing Guidelines*[25] have been treated by some corporations as a checklist to be gone though by their lawyers: draw up a code, have employees sign it, have the CEO give an annual address on ethics, and the matter is taken care of. In other words, although such external pressures can offer some incentive to develop ethics programs, they can also lead to mere conformism[26] or to a minimalism that has nothing to do with ethics and everything to do with insuring against a heavy sentence in the event of failure to comply.

Some of the mechanisms advocated for developing and sustaining an ethical culture are publicly stated commitments to ethical practices emanating from top management: establishing an ethics officer or committee; ethics training programs for all staff at induction and updating this training periodically; channels for internal reporting of unethical conduct; and rewards (never penalties) for ethical behaviour and penalties (never rewards) for unethical behaviour, even if it improves the bottom line.[27] The main point here is to send an unambiguous message to all employees that what is expected of them is ethical behaviour first and last. There should be no hidden agenda about results at any cost. The expectations of employees should match those of the organization. This means that staff are not placed in situations where competitive pressures can motivate unethical conduct. It also means making moral decisions collegially whenever possible, rather than placing ethical burdens on the shoulders of individuals.[28] This ensemble of measures to support an ethical culture in an organization has the virtue of sustaining an open and sharing ethos that is self-correcting.[29]

Review Questions

1. Why might a business want to develop a code of ethics?
2. What would be ways of introducing and maintaining systematic attention to good ethical decision-making by those people in an organization who are authorized to make such decisions? What "resources" could be available to these people?
3. What are the limits on codes of ethics? What won't they do?

Suggested Websites

Canadian Bankers Association, Voluntary Commitments and Codes of Conduct:
http://www.cba.ca/en/consumer-information/43-rights-responsibilities/78-voluntary-commitments-and-codes-of-conduct.

Canadian Bar Association, Code of Professional Conduct:
http://www.cba.org/cba/activities/code/.

Canadian Medical Association, Code of Ethics:
http://policybase.cma.ca/dbtw-wpd/PolicyPDF/PD04-06.pdf.

Toronto Stock Exchange Employee Code of Conduct:
http://www.tmx.com/en/pdf/TSXGroupEmployeeCodeOfConduct.pdf.

Treasury Board of Canada Secretariat, Values and Ethics Code for the Public Service:
http://www.tbs-sct.gc.ca/pubs_pol/hrpubs/tb_851/vec-cve-eng.asp.

11

The Environment

Chapter Outline

How should corporations go about protecting the environment from damage caused by their operations? The question sounds simple, and in the case of rogue organizations, so might be the answer—"Don't do it; don't damage the environment!"—but for corporations that try to work within community standards, answers are not always easy or simple. If they were, then major corporate headaches, such as the legacy of environmental contamination left on Marinduque, a small island in the Philippines, by Canadian mining firm Placer Dome, could be solved with a plan and an aspirin. Barrick Gold Corp., Canada's largest gold-mining firm, has been left the pollution problem by its forebear, Placer Dome, which it acquired in 2006. Three decades of operation on Marinduque have badly contaminated groundwater and seen 200 million tons of mine waste dumped into Calancan Bay. Approximately 80 square kilometres of mine waste has decimated coral beds and devastated fish habitats. The toxic mine waste continues to flow into the Boac and Mogpog rivers every time it rains. The question is whether a stronger sense of responsibility to the environment would have prevented this problem from arising in the first place. Specifically, if Placer Dome had taken responsibility in the latter half of the twentieth century instead of waiting for government regulators to act, would remediation have been necessary now? What does hindsight tell us: that Placer Dome was morally blind or morally negligent? Perhaps ignorance and indifference were to blame for belated recognition of a problem. For much of the last century, an attitude prevailed that the solution to pollution was dilution, as the historical discharge of effluent by Halifax and Victoria into their respective adjacent oceans illustrates. Behind the Marinduque legacy of contamination is a story of ethical failures that any number of actors, from governments and senior managers to shareholders and community leaders, could have addressed but did not recognize or think it their business to do anything about.[1] Even small-scale failures accumulate, and now there is a large problem for a corporation and its stakeholders.

Closer to home, there exist an estimated 10,000 abandoned mine sites in Canada that, if not properly cleaned up, could pose environmental health risks to neighbouring communities. The fundamental lesson here is that the problem would not arise in the first place if environmental consequences were given sufficient attention and all employees were informed that their responsibilities in this area were serious.

There is no question about whether business has some responsibility for the environment. Laws require employers to provide safe work places and businesses to offer goods and services that are safe to consumers and the public. Industries must comply with waste and pollution regulations. There are issues that arise for business in connection with the environment. The first is whether businesses that ignore environmental factors in their operations are sustainable. This is a prudential issue rather than a moral one, but ethical questions are not far behind. Too often, however, these are couched in the familiar terms of fiduciary duties to shareholders. Once prudential and fiduciary obligations are accounted for, are there any ethical matters left? Does business have ethical responsibilities towards the environment in addition to prudential, fiduciary, and legal ones? And if so, what are the nature and extent of the responsibilities?

Recall Milton Friedman's objections to business engaging in socially responsible activity. First, such activity diverts profits from shareholders. It is up to them to decide how to spend their money on worthy causes, not for the directors of their corporations to do this for them. Second, business should not trespass on the role of governments. Governments have the role of setting social policy agendas, and they have the mandate of voters to do so. Business has neither. It is for governments to set the legal frameworks in which business operates and for business to generate wealth within the laws and regulations established by governments. Social responsibility is not a part of the obligations of business.

We repeat these arguments because they have figured and continue to figure in the positions of corporations that wish to reject a role in environmental protection. These corporations are, as it happens, out of date. The rise of the *No Logo*[2] attitude, a skepticism about corporate citizenship, and genuine concern for social responsibility, along with shareholder activism and the greater spread of share ownership, mean that directors have a more complex duty to the owners of listed companies than 40 years ago. Many activities once thought extraneous to business purposes are now an ordinary part of commercial enterprises.

Even Friedman would have allowed as exceptions socially responsible actions that support the reputation of a corporation and hence its capacity to earn profits. If environmentally responsible conduct can enhance a company's reputation, then it has added value to the shareholders' investments. Levi's, Saturn cars, Proctor and Gamble, Johnson & Johnson, and The Body Shop have all benefited from good reputations. Then there are cases of damaged reputations because brand names came to be associated with socially irresponsible practices: Nestlé, Shell, Nike, Union Carbide, Exxon, and Alcoa are a few examples. In 1990, McDonald's had to protect its reputation by replacing its polystyrene hamburger boxes with paper packaging. There was no clear scientific evidence that paper was more environmentally friendly than plastic, but consumer sentiment was against polystyrene and McDonald's took a precautionary strategy and changed its packaging. Because reputation is valuable, it is both a strength and a weakness. It can be a mark of trust in the marketplace, but it also exposes a company to activism as well as customers' attitudes and beliefs. In 2003, for example, an activist group called People for the Ethical Treatment of Animals (PETA) organized a boycott of Kentucky Fried Chicken (KFC) outlets. By placing pressure on the point of sale, the group hoped to improve the conditions in which chickens were held by KFC suppliers. The KFC brand, like other fast-food chains, was under pressure from lawsuits brought by litigants claiming that fast food had contributed to their obesity. In other words, PETA took advantage of the public mood about fast food to leverage better conditions for chickens, and the KFC brand name was the lever.[3] So, far from being a diversion of shareholders' money into causes unrelated to the purposes of the business, socially responsible action may enhance the bottom line. And neglect of such action might well weaken the performance of the business, especially if competitors have taken a proactive position.

As for Friedman's objection about business intruding into the domain of governments, it is clear that there is no clear boundary to be crossed here.[4] Social concerns—including environmental issues—are now very much within the responsibilities of business. The example of the potential effects on reputation is an indication of this.

The Canadian public feels strongly about environmental issues, whether from dissatisfaction with the nation's environmental record or from a concern for the future.

However, the strength of that feeling does not make the environment an ethical issue or an issue for business.

Richard De George suggests that some very important matters are for political, rather than moral, decision-making.[5] We touched on De George's point in chapter 5. In some areas, although regulation would not be morally objectionable, neither is it morally necessary. Some matters can be matters of general preference without being matters of morality, and, De George suggests, sometimes it is permissible to legislate because of preference. It can be a matter of politics rather than ethics. This is an important point: not all preferences—even strongly felt ones—are matters of morality, and some things that are not matters of morality should not therefore necessarily be considered as beyond governmental interference or regulation. The enthusiasms and passions of individuals do not make their concerns ethical issues. Conversely, however, just because business groups are uninterested in environmental issues or are immersed in their own values does not mean that the environment is not an ethical issue.

Business hostility to the environment is difficult to understand in the light of the history of industrialism. Among the great number of articles and books on the fate of the environment under industrial capitalism, one of the most interesting discussions has been over the "tragedy of the commons"—the fate of commonly held property or resources. Where things belong to everybody, it is often the case that they belong to nobody, and nobody expends sufficient time on their care and upkeep. Or, worse still, they are regarded as "free" resources to be used at will, as in the case of manufacturers who pollute the air and water because there is no "owner" to harm in the process. This is, of course, freeloading on a huge scale, and it is puzzling that some people cannot recognize this as a moral problem. Ultimately such individual opportunism is harmful to all. As Garrett Hardin observed nearly two generations ago, its cumulative effects end up destroying everyone.[6]

This has long been foreseeable. In 1833, W.F. Lloyd observed that cattle grazing on common land in England were leaner than those grazing on private property. The feed on the commons was poorer because of overgrazing. Over time, each farmer had increased his herd by only one or two cows—not much for each individual and not enough in each case to make a difference to the commons. But the combined effect of such increases in individual herds meant the destruction of the commons. The message here is clear: the earth's resources are finite, and the demands already made on them by human populations have produced changes in the atmosphere, the oceans, and the soils.

The exercise of even small economic liberties can have devastating social and environmental effects. DuPont, for example, used to dump 10,000 tons of chemical waste each month into the Gulf of Mexico from its West Virginia plant because it was cost free. Even with this level of dumping, the contribution to the pollution of the gulf would be negligible. But if every plant along the gulf acted in this way, the gulf would suffer the same fate as the commons.[7]

The environment is not a source of "found" resources. While the environment does not "belong" to anyone, this does not mean that people's rights are not violated by excessive exploitation and abuse. Our ethical obligations are not confined to privately owned property. Someone in the present or in a future generation will have to bear the cost of exhausted soils, depleted energy resources, or pollution. When old coal-fired power stations generated electricity, not all the costs were included in the bills consumers paid. There was no charge for the atmosphere, for the greenhouse gases, or for the fallout on neighbours.[8] With nuclear energy, will the same attitudes prevail? Will the costs of safe disposal of radioactive waste be reflected in the cost of electricity? There are no free lunches: someone has to pick up the bill, and it really should be the "user." The true costs, including the environmental costs, of doing business should be reflected in the price of the goods and services produced. Prices should include a component for social costs and not just the private costs—wages, raw materials, taxes, interest charges, and rents—of production. Then we could make informed economic choices about whether we could really afford some products and whether we would be prepared to live well at the expense of others in the present and perhaps in the future. If it is not to be the user who pays, we must recognize that someone must. Where and upon whom those costs fall is a question of justice.

The care of the environment, then, is a matter of ethics, even if not all environmental issues raise ethical questions. Still, we need to be clear about the nature of environmental ethics. To whom is business ethically accountable for environmental decisions? To nature or to humanity? To future generations? Answers to these questions divide into two broad groups: the humanistic and the naturalistic.

The Humanistic Argument

The first kind of answer is that the environment is an ethical matter because without a clean environment, human health will be harmed, and without a natural world with a diversity of species, human life will be diminished. Similarly, without a stock of non-renewable resources for future generations, their lives will be of a poorer quality than our own. This is the anthropocentric or humanistic argument. It is clear that chemical companies that pollute streams and bays with mercury have a direct influence on the food chain, one that can lead to ill health in humans. Factories that pollute the air can cause respiratory problems in young children and elderly people. When business pollutes, there is a cost to be paid, whether it be financial, in health, or in amenity. This payment is a subsidy from the person who pays it to the business, and such an imposition is unfair. Such instances of environmental free-riding have been relatively common and illustrate the anthropocentric argument about environmental ethics.

William Blackstone argued that everyone has a right to a livable environment and that therefore others have an obligation to allow the free enjoyment of this right.[9] A person cannot flourish or develop potential without an environment that provides clean air and water, natural beauty, and so on. The right to these overrides considerations of property and economic development. This argument is an extension of Immanuel Kant's requirement that one should treat people with respect. If respect for persons entails respect for those things that are necessary for their well-being, then we must respect nature.

The difficulty with Blackstone's position is that it does not tell us how we are to live and still respect nature. If we do not use the resources of the earth, then we might be showing a lack of respect to persons who, as a consequence, will live a diminished life. There has to be a compromise.

The problem lies in brokering a compromise between the green movement and business and industry. Ultimately, economics bites, but if compromise means waiting until either the environment is degraded or industry shuts down, then the outcome is more in the nature of an accident than a decision. A clear instance of this is the gradation of difficulties attending the introduction of a carbon emissions trading scheme (ETS) in Canada.[10] The implementation of an effective ETS across Canada is hampered by the uncertain regulatory environment created by the jurisdictional inconsistencies and conflicts across provinces and between the provincial and the federal governments.The Canadian government originally wanted to cut carbon emissions in accordance with the Kyoto Protocol.[11] Many in business thought it would be a bad idea unless other countries—particularly China and the United States—also signed on to ETS provisions because Canada's emissions are such a small percentage of the total that we would impoverish ourselves for no appreciable result. Many in the scientific community, on the other hand, thought the government's proposals did not go far enough in reducing emissions. With the change in federal government and Canada's withdrawal from the Kyoto agreement, plans for a federally mandated ETS were deferred. Then, with the global financial crisis, the pressure to defer the introduction of an emissions trading scheme became too great and the government further delayed its introduction.[12] Such is the difficulty of getting anything like agreement on this policy.[13]

The Naturalistic Argument

The second kind of answer is that nature has intrinsic value. As but one part of nature, humans have no dominion over it, no unqualified right to harm or extinguish the lives of plants and animals or to destroy the ecosystems that support them. The right to exploit the resources of the planet is qualified by the gravity of reasons that support the inherent right of nature to our respect. With the world's population growing alarmingly and placing demands on non-renewable resources as all nations seek a share of the lifestyle of the developed world, the problems of resource and pollution management are now critical. But environmental ethicists want more than protection for economically valuable and life-sustaining resources. They want respect for the natural world, an ecological or naturalistic ethic.

Michael Hoffman, for example, believes that placing a humanistic value on the environment provides no protection in the long run. If business is convinced of the validity of the slogan "Good environmental ethics is good business," then protection of the environment comes to depend on the profitability of responsible practices. It is the same potentially misleading promise of the parallel slogan, "Good ethics is good business": there is the suggestion that an ethical position is just one more way to make a profit. It would follow that if environmental irresponsibility were better business, then one ought to take that position—good business being the relevant standard for all policy. But neither ethics nor environmental care is cost free. According to Hoffman, it is important that the natural world be valued for the right reason, and that involves according the environment the kind of intrinsic respect we give to human beings.[14]

A number of writers, led by Peter Singer, have argued that as sentient beings, animals have interests that deserve consideration by humans. To disregard those interests is "speciesism," an analogy with racism. Speciesism "is a prejudice or attitude of bias in favour of the interests of one's own species and against those of members of other species."[15] Of course, the problem here is that racism is unjust discrimination within a species, whereas speciesism is one species making use of another. It is a genuine question whether the term "discrimination" can be used in relation to the way that humans treat animals. To deny equal consideration to people on the grounds of irrelevant differences such as ethnicity or skin colour is discrimination precisely because we all belong to the same species. To deny equal consideration to animals on the grounds that they are not human is not so obviously unjust. Singer argues that because animals can suffer and feel pleasure, it is unwarranted to give consideration to humans at the expense of the pain (and pleasure?) of animals. He does not require that animals be treated equally with humans, just that their interests should receive equal consideration. How one gives equal consideration without giving equal treatment is not clear. Singer nonetheless makes an important point about the intrinsic value of animals: if they are the kind of beings that can suffer and feel pleasure, then our attitudes to them are not the only things that count morally. Cruelty is reprehensible whether inflicted on humans or animals. Almost 500 years ago, Thomas More condemned the widely accepted sport of hunting:

> [I]f you want to see a living creature torn apart under your eyes, then the whole thing is wrong. You ought to feel nothing but pity when you see the hare fleeing from the hound, the weak creature tormented by the stronger. . . . Taking such relish in the sight of death, even if only of beasts, reveals . . . a cruel disposition.[16]

The case for respecting animals and their habitats is easier to make than that for inanimate nature. Humanity is enriched by animals.[17] Domestic pets and animals in the wild are loved and valued, even by meat eaters, graziers, and poultry farmers, just as forests and gardens are loved by wheat farmers and rice growers. The world is a lesser place when it loses a species of plant or animal. But do we weep for such losses? And what of inanimate nature? What intrinsic rights does nature have? Most of the universe is cold, dark, and lifeless. Should these desolate places count ethically?

Imagine that we could conduct an experiment that would reveal some fundamental facts about the universe. This experiment would be very dramatic but completely safe to humans. It would involve crashing one of the moons of Jupiter into the surface of the planet. What reasons could there be against such an experiment? Would it matter that Jupiter had one less moon? Would we even need to justify this experiment in terms of the value of the knowledge to be gained? In what possible ways could this experiment be unjustifiable? Imagine another scenario much closer to home. Say we have devised a way to produce electricity that is a cheap and safe replacement for fossil fuel generators. It will save hugely on carbon dioxide emissions, but alas will produce a large quantity of nuclear waste if it is widely adopted. Thankfully, we can solve the waste problem through using the latest generation of space vehicles to ferry the waste to the moon. This should not be a problem because the waste dumps will be on the dark side of the moon, and not visible to Earth. What possible objection could there be to such a plan? We could dispose of our waste on an uninhabitable space object and forget all about it. As it is, tonnes of debris fall every year on the moon, so adding a bit more from earth will not matter.

An appeal to intrinsic value might cause us to pause before destroying Jupiter's moon or dumping on ours. But how can we justify such a valuation? Is it just an appeal to the strength of our preferences that makes us claim intrinsic value? Is it not rather that what is valuable is what we value? If we were dealing with animals, we might appeal to Singer's argument and the extension of regard for animal life to the protection of the habitat on which animals depend. In short, appealing to the intrinsic worth of inanimate nature only seems to work with people who share one's appreciation of nature. Or does it? If a person defaced a work by Rembrandt or Picasso, would we not be shocked and saddened? When the Taliban destroyed Buddhist statues with dynamite in Afghanistan, were not all decent people horrified? One does not have to be an art lover or a Buddhist to be appalled by vandalism and wanton destruction, just as one does not have to be an animal rights campaigner to react to cruelty to animals. We can understand barbarity and appreciate that a good is being destroyed even if we do not participate in the full meaning of that good. That is how it is with the moons of Jupiter and with our moon. We do not destroy the environment wantonly and should not cause major disturbances without the strongest reasons for doing so. There is a good even in the things we do not see, and the life of humans is diminished when species, habitats, and even cold and lifeless rocks in space are the victims of rapacity. We should not deface our heritage, but enhance it for transmission to future generations.

Growth

An ethically responsible policy towards the environment must deal with the problem of growth. There are strong arguments that the earth cannot sustain present growth patterns, let alone extend them to cover more of the world's population. Affluence is the problem.[18] Yet, in times of recession, growth is the watchword of those seeking employment and profits. Whether we must have economic growth or can develop a sustainable steady-state economy are questions that cannot be answered by an ethicist. One can simply take note of the increasing demand on fossil fuels and the polluting effects these will continue to have unless curbed, and of the increasing demands of expanding economies in China and Southeast Asia and the pressure these will place on known energy reserves and arable land. It hardly makes sense to talk of globalization in business and restrict this to profits and growth. Collateral effects such as rising expectations, limited resources, and pollution must also be considered. Moreover, we should not take the solutions of conventional economists at face value. Growth statistics do not tell us much aside from the size of the economy. Although Canada's gross domestic product more than doubled in the 1980s, poverty and unemployment increased, and real wages stagnated.[19] Public infrastructure declined as railway services were cut back, hospital waiting lists increased, and the gap between rich and poor widened. Growth benefited relatively few. The same is true of the United States, which on one index of economic well-being that takes account of social and environmental factors had, by 2008, become worse off after years of economic growth.[20]

Intergenerational Issues

No generation has an unfettered right to use the world's resources for its own advantage without regard for the fate of future generations. Because the possibility of such misuse exists, it is something that must concern business, not only in a strategic sense but ethically.

But why should we assume responsibilities that no other generation has had to assume? Why is there a moral obligation here? John Rawls argued that we should adopt a "just savings principle" or "an understanding between generations to carry their fair share of the burden of realizing and preserving a just society."[21] Each generation should preserve the social and economic gains it has received, and put aside for the next generations what it would consider fair to have received from its predecessor.[22] We should leave the world in no worse a state than we found it. After all, that is what we should be grateful for from our parents. This has implications for the use of non-renewable resources and energy, the production of waste and pollution, and the release of potentially harmful substances into the environment.[23]

The following case illustrates some of these issues.

CASE 11.1: Carson and DDT

Rachel Carson achieved enduring fame for her classic study of the effects of the miracle pesticide, DDT, on the environment. That work, *Silent Spring*, was published in 1962 and had such an impact that DDT was progressively banned around the world. One of Carson's main allegations against DDT was that when it entered the human food chain, it was carcinogenic. These claims gained wide currency, and many scientists backed the banning of DDT. The problem is that the claims were not supported by evidence, and there has been in consequence a backlash against Carson. The main charge of the critics is that the banning of DDT allowed mosquitoes bearing the malaria parasite to spread unchecked. Had DDT been available, the health and lives of millions of people could have been spared.[24]

Michael Crichton, author of *Jurassic Park*, was one of Carson's critics. He attacked the environmental movement for being quasi-religious (working from faith, ideology, and passion) rather than empirical (getting the data and interpreting them scientifically). According to Crichton, only genuine scientists are in a position to make sound judgments about environmental policy. Proper policy debates are not possible with people who will not accept facts. You cannot talk somebody out of a religious position, asserted Crichton, and that is exactly the position knowledgeable people find themselves in when confronted with the unshakeable beliefs of ideological environmentalists.

continued . . .

> I can tell you that DDT is not a carcinogen and did not cause birds to die and should never have been banned. I can tell you that the people who banned it knew that it wasn't carcinogenic and banned it anyway. I can tell you that the DDT ban has caused the deaths of tens of millions of poor people, mostly children, whose deaths are directly attributable to a callous, technologically advanced western society that promoted the new cause of environmentalism by pushing a fantasy about a pesticide, and thus irrevocably harmed the third world. Banning DDT is one of the most disgraceful episodes in the twentieth century history of America.
>
> . . . I can tell you that second hand smoke is not a health hazard to anyone and never was, and the EPA [Environmental Protection Agency] has always known it. I can tell you that the evidence for global warming is far weaker than its proponents would ever admit. I can tell you the percentage of the US land area that is taken by urbanization, including cities and roads, is 5%. I can tell you that the Sahara desert is shrinking, and the total ice of Antarctica is increasing. I can tell you that a blue-ribbon panel in *Science* magazine concluded that there is no known technology that will enable us to halt the rise of carbon dioxide in the 21st century.[25]

Crichton's argument at its root is not anti-environmentalist; rather, it is the stance that ideology must not be allowed to trump science when the decisions being made or the legislation being enacted has an impact on the environment. One criticism of Crichton's argument is that scientific investigation can often lag behind the adoption of new products and processes that may affect the environment. Some time may be required for the negative environmental effects to emerge that initiate scientific investigation. This is the case with genetically modified foods. Proponents point to the already evident capacity of genetic modifications to increase agricultural productivity, to reduce susceptibility of crops to pests and disease, and to lengthen growing seasons. Those who object to the increasing use of genetically modified foods can only do so on the basis of non-scientific or ideological grounds: that genetically modified foods might be dangerous; that it is wrong to manipulate nature, and that dangers exist that we have yet to discover. While it may or may not be true that GM foods may be harmful to the environment or to human health, there currently exists no scientific evidence either way. No long-term scientific studies of the effects of GM foods have so far been completed.

Likewise, in the case of global warming, the detractors from the argument that the production of carbon as a result of human activity is irreversibly altering the planet's climate point to a lack of scientific evidence. The scientific community has been scrambling to provide hard evidence in support of their claims that human activity and the burning of fossil fuels is responsible for climate change. Even as the scientific evidence builds that the earth's climate is indeed changing as a result of human activity, it must be acknowledged that for decades there has been a reluctance of governments and businesses to embrace the possibility of climate change. This reluctance to admit the possibility that climate change may be a real threat existed not just because of the negative economic effects that mandated reduction of carbon output would have had on economies and business performance, but because there was a real or perceived lack of scientific evidence to support the threat of climate change.

In addressing developing issues such as climate change and GM foods, environmentalists have no choice but to rely on ideological arguments until these arguments can be backed up, or disproved, by scientific evidence. Criticisms like Crichton's and the divide that can exist between ideology and science point to a difficulty for business.

Case Questions

1. Should environmental responsibility take the form of specific responses to problems or should it be a commitment to a belief system or ideology?
2. Does business have to subscribe to a package of environmental beliefs in order, say, to reduce waste or to ensure a safe workplace?

It is clear that some environmental groups want nothing less than fundamental social and economic change, and that is a difficult proposition for business to support. This concern is not misplaced. Even reputable green groups make mistakes, and sometimes those mistakes arise from zealotry. The following case shows what can happen.

CASE 11.2: Shell and Greenpeace

Greenpeace and other environmental groups organized a campaign against Shell over the disposal of its obsolete Brent Spar oil rig. The campaign included boycotts of Shell petrol, demonstrations, and publicity offensives. The problem was that Greenpeace was wrong. They mistakenly believed that Brent Spar contained 5,000 gallons of waste oil and protested against its disposal in the North Sea. In the face of sustained public opposition generated by the environmentalists, Shell decided to move the rig to Norway for breakup and disposal. This proved to be not only a more expensive but also a more environmentally hazardous option.

This incident could be instanced as an example of the dangers of knee-jerk responses made on the basis of ideology rather than facts—the kind of reaction that Crichton warned against. It could be seen as an opportunity for a corporation with less than satisfactory systems to change them. Shell did so by changing to triple bottom line reporting (discussed below), aligning its business principles with social and environmental objectives,[26] and thereby projecting a strong image as an ethical and responsible corporation. In 2001, Shell was joint winner of the British Social Reporting Award for its 1999 report.[27]

While the demand for better scientific evidence in environmental decisions, standards, and policies is reasonable in theory, in practice it can take a very long time to produce and interpret such evidence. In cases like the Brent Spar, a less emotional atmosphere in discussing the issues might have produced a more satisfactory environmental outcome. The evidence should have prevailed. Not all environmental issues, however, are like this. In some—the impact of mining on an environment, the planting of genetically modified crops, or the effect of farming on atmospheric conditions—the evidence takes a long time to accumulate and be analyzed, and by then irreversible damage might have been done. This is not to imply that warnings based on environmental ideology all have merit; some may be exaggerated to varying levels while others may be sheer conjecture and eventually be found to have no bearing whatsoever on the quality of the environment. The important lesson here for business is that it must be aware of these warnings and make make its own judgments on how to react to them in light of the lack of scientific validation and the significant public opinion that may be attached to these ideological positions.

The Precautionary Principle

In 1992, the United Nations Conference on Environment and Development was held in Rio. One of the resolutions contained in the Rio Declaration stated,

> In order to protect the environment, the precautionary approach shall be widely applied by States according to their capabilities. Where there are threats of serious or irreversible damage, lack of full scientific certainty shall not be used as a reason for postponing cost-effective measures to prevent environmental degradation.[28]

What is the precautionary principle? The widely quoted Wingspread Statement, drafted in 1998, puts it like this:

> Where an activity raises threats of harm to the environment or human health, precautionary measures should be taken even if some cause and effect relationships are not fully established scientifically.[29]

The precautionary principle asks business to scan the horizon and even to look over it for the unintended harms that might come from its activities. The absence of clearly established scientific proof has often prevented environmental concerns from being taken seriously, but the precautionary principle reverses the burden so that it falls on those who wish to engage in potentially harmful activities.

> In essence, the precautionary principle provides a rationale for taking action against a practice or substance in the absence of scientific certainty rather than continuing the suspect practice while it is under study, or without study.[30]

This is a higher standard than the law in environmental matters. The precautionary principle should be a check on rashness, but reversing the onus of responsibility is not a universal remedy in environmental controversies. Think of the example of DDT: it might have seemed precautionary to ban it, but it was simply wrong to continue that ban when the evidence did not show that it caused cancer and suggested that it might be used without wholesale environmental damage.

The precautionary principle operates in areas where such evidence is absent but there are real concerns about harm. It is meant to serve as a restraint where there is concern but where no causation is yet known to exist. An activity might not be known to damage health, but one might reconsider it or restrict it until concerns are allayed. This kind of thinking is really common sense, but it has been elevated to the status of a principle because those who oppose it ask for scientific proof. Such proof cannot always be produced, so the precautionary principle is now invoked to change the onus of responsibility, sometimes provocatively—"Prove that the activity is not dangerous!" The principle could, however, be usefully extended. It could prompt corporations to ask the following questions. What could go wrong? What systems do we need to ensure that the risk of things going wrong is minimized? What would we do if something did go wrong? What backup facilities and safe exits should we build into this project? Space engineers have learned about safe exits from incidents like the *Challenger* and *Columbia* shuttle disasters, but business needs to think of exit strategies for the public and the environment—not for managers and directors—should a system fail.

The precautionary principle is not cost free and can bring about its own unintended consequences. One critical supporter argues that its widespread introduction would have costs beginning with the introduction and implementation of regulations; it would then have an impact on productivity, wages, and prices; and it would end up diverting money available for other public health priorities.[31] In other words, application of the precautionary principle might end up harming health more than it would protect it. That is what might have happened had the precautionary principle been applied to the banning of DDT. As it was, that pesticide was banned on the basis of scientific evidence, but the case illustrates that one cost of applying the precautionary principle could be the loss of a health-protecting chemical. Just as some toxins reveal themselves only in cumulative effects, so the removal of a useful substance as a precautionary measure can have long-term deleterious effects.

The precautionary principle changes the default position. Instead of requiring a business to determine an acceptable level of risk, it asks whether risky action can be avoided. It encourages the asking of questions from a broader social perspective. While a development such as the genetic modification of foods might present a business opportunity, application of the precautionary principle would pose the question of whether there might not be other ways of making a profit in the food industry. The precautionary principle is an amber light to technology. It warns of a stoppage, whereas a risk assessment weighs the odds of getting through an intersection before the red. Risk assessment can sometimes resemble a green light rather than an amber—proceed with caution. If a new technology has the potential to harm, it is better to re-examine its use rather than to wait and see if the harm eventuates. Genetically modified crops and animals are obvious candidates for the application of the precautionary principle.

Waste or Fertilizer

What happens to the waste material of steel mills, power stations, aluminum smelters, and concrete kilns? Some of it is sold to farmers as fertilizer. It finds a ready market because it sells for much less than traditional fertilizers. The problem is that these products of industrial waste are not tested by agricultural authorities. Their benefits might be short term, and they might even be potentially harmful. This waste does legitimately contain compounds such as nitrogen and magnesium that promote agricultural growth and are found in many fertilizers. The problem resides with the toxic chemicals and heavy metals that accompany these compounds when acquired as industrial waste. The slag from steel mills, for example, contains heavy metals such as chromium, lead, and arsenic. There is weak legislation in Canada, and virtually none in the United States, against labelling such wastes as fertilizer, and they can even be legally labelled as organic. Even where regulation prevents the sale of waste as fertilizer, it can still be sold as soil conditioner.[32] This discovery was shocking to Canadians and Americans alike, but the disposal of industrial waste as fertilizer has been occurring in the less-regulated markets of the United States for years. According to the president of one waste "recycler," "When it goes into our silo, it's a hazardous waste. When it comes out of the silo, it's no longer regulated. The exact same material. Don't ask me why. That's the wisdom of the EPA."[33]

Clearly, the precautionary principle indicates that this is an area that should be more extensively regulated, but if the precautionary principle were applied by the suppliers, they would do their own testing. The question is complicated in this case because producers, like Australian mining giant BHP Billiton, are not the suppliers. BHP has professed ignorance of the fate of its slag, which is marketed by Australian Steel Mill Services. The latter disposes of the material to farmers and there is no deception about its source. Does this absolve BHP of any responsibility to ensure the safe disposal of its waste? Considering the potential costs to BHP Billiton's reputation (Australian Steel Mill Services does not enjoy the same profile) if toxins were to enter the food chain, the precautionary principle could work to the advantage both of producer and the public here.

The following cases illustrate these issues.

CASE 11.3: Dow Chemical's "Blob"[34]

In 1985, an equipment malfunction at the Dow Chemical plant near Sarnia, Ontario, spilled approximately 11,000 litres of a chemical solvent used in dry cleaning called perchlorethyline into the St Clair River. Because perchlorethyline is heavier than water, the chemical pooled into a basketball court–sized mass at the bottom of the river. Once the mass, or "blob" as it came to be known, was discovered, Dow spent over one month and $1 million vacuuming it up, placing it in a protective pond, and recycling the chemicals where possible.

The alarming thing about this incident was not necessarily the spill itself, but the findings subsequent to the chemical analysis of the blob. Perchlorethylene's purpose as a solvent used in the dry-cleaning process is to absorb contaminants so that they can be effectively removed. When spilled into the St Clair River, the perchlorethylene proved its effectiveness by proceeding to absorb a number of chemical contaminants contained in the water and the river sediments. While perchlorethylene is in itself fairly benign, the blob that formed at the bottom of the river contained no fewer than 18 chemicals, including some deadly dioxins.

In 1985, the area near Sarnia referred to as "Chemical Valley" contained 13 major chemical plants producing petrochemicals, plastics, and glass. In the decade from 1975 to 1985, there were 275 reported chemical spills near Sarnia. Dow Chemical was responsible for 11 of these accidental discharges in 1985 alone. While no single one of these chemical spills may have created any significant danger either to the public or to the environment, the formation of the blob and the results of its subsequent chemical analysis illustrate the tendency of chemical pollutants to linger and accumulate. Surely the cautious approach for companies producing hazardous chemicals should be to minimize the risk of any spill occurring, not just because of the dangers posed by the chemical involved in the particular spill, but also because of the unknown dangers that may result from the long-term and/or cumulative effects of multiple discharges emitted from a number of companies clustered together in an industrial complex.

If the scientific evidence eventually supports the cautious approach, then Dow may be storing problems for itself in the future.

CASE 11.4: Alcoa Emissions

In 1996, the US aluminum producer Alcoa, Inc. commissioned a refining incinerator, called a liquor burner, at its plant in Western Australia in order to improve productivity and cut costs. This device burned impurities from aluminum ore but emitted a cocktail of noxious fumes containing benzine, xylene, toluene, and naphthalene.[35] Workers and local residents began to complain about the stink and then about sudden illnesses, unprecedented allergies, increased sensitivity to chemicals, and pitted enamel on cars. Animals began developing unusual diseases. When Alcoa's new publicist, recruited to improve the company's image, complained about the fumes, she was issued with a respirator—to wear in her office.[36]

Alcoa has since bought properties around its plant and had to face inquiries and audits. A precautionary approach would have obviated much of this. Alcoa always knew that there would be some negative reaction to the liquor burner, but it was too sanguine about its own measures. A useful device in this situation would have been to have an environmental "devil's advocate" to put the case against the liquor burner and to challenge the responses of the firm to potential complaints. Alcoa did bring in its chief medical officer from the United States, Professor Mark Cullen of Yale University. Cullen found minimal risk of illness as a result of the plant. "If I had any other view I would recommend the immediate closure of the facility—in line with Alcoa values," he is reported as saying.[37] Fine, but it is not unknown for corporations to bring in their own experts to counter public concerns by creating uncertainty.

Even before extensive investigations and modifications became necessary, Alcoa could have taken a precautionary posture. Andrew Harper, fellow of the Faculty of Occupational Medicine, told the Western Australian parliamentary inquiry that "[t]he level of a given chemical may well be below the safety level defined by government standards, but when the chemical is mixed with others in the body it can be toxic."[38] Given the nature of the toxins emitted—even in small doses—from the Alcoa plant, there was a reason for the corporation to be cautious. At the very least, the company should have been conscious that in seeking to cut the costs of aluminium production, it was imposing social costs on the local residents, many of whom were also its employees. Why did not the social costs of installing the liquor burner rank as high as the economic ones? A more prudent and environmentally proactive course of action might have satisfied the demand to make a profit and the obligation to do so without harming the welfare of the town or its environment.

The Canadian aluminum producer Alcan faced a similar problem with its smelter near Lynemouth in the northeast of England. When construction began on the smelter in the early 1970s, local farmers expressed concern that the resultant pollution from the operation of the smelter would endanger the quality of their crops and health of their livestock. In this case, Alcan took the precautionary measure of buying the land from the farmers, eventually acquiring 4,500 acres of surrounding property. Alcan employed a farming director, and the land purchased continues to produce crops and grow livestock. The uncertainty and concerns surrounding the effects of the pollution from Alcan's Lynemouth smelter were ultimately dispelled. Had the smelter's operation adversely affected local crops and livestock, Alcan's precautionary action would have mitigated at least some of the risk of legal action from the local community.

Voluntary Action

Ethics is quite often the realm of the voluntary. Ethics sets higher standards than the law. The perennial problem for responsible businesses that meet ethical requirements is that less-responsible competitors will take the opportunity to enlarge their market share. Christine Parker has argued that deterrence alone cannot explain corporate adoption of environmentally responsible policies. Usually such policies emerge from the context of crisis and the threat or actuality of harm to the corporation. But beyond enforcement and deterrence, Parker shows that management engages with environmental policy for a variety of reasons. An example of such engagement is the Green Challenge.[39]

Facing moves to recommend a carbon tax at the 1995 Berlin conference on climate change, corporations and industry associations devised the Green Challenge.[40] Several countries agreed to the challenge as an alternative to the tax and began a partnership program to lower greenhouse gas emissions in 1996. Membership of the Green Challenge is entirely voluntary, but the performance of members is audited. Action that could potentially harm the interests of any one business becomes viable if it is collaborative. Collaboration can forestall government action and exert pressure on other businesses to self-regulate.

An example of Canadian business voluntarily taking on environmental responsibilities is found in its subscription to the International Organization for Standardization's 14001 environmental management systems standards. By January 2007, 2,578 Canadian companies had signed up.[41] Japan ranked first, with 21,779 signatories, then China, Spain, Italy, and the United States. Canada occupies eleventh position. Taking into consideration Canada's relative size and population, these statistics indicate that, at least by international standards, Canadian business is well disposed towards adopting environmental standards.

A further indication of this is the rate of voluntary compliance with what has become the global standard in environmental reporting. In the late 1990s, John Elkington coined the term "triple bottom line reporting" to indicate that the social and environmental aspects of a corporation's operations were as important as the economic ones.[42] The idea joins corporate social responsibility with profits. One of the ways in which this reporting has been promoted is through the Global Reporting Initiative (GRI) begun in 1997 by the Coalition for Environmentally Responsible Economies (CERES) but now a separate organization. The object of the GRI is to promote the *Sustainability Reporting Guidelines* on the economic, environmental, and social dimensions of business activities, which it does in collaboration with the United Nations. By 2009, more than 1,500 companies had adopted the guidelines, which are now in their third iteration (G3). The GRI claims that the G3 guidelines "have become the de facto global standard for reporting."[43] None of this should suggest that regulation is now superfluous, but, as Parker suggests, compliance is more complicated than threatening corporations with penalties.

The CERES Principles

Business attitudes have changed over the past few decades, and it would be incorrect to characterize them as hostile to the environment or even as defensive. These changes, however, have generally come as a result of crises. One of the best-known examples of a proactive stand on environmental protection by business is the work of a coalition of concerned investors, environmentalists, religious groups, and pension trustees called the Coalition for Environmentally Responsible Economies (CERES), which produced the CERES Principles (formerly called the Valdez Principles after the environmental disaster that took place when the *Exxon Valdez* ran aground in King William Sound, Alaska, in 1989).[44]

The CERES Principles attempt to extend environmentally responsible business practices across the globe and across all kinds and sizes of business. The scope of the principles is broad, covering environmental protection, conservation, waste reduction, risk reduction, and public accountability. Although the principles seem to add to an ever-increasing list of standards, experience has shown that if business is unprepared to regulate its own operations, government agencies are not reluctant to do the regulating for them. So, for all the difficulties of adopting standards like the CERES Principles, there are incentives for large corporations at least to support them and use them credibly.

There are 10 principles:

1. *Protection of the biosphere*. Provides for the elimination of pollution, protection of habitats and the ozone layer, an d the minimization of smog, acid rain, and greenhouse gases.
2. *Sustainable use of natural resources*. Commits signatories to conservation of nonrenewable resources, the responsible use of renewable resources, and the protection of wilderness and biodiversity.

3. *Reduction and disposal of waste.* Obliges signatories to minimize waste, to dispose of it responsibly, and to recycle wherever possible.
4. *Energy conservation.* Commits signatories to conserve energy and use it more efficiently.
5. *Risk reduction.* Provides for minimizing health and safety risks to employees and the public by using safe practices and being prepared for emergencies.
6. *Safe products and services.* Seeks protection of consumers and the environment by making products safe and providing information about their impact on the environment.
7. *Environmental restoration.* Accepts responsibility for repair of environmental damage and compensation to those affected.
8. *Informing the public.* Obliges management to disclose to employees and the public information about environmentally harmful incidents. It also protects employees who blow the whistle about environmental or health hazards in their employment.
9. *Management commitment.* Commits signatories to provide resources to implement and monitor the principles. This also means that the CEO and the company's board are kept abreast of environmental aspects of the company's operations. The selection of directors will give consideration to commitment to the environment.
10. *Audits and reports.* Commits signatories to an annual assessment of compliance with the principles that it will make public.

Canadian Standards and Principles

The Canadian government is committed to the protection of the environment and the conservation of the country's natural heritage.[45] The government endorses a balanced approach to environmental policy-making that ensures solutions that provide both environmental and economic benefits for Canadians.[46]

The Canadian approach to developing policy has been multi-faceted, with working groups producing major policy papers on sustainable development, corporate environmental innovation, corporate sustainability reporting, and sustainable finance. The individual ministries approach environmental issues sectorally, focusing on each of their respective economic sectors—agriculture, energy, fisheries, forests, manufacturing, mining, tourism, and transport. Particular emphasis is also placed on major environmental issues, including air, water, nature, climate change, pollution, and waste. With each ministry and industry sector presenting its own issues and appropriate methods of enhancing environmental protection, environmentally sustainable development in many respects must be regarded contextually. Ecologically sustainable development is difficult to define closely and is not readily specified in terms of pre-cast criteria.

As an example of this sectoral approach to environmental policy formulation in Canada, the relevant policy of Fisheries and Oceans Canada consists of a general prohibition of harmful alteration, disruption, or destruction (HADD) of fish habitat. The HADD policy, which represents a significant part of the Canadian Fisheries Act (subsection 35(1)), asserts that any undertaking that results in HADD is a contravention of the Act.

The only exception to this general prohibition occurs when a subsection 35(2) Authorization is issued for the HADD. This authorization authorizes the HADD and not the project resulting in the HADD. A project does not need an authorization to proceed, but if a HADD results and an authorization was not issued, the proponent may be guilty of an offence. Many proponents prefer to obtain an authorization before they proceed considering that the penalties for violating the Act can include fines of up to $1,000,000 and imprisonment up to six months, or a combination of both.[47]

The dredging of the harbour in Sydney, Nova Scotia, that commenced in 2011 is an example of the HADD policy at work. In a seminar held in Ottawa on 14 April 2012, Dr Bruce G. Hatcher, chair in Marine Ecosystem Research, Cape Breton University, Sydney, Nova Scotia, described the dredging project and its relevance to the HADD policy:

> The dredging of the Sydney Harbour in 2011–2012 generated the largest Harmful Alteration, Damage or Destruction [HADD] of Fish Habitat in Canadian history. A complicated application of DFO's [Department of Fisheries and Oceans] HADD Policy under Section 31 of the Fisheries Act requires an effort to relocate marine macro-fauna from the path of the dredge, and the construction of 300 artificial reefs within the harbour. The work is being done by an unlikely partnership among the projects proponent (Sydney Ports Corporation), the Sydney Harbour fishermen (Association), the Regulator (Fisheries & Oceans Canada) and the local university (Cape Breton University). Impressive accomplishments and errors have been made to date by all parties. We have learned from them and will continue to do so. The process and outcomes highlight the profound significance of the current HADD policy as a mechanism for "polluter pays" in Canadian marine environmental law. The project also identifies three significant deficiencies in [the process]: a) it does not involve the fishing industry; b) it takes a very limited approach to ecosystem-based management of marine resources; c) it does not apply adaptive, outcomes-based management methods in a very challenging regime. We know enough to improve this important process.[48]

The Brundtland Report (of the World Commission on Environment and Development) defines ecologically sustainable development as "development that meets the needs of the present without compromising the ability of future generations to meet their own needs."[49] Ecologically sustainable development attempts to integrate economic, social, and ecological criteria, and to balance present economic and social goals and the just-savings principle. In other words, ecologically sustainable development tries to get some perspective on the just requirements of future generations while paying regard to the demands of equity in the present. Of course, the issue facing our heirs might not be the degree of comfort available to them on a planet with depleted resources, but survival itself. In resolving the inevitable clashes that will occur in distributing equitably for the present and saving adequately for the future, the issue of survival should indeed be kept in mind.

Implementation of ecologically sustainable development faces obstacles; people are often unwilling to begin paying for the environmental subsidies they are accustomed to receiving.[50] As already noted, someone, even if not the ostensible user, is paying these costs. An example might be the use of lead in petrol. When the government put a surcharge on leaded gasoline, there was an outcry from the welfare lobby in particular. They argued that less well-off people had older cars and so would be paying more than those people who were better off. This violated equity, they said. But someone was already subsidizing those using leaded gasoline, and that someone was not just the environment polluted with lead; it was children with high lead concentrations in their bodies.

Resistance to measures for intergenerational equity, such as an economic rent on gasoline, could also be anticipated. Proceeds from rents for non-renewable resources could be invested to provide "a continuous stream of income . . . and this is equivalent to holding the stock of that capital constant."[51] Obtaining public and business support for such a measure is another matter.

Perhaps the most prominent environmental issue facing Canada is the continuing development of Northern Alberta's oil sands. The economic benefits provided by oil sands development projects to the province of Alberta are pitted against the significant negative environmental impacts created by these same projects, creating significant discord both domestically and internationally.

CASE 11.5: Alberta Oil Sands

Canada has a large quantity of unconventional petroleum deposits known as the Alberta oil sands located in the northern part of that province. The oil sands are actually a mixture of sand, clay, water, and a dense semi-solid or viscous form of petroleum. The extraction of oil from the oil sands is significantly more expensive and labour intensive than the drilling and refining normally associated with the extraction of conventional petroleum, producing two to four times the greenhouse gases and using significant amounts of water and energy for the steam injection processes required for this type of extraction.

The Alberta oil sands contain the second-largest known oil reserve globally. The development of the oil sands has driven unprecedented economic growth in Alberta, but not without significant environmental consequences. These environmental impacts include the following:

- *Production of greenhouse gases:* the oil sands are responsible for one-third of Alberta's greenhouse gas emissions and represent Canada's largest single source of greenhouse gases.
- *Increases in water consumption:* oil sands production requires up to 4.5 barrels of water to produce one barrel of oil. This large quantity of water comes primarily from the Athabasca River, threatening fish stocks, the stability of the water table, and future freshwater supplies for local and indigenous communities.
- *Negative impacts on Northern Alberta's boreal forests:* exploration, open-pit mining, and supporting urban development have contributed to large-scale deforestation, habitat fragmentation, and species loss.

The late Alberta premier Peter Lougheed argued that the rate of oil sands development is not socially or economically beneficial for the province. The Alberta government is responsible for the formulation of the policies surrounding oil sands development, including the resolution of numerous competing and complex policy issues. To date, the provincial government has been unwilling to heed any calls for the slowing of the growth in oil sands development. The Canadian federal government has historically maintained a hands-off position, remaining largely content to leave governance issues surrounding the development of the oil sands to the Alberta government.

Canada has received unprecedented criticism both domestically and internationally for the negative environmental impacts inflicted by its continued support for the development of its oil sands. This, combined with its withdrawal from the Kyoto Protocol, has moved Canada from a recognized world leader in environmental stewardship to a position of pariah in the eyes of environmental groups and other concerned stakeholders worldwide. Peter Kent, federal minister of the environment, maintains that Canada's focus is "ensuring future growth is done in a responsible and sustainable manner."[52] In order to achieve this, the federal and provincial governments have joined forces to develop the Joint Canada-Alberta Implementation Plan for Oil Sands Monitoring, with the rationale that comprehensive environmental monitoring will encourage sustainable practices among the industry participants in oil sands development.[53] Critics argue that simply monitoring development does little to stop or repair the environmental degradation caused by continued activity in the oil sands.

Policies of recycling at all cost can ultimately lead to the exporting of waste, and in the face of low demand, this means paying for waste to go offshore—a growing practice condemned by green activists. In many countries, the requirement to recycle rather than incinerate resulted in an oversupply of paper produced from recycled waste that ultimately led to continuing international price collapses. American and European waste had flooded the market and driven the price down. Successful recycling campaigns had resulted in an oversupply of old newspapers. This oversupply had created a situation where the collection, baling, and shipment of old newsprint cost significantly more than the international market would pay.

The problem of recycling waste seems again to be one of perplexity with a moral aspect. If the problem was not generated, then remedies would not be necessary. Recycling massive amounts of waste material shifts the problem; it does not address it. Treating the symptoms rather than the causes will eventually be unsustainable. The prudential and ethical obligation is not primarily to dispose of waste responsibly—a difficult task when waste continues to be produced on a massive scale—but to avoid producing it in the first place. Whatever theory of environmental protection you might subscribe to, the fundamental responsibility is to use resources responsibly and avoid using industrial waste disposal—including recycling—where possible. The case of Ok Tedi takes us back to the kind of issues we saw first with Placer Dome or Barrick. This case, like the earlier ones, also illustrates the immense financial and reputational costs to corporations of persisting in a course of action—often with governmental approval—that is inevitably calamitous. Like the other cases, Ok Tedi is a classic illustration of poor decision-making that had large-scale repercussions for core stakeholders and for the commercial well-being of one of the world's major mining corporations.

CASE 11.6: BHP and Ok Tedi

In the early 1980s, the Australian mining firm BHP (now BHP Billiton), with its partners the Papua New Guinea (PNG) government and the Canadian Inmet Mining Corporation, formed Ok Tedi Mining Limited (OTML). OTML sought to develop a huge copper and gold lode, but the project was fraught with problems from the beginning. These ranged from difficulties with venture partners, to strikes, droughts, and landslides. The ore deposits are situated on Mount Fubilan in the Star Mountains near the border with West Papua. This area is geologically unstable. Drenched by 10 metres of rainfall a year, it is subject to powerful erosion, which carries sediment into the Ok Tedi River, thence into the Fly River and the Gulf of Papua.

During construction of a tailings dam for the Ok Tedi mine in 1983–4, the foundations collapsed and an investment of $70 million was washed into the river system. This set the scene for all the ensuing problems for BHP and the Ok Tedi peoples. In brief, the mine was developed without a tailings dam, and tailings were thenceforth released into the Ok Tedi River. The result was that the Ok Tedi and Fly rivers were seriously contaminated. Much of the Ok Tedi became unusable, and people who relied on the river for water and fishing could no longer do so.

While a safe tailings dam could not be constructed initially, BHP insisted that it would continue searching for a way to manage the problem—including construction of a dam. BHP did not cease its mining operations in light of this. Its investment in the project was too great. OTML did employ about 40 environmental officers who reported to the PNG government and were audited by independent scientists.

Despite these measures, local landowners called the OTML operations at Ok Tedi "a disaster" and lobbied for the Australian government to introduce a code of conduct for Australian mining companies operating abroad.[54] In May 1994, they launched a $4-billion action against BHP in the Supreme Court of the Australian State of Victoria. Two billion dollars were sought for exemplary damages and the building of a tailings dam, and another $2 billion in compensation. An injunction against further mining until a dam was constructed was also sought. The reaction of the PNG government was immediately hostile. In repeated statements, Prime Minister Wingti warned of the damage that such actions could do to overseas investment confidence in his country. He stressed the importance of dealing with such legal issues inside PNG, not through foreign courts. "The Ok Tedi matter is a matter taking place in PNG and we are going to make it so we handle this within our own country under our own laws," he said shortly after the action was launched.[55] This determination to deal with such actions within his own country led Wingti to consult with BHP over the preparation of legislation to secure a favourable outcome. By the time the legislation was introduced into Parliament in December 1995, it had caused a public relations nightmare for BHP and produced its own legal difficulties.

The Combined BHP/PNG Government Case

In order to make any judgment about the issues involved here, it is necessary to place OTML's mining in context. Each year (drought years excluded), rainfall washes over 90 million tons of sediment into the Fly River. Mining has added another 40 million tons to this, which is mainly deposited over a 20-kilometre stretch of the 1,000-kilometre Fly River. The company, however, forecast that, by the time mining was completed in 2013, this sediment would be washed to the sea by the large volumes of water from the catchment. BHP claimed that the main problem was the amount of sediment, not its toxicity, and it produced evidence to show that the copper levels of fish in the Fly River were lower than in metropolitan Sydney. This analysis proved to be optimistic, as toxic damage to the environment from acid rock drainage emerged.[56]

The Ok Tedi mine is the largest enterprise in PNG, it contributes about 20 per cent of the country's export income, and it has provided employment for thousands of local people. Since it commenced operations, benefits from the Ok Tedi mine have included the investment of $300 million in infrastructure, including roads, power, water, communications, schools, and medical facilities; the education and training of over 1,500 workers; a decline in infant mortality rates from around 33 per cent to less than 3 per cent; generally improved health, with a dramatic decline in malaria infections and an increase in the average life span from 30 to 50 years; and greatly expanded educational opportunities for children. Apart from voluntary compensation initiated by BHP for disturbance of traditional ways of life among the Western Province peoples, a trust fund has been established for community development in areas such as school buildings and small business assistance. By 2010, the time that mining was originally expected to be concluded, the value of this trust fund exceeded $80 million. The mine life has since been extended to 2013, which should further increase the ultimate value of the trust.

BHP summed up its position in these terms:

> BHP is proud of what has been achieved at Ok Tedi but recognizes the difficulties the mine has created due to its environmental impact and its effects on the lifestyles of some of the people living along the river. The Company would very much like to find a better solution to the problem it confronts. Closing the mine is not an option—it is too important to the economic and social welfare of Papua New Guinea and is not advocated by any but a small number of people in the region.[57]

Case Questions

1. What is the ethical issue here? This is an important question. Is it the despoliation of the environment?
2. Should the economic, health, and social benefits to the people of PNG be allowed to eclipse the environmental issues?
3. Are tailings in the Fly River the main issue? If so, how should this ethical obstacle be explained? Under what circumstances could the obstacle be overcome, or is it absolute? Does the issue arise because local residents have had their lifestyle changed or destroyed? Why is this a problem if the nation as a whole benefits from the mining? Is it because these particular stakeholders were insufficiently compensated?

Geoffrey Barker, a journalist who takes an interest in ethics, identifies three ethical questions related to the Ok Tedi affair:

1. Should companies be able to do abroad what they cannot do at home? Should there be universal standards for environmental protection? Should global consistency be demanded of firms like BHP?
2. What is the proper relationship between multinational firms and the governments of poor countries desperate for development and foreign exchange? More precisely, how closely should firms be involved in drafting the regulatory frameworks in which they are to operate?
3. If local villagers are to suffer losses for wider national gains, should they be consulted by incoming firms? This raises fundamental issues of autonomy and justice: how much notice should firms take of villagers' desires to preserve traditional lifestyles if national governments are eager for development? On what basis should compensation be paid for environmental and other losses?[58]

In June 1996, BHP agreed to a $400-million out-of-court settlement for the landholders, which included $110 million in compensation, $40 million to relocate 10 villages, and $7.6 million in legal expenses. BHP also agreed to sell 10 per cent of OTML to the PNG government for the benefit of local communities. BHP did not undertake to build a tailings dam, but did promise to look at all feasible options for tailings containment. In 2002, BHP gave its 52 per cent share of the mine to the PNG government, which formed The Papua New Guinea Sustainable Development Program to continue operations at Ok Tedi.

1. If BHP had offered such a package before it commenced mining, would the ethical issues identified by Barker have been avoided?

Consider the second and third of Barker's questions.

2. Say the PNG government and BHP had been at arm's length during all negotiations about the mine. And suppose that BHP had consulted local villagers and obtained their consent to mining on terms identical to those that applied later. Would the Ok Tedi operation then have been ethically trouble free? If you believe not, then consider this: what amount of compensation would have removed ethical obstacles to the mine?

BHP and the PNG government were not at arm's length. They were partners, and one of the partners (the government) was, among other things, responsible for regulation of the other.

3. Is there an issue here of conflict of interest? Are there other ethical concerns that arise in virtue of the partnership?

A government has responsibilities to its people as a whole, but also to each of its people individually. It has responsibilities to sustain the economy and attract productive investment, but it also must protect its environmental heritage. As a partner in OTML, the PNG government was in a position that made it difficult to discharge its responsibilities. Consider the ethics of the situation in PNG.

These questions pursue only two of the issues raised by Barker. Let us move to his question about standards of environmental protection. Is the central issue here whether the standards of BHP in PNG differ from those in the mining company's home country, or is it the impact of mining on the Ok Tedi ecosystem? Both issues are important, of course, but the question of standards would not arise unless mining had had a major impact there.

1. How is it possible to legislate regarding practices from one setting to another?
2. Would not any acceptable code require interpretation that might permit another Ok Tedi?

Corporations have learnt from confrontations with stakeholders, as Shell learned from Brent Spar, and BHP Billiton learned from Ok Tedi. Both now subscribe to triple bottom line reporting, and BHP Billiton has taken a positive attitude to sustainable development.[59] This does not mean that the corporation does not raise environmental questions, such as the fate of its blast furnace waste.

Understandably, such changes are often greeted with cynicism by those who see economic activity in Marxist or quasi-Marxist terms—as the result of forces alone and not of human intentions. If this is so, then all the activism to bring about change in corporate conduct seems wasted. If reforms are rejected as cosmetic, the answer must lie in systemic change—the replacement of capitalism and its institutions altogether. It is not clear just what political and economic substitute would dissolve the problems of waste, pollution, and energy consumption, especially as many of these problems are historical in nature. This is not to deny that prevention is preferable to remediation. Still, for those with less revolutionary ambitions than the replacement of the capitalist economy, it seems unfair to demand change from corporations on the one hand, while on the other claiming that efforts to be more environmentally responsible are no more than "greenwashing."

All of this suggests that the place to begin discussions of environmental ethics is not with Friedman's objections, but with the reasonable expectations of business in a sustainable future. While environmental ethics needs the support of enforceable regulations, these will not be effective without the willing collaboration of business.

Review Questions

1. We asked, "Is it not just an appeal to the strength of our preferences that makes us claim intrinsic value for the environment?" What else could it be?
2. Could there be a systematic statement of, and then enforcement of, the precautionary principle?
3. Could there be such a statement that would do justice to all stakeholders in a proposal?
4. What are the practical limits of the precautionary principle?

Suggested Readings

Carson, Rachel, L. *Silent Spring*. Boston: Mariner Books, 1962.

Daly, H., and J. Cobb. *For the Common Good*. London: Greenprint, 1989.

Jamieson, Dale. *Ethics and the Environment: An Introduction*. Cambridge: Cambridge University Press, 2008.

Singer, Peter. *Animal Liberation*. 2nd edn. New York: Thorsons, 1991.

Trainer, Ted. *Abandon Affluence*. London: Zed Books, 1985.

Suggested Websites

The Brundtland Report:
http://www.earthsummit2012.org/historical-documents/the-brundtland-report-our-common-future.

Environment Canada:
http:/www.ec.gc.ca/.

International Standards Organization:
http://www.iso.org/.

Pembina Institute:
http://www.pembina.org/.

United Nations: Framework Convention on Climate Change:
http://unfccc.int/kyoto_protocol/.

World Wildlife Fund Canada:
http://wwf.ca/.

12
International Business Ethics

Chapter Outline

- Competition or Trust?
- Ethics and Cultural Difference
- The Global Social Responsibilities of Business
- Business and Human Rights
- Affordability
- A Double Standard?
- Supportive Institutions
- Review Questions
- Suggested Readings
- Suggested Websites

International business dealings raise in a special way many of the ethical issues outlined at the beginning of this book. One kind of challenge is presented by the responsibilities of multinational corporations (MNCs) that operate in environments that are less regulated, that are not democratically governed, and in which corruption flourishes. Another challenge is respecting the cultural differences that MNCs encounter in the countries in which they operate. Another is the difficulty of regulating commerce in globalizing markets. We shall consider just some of these issues in this chapter.

Competition or Trust?

Competition in international business is such that ethics can appear to be a handicap, if not downright irrelevant. Too often, business people argue in polarized terms, as though business had only two choices: to behave unethically or to fail. It is easy to think of the standard slogans: "It's kill or be killed"; "It's a jungle out there"; "It's dog eat dog." Leaving aside the view that ethics is irrelevant, it can be argued that the survival of a firm should not be jeopardized in order to fulfill an ethical obligation when one's competitors are not ethical. A case could be made that paying a **bribe** to an official to secure a contract in a host country could mean the viability of the firm, it could help local employment, and it could even promote economic efficiency. Of course, making such a case is saying that paying the bribe is not really unethical (see chapter 2 on dirty hands). But how many cases are there in which the survival of a firm depends on a bribe? Just how much of a hurdle is ethics to achieving international competitiveness? It is unconvincing, both in domestic and international business, to dramatize the difficulties of matching competitors ethically by claiming that the competitor's tactics are designed to destroy all rivals. The survival of most businesses does not depend on one decision, and if the matter is very serious, then being unethical in order to save the company simply changes the nature of the risk.

bribe *the provision of money or gifts with the intention of influencing an individual with official, public, or legal decision-making responsibilities*

For a company to embark deliberately on unethical conduct under the guise of "necessity" is morally indefensible. This might seem a harsh view, especially when the livelihood of a community is related to the survival of a business enterprise. In a time of economic restructuring, we are only too familiar with the human cost of business collapse. But the way to mitigate human tragedy is to appeal to public policy, not to toss regulations, and human decency, off to the side. Corporations are not natural persons who may legitimately steal when survival is on the line. A business conducted as though each sale is "make or break" has serious problems that breaches of ethics will only make worse, not resolve. But it is not only failing businesses that argue from necessity: as mentioned in chapter 2, necessity is often the excuse for a hard-nosed business culture that seeks to normalize indifference to moral principles in business—at least in relation to its own actions.

The link made between competition and survival is a parody of the work of Charles Darwin—social Darwinism. It imagines a world where only the fit should survive. Interestingly, another great English thinker, Thomas Hobbes, suggested a different requirement for corporate survival in the arena of international competition. Hobbes believed that a world where people do whatever is required to maintain their own security is in a state of war. Such an unpredictable and unstable state is likely to result in an unpleasant life and an early death.[1] The remedy for this vulnerability is enforceable authority, which brings people under the common regime of the state. By analogy, if international markets are to work, then a Hobbesian solution is needed. An international legal and normative infrastructure is necessary among states. The point that is often lost in analogies with war, however, is that a great deal of this infrastructure already exists in private and public international law. It enables the most complex kinds of global transactions to be conducted with a degree of trust and predictability that is often taken for granted. Moreover, business itself has initiated a number of bodies to set standards of conduct internationally. We will discuss these in a later section.

Ethics and Cultural Difference

One of the difficulties of doing business internationally stems from the variety of social and legal standards that apply around the globe. What might be acceptable or legal in the home country of a business might be offensive or bring penalties in a host country. Whatever the differences between other cultures and Canada, the problem for business is arguably not primarily one of a conflict in basic values but of cultural, economic, and political differences. Corruption can exist in any context. It is the reaction of business to that corruption that matters. There are more safe exits for businesses faced with pressures to behave unethically in Canada than exist in some other countries, such as Thailand or Vietnam. But the lack of strong formal regulatory environments does not indicate an absence of values that we should respect and upon which the regulatory infrastructure of business can be built.

When we observe foreign cultures, we tend to be struck more by differences than by similarities. That is, after all, why we travel and take an interest in other peoples: to experience the breadth of human diversity. Ethical practices are among such differences in the customs and ways of life of our hosts. As we noted in chapter 1, the words "ethics" and "morals" originally referred to the standards of a culture—the social mores, understandings, conventions, and norms by which conduct is judged. But there is a limit to the relevance of social and cultural difference. While we speak of the respective mores and norms of the French, Germans, and Japanese, we do not usually speak of French ethics, German ethics, and Japanese ethics. A particular emphasis on certain values in these countries need not suggest a different ethical universe. If multiple sets of ethics are applied—"when in Rome . . ."—then not only can one culture not criticize another, but there can be no real basis for one culture to learn from another's values. Each culture would have to reject the positive as well as the negative aspects of foreign societies. Not only does common experience contradict such cultural isolationism, but empirical work—such as that of the highly regarded mythographer Joseph Campbell—shows that the notion of a common humanity is not some Western ideal born of the eighteenth-century Enlightenment.[2]

It is not unreasonable, then, to suggest that ethics is universal as well as rooted in particular contexts. We expect some moral principles to transcend particular cultures.

What values might these be? High on the list would be respectfulness, honesty, trust, integrity, sincerity, loyalty, and diligence. Of course, these values are expressed in different and distinctive ways. Let us distinguish between primary and secondary values.[3] The list above identifies primary values. Secondary values would relate to the expression of these primary values in certain ways, such as marriage customs, social stratification, kinship obligations, and so on. In the case of Japan, it would be important to understand the significance of harmony, consensus, and loyalty within a group or company—*wa*—which could lead a subordinate, for example, to cover for a superior accused of accepting bribes. According to one research group, "loyalty to one's group is a respected personal trait, which may be compared in importance to the personal integrity of Westerners."[4] In China, trust—*xiyong*—is the fundamental value of business, much of which is conducted by verbal agreements in under-regulated environments.[5] In Vietnam, Indonesia, and Thailand, the reluctance to say "No" directly to a request may seem evasive when in fact it is a mark of respectfulness to those making the request. Understanding these differences can increase one's regard for those with whom one is doing business, especially if one recognizes that many of the cultural mores of Asians and Canadians rest upon the same primary values and, in terms of ethics, differ only in their secondary values.

Of course, the distinction between primary and secondary values does not help business in a situation where secondary values are the problem. The point of making the distinction, however, is that differences in secondary values might indicate cultural differences other than ethically divisive ones. It might be appropriate to give a gift as a matter of cultural sensitivity rather than to gain an uncompetitive advantage. So while we are not trying to reduce ethical questions to primary values shared universally, we would suggest that the traditions of a foreign culture are directed towards preserving certain primary values and that when this is understood, unfamiliar customs become more intelligible and are not confused with ethical transgression. Moreover, this distinction between primary and secondary values helps us identify fundamental issues and permits legitimate and sensitive criticism of practices that are believed to protect primary values but may not. Argument or discussion about primary values is more likely to come to a sudden halt: if there is disagreement, there may be nothing more to argue about. But secondary values thought to protect more fundamental goods through cultural and legal mechanisms invite the kind of discussion and dialogue that can benefit critics and defenders alike and can invite imaginative solutions to differences.

Take the example of "face," a crucial value common in many Asian societies. Causing a person to lose face in a business deal cuts through secondary values to primary values of respect and trust. Westerners do not like to be publicly embarrassed or to have their self-esteem or dignity damaged, so why should it be different for others? Given that Asian societies are more communal and relationship based and that family obligations extend beyond the nuclear and blood relationships familiar in the West, the nature of face needs to be examined on a case-by-case basis. The issue of face also illustrates how ethics must go beyond rules in order to be culturally sensitive. It takes an ethical imagination to do well in situations in which values collide. This sort of imagination was shown by a prominent Western businessman who was managing an MNC in Thailand.

At Christmas, a lavish gift of food and wine was given to him. He felt that it would be awkward to accept this gift but also awkward to refuse. His imaginative solution to this problem was to thank the gift-giver by saying how much his staff would enjoy it. The gift-giver's insistence that the gift was for the CEO was countered by a face-saving strategy of modesty and generosity: the staff must be permitted to share in the gift because they had worked hard. Dissipating the contents of the gift also dissipated the concern about the creation of a direct obligation to reciprocate by offering some business favour to the giver. Eventually the gifts stopped coming, perhaps indicating that their true purpose had not been achieved.

Is Corruption Acceptable in Foreign Cultures?

In December 1996, the German newspaper *Der Tagesspiegel* ran a story under the headline "Corruption part of traditional Thai culture." This extraordinary claim was not made by the newspaper, however, but by the Thai deputy minister of the interior, Mr Pairoj Lohsoonthorn, who publicly told officials that his department's policy was to accept bribes:

> He had ordered staff of the land sales department of his ministry to accept any money offered to them, he told "Matichon" newspaper. However, civil servants were not allowed to ask for bribes or to circulate price lists. "This is part of traditional Thai culture," Mr Pairoj said. The acceptance of bribes was justified by the low level of pay in the civil service.[6]

From such reports, one might conclude that corruption is acceptable to the citizens of Asian countries or that their authorities are indifferent to it. This inference would be unjustified. First, as Johann Lambsdorff points out, alleging corruption in foreign business environments shifts responsibility from those who offer bribes to those who accept them: both sides of the equation need to be examined.[7] Second, although high levels of corruption remain, the financial and political instability of 1997 put new fight into anti-corruption programs already instituted by the Chinese, Thai, Malaysian, and Vietnamese governments. In 1999, Indonesia passed laws on "clean government," requiring public officials to disclose their wealth, and on the "eradication of criminal acts of corruption" to identify and punish corrupt practices. In China, serious penalties—including death—apply to corruption, and new institutions, such as the Chinese National Bureau of Corruption Prevention, which was opened in 2007, have been introduced. Such corruption-fighting measures may be embryonic from a Western point of view, but they are clear signs that corruption cannot be dismissed as cultural difference. Together with improved legal infrastructures and the economic resources to support them, such measures will lead to changes in the business cultures of these countries. If corruption were acceptable in Asia, it would follow that Westerners could engage in corruption in Asia without drawing comment. The hostile reaction of Indonesian commentators to a Canadian company's mining scam shows the falseness of this.[8] Anti-corruption measures now reach into the elite ranks of Asian states. In Vietnam, the government has launched a campaign against corruption that involves the death penalty for some crimes. Some estimates put losses from corruption at over C$194 million in 1996. Because corruption involves top party officials, there has been some skepticism about whether the new laws will be enforced diligently, but already two executives have been convicted and sentenced to death in absentia after fleeing to Cambodia with millions of dollars. Similar stories are increasingly common. The director of an import-export company owned by the Vietnamese Communist Party, Tamexco, has been charged with fraud costing A$33.2 million in a scheme involving 19 others and a total of $62 million. One of these is the former deputy of Vietnam's biggest state-owned bank, who was convicted on charges of making illegal loans and sentenced to death by firing squad.[9]

Oddly enough, Japan, one of the world's most spectacular economies, is driven by an ethos that is based not on profit-maximization but on values such as honour.[10] Corruption is consequently a great source of shame, even in the face of "necessity." In March 1997, Hideo Sakamaki, president of Nomura Securities, the largest stockbroking firm in the world, resigned because his vice-president and two managing directors had complied with the demands of corporate extortionists.[11]

Would it be possible to splash the details of secret dealings over the front pages of local Asian newspapers and find approval among readers? Clearly not. Perhaps the most famous scandal involving an overseas company in corruption was Lockheed's channelling money to the Japanese Liberal Democratic Party and the eventual charging of two former Japanese prime ministers. When one considers the magnitude of buying influence at the political summit of one of the world's leading economies, one wonders how such a thing could have happened.[12] The audacity of the company cannot be excused on the grounds of commercial necessity and the absence of regulation in the United States at the time. It was blatantly unethical, and Lockheed could not evade responsibility by shifting the blame onto the Japanese. This scandal should serve as a lesson for all those who wish to justify the payment of bribes by invoking its commercial necessity in an environment where bribery is alleged to be "normal." In 1977, the United States Congress passed the **Foreign Corrupt Practices Act**, which prohibits American corporations making payments to foreign governments to advance their business interests. Contrary to the expectations of US legislators, the international community did not follow the American lead and failed to enact anti-corruption legislation along similar lines for several years. In Canada, the Corruption of Foreign Public Officials Act was not enacted until 1998.

Foreign Corrupt Practices Act *the 1977 US law prohibiting American corporations from making payments to foreign governments in order to advance their business interests. This was the first example of extraterritorial legislation governing citizens beyond the borders of the enacting jurisdiction.*

Scandals like the Lockheed bribe are not rare in Japan. Although they have brought leading business people and high-ranking politicians before the courts, the shame has not been sufficient to avert other corporate disgraces involving such major corporations as Nomura and Daiwa. Some might assume from cases such as these that Japanese business relies on fraud and corruption. If everybody is doing it, then it must be normal. Hence, it is legitimate for foreign firms operating in Japan to give bribes or indulge in other forms of corruption. If home country laws forbid such corrupt practices, then a firm might form an alliance or partnership with an indigenous company that would handle culturally and legally sensitive issues such as "facilitation fees" and undisclosed commissions. Yet it is no more acceptable in Japan to offer or accept bribes than it is in the

United States. In both countries, it is necessary to hide this conduct because it is shameful and unethical. When the *Asahi* newspaper reported that Osaka oil dealer Junichiro Izui, charged with tax evasion, had been a conduit for senior Mitsubishi Oil officials to channel several million dollars to Japanese politicians, there was a public outcry.[13] Again, the "light of day" test makes the point: once bribery is publicly exposed, people are incensed.

CASE 12.1: Niko Resources in Bangladesh

In 2011, approximately six years after the incident, the Canadian energy company Niko Resources pleaded guilty to bribing a Bangladesh state minister responsible for energy and mineral resources. On 7 January 2005, Niko's first drilling operation in Bangladesh initiated a massive early-morning natural gas explosion that left a 100-metre in diameter crater. Fortunately, no one was killed, but there ensued a huge public outcry in Bangladesh, with demands for retribution for and compensation from the "faulty and negligent" Canadian company.

The Bangladeshi government found Niko Resources to have been liable for the accident and responsible for payment of a significant fine. The amount to be paid by Niko Resources could be significantly influenced by A.K.M. Mosharraf Hossain, the Bangladeshi state minister for energy and mineral resources at that time. On 23 May 2005, two representatives of Niko Resources delivered a brand new Toyota Land Cruiser to Mr Hossain. Investigations were launched by the Royal Canadian Mounted Police (RCMP) into the business practices of Niko Resources as part of the Canadian federal government's crackdown on corruption.

This landmark case was the first example of a successful prosecution of a Canadian firm under the 1998 Corruption of Foreign Public Officials Act. Niko Resources was fined $9.5 million in an Alberta court. The investigating RCMP officers were said to have significant evidence of additional illegal behaviour under the Act, but the iron clad case involving the bribery of Mr Hossain with the gift of the Land Cruiser led them to pursue a conviction based on that one specific incident rather than engaging in a protracted multi-faceted investigation.[14]

Cultural Relativism

The mere fact of cultural difference does not imply its acceptability. Although respect for persons is basic to civilized interaction, we are not obliged to respect every kind of belief that people might hold simply because we wish to show them due regard. On the contrary, while courtesy should prevail, we might on occasion feel obliged to criticize certain beliefs on the basis of what we believe is a stronger position in our own belief system. Were this not so, different peoples could never learn from one another. Examples of resistance to beneficial cross-cultural criticisms are common. Slavery flourished in the United States long after its abolition in Great Britain. Women's suffrage was achieved only gradually—New Zealand in 1893, Australia in 1902, Canada in 1919, the United States in 1920—with Switzerland granting women the vote as late as 1969. Respect for individuals does not mean sacrificing one's own values for those of others. Such respect is, however, likely to reveal that there is more common ground between cultures than is at first apparent. An increasing body of data is being gathered as a result of a number of surveys conducted by professional organizations, NGOs, and research groups on the ethical behaviour of corporations that conduct business internationally. In its 2012 global survey on business ethics, the Certified Global Management Accountants received 1,966 responses from over 80 countries. Summarizing the responses from the 10 countries with the highest response rates provides a high-level view of company performance in addressing ethical misconduct.[15] An Ernst and Young annual survey on corruption released in 2012 showed an increase from 9 to 15 per cent over the past year in the proportion of senior executives willing to pay cash to secure business.[16] The Institute of Business Ethics in the UK produces an annual briefing with a summary of various surveys on business ethics, many of which address issues in international business.[17] With respect to specific perceived ethical problems in international dealings, however, a paper published in the *Journal of Business Ethics* in 1992 on a survey of 150 randomly chosen companies among Australia's 500 largest exporters identified the 10 most commonly perceived ethical problems in international dealings. In order of frequency, they were[18]

1. gifts and favours: large sums of money, call girls, travel, lavish gifts
2. cultural differences: misunderstandings about cultural matters such as the significance of gifts and tokens of esteem
3. traditional small-scale bribery: for example, small sums of money to speed up a routine bureaucratic procedure
4. pricing practices: differential pricing, requests for invoices that do not reflect actual sums paid—for example, for dumping or price-fixing
5. questionable commissions: large sums paid to middlemen, consultants, and so on
6. tax evasion: transfer pricing
7. political involvement: political influence of multinationals, illegal technology transfers
8. large-scale bribery: political donations, sums paid to evade laws or influence policy
9. illegal or immoral activities in a host country: pollution of host country, unsafe working conditions, flouting patent and copyright provisions
10. inappropriate use of products: use of technology in a host country that is banned in the home country.

These problems were ranked in importance as follows:

1. large-scale bribery
2. cultural differences
3. involvement in political affairs
4. pricing practices
5. illegal or immoral activities in a host country
6. questionable commissions
7. gifts or favours
8. tax evasion
9. inappropriate use of products
10. traditional small-scale bribery.

The dominant problem for businesses operating in Asia concerned bribes, gifts, and commissions. But serious breaches need to be distinguished from minor ones. There is a difference between a payment to expedite business that is already in train and a payment to influence the awarding of a contract. While both involve departures from ethics, one is akin to queue jumping and the other is plain crooked. While small failings can lead to larger ones—for even small collusions have their costs—there are degrees of seriousness.

Western perceptions of ethical problems in Asia are mirrored by the perceptions of Asian managers. Indonesia, for example, was perceived by nearly 17 per cent of Australian companies surveyed as the trading partner with which they experienced the greatest ethical difficulties, while China had a 10 per cent rating. In a survey of 280 Asian executives by Political and Economic Risk Consultancy Ltd (PERC) of Hong Kong, corruption was perceived as declining only in the Philippines and Singapore.[19] (See also the discussion of Transparency International's Corruption Perception Index on pages 297–300.) The PERC report found China to be near the top of the corruption list. South Korea (plagued by scandals such as the Hanbo collapse)[20] and Vietnam also ranked highly in the corruption stakes. According to PERC, control of corruption "requires an institutional framework that is lacking in many countries . . . and can take years to develop." Vietnam's corruption problems have hampered the operations of business. A downturn in the property market and the consequent non-performance of many loans has badly affected the banking system. Poor management and corruption are to blame.[21]

Judgments about corruption are influenced by cultural factors, but what the surveys above reveal is a great deal of overlap among many cultures in what is regarded as unacceptable conduct. Crime and corruption in Canadian and other Western business circles are often invisible,[22] while highly visible instances in other parts of the world can confirm certain stereotypes. A different reality might be hidden beneath such perceptions. One cross-cultural study of marketing ethics suggests that collectivist societies, such as those found in Asia, are more likely to conform to organizational ethical standards and requirements than are individualist societies, such as Canada or the United States.[23] It is useful to issue such cautions in order to balance stereotypical judgments, and to point out that the problems Canadian firms face in dealing with corruption and unethical conduct in Asia are often the very ones encountered by Asian firms as well.

It is not uncommon for a company to bring new skills and processes to a foreign country. If trained staff are not available, they are trained. If infrastructure is absent, it is built. With ethics, it is the same: insistence on certain standards of conduct, clear statements of guiding principles, and the introduction of values and priorities unfamiliar in the foreign environment are all part of building ethical infrastructure. If it is absent, it is built. The point is to do it reflectively and sensitively—that is, without imposing home country values as though they are some improvement on the host country's ethics. Foreign firms should consider the impact of their activities on local communities and build commercial and ethical infrastructure that respects the traditions and values of the host country.

These principles are easy to preach and hard to implement. In Indonesia, for example, the nobility (*priyayi*) of the Javanese majority divide the world into two: "refined" or elevated elements and occupations, called *alus*, and the "crude" or tainted elements and activities, called *kasar*. Tradition places business under *kasar*, which implies that it is inherently "immoral." The attitude that business is distasteful—familiar in the West until relatively recently—can make unethical conduct self-fulfilling: "[S]ome businessmen . . . show immoral conduct because they think that their activity is by definition immoral. Those who don't want to be dirty never ever enter business enterprises."[24] An understanding of these values would help an MNC strategically but could also assist Indonesia in building culturally appropriate economic infrastructure. It would not excuse unethical conduct by the MNC in Indonesia.

Corruption is, by definition, not an ethical value for any country, and so, as long as the ways of minimizing corruption are not offensive or culturally inappropriate, there is no reason to be anxious about shaping or enhancing the ethical environment of an overseas operation. This is well illustrated by the problem that confronted Julius Tahija, who was managing director of Caltex Pacific Indonesia from 1967 to 1977. When he was first approached with a kickback (which he rejected), Caltex had no formal training programs in ethics. Tahija believes that such programs can be an effective antidote to spurious claims of culturally relative standards:

> Many people mistakenly believe, or convince themselves, that honesty and dishonesty translate differently in different parts of the world. This is self-deception. To be honest is to be honest. . . . If culture pressures people toward a certain type of business duplicity, then the transnational must counteract these pressures. Ethics classes should be integrated into training programs to strengthen each employee's personal sense of ethics and to clarify what the company expects.[25]

Here, the crucial goal is to meet the MNC's expectations, not to attempt wholesale reform of a foreign business environment. It is not unusual for MNCs to require consistency across corporate culture, no matter where it is located. If they are American corporations, the Foreign Corrupt Practices Act will support such requirements. For example, Honeywell's Code of Ethics and Business Conduct has, like those of all large American multinationals, specific provisions against overseas misconduct. In clear and direct terms, the code prohibits international price-fixing, bid-rigging, collusion, bribery, kickbacks, or any kind of inducement to influence a transaction.[26] To the extent that such standards become global, the MNC is influencing the business environment of its hosts.

There is, however, some merit in the complaints of MNCs about competing ethically in an unfair marketplace. If all businesses are to be on a level footing, then public policy should enforce at least a rough equality among competitors. If this does not happen, how can people entering the market be expected to behave fairly? Why does any particular company have an obligation to put itself at a disadvantage in relation to its competitors? Any company doing so would go under in a market where the less scrupulous prevail. Such reasoning is a moral evasion, but one derived from a sound notion. We do not blame a bank teller for handing over cash when confronted by an armed robber. Whenever duress is applied, we reduce responsibility accordingly. In some environments, business can be confronted with operating conditions that are analogous to coercion, so no ethical blame should attach to them for conforming. The reason that it is an evasion nonetheless is that it makes an exception to the rule. In making necessity a virtue, it abandons reasonable responsibility. Companies can be caught in difficult situations that may be exculpating, but to make the operating environment the justification for corrupt behaviour is unacceptable. General or stereotypical excuses will not convince. Corporations no less than individuals are required to make sacrifices at times: profits do not outrank morality, a point tacitly conceded by the necessity of reaching for excuses. The answer is not to deny the wrongfulness of the conduct, but to stop it. In the words of Richard De George, "Some firms that operate in corrupt environments claim implicitly or explicitly that it is ethically justifiable for them to do whatever they must to stay in business. But their claim is too broad to be defensible. Ethics does not permit a company to capitulate to corruption."[27]

Richard De George has specified moral guidelines for multinational corporations. The problem of doing business internationally is not only the relative underdevelopment of legal and commercial institutions in some countries, but also the absence of international background institutions, such as laws, shared norms, and social requirements. Rather than providing an excuse for substandard ethical practices, such differences place greater responsibilities on international business than those that apply at home. De George suggests that the most important criteria for responsible business operations abroad are for companies to

- do no intentionally direct harm in the host country
- benefit the host country and contribute to its development
- respect the human rights of workers in the host country
- respect the values, culture, and laws of the host country, as long as these do not involve moral inconsistency or the abridgment of human rights, as apartheid did
- pay their taxes
- assist in the building of just background institutions in the host country and internationally.[28]

If a corporation cannot meet its responsibilities abroad, then De George suggests that an ethical manager might have to consider sacrificing survival:

> At times, acting ethically takes some toll on a company, and it may even threaten its existence. Although we are told human life is sacred, it is sometimes right to lay down one's life for a friend, for one's family, for one's country. . . . Similarly, might not a CEO justifiably lay down the life of the corporation for a cause or principle?[29]

This is a course that many writers on business ethics would find unacceptable because of the limited moral personality of the corporation. As an "artificial person," it cannot lay down its life for others as natural persons (people) can. We discuss this issue below.

The Global Social Responsibilities of Business

CASE 12.2: Kader Industrial Toy Company Factory Fire

On the afternoon of 10 May 1993, a fire broke out in a four-storey factory complex owned by Kader Industrial Toy Company in Nakhon Pathom Province near Bangkok in Thailand. Of the 188 workers killed in this tragedy, 174 were women and children. The Kader factory was a notorious sweatshop, but it supplied toys under subcontract to some of the leading toy-makers in America.

Just before Christmas 1994, the American journalist Bob Herbert published a commentary on the fire. He did not mince words in apportioning responsibility:

> In the United States, toy company executives are immersed in the sweet season of Christmas. It is jackpot time and they do not want the holiday mood spoiled by reminders of the Kader horror. These executives know that their profits come from the toil of the poor and the wretched in the Far East; they can live with that—live well, in fact. But they do not want to talk about dead women and girls stacked in the factory yard like so much rubbish, their bodies eventually to be carted away like any other industrial debris.
>
> It is just for such occasions that God gave us the gift of denial. Much better to think of the happy American shoppers clutching the stuffed animals and other toys as they wait in line at the register. . . . US executives keep the misery at a distance through the mechanism of contracts and subcontracts. They act as if they bear no responsibility for the exploitation of the men, women and children upon whom so much of their corporate profits rest.[30]

While Herbert concludes that corporations will always chase profits no matter how tragic the circumstances in which they are generated, he hopes that consumers will be more ethically sensitive than corporate executives to scandals such as the Kader fire. He believes that when consumers realize that the lives and health of child labourers are at risk in the production of toys they buy for their own children, they will not buy them.

There are grounds for this belief, as successful campaigns against Nestlé and Shell have shown. Nike offers another example of a high-profile corporation successfully targeted in campaigns by human rights organizations.

CASE 12.3: Nike "Sweatshop" Allegations

According to a 1997 report, girls were subjected to abuse by Vietnamese factories supplying footwear to Nike. "Supervisors humiliate women, force them to kneel, to stand in the hot sun, treating them like recruits in boot camp," Thuyen Nguyen, spokesman for Vietnamese Labor Watch, said after a 16-day inspection of four factories supplying Nike. Nguyen, an investment banker from New Jersey, issued a report detailing abuses such as 12-hour working days in overheated and noisy conditions; all-up labour costs of less than US$2 for items retailing for as much as US$149; wages of US$1.60 for eight hours' work; and workers being allowed only one toilet break and two drinks of water in an eight-hour shift. At one subcontracting factory, the Taiwanese-owned Pou Chen Vietnam Enterprise, a manager forced 56 women to run in the hot sun as punishment for not wearing regulation shoes. Twelve women were hospitalized as a consequence. Nike later instituted an inquiry and suspended the manager. But Nguyen alleged that "Nike clearly is not controlling its contractors, and the company has known about this for a long time."[31] Nike denied this but was clearly spurred into damage control. The markets for its products are highly competitive and sensitive to the tarnishing of a clean, healthy, sporting image.

Across the world, this image has come under attack. In 1997, United Students Against Sweatshops (USAS), a student organization representing 250 colleges and universities across Canada and the United States, set up an independent monitoring arm to investigate and monitor labour conditions in factories internationally that produce collegiate apparel.[32] In a report entitled "Nike's Satanic Factories in West Java," the author, Peter Hancock, spent eight months in Indonesia documenting sweatshop conditions in Vietnam. Employees worked an average of 11.5 hours a day, and 80 per cent of them were forced to work seven days a week; girls as young as 11 years old were employed; workers were sacked on the spot for taking sick leave; verbal abuse of female workers was endemic; and most workers earned the legal minimum wage of about $2.50 per day and some overtime. According to Hancock, this contrasted with the better conditions of Nike's competitors, such as Reebok. Nike's response to such allegations was to deny control, and therefore responsibility, over its suppliers. Hancock rejected this defence. He claimed to have observed two American representatives of Nike working on the factory floor.[33]

The responsibilities of boards of directors and senior managers for offshore operations cannot be evaded by claims that cultural differences preclude intervention or that subcontractors are beyond their reach. Why, for example, do they deliberately locate in countries where unions are illegal? As the Bhopal disaster showed, it is easier to export the plant than responsibility.[34] In the cases cited above, there was not even an attempt to assume a proper responsibility for work practices abroad until they were exposed. The "light of day" test (as set out in the discussion of various decision-making models in Appendix 1) dictated a response from Nike: if the publicity did not subside, it could be forced to change its contracting terms to relieve public pressure. President Clinton introduced a code of practice for corporations operating overseas; while this did not eliminate sweatshops—and might even have given a facade of respectability to some companies that use them—it was a necessary first step in mobilizing public opinion against oppressive labour conditions.[35]

Business and Human Rights

In 1993, representatives of Asian governments met in Bangkok prior to the Vienna conference on human rights. In a joint declaration, they claimed that "[w]hile human rights are universal in nature, they must be considered in the context of a dynamic and evolving process of international norm-setting, bearing in mind the significance of national and regional peculiarities and various historical, cultural and religious backgrounds."[36]

Chris Patten, last British governor of Hong Kong, read this equivocal endorsement of human rights as a camouflaged attack on their universality. Specifically, he argued that the rhetoric hid a belief that human rights hamper economic development: they are bad for business.[37]

Yet Hong Kong exemplifies, Patten maintains, the constructive role of the rule of law and "a proper regard for human rights" in the creation of prosperity. He takes the Hong Kong experience to be "living proof" that human rights are as relevant to Asia as they are to the West. They are not some colonial relic or a new imperialism. Patten believes that if the critics had had their way, Hong Kong should have reached a certain undefined level of affluence before starting to take human rights seriously. Otherwise rights might have got in the way of economic progress, much as the Bangkok delegates implied.

Patten's view is a welcome change from the weasel words of conditional supporters of human rights, even though there is no more evidence for his claims than there is for the belief that ethical business people will prosper. Moreover, his position seems to suggest that human rights are cost free. Human rights that mean anything in practice are not without costs.[38] At the very least they require the removal of **negative externalities** and sometimes considerably more. Rights that rely on non-interference and governmental forbearance (often called **negative rights**) seem to be what Patten had in mind. The protection of negative rights is not free, but is less costly than the protection of **positive rights**, which entail the allocation or redistribution of resources. Acknowledging such costs up front, even though this might seem to subject rights to an affordability test, is important if the role of business in human rights protection is to be serious. We discuss this further in connection with South Africa and in arguments about affordability below.

negative externality *the external cost of a transaction, not transmitted through prices, that is incurred by a party who was not involved as either a buyer or seller of the goods or services causing the cost or benefit*

negative rights *rights that require or involve only freedom from interference*

positive rights *rights that require assistance or provision in order to be exercised*

Patten is on firmer ground in demanding evidence to support the view that human rights slow the material development of peoples. This demand does not address the question of whether material prosperity should be pursued at the expense of human rights—a question that the Bangkok conference probably had on its mind. It is a question that is much on the minds of business people in the West as well: it would be wrong to suggest that Canada has problems of business ethics and less-developed countries have problems of human rights. Economic justifications for ignoring human rights problems in the conduct of business are as familiar in Canada as anywhere around the globe. The labour conditions of immigrant workers in the clothing industry in this country are as much a human rights matter as those in China or India. Of course, garment manufacturing has all but totally moved offshore, reducing the occurrence of domestic exploitation in Canada. The West remains concerned for human rights as exhibited by the inroads that Canada and other countries have made into rectifying exploitation in Asia. Still, the fact that domestic firms find it virtually impossible to compete on a cost basis with firms exploiting developing-country labour markets can make ethical considerations seem unattainable. If offshore competitors have lower labour costs, Canadian producers are in a difficult position and the use of immigrant labour can assume the colour of necessity, as in the case of Canadian domestic textile and clothing manufacturers who feel pressured to compete on a strictly price basis. It is difficult to obtain accurate data on sweatshop activity in Canada, as it is largely part of the underground economy, but activity on immigrant worker help lines and anecdotal information from community service organizations indicate that sweatshop activity remains pervasive in the Canadian garment industry. Many employers are small subcontractors that change their company names and locations to avoid detection and prosecution for illegal labour practices.[39]

The problem with arguments that sweatshop labour is required in order to be competitive is that they open the door to compromise on rights if advantages—Canadian advantages—are at stake. Fortunately, the Canadian government continues to place human rights at the forefront of its international and foreign affairs agenda. In 2007, Canada imposed significant and comprehensive trade sanctions against Burma in order to further isolate its military junta. This included a ban on all new Canadian investment in Burma and on the import and export of all goods with the exception of those required for humanitarian purposes.[40] Not all Western countries have been as ready to take a stand on human rights through the implementation of trade sanctions. Despite calls from the Burmese democracy leader, Aung San Suu Kyi, for economic sanctions against the military dictatorship, the United States and the European Union only threatened to impose trade and investment sanctions if political repression worsened. The Australian deputy prime minister, Tim Fischer, ruled out sanctions against Burma on the grounds that they would be ineffective and therefore would do nothing for human rights. Fischer rejected trade sanctions as a course of action because, as he put it, "[t]hey are not practical with regard to the Burma situation. It is, therefore, the view of Australia that they are not practical." Business leaders have been too ready to treat questions of human rights in host countries as internal matters that have nothing to do with them, even when their operations and investments are enmeshed with rights issues. Political leaders have shown a similar reluctance to confront rights abuses squarely when trade might be jeopardized by such action. The only reasonable conclusion that may be drawn is that human rights are taken to be less important than profits.

In a series of influential works, Thomas Donaldson has argued that multinational corporations ought not to deprive workers in host countries of their rights and should even assist in protecting some rights—minimal education and subsistence—but that they have no duty to provide direct aid to those whose rights have been abridged.[41] The reason for this is that such direct aid "would be unfair [to the] profit-making corporation [which] is designed to achieve an economic mission and as a moral actor possesses an exceedingly narrow personality."[42] The economic mission of the business corporation makes it a poor substitute for a government in dispensing welfare. It is neither a real (moral) person nor a democratic institution, and it has no mandate to render more than minimal assistance except in unusual circumstances (Donaldson gives the example of an earthquake). It is not within the moral capacity of a corporation to rectify deficiencies in human rights, such as minimal education and subsistence, even if such rectification is notionally within its capacity. Quite simply, argues Donaldson, the languages of personal morality, of virtue and vice, of personal perfection and the maximization of human welfare are inappropriate to considerations of corporate responsibility. The business corporation is a very restricted, artificial person, and only restricted, moral responses may be expected of it. These are not responses that presuppose a human psychology, but those that relate to legal and contractual duties and rights, responsibilities and benefits.[43]

The application of such reasoning to concrete cases can be complicated, as the following case study shows.

CASE 12.4: Shell and Nigeria

Geraldine Brooks, a journalist on the *Wall Street Journal*, was arrested by the Nigerian State Security Service for delving too deeply into the fate of the Ogoni people, among whom she found conditions far worse than she expected:

> I suppose that 10 years of working on a conservative pro-business paper had taught me that self-interest, if nothing else, usually prompts corporations to behave with a measure of decency. Oil companies, dogged by poor records in developing nations, have tried in recent years to better their image.
>
> But three days in Nigeria's Ogoniland had quickly revealed a picture much grimmer than anything the Ogoni leader, Sari Wewa, had described. Since Shell struck oil there in 1958, an estimated US$30 billion . . . worth had been extracted and sold. Yet the poverty of the 500,000 Ogoni remained desperate, even by the harsh yardstick of the poor world.
>
> As subsistence farmers dug for yams with sticks, their naked children drank from streams polluted by the toxic chemicals of neglected oil spills. Oil pipelines snaked hard up against the farmers' mud brick huts, even though current industry practice is to site them far from human habitation. I spoke to a woman burned in one of the inevitable oil fires that had resulted from this perilous practice. Still in pain almost three months later, she lay on the earthen floor of a traditional healer's hut, her burns wrapped in poultices of leaves. When I asked a Shell spokesman about her, he said the company was "hazy" on the details of the accident, and couldn't investigate because of tensions in the area.[44]

Case Questions

1. Is it inappropriate to make an adverse moral judgment about a company such as Shell, which has had an appalling environmental record in Nigeria and a disastrous effect on the Ogoni people?
2. Can a multinational be an innocent bystander when it operates in a country ranked 143 (out of 182) on Transparency International's 2011 Corruption Perception Index?[45]
3. And what is Shell's position when that oppressive regime executes dissenters such as Ogoni leader Ken Sari Wewa?

A supporter of Donaldson's view might argue that Shell is responsible for the evils it causes, but should not be expected to become involved in supplying remedies for rights violations for which it is not responsible. To impose such obligations would not only mistake the purpose of corporations and their restricted moral personality, but also commit the additional error of believing that they were fitted for such a role. On Donaldson's analysis of corporate duties, it would seem that Shell should assist the Ogoni people in overcoming the hardship inflicted upon them from oil drilling, but should avoid the political questions arising from protests against drilling on their land. Such a position, however, while plausible on paper, would be absurd in practice. Shell is producing oil with government approval but without the consent of the Ogoni. The political question is inseparable from the business issue, just as the economic and political issues in slavery were entwined. Moreover, the hardships of these people are not exceptional—they are an everyday occurrence; they are "normal." And Shell, by taking the posture of innocent bystander, helped to normalize them.

To argue otherwise would be to partition one kind of public institution in one sector of social life—the business corporation in the economy—from the kinds of burdens and costs that have to be carried by others. Whatever the limitations on the corporate personality, it cannot be suggested that the corporation is incapable of conferring and enjoying political benefits, of being criminal, or of behaving justly. Ultimately, it would be reductionist to hold that because the business corporation has limited purposes, its moral accountability can be described only in terms of these purposes; that it is such a restricted vehicle for economic advantage that it cannot be responsible for matters that are not its legal or causal responsibility; and that deviations from such conceptions of the business corporation are warranted only in exceptional circumstances, such as natural disasters. Corporations do not behave according to such a limited conception of their (moral) capabilities, and the public clearly expects more than a minimal standard of conduct from business in circumstances less unusual than an earthquake. As Kevin Jackson has remarked, given the widespread nature of poverty and disease in less-developed countries where multinationals operate profitably, "[t]he Donaldsonian exception ought . . . to be the rule."[46] Specifying the extent of the moral obligation is not easy, but that does not amount to an objection in principle. Shell's conduct subsequent to the repression of the Ogoni, which included the execution of prominent dissidents by the government, shows that corporations are not immune from moral responsibility. As noted in chapter 11, Shell took seriously the impact of its actions on the peoples and environments in which it operated, and adopted a corporate social responsibility approach, winning a British Social Reporting Award in 2001 for its 1999 report.

The test of business probity is not only observance of procedure in the matter of basic rights (such as the law), but also respect for human goods more generally. In the words of George Brenkert, "morally significant human rights [cannot be obtained] by appealing to utterly minimal duties."[47] Some conception of the goods necessary to human flourishing is also required, and no society, government, or business is entitled to trade them for more general benefits, as some forms of utilitarianism would allow. It took decades of argument and hard campaigning to get rid of slavery, to secure fair wages and conditions for workers, and to abolish child labour. These are matters that, at one time or another, were opposed on the grounds that they were unaffordable—that is, on grounds that claimed exemption from moral appraisal. An unwillingness among those who benefit from the exploitation of others to recognize their moral responsibilities is not a sufficient ground on which to pronounce an issue non-moral. Such an unwillingness betrays a move from the view that the corporation has severely limited moral capacities to the view that those who benefit from the corporation have similarly limited moral responsibilities. The thin moral personality of the corporation can be a very thick barrier between its beneficiaries and the moral problems encountered in producing earnings.

It is difficult for those businesses that differ with the hostile policies of host governments to stand up for human rights, and the decisions must be made on a case-by-case basis. Each case has to be argued, not merely proclaimed. This is a large demand to place on human rights activists: moral argument is difficult enough in a community that seems to accept cultural relativism and moral pluralism unreflectively. But moral argument of various kinds does go on. The case of Australian resources company BHP Co. Ltd's mining activities in Ok Tedi (discussed in chapter 11) was argued by that company and its critics and was resolved when BHP acknowledged its responsibilities in a fashion too rarely seen among transnational corporations. The questions it faced were not simple. The case was not only about investment and tailings in a river; it was also a case of the different aspirations of the peoples who work in that region; of just compensation for losses; and of the costs and benefits, the losers and beneficiaries from mining. The BHP decision to compensate says something about the moral community in which the company's owners live, and may signal the effect of ethical investment and moral suasion on such global businesses.

Ethical questions such as those surrounding the involvement of BHP in Ok Tedi are difficult: they require argument about the issues mentioned above. Whether companies should co-operate with evil is one of the most significant and common questions faced by businesses based in countries that claim to uphold human rights. If business is to further human rights, mere withdrawal from the site of conflict might not always be the ethical thing to do. It might be better to leave, as Levi's did in China (see Case 12.5 on page 290); on the other hand, it might be better to stay and prevent things from becoming worse for the host population. Such decisions, like Oskar Schindler's reversal of support for the German cause when he witnessed atrocities in Nazi-occupied Cracow, are not made as a result of slogans, but as a result of the ability to unite an appreciation of context with principle.

Realistically, business will not lead the way on human rights. Indeed, it would be enough if business were to follow in the wake of human rights activism and support its advances. At the very least, business may be forced to protect its interests (that is, its reputation) in the face of pressure from ethical investment organizations[48] and public interest groups. This is the argument from self-interest.[49] It is not to be despised, particularly if it assists the recognition of human rights in practice. Ultimately, the argument for international business ethics must be in terms of humanity, not commercial advantage, but at a less sublime level, self-interest is an aspect of the work of organizations dedicated to ethical standards in global business, such as Transparency International and the Caux Round Table (see pages 296–7).

Affordability

According to Donaldson, one of the three conditions for a human right is that "the obligations or burdens imposed by the right must satisfy a fairness-affordability test."[50]

This is simply the familiar moral requirement that agents must be capable of realizing—or of preventing—an action for which they are to be held responsible. If they were not in a position to act, then they could not be held accountable. So, too, with rights: corporations that are not able to prevent breaches of human rights are not to be blamed. And, because of their limited moral personalities, business corporations are less able to give effect to rights claims than are real persons, governments, or aid organizations. Donaldson does not adequately distinguish between the possession of a right and the blame attributable to those who do not, or cannot, recognize it. That is what the affordability condition is really about: blameworthiness in cases where rights are not observed, not the possession of a right.[51] Even if corporations cannot afford to act positively in defence of rights in a particular context and so cannot reasonably be blamed for this, it does not follow that the people making the rights claims do not have a legitimate case.

The failure to make this distinction clearly could have unfortunate consequences for the defence of human rights. It also underlines the importance of giving an unambiguous sense to "fairness" and "affordability" in this context. The danger is that ethics might be seen as tradable, something that Donaldson does not endorse. Nevertheless, moral rights appear to be expensive and perhaps unaffordable in situations where rights are regarded as having equal standing with economic development, profits, property, and the exploitation of a resource. Objections to mining, bridge-building, forest-felling, tourism development, child labour, less-regulated labour markets, self-regulation of occupational health and safety, and so on could well be met with the response that choices that protect human rights are too costly, that they destroy competitive advantage, and that they will cause the loss of jobs or the flight of capital.

Questions of economic benefits should take into account who is being asked to bear the costs. For whom is the business activity affordable? Are social costs being fairly compensated? In concrete terms, this means questions such as these: What if the Ogoni told Shell that they could not afford to have petroleum drilling in their midst? What if the people of Ok Tedi told BHP that they could not afford mining because it increased effluent in their river? What if Southeast Asian sweatshop workers were to ask Nike executives why they thought we could afford the current system and why we could not afford fair wages for all workers in the garment industry?

The notion of affordability suggests that we can decide when and where human rights will have currency rather than determine the answer to the different question of whether particular rights claims can be met. The notion that, in argument, morals are trumps implies that other factors should carry less weight in governing action. If that is so, then decisions about what can be afforded by a business—as distinct from a society—have already shifted ground to the detriment of human rights. If affordability is an issue for a corporation, it might have to forgo operations in a particular country. It is not entitled to evade human rights to prevent this outcome. There is a maxim in ethics that "ought" implies "can"—that is, that we should only ask someone to do something if they are able to do it. In the case of business, as with individuals, this means—among other things—that some ethical actions are subject to an affordability criterion. But affordability is a slippery notion that can easily slide over into suggesting that human rights are conditional on profitability—that we can decide when and where human rights will operate or, worse still, that we can decide when and where human rights exist at all. Peter Drucker has expressed the matter soundly:

> An organization has full responsibility for its impact on community and society. . . . It is irresponsible of an organization to accept, let alone to pursue, responsibilities that would seriously impede its capacity to perform its main task and mission. And where it has no competence it has no responsibility. . . . But—and it is a big "but"—organizations have a responsibility to try to find an approach to basic social problems which fits their competence and which, indeed, makes the social problem into an opportunity for the organization.[52]

There are, however, many instances of businesses refusing to compromise ethically and prospering nonetheless, as the following cases show.

CASE 12.5: Levi Strauss Leaves China

Because of systematic human rights violations in Myanmar and China, Levi's pulled out of these countries. The decision to leave China has been described as one of the most difficult for Levi's to make because it meant sacrificing large market opportunities. Explaining the decision, Levi's communications manager, Linda Butler, said,

> Last year we issued our global sourcing guidelines, which help us make decisions about what countries we should be in and what business partners we should be doing business with. There is a provision in those guidelines concerning human rights violations, and in light of that and in light of the current human rights situation in China, we have decided that we will not pursue a direct investment at this time and that we will begin a phased withdrawal of our contract sewing and finishing work in China.[53]

Despite the potential costs, Levi Strauss CEO Bob Hass said "never has an action by the company been met with such immediate, spontaneous, large and mainly supportive reaction from people all over the world."[54]

Another MNC that has moved beyond an ethics of minimal duty to take a more proactive role in securing the goods necessary to human development—often called corporate citizenship—is Grand Metropolitan, a leader in the international consumer goods market.

CASE 12.6: Grand Met and Corporate Citizenship

Grand Met has taken an expansive view of affordability because "[i]t shows that the company is not content just to comply with high standards of behaviour; we also want to contribute actively to the community. This proactive approach to corporate citizenship . . . sees [it] as a two-way street where value flows to the company as well as from it."[55]

A stakeholder approach, similar to that advocated by the Caux Round Table (see pages 296–7), underlies Grand Met's model of corporate relationships.[56] In India, for example, Grand Met's managers were faced with the problem of being accepted in a host society, not just in a legal sense but also in a social sense. They wanted Grand Met to be clearly seen to be adding value to Indian society and to be setting an example to other firms, both foreign and Indian. More specifically, they wanted to be in tune with the transcendent Indian goal of *sarbodaya* (moral and material well-being) and were keen to focus mainly on the needs of the most disadvantaged members of Indian society.[57]

Accordingly, they sponsored community-development programs that could become self-sustaining. Although Grand Met describes such activities in terms of charity or philanthropy, leading advocates of corporate citizenship, such as Chris Marsden, relate them to self-interest. Marsden, like many of those who are impressed by Milton Friedman's argument that managers have no business giving their owners' money to worthy causes,[58] sees so-called corporate philanthropy as strategic. Thus Grand Met's corporate citizenship in India could, in Marsden's terms, be described as "earning its 'licence to operate.'" It is a strategic move by a business that benefits its operating environment but also, and intentionally, benefits other stakeholders in that environment.[59] It goes beyond ethics, in the minimalist sense of avoiding wrongdoing, and attempts to do good. But this is not the disinterested good of the philanthropist. In the words of Julius Tahija, "Promoting goodwill in a host country is critical to a transnational's survival. But for corporate development programs to be more than stopgap measures, transnational managers must make a serious commitment to the more ambitious long-term goal of transferring business, technical, and social competencies to people in the developing world."[60]

Caltex Pacific Indonesia provides another example of active international corporate citizenship.

CASE 12.7: Caltex Pacific Indonesia

Caltex Pacific Indonesia spent 30 years repairing damage done during drilling in the Indonesian province of Riau in Sumatra. Yet, in building infrastructure, they went beyond the expected minimum. They built bridges that could also be used by local people; drained swampy land, which then became available for agriculture; promoted local businesses so that Caltex could be supplied by the people among whom it operated; avoided environmental destruction at monetary cost but with a gain in goodwill; and provided a relatively high standard of living to Indonesian workers so that they would not feel uncomfortable working beside better-favoured American expatriates.[61]

The decisions to provide benefits to local stakeholder groups must have been taken not only in the light of ethics, but also with some vision—perhaps in the belief that such actions would enhance Caltex's long-term fortunes in Indonesia, that they were affordable in terms of investment.

A Double Standard?

Richard De George has argued that the same standards are not always applicable to small entrepreneurs and MNCs in international business.[62] His argument is based on a fundamental principle of moral philosophy: we are morally responsible only if we are able to act (once again, the moral "ought" implies the practical "can"). If, for example, you say that I ought to pay my debt to you now, I must have the money to do so. It makes no sense to impose a duty on a person who is unable to undertake it for reasons beyond their control. De George argues that this consideration applies to relative assessments of multinational and domestic business operations.

De George argues that context changes the application of ethical principles. In the case of apartheid, the Sullivan Code (see pages 293–5) was an effective brake on US companies using a structurally unjust political system to their commercial advantage. International outrage at the appalling racism in South Africa at least restricted the exploitation of blacks by MNCs. But what of the case of a white South African business person employing blacks: is that person guilty of exploitation in a similar manner to the multinational that takes advantage of cheap labour? De George regards placing the local enterprise and the MNC on the same level as "both logically necessary and too strong."[63] Any whites who wished to remain ethical would be precluded from engaging in business. Paradoxically, this would mean that blacks could only work for whites who were unethical. Even living in such an unjust environment would make one a party to the unjust system—a participant in black exploitation. Hence the position of the white in South Africa seems to have been "necessarily unethical": "But any doctrine that says that people are necessarily unethical is too strong because one can only be held responsible for doing what it is possible for them to do."[64]

Bribery poses another challenge to De George's position. There seems to be a clear distinction between the obligations of international businesses and those of local business operations. In many countries—such as Indonesia, Russia, and Thailand—bribes, favours, "gifts," or secret commissions are commonplace. There is no question that each individual payment of this kind reinforces the corruption of the system and introduces injustice at personal, market, administrative, and political levels. But the system is not primarily the individual's responsibility. Systemic corruption is a collective responsibility, and the individual can only be asked to do so much to remove it.[65] While multinationals have the option of resisting demands for bribes and even of moving their operations elsewhere, local entrepreneurs might have no real choice. If a local business refuses to comply with corrupt practices, it might go out of business. Then the field will be left to those who do not mind paying bribes, and the chances of reform will be lessened. If a local business pays bribes, it is complicit in corruption, but De George argues that this is the lesser of two evils. At least the ethically disposed local business can try to change the system—something not to be expected of businesses that do not even recognize that bribery is a problem.[66]

In the cases of both apartheid and bribery, the contexts of operation for local and multinational operators differ, even in the same country. Both practices are wrong, but responsibility differs for the local and the multinational company. The local operator has limited resources and nowhere else to go; the multinational has extensive resources and other locations. The multinational could—like Levi's—challenge corruption in a host country; the local company would be unlikely to succeed and is therefore unlikely to try.

It is true that some local entrepreneurs are condemned in their own countries as exploiters, but can this judgment be generalized in countries where corruption is systemic? De George argues that it cannot. While a multinational might be embarrassed about offering bribes in a country notorious for this form of corruption, the same judgment would probably not apply to the local owner of a small transport company or retail outlet or factory. While rejecting relativism, De George argues with some force that the same judgments cannot be applied to both types of business. Of course, it would be better to change the system and to make it fair and just. But if "ought" implies "can," then the small entrepreneurs, just as the individual workers, may plead that they cannot change the system. The conclusion that it is better for them to suffer injustice than to try to improve their lot, if this means engaging in the system, is a harsh doctrine indeed.[67]

Supportive Institutions

Too often, campaigns against business decisions are driven by external interests. This typecasts business as reactive rather than responsive. Initiatives such as the Sullivan Code, the Caux Round Table, and Transparency International (see below) are important because they model a more engaged and responsive form of business conduct. Sometimes businesses can surprise themselves by taking the initiative on issues such as the environment.[68]

Institutional support for the ethical conduct of international business is important in both the domestic and international arenas. Most of that support is not in a legal form, although important legislation, such as the Foreign Corrupt Practices Act, 1977, obliges US multinationals to avoid corruption. Support for ethics is more visible in the institution of international business, fragmented as it is, and in civil society organizations born of a growing need for international standards of ethical business. The Sullivan Code, the Caux Round Table, Transparency International, and the UN Global Compact all illustrate the work of international business to support ethical international transactions.

The Global Sullivan Principles

In 1977, the Reverend Leon Sullivan, an African-American minister from Philadelphia and a board member of General Motors, drafted a set of principles for investment and operation in South Africa by US companies that came to be known as the "Sullivan Code." The code was an attack on apartheid through the morality of American investors, corporate directors, and managers. It aimed to get corporations operating in South Africa to defy apartheid by rejecting its operation in the workplace and, to some extent, beyond it. According to the code, black workers should receive equal pay, opportunity, facilities, and respect. Unions should be recognized and living conditions improved. The stability of the South African government, the cheapness of black labour, the natural resources of the country, and the expanding market for American products in a nation of 28 million people were powerful incentives for over 300 US companies to operate there. Perhaps surprisingly, many American firms—including General Motors, IBM, Mobil, 3M, and International Harvester—voluntarily adopted the Sullivan Code, thereby lessening their profits but keeping their investors happy and their image at home clean. Critics argued that the code allowed apartheid to continue with sanitized American support. Eventually, Sullivan agreed with the critics and set a deadline of 1987 for the removal of apartheid, just a few years before Nelson Mandela's release from prison. When that deadline passed, he vigorously opposed investment in South Africa, and many American firms either pulled out or sold off their interests to South African concerns. Products no longer available from American sources were replaced with those from other countries, but, even so, there were important moral victories as a result of the code. Some firms, like Kodak, not only pulled out of South Africa, but also refused to sell any of their products there. Hindsight has shown the Sullivan Code to have been more constructive as a challenge to injustice than its critics believed. Although limited, it added to the accumulation of world opinion and translated that opinion into action. Considering the way sanctions against Rhodesia were evaded, the Sullivan Code was a strategy that immediately did away with bottom-line justifications for breaches. The code required companies to take a cut in profits in South Africa. That was upfront.

Sullivan's success became the springboard for the development of his original principles into a set of aspirational principles with a global reach. These principles support justice, advocate recognition of human rights, and encourage corporate social responsibility through business collaborating with host communities.[69] The Global Sullivan Principles was launched by the Reverend Sullivan and then United Nations Secretary General Kofi Annan in 1999. By signing on to the principles, corporations commit themselves to implementing them in their global operations, but the principles are avowedly collaborative, flexible, and sensitive to the difficulties of particular environments. "The aspiration of the Principles is to have companies and organizations of all sizes, in widely disparate industries and cultures, working towards the common goals of human rights, social justice, protection of the environment and economic opportunity."[70] The website of the Global Sullivan Principles lists actions taken by corporations such as General Motors and Procter and Gamble to give effect to the principles.[71] Corporations that sign on to the principles commit to more than the following propositions, but these indicate the scope and depth of the demands on signatories.

> *The Global Sullivan Principles*[72]
>
> As a company that endorses the Global Sullivan Principles we will respect the law, and as a responsible member of society we will apply these Principles with integrity consistent with the legitimate role of business. We will develop and implement company policies, procedures, training and internal reporting structures to ensure commitment to these Principles throughout our organization. We believe the application of these Principles will achieve greater tolerance and better understanding among peoples, and advance the culture of peace.
>
> Accordingly, we will
>
> - Express our support for universal human rights and, particularly, those of our employees, the communities within which we operate and parties with whom we do business.

- Promote equal opportunity for our employees at all levels of the company with respect to issues such as color, race, gender, age, ethnicity or religious beliefs, and operate without unacceptable worker treatment such as the exploitation of children, physical punishment, female abuse, involuntary servitude or other forms of abuse.
- Respect our employees' voluntary freedom of association.
- Compensate our employees to enable them to meet at least their basic needs and provide the opportunity to improve their skill and capability in order to raise their social and economic opportunities.
- Provide a safe and healthy workplace; protect human health and the environment; and promote sustainable development.
- Promote fair competition including respect for intellectual and other property rights, and not offer, pay or accept bribes.
- Work with governments and communities in which we do business to improve the quality of life in those communities—their educational, cultural, economic and social well-being—and seek to provide training and opportunities for workers from disadvantaged backgrounds.
- Promote the application of these Principles by those with whom we do business.

We will be transparent in our implementation of these Principles and provide information which demonstrates publicly our commitment to them.

The UN Global Compact

In 2000, the United Nations—or rather, the Secretary General of the time, Kofi Annan—began a Global Compact initiative. The Global Compact is supported by businesses around the world rather than by governments. It states that it "seeks to combine the best properties of the UN, such as moral authority and convening power, with the private sector's solution-finding strengths, and the expertise and capacities of a range of key stakeholders."[73] It does this through the usual methods: producing literature, hosting conferences, and developing "tool kits" for corporate decision-makers. Although the Global Compact has attracted support and membership from over 4,000 corporations, its impact is yet to be felt, and its aim of shaping business practices according to its 10 principles seems to duplicate other initiatives—notably the Global Sullivan Principles—and thereby to lessen the force of the 10 principles. Indeed, the 10 principles, whose values are derived from UN declarations and conventions, have the obviousness of motherhood statements about them. Principles 1 and 2 state that businesses should support human rights and ensure that they do not collude in human rights abuses. Principle 3 recognizes the right to bargain collectively, 4 and 5 oppose forced labour and child labour, and Principle 6 calls for the elimination of discrimination in employment. Principles 7, 8, and 9 recommend adoption of the precautionary principle and encourage greater environmental responsibility and the development of environmentally friendly technology. Principle 10 helpfully suggests that "[b]usinesses should work against corruption in all its forms, including extortion and bribery."[74]

Signing up to the principles could probably enhance reputation, but some members of the Global Compact have not been ethically pristine. The danger in such well-meaning programs is that they can disguise problems rather than do something about them, allowing business—even if dubious—to continue as usual.

The Principles of the Caux Round Table

The Caux Round Table (CRT) evolved from a meeting of Japanese, American, and European business leaders in the Swiss mountain retreat of Caux in 1986.[75] The meeting had been called by Frederik Philips, the Dutchman who rebuilt Philips Electrical Industries after the Second World War. Philips had had extensive contacts with Japan since 1950 and was concerned about growing anti-Japanese sentiment in the light of successful Japanese car and electronics exports to Europe and the United States. Japan's high-quality and low-priced exports had placed enormous pressure on European and American industries, and now the Japanese were accused of using protectionism, dumping, theft, and blackmail to expand their international market share. Concerned that these accusations would lead to trade wars or worse, Philips contacted his Japanese friends to propose a meeting at Caux.

The first meeting was marked by frankness and openness, and these became the founding principles for the continuing forum. Jean-Loup Dherse, chair of the CRT steering committee, compares its meetings to chemical reactions "in which the experience of being honest over real conflicting situations has allowed trust to develop to such an extent that there now is a common philosophy."[76] From this beginning, an informal institution emerged. The informality arose from the friendships among the members of the group, who were senior executives from such major MNCs as Philips, Canon, Matsushita, Chase Manhattan Bank, Prudential Insurance, Mitsubishi, Toshiba, Procter and Gamble, Nissan, Schock, Ambrosetti, Medtronic, and Royal Dutch Petroleum. These are not, however, just social gatherings. The members meet twice yearly, once in Caux and once elsewhere, and sometimes guests are invited. These meetings seek to advance the aims of the CRT.

A basic aim of the CRT is to encourage business to contribute to global economic and social development. The late Ryuzaburo Kaku, chair of Canon in the 1990s and a founder of the CRT, focused the Round Table's attention on the global responsibilities of business to foster world peace and economic stability. Hence, the CRT "emphasizes the development of continuing friendship, understanding and cooperation, based on a common respect for the highest moral values and on responsible action by individuals in their own spheres of influence." Underlying this aspiration are two basic ethical principles: *kyosei*, a Japanese term coined by Kaku meaning "working together for the common good," and respect for human dignity in the Kantian sense.

In 1994, the CRT published its "Principles for Responsible Business" as "a world standard against which business behaviour can be measured." This was, in effect, the first international code of business ethics. The principles were not new, but the attitude of the CRT was distinctive. While publishing principles that they believed had global application, the members "place[d] their first emphasis on putting one's own house in order, and on seeking to establish what is right rather than who is right." In other words, they have emphasized leadership by good example and responsibility, and have tried to avoid moralizing. Corporations that want to grow ethically will put their own houses in order according to *kyosei* rather than wait to be regulated. ("The Caux Round Table Principles for Responsible Business," as slightly revised in 2009, are set out in Appendix 2.)

The CRT identifies six sets of stakeholders—customers, employees, owners or investors, suppliers, competitors, and communities—but seeks to move business beyond even these towards a new international perspective. This is in keeping with Kaku's vision of *kyosei* and the fullest conception of stakeholder responsibility in a global community. To respect these stakeholders and secure the place of business in the global economy, the CRT enjoins business to observe the principles of business ethics and "to go well beyond the requirements of the law."[77] The Caux principles set out the basic requirements of fairness, integrity, social responsibility, obligations to stakeholders, and observance of the law and human rights that one would expect of a company operating under the rule of law in any country, and then apply them internationally. There is no blueprint for the future in the CRT principles. Their strength derives from the authority of those who devised and continue to endorse them, and from their appeal to the moral sense of ethical business leaders.

Transparency International

Transparency International (TI) was founded in 1993 and commenced its campaign against international corruption in 1994. It has chapters all around the world, including an active chapter in Canada. Transparency International is best known for its annual Corruption Perception Index (CPI), which scores countries across a range of criteria. Based on a number of surveys, the CPI ranks countries according to the propensity of public officials to accept bribes. Although TI has a strong focus on developing nations, its strongest criticisms are reserved for multinational companies that indulge in corrupt practices, such as bribery, that would be condemned at home. In the words of TI's founder, Peter Eigen, the index is "a measure of lost development opportunities as an empirical link has now been established between the level of corruption and foreign direct investment. Every day the poor scores in the CPI are not being dealt with means more impoverishment, less education, less health care."[78]

TI-Canada began in November 1996 to assist in the exposure of, and fight against, international business corruption in Canada. Among its corporate members are Barrick Gold Corporation, GE Canada, Talisman Energy, Nexen Energy, and Teck Cominco Ltd. TI-Canada also enjoys the support of the accounting and legal professions, law enforcement agencies, academics, political leaders, non-government organizations, and concerned citizens. It implements the mission statement of its parent organization to forge alliances, and it participates with its government partners—the Canadian International Development Agency and the Export Development Corporation—and with international organizations such as the World Bank, the OECD (Organization for Economic Co-operation and Development) and the OAS (Organization of American States) in corruption-prevention ventures in a multitude of developing countries.

Table 12.1 Selected countries in Transparency International's Corruption Perception Index, 2011

Rank	Country	Score out of 10
1	New Zealand	9.5 (evaluated best in terms of its public officials being unlikely to accept bribes)
2	Denmark, Finland	9.4
4	Sweden	9.3
5	Singapore	9.2
6	Norway	9.0
7	Netherlands	8.9
8	Australia, Switzerland	8.8
10	Canada	8.7
12	Hong Kong	8.4
13	Iceland	8.3
14	Germany, Japan	8.0
16	Austria, Barbados, United Kingdom	7.8
19	Ireland	7.5
24	United States	7.1
32	Taiwan	6.1
36	Israel	5.8
57	Saudi Arabia	4.4
61	Cuba	4.2
69	Italy	3.9
75	China	3.6
80	Greece	3.4
95	Tonga	3.1
100	Argentina, Indonesia	3.0
120	Bangladesh, Iran	2.7
129	Philippines	2.6
134	Pakistan	2.5
143	Nigeria, Russia	2.4
172	Venezuela	1.9
175	Iraq	1.8
177	Sudan	1.6
180	Afghanistan	1.5
182	Somalia	1.0

Source: Adapted from Corruption Perception Index 2011. Copyright 2011 Transparency International: the global coalition against corruption. Used with permission. For more information, visit http://www.transparency.org.

Since 1999, TI has also compiled a Bribe Payers Index (BPI). This is an index of the propensity of businesses in developed countries to offer bribes in order to gain or keep business in developing countries.

> The [2011] BPI is a ranking of 28 of the world's wealthiest and most economically influential countries according to the likelihood of their firms to bribe abroad. It is based on two questions asked of 3016 senior business executives from companies in 30 countries. To assess the international supply side of bribery, senior business executives were asked about the likelihood of foreign firms, from countries they have business dealings with, to engage in bribery when doing business in their country. In short, senior business executives provide their perception of the sources of foreign bribery, and these views form the basis of the 2011 BPI.[79]

Table 12.2 Countries in Transparency International's Bribe Payers Index, 2011

Rank	Country	Score out of 10
1	Netherlands, Switzerland	8.8 (evaluated as best in terms of businesses being least likely to offer bribes)
3	Belgium	8.7
4	Germany, Japan	8.6
6	Australia, Canada	8.5
8	Singapore, United Kingdom	8.3
10	United States	8.1
11	France, Spain	8.0
13	South Korea	7.9
14	Brazil	7.7
15	Hong Kong, Italy, Malaysia, South Africa	7.6
19	India, Taiwan, Turkey	7.5
26	Mexico	7.0
27	China	6.5
28	Russia	6.1

Source: Adapted from Bribe Payers Index 2011. Copyright 2011 Transparency International: the global coalition against corruption. Used with permission. For more information, visit http://www.transparency.org.

Unlike the CPI, the BPI has not been published annually. It has been published only five times. Canada's position in the most recent BPI is noticeably lower than it was in the previous surveys: number 6 out of 28 in 2011, number 1 out of 22 in 2008, number 5 out of 30 in 2006, number 5 out of 22 in 2002, and number 2 out of 19 in 1999.

The mission of Transparency International is to forge coalitions internationally; to combat corruption through law reform and anti-corruption policies; to build public support for anti-corruption measures; to promote transparency and accountability in public administration and international business; and to encourage all involved in international business to adhere to high standards of ethics, such as those proclaimed in TI's Standards of Conduct. The main instrument used to pursue this mission is the global building of coalitions of like-minded individuals and organizations. TI was heavily involved in the International Anti-corruption Conference in Lima, Peru, in 1997 and the Lima Declaration, which issued from it.[80] TI sponsors conferences and studies, and publishes information about the costs of corruption in international business.

International norms of business conduct are very much like those that prevail at the domestic level: many who know of them observe them in the breach, many are cynical about the notion for self-interested reasons, and some have yet to make their acquaintance. Efforts to build a global business culture have begun and have the strong support of some of the largest MNCs, as well as a host of governments. But all of these efforts must be based on sound reasoning about the issues. That is what this chapter has tried to elicit.

Review Questions

1. Is ethics a handicap to successful international business? Does the nature of international business mean that it must be? Is this the right way to look at it?
2. Does the distinction between primary and secondary values itself have any practical value in dealing with apparently different and conflicting ethical practices?
3. If we can speak of being tolerant and even accepting of some cultural and ethical differences, can we also speak of a limit to such toleration and acceptance? Can we identify criteria for determining whether and where such lines should be drawn?
4. In Transparency International's Corruption Perception Index of 182 countries, roughly the bottom 50 per cent of the countries listed are poor countries. So, the poor countries are those in which public officials are most likely to take bribes. From this fact, should we draw the conclusion "Ethics is okay, but, really, it is a luxury that only the wealthy can afford"?

Suggested Readings

Baker, H.K., and J.R. Nofzinger, eds. *Socially Responsible Finance and Investing: Financial Institutions, Corporations, Investors, and Activists*. Hoboken, NJ: John Wiley and Sons, 2012.

De George, Richard. *Competing with Integrity in International Business*. New York: Oxford University Press, 1993.

Donaldson, Thomas. *The Ethics of International Business*. New York: Oxford University Press, 1989.

Drucker, Peter. *Post-Capitalist Society*. New York: Harper Business, 1993.

Hartley, R.F. *Business Ethics: Mistakes and Successes*, chap. 12. 1st ed. Hoboken NJ: John Wiley and Sons, 2005.

Landier, A., and V.B. Nair. *Investing for Change: Profit from Responsible Investment*. New York: Oxford University Press 2009.

Suggested Websites

Bhopal Information Centre, Chronology:

http://www.bhopal.com/chronology.

The Caux Round Table:

http://www.cauxroundtable.org/.

Certified Global Management Accountants, "Managing Responsible Business: A Global Survey on Business Ethics":

http://www.cgma.org/Resources/Reports/DownloadableDocuments/CGMA%20Ethics%20Report%20FINAL.pdf.

Global Sullivan Principles:

http://www.thesullivanfoundation.org/gsp/principles/gsp/default.asp.

Institute of Business Ethics, "Surveys on business ethics, 2011," ***Business Ethics Briefing*****, no. 23 (February 2012):**

http://www.ibe.org.uk/userfiles/surveys_2011.pdf.

"Overview of the UN Global Compact":

http://www.unglobalcompact.org/AboutTheGC/index.html.

"The Ten Principles" of the UN Global Compact:

http://www.unglobalcompact.org/AboutTheGC/TheTenPrinciples/index.html.

Transparency International:

http://archive.transparency.org/.

Transparency International Canada:

http://www.transparency.ca/.

Appendix 1
Ethical Decision-Making Models

An "ethical decision-making model" is a suggested device for use in working through ethical problems and reaching a decision about a course of action in a structured and systematic way. In recent years, a great number of ethical decision-making models have been proposed, and various models have been officially adopted or endorsed by several professional and business organizations. A number of decision-making models are reproduced here for your consideration. These models are not provided as the only ways to go about dealing with ethical issues. Indeed, some people have expressed concern about the wisdom of using decision-making models at all. The concern has largely been that decision-making models can give the impression that ethical decision-making is an algorithmic and mechanical process when, in fact, it is usually much more complex and subtle than that. In addition, the fact of there being so many different decision-making models can give the impression that just any old decision procedure, involving any considerations, will do, as long as it can be represented as steps that can be followed in reaching a decision. Ethical decision-making models do, however, have the important characteristic of representing ethical deliberation as a systematic process rather than simply as a "touchy-feely" experience or as a matter of one's gut reaction to a situation. Ethical decision-making models emphasize that there is, in fact, deliberation associated with making ethical decisions—there is something to deliberate about, and the various contributing factors can be articulated and dealt with.

In considering the following proposed ethical decision-making models, you should give some thought to the appearance of common elements in some or most of them (for instance, they almost all include a "light of day" test, a suggestion that you imagine how you would feel if the proposed action came to be widely known). You should also give some thought to whether any of the steps or elements in these models seem to be particularly insightful, potentially fruitful, or helpful in dealing with ethical matters systematically. You will notice that all the models allow for what was earlier referred to as "ethical pluralism"; none of them is couched in terms of a purported correct moral theory.

1. The American Accounting Association Model: Seven Steps

In 1990, the American Accounting Association (AAA) published a casebook, *Ethics in the Accounting Curriculum: Cases and Readings*. These cases illustrate ethical issues that accountants may encounter in the context of their professional activities. Each case is analyzed using a seven-step decision-making model.[1]

1. **Determine the facts—what, who, where, when, how.**
   What do we know or need to know, if possible, that will help define the problem?
2. **Define the ethical issue.**
   a) List the significant stakeholders.
   b) Define the ethical issues.
   Make sure you know precisely what the ethical issue is—for example, conflict involving rights, question over limits of an obligation, etc.

3. **Identify major principles, rules, values—for example, integrity, quality, respect for persons, profit.**
4. **Specify the alternatives.**
   List the major alternative courses of action, including those that represent some form of compromise or point between simply doing or not doing something.
5. **Compare values and alternatives. See if a clear decision is evident.**
   Determine if there is one principle or value, or combination, which is so compelling that the proper alternative is clear—for example, correcting a defect that is almost certain to cause loss of life.
6. **Assess the consequences.**
   Identify short- and long-run, positive and negative consequences for the major alternatives. The common short-run focus on gain or loss needs to be measured against long-run considerations. This step will often reveal an unanticipated result of major importance.
7. **Make your decision.**
   Balance the consequences against your primary principles or values and select the alternative that best fits.

2. The Laura Nash Model: Twelve Questions[2]

Nash wants to make decision-making more practical, rather than relying on abstract philosophical concepts.

1. **Have you defined the problem accurately?**
   Gain precise facts and many of them.
2. **How would you define the problem if you stood on the other side of the fence?**
   Consider how others perceive it; alternatives?
3. **How did this situation occur in the first place?**
   Consider the history, problem, or symptoms.
4. **To whom and what do you give your loyalties as a person and as a member of the corporation?**
   Private duty vs corporate policy or norms.
5. **What is your intention in making this decision?**
   Can you take pride in your action?
6. **How does this intention compare with the likely results?**
   Are results harmful even with good intentions?
7. **Whom could your decision or action injure?**
   A good thing resulting in a bad end? Wanted A; got B.
8. **Can you engage the affected parties in a discussion of the problem before you make your decision?**
   Example: talk to workers before closing the plant.
9. **Are you confident that your position will be valid over a long period of time as it seems now?**
   Look at long-term consequences.
10. **Could you disclose without qualm your decision or action to your boss, your CEO, the board of directors, your family, or society as a whole?**
    Would you feel comfortable with this on TV?

11. **What is the symbolic potential of your action if understood? If misunderstood?**
    Sincerity and the perceptions of others.
12. **Under what conditions would you allow exceptions to your stand?**
    Speeding to a hospital with a heart attack victim.

3. The Michael Rion Model: Six Questions[3]

1. **Why is this bothering me?**
   Is it really an issue? Am I genuinely perplexed, or am I afraid to do what I know is right?
2. **Who else matters?**
   Who are the stakeholders who may be affected by my decisions?
3. **Is it my problem?**
   Have I caused the problem or has someone else? How far should I go in resolving the issue?
4. **What is the ethical concern?**
   Legal obligation, fairness, promise keeping, honesty, doing good, avoiding harm?
5. **What do others think?**
   Can I learn from those who disagree with my judgment?
6. **Am I being true to myself?**
   What kind of person or company would do what I am contemplating? Could I share my decision "in good conscience" with my family? With colleagues? With public officials?

4. Mary Guy: Values, Rules, and a Decision-Making Model[4]

Before offering a decision-making model, Guy suggests that one might keep "ten core values" in mind: "By evaluating how these values relate to an issue under consideration, and by analyzing who the stakeholders are in the decision, the ethical implications of an action become clearer."

- *Caring*—treating people as ends in themselves, not as means to ends. This means having compassion, treating people courteously and with dignity, helping those in need, and avoiding harm to others.
- *Honesty*—being truthful and not deceiving or distorting. One by one, deceptions undermine the capacity for open exchange and erode credibility.
- *Accountability*—accepting the consequences of one's actions and accepting the responsibility for one's decisions and their consequences. This means setting an example for others and avoiding even the appearance of impropriety. Asking such questions as "How would this be interpreted if it appeared in the newspaper?" or "What sort of person would do such a thing?" brings accountability dilemmas into focus.
- *Promise keeping*—keeping one's commitments. The obligation to keep promises is among the most important of generally accepted obligations. To be worthy of trust, one must keep one's promises and fulfill one's commitments.
- *Pursuit of excellence*—striving to be as good as one can be. It means being diligent, industrious, and committed, and becoming well informed and well prepared. Results are important, but so is the manner and the method of achievement.
- *Loyalty*—being faithful and loyal to those with whom one has dealings. This involves safeguarding the ability to make independent professional judgments by scrupulously avoiding undue influence and conflicts of interest.

- *Fairness*—being open-minded, willing to admit error, and not overreaching or taking undue advantage of another's adversities. Avoiding arbitrary or capricious favouritism; treating people equally and making decisions based on notions of justice.
- *Integrity*—using independent judgment and avoiding conflicts of interest, restraining from self-aggrandizement, and resisting economic pressure; being faithful to one's deepest beliefs, acting on one's conviction, and not adopting an end-justifies-the-means philosophy that ignores principle.
- *Respect for others*—recognizing each person's right to privacy and self-determination and having respect for human dignity. This involves being courteous, prompt, and decent, and providing others with information that they need to make informed decisions.
- *Responsible citizenship*—having one's actions in accord with societal values. Appropriate standards for the exercise of discretion must be practised.

Guy also suggests five rules that integrate these values and that might be of assistance in codifying one's ethical decision-making:

- *Rule 1*—Consider the well-being of others, including nonparticipants. This rule emphasizes caring and respect for others.
- *Rule 2*—Think as a member of the community, not as an isolated individual. This emphasizes loyalty, integrity, respect for others, and responsible citizenship.
- *Rule 3*—Obey, but do not depend solely on the law. This emphasizes integrity and responsible citizenship.
- *Rule 4*—Ask, "What sort of person would do such a thing?" This emphasizes all the values by calling each into question.
- *Rule 5*—Respect the customs of others, but not at the expense of your own ethics. This emphasizes accountability, fairness, integrity, and respect for others.

Guy's decision-making model:

1. **Define the problem.**
   Isolate the key factors in question and diagnose the situation to define the basic problem and to identify the limits of the situation. This step is critical, because it prevents solving the wrong problem.
2. **Identify the goal to be achieved.**
   If you do not know where you are going, you will never know when you get there. For this reason, it is essential that a goal is clearly declared.
3. **List all possible solutions to the problem.**
   All alternatives that will address the problem and achieve the goal are placed under consideration.
4. **Evaluate each alternative to determine which one best meets the requirements of the situation.**
   This requires a thorough analysis of each alternative. The analysis involves measuring the benefits, costs, and risks of each, as well as identifying the likely intended and unintended consequences of each. This step provides information about the utility of each alternative in terms of the efficiency with which it maximizes desired values and still achieves the goal.
5. **Identify the one course of action that is most likely to produce the desired consequences within the constraints of the situation.**
   This requires selecting the alternative that maximizes the most important values and holds the most promise of achieving the goal while solving the problem as effectively as possible.

6. **Make a commitment to the choice and implement it.**
   This requires converting the decision into action.

Guy further suggests that a slightly larger, 10-step, model is more appropriate for complex problems:

1. **Define the problem.**
2. **Identify the goal to be achieved.**
3. **Specify all dimensions of the problem.**
4. **List all possible solutions to each dimension.**
5. **Evaluate alternative solutions to each dimension regarding the likelihood of each to maximize the important values at stake.**
6. **Eliminate alternatives that are too costly, not feasible, or maximize the wrong values when combined with solutions to other dimensions.**
7. **Rank the alternatives to each dimension according to which are most likely to maximize the most important values.**
8. **Select the alternative to each dimension that is most likely to work in the context of the problem while maximizing the important values at stake.**
9. **Combine the top-ranking alternatives for each dimension of the problem in order to develop a solution to the problem as a whole.**
10. **Make a commitment to the choice and implement it.**

5. The Kent Hodgson Model: The Three-Step Process[5]

1. **Examine the situation.**
   - Get the critical facts. What does the situation look like? What has happened? What are the circumstances involved?
   - Identify the key stakeholders. Who are the significant players? Include all the key stakeholders significantly affected by the situation and by any decisions you might make.
   - Identify each stakeholder's options (what each stakeholder wants done). State the options for action that represent each stakeholder's interest. Put yourself in the stakeholders' shoes and think from their point of view. This is not the time to make final judgments or slant stakeholder options from your own perspective.
2. **Establish the dilemma.**
   - Identify the working principles and norms that drive each option (why each stakeholder wants it done). Pinpoint, as best you can, the business reasons for each option. Why is this stakeholder in favour of this option for action? The answers show you what the stakeholders' value and the working principles that flow from those values.
   - Project the possible outcomes (consequences) of each stakeholder option. Do any violate your principles or those of your organization? What will each stakeholder option cause to happen? You are trying to discover what the stakeholder wants to have happen in this situation. Then ask, "Do any of the outcomes resulting from these options violate my principles, or those of my organization?"
   - Determine the actions (means) necessary to produce each outcome. Do any violate your principles or those of your organization? What will stakeholders have to do to get the result they want? What steps will they take to make their desired options

happen? Then ask, "Do any of the actions they will take to make their options happen (means to the end) violate my principles or those of my organization?

- State the dilemma. Through the activities completed, you know the stakeholders, the options they represent, the validity of the working principles behind their options, and the validity of the means to implement their options. You are now in a position to decide if what you are facing is a true dilemma (balanced opposite interests). You are now able to state, even write down, the dilemma exactly.

3. **Evaluate the options.**
   - Identify the General Principle(s) behind each stakeholder option. Is the option driven primarily by dignity of human life, autonomy, honesty, loyalty, fairness, humaneness, or the common good (the "magnificent seven")? The answer is not automatic or expedient; rather, it is a matter of honest judgment on your part.
   - Compare the General Principle(s) behind each option. Which is the most responsible General Principle(s) in this situation? In your mind, in this situation, which of the "magnificent seven" holds top priority as an ethical reason for this or that option? The object is to choose an option for action that represents the most responsible General Principle (or Principles) for you, now, in this situation.
   - The option with the most responsible General Principle(s) is your choice for action. Your decision is not a guess, a choice from ignorance, or a choice from expediency. It is choice for action derived from principles. And it is a decision that is defensible on the grounds of principle and an attitude of cooperative responsibility.

6. The Cottell and Perlin Model: Five Steps[6]

1. **Describe all the relevant facts in the case. Be certain to note any assumptions not directly presented in the case.**
2. **Describe the ethical and legal perspectives and responsibilities of the parties. Try to distinguish between legal and ethical responsibilities. Take note of potential value conflicts among participants in the case.**
3. **State the principal value conflicts in the case.**
4. **Determine possible courses of action. Note both short- and long-term consequences. Describe the principles affirmed or abridged in projected courses of action. Distinguish utilitarian (consequences) from deontological (principles) justifications in each case. Would ethical realism as it exists in the accounting profession assist in resolving the dilemma?**
   ["Ethical realism" is an important notion for Cottell and Perlin. Basically, it means trying to consider what the leaders in the profession would think is right or wrong. This relies on the premise that "the leadership has an ethical insight." By "leaders," they mean the "intellectual authorities . . . the big guns. Each of us can name the national leaders in the profession. They are the managing partners of large firms, the heads of professional bodies, the members of standard-setting boards. In short, they are the men and women who have risen up through the ranks to positions of respect."]
5. **Choose and defend a decision. State why one value (or set of values) was chosen over another in the case. Discuss the result of such a choice for participants in the case, for the accounting profession, and for society in general.**

7. David Mathison: The Synthesis Model[7]

First, understand three foundational concepts:

- *Obligations*—restrictions on behaviour, things one must do or must avoid; for example, business relationships, fidelity in contracts, gratitude, justice.
- *Ideals*—notions of excellence, the goal of which is to bring greater harmony to self and others; for example, concepts as profit, productivity, quality, stability, tolerance, and compassion all fit here.
- *Effects*—the intended or unintended consequences of a decision; for example, oil rigs on the high seas, a spillage.

This requires a three-step process:

1. **Identify the important issues involved in the case using obligations, ideals, or effects as a starting point. The goal here is to expand one's view.**
2. **Decide where the main emphasis or focus should lie among the five or so issues generated in Step 1. Which is the major thrust of the case? Is it a certain obligation, ideal, or effect? For example, it may be a choice of remaining silent about a wing design defect with the effect of people dying in a plane accident versus going to the media with the effect of damaging a plane manufacturer's credibility on a personal "hunch."**
3. **With the well-focused issue worked out in Step 1, now you apply the "Basic Decision Rules":**
   a) When two or more obligations conflict, choose the more important one.
   b) When two or more ideals conflict or when ideals conflict with obligations, choose the action that honours the higher ideal.
   c) When the effects are mixed, choose the action that produces the greatest good or lesser harm. For example, in the case of the questioning engineer, clearly saving human lives is the greater good over saving a manufacturer's image.

8. Anthony M. Pagano: Six Tests[8]

Pagano proposes six tests rather than outlining a particular approach or model. His idea is that these tests can provide useful insights into the ethical perspective of a proposed action:

1. **Is it legal?**
   This is the core starting point.
2. **The benefit-cost test.**
   This is the utilitarian perspective.
3. **The generalization test.**
   Do you want this action to be a universal standard? If it's good for the goose, it's good for the gander.
4. **The light-of-day test.**
   What if it appeared on TV? Would you be proud?
5. **Do unto others—the golden rule test.**
   Do you want the same thing to happen to you?
6. **Ventilation test.**
   Get a second opinion from a wise friend with no investment in the outcome.

Appendix 2

The Caux Round Table Principles for Responsible Business[9]

Principle 1: Respect Stakeholders beyond Shareholders

A responsible business

- acknowledges its duty to contribute value to society through the wealth and employment it creates and the products and services it provides to consumers.
- maintains its economic health and viability not just for shareholders, but also for other stakeholders.
- respects the interests of, and acts with honesty and fairness towards, its customers, employees, suppliers, competitors, and the broader community.

Principle 2: Contribute to Economic, Social and Environmental Development

A responsible business

- recognizes that business cannot sustainably prosper in societies that are failing or lacking in economic development.
- therefore contributes to the economic, social, and environmental development of the communities in which it operates in order to sustain its essential "operating" capital—financial, social, environmental, and all forms of goodwill.
- enhances society through effective and prudent use of resources, free and fair competition, and innovation in technology and business practices.

Principle 3: Respect the Letter and the Spirit of the Law

A responsible business

- recognizes that some business behaviours, although legal, can nevertheless have adverse consequences for stakeholders.
- therefore adheres to the spirit and intent behind the law, as well as the letter of the law, which requires conduct that goes beyond minimum legal obligations.
- always operates with candour, truthfulness, and transparency, and keeps its promises.

Principle 4: Respect Rules and Conventions

A responsible business

- respects the local cultures and traditions in the communities in which it operates, consistent with fundamental principles of fairness and equality.
- everywhere it operates, respects all applicable national and international laws, regulations, and conventions, while trading fairly and competitively.

Principle 5: Support Responsible Globalization

A responsible business

- as a participant in the global marketplace, supports open and fair multilateral trade.
- supports reform of domestic rules and regulations where they unreasonably hinder global commerce.

Principle 6: Respect the Environment

A responsible business

- protects and, where possible, improves the environment and avoids wasteful use of resources.
- ensures that its operations comply with best environmental management practices consistent with meeting the needs of today without compromising the needs of future generations.

Principle 7: Avoid Illicit Activities

A responsible business

- does not participate in, or condone, corrupt practices, bribery, money laundering, or other illicit activities.
- does not participate in or facilitate transactions linked to or supporting terrorist activities, drug trafficking, or any other illicit activity.
- actively supports the reduction and prevention of all such illegal and illicit activities.

Notes

Introduction

1. Andrew Clark, "Thain says sorry for $1.2m furniture bill," *Guardian*, 27 January 2009, http://www.guardian.co.uk/business/2009/jan/27/merrill-lynch-john-thain-citigroup.
2. "Bank of America CEO subpoenaed over Merrill Lynch bonuses," Syracuse.com, 20 February 2009, http://www.syracuse.com/news/index.ssf/2009/02/bank_of_america_ceo_subpoenaed.html.
3. Maureen Dowd, "Wall Street's socialist jet-setters," *New York Times*, 27 January 2009, A31.
4. "Stand-off over Sir Fred's pension," BBC News, 27 February 2009, http://news.bbc.co.uk/2/hi/uk_news/politics/7912651.stm.
5. "Lehman boss sells mansion for just $15," *Australian Financial Review*, 28 January 2009, 10.
6. Michael Lewis "The irresponsible investor," *New York Times*, 6 June 2004, http://query.nytimes.com/gst/fullpage.html?res=9A01E1DA1431F935A35755C0A9629C8B63&scp=1&sq=The%20Irresponsible%20Investor&st=cse.
7. Ibid.
8. Richard De George, *Business Ethics*, 6th edn (Upper Saddle River, NJ: Pearson Education, 2006), 5–8.
9. M. McCuddy, K. Reichardt, and D. Schroeder, "Actions speak louder than words: Organizational ethics, success, and reputation from the perspective of members of the Institute of Management Accountants," *2007 Oxford Business & Economics Conference Proceedings* (Oxford, 2007) (published on CD without sequential pagination), http://www.gcbe.us/2007_OBEC/data/confcd.htm.
10. Stephen Cohen, *Moral Reasoning: The Framework and Activities of Ethical Deliberation, Argument and Decision-Making* (Melbourne: Oxford University Press, 2004).

Chapter 1

1. Aristotle, *The Ethics of Aristotle*, trans. J.A.K. Thomson et al. (Harmondsworth, UK: Penguin Books, 1976), 64–5.
2. Merriam-Webster online dictionary defines "sharp practice" as the act of dealing in which advantage is taken or sought unscrupulously.
3. James Rachels, *The Elements of Moral Philosophy*, 2nd edn (New York: McGraw-Hill, 1993), 13.
4. Lawrence M. Hinman, *Ethics: A Pluralistic Approach to Moral Theory*, 4th edn (Belmont, CA: Thomson Wadsworth, 2008), 4.
5. Peter Singer, ed., *Ethics* (New York: Oxford University Press, 1994), 4, 10.
6. Peter Singer, *Practical Ethics*, 2nd edn (New York: Cambridge University Press, 1993), 10, 12.
7. David Elias, "Tweed finds profit preying on old folk," *Sydney Morning Herald*, 30 December 2004, http://www.smh.com.au/news/Business/Tweed-finds-profit-preying-on-old-folk/2004/12/29/1103996611426.html.
8. *New York Times*, 23 September 1969, 34.
9. Tony Paterson, "Josef Fritzl: The making of a monster," *Independent*, 3 May 2008, http://www.independent.co.uk/news/world/europe/josef-fritzl-the-making-of-a-monster-820370.html.
10. Kate Connolly, "I'm no monster, says dungeon father in attack on 'biased' media," *Guardian*, 8 May 2008, http://www.guardian.co.uk/world/ 2008/may/08/joseffritzl.austria.
11. "I'm no monster, says dungeon dad," *Sydney Morning Herald*, 8 May 2008, http://www.smh.com.au/articles/2008/05/08/1210131101774.html.
12. Albert Jonsen and Stephen Toulmin, *The Abuse of Casuistry* (Berkeley: University of California Press, 1988).
13. John Rawls, *A Theory of Justice* (Cambridge, MA: Harvard University Press, 1971).
14. Roger P. Ebertz, "Is reflective equilibrium a coherentist model?," *Canadian Journal of Philosophy* 23 (1993): 194.
15. J.S. Mill, *Utilitarianism* (Indianapolis: Bobbs-Merrill, 1957), 22.
16. Deontological theories of ethics have been invigorated in two very different theories by philosophers John Rawls and Robert Nozick. Although they argue for radically differing views concerning the role of government in a just society, both take a strong position on respect for persons as a matter that is independent of concern for consequences. See Rawls's *A Theory of Justice* and Nozick's *Anarchy, State and Utopia* (New York: Basic Books, 1974).
17. Immanuel Kant, *Foundations of the Metaphysics of Morals*, trans. L.W. Beck (New York: Macmillan, 1990).
18. Ibid., 38.
19. Ibid., 46.
20. Depending on how they are counted, Kant offers five or six formulations of the categorical imperative.

21. Adam Smith, *The Theory of Moral Sentiments* (Indianapolis: Liberty Press, 1982). See also E.W. Coker, "Adam Smith's concept of the social system," *Journal of Business Ethics* 9 (1990), 139–42.
22. William Frankena, *Ethics*, 2nd edn (Englewood Cliffs, NJ: Prentice Hall, 1973), 47.
23. See Edmund L. Pincoffs, *Quandaries and Virtues* (Lawrence, KS: University of Kansas Press, 1986).
24. Mill, *Utilitarianism*, 30.
25. This is discussed more in Stephen Cohen, *The Nature of Moral Reasoning: The Framework and Activities of Ethical Deliberation, Argument, and Decision-Making* (Melbourne: Oxford University Press, 2004), 84–7.
26. Cicero, *De officiis*, trans. Walter Miller (Cambridge, MA, and London: Loeb, 1913), vol. 3, 99–101.
27. For an accessible presentation of a variety of positions concerning relativism, see *Social Philosophy and Policy* 11, no. 1 (1994).
28. Marcus G. Singer, *Generalization in Ethics* (New York: Russell and Russell, 1971), 327–34; John Finnis, *Natural Law and Natural Rights* (Oxford: Clarendon Press, 1980), 81–5.
29. However, at this point a very important question can sometimes be asked concerning whether and why such-and-such convention is itself worthy of respect. It is not worthy of respect just because it is a group's convention.
30. Walt W. Manley II and William A. Shrode, *Critical Issues in Business Conduct* (New York: Quorum Books, 1990), chap. 14.
31. Famously, Immanuel Kant argued for this view in his nonconsequentialist position in *Foundations of the Metaphysics of Morals* (1785). Recently, in *Moral Animals* (2004, chap. 3), Catherine Wilson argued that this is the hallmark of an ethical consideration, whether consequentialist or nonconsequentialist.
32. Here is an example of something quite like moral blindness. In a recent Clemenger BBDO television advertisement for Hahn Premium Light beer, titled "Sex Bomb," a woman sets the relaxed, romantic mood and begins to luxuriate in a serene bubble bath. A short while after she has begun, her male partner enters and does a "bomb" into the bath, thus destroying the mood. She is clearly annoyed by what has happened. As he then pops the top on his Hahn Premium Light, he notices her expression and, with a nonplussed look on his face, says, "Whaaaat?" He simply has no idea as to how what he has just done could have been other than enjoyed. He just did not see it. We could even imagine that he considered the mood, his partner's enjoyment, and "decided" that this would be a good thing to do. He was blind to the situation. It is not difficult to imagine that someone would behave in this way in the face of—and with some sort of recognition of—a serious moral dimension to a situation. So, "Did you think about this?, . . . this?, . . . this?, . . ." The answer is "Yes," "Yes," and "Yes"; but they did not really see those things in any serious way.
33. Ethical decision-making models are discussed at somewhat more length and some examples are offered in Appendix 1.
34. This point is discussed more fully in Cohen, *The Nature of Moral Reasoning*, 113–18.
35. Adam Smith, *An Enquiry into the Nature and Causes of the Wealth of Nations* (New York: Modern Library, 1937). See, for example, page 423.
36. Cicero, *De officiis*, vol. 3, xiii.
37. Peter Drucker, "What is 'business ethics'?," *Public Interest* 63 (1981): 18–36.
38. Milton Friedman, "The social responsibility of business is to increase its profits," *New York Times Magazine*, 13 September 1970, reprinted in T. Donaldson and P. Werhane, eds, *Ethical Issues in Business: A Philosophical Approach*, 2nd edn (Englewood Cliffs, NJ: Prentice Hall, 1983), 239–42.
39. Jonathan Dancy, *Moral Reasons* (Oxford: Blackwell, 1993), 211.
40. See, for instance, Lawrence Hinman, *Ethics: A Pluralistic Approach to Moral Theory*, 4th edn (Belmont, CA: Thomson Wadsworth, 2008). Hinman also maintains a website that includes references to and discussions about moral pluralism: http://ethics.acusd.edu/ and, in particular, http://ethics.acusd.edu/theories/Pluralism/index.html.
41. Geoffrey Barker, "Ethics: The glove that tempers the iron fist," *Australian Financial Review Magazine*, 7 July 1995, 14–20.
42. Much of the following discussion of "good ethics is good business" is revised from Stephen Cohen, "Good ethics is good business—revisited," *Business and Professional Ethics Journal* 18, no. 2 (1999): 57–68.
43. Barker, "Ethics," esp. 20.
44. Paul Simons, former chairman of Woolworths Ltd, was in this camp. See, for instance, Paul Simons, "Be interested in the people you serve and your life will be happy," Fourth Annual Lecture, St James Ethics Centre, Sydney, November 1994.

45. We realize that, strictly speaking, an enhanced bottom line is not identical to, and is sometimes not a good indicator of, enhanced self-interest. For convenience here, however, we will use the expressions as though they were equivalent.
46. Thomas Hobbes (1588–1679) argued in *Leviathan* (1651) that ethics is founded on self-interest, which provides the sole motivation for behaving ethically.
47. Padraic P. McGuinness, former social commentator for (among other places) the *Australian Financial Review*, held this view. See his "Elusive ethics," *Sydney Morning Herald*, 17 November 1994, 20.
48. Kant argued in *Foundations of the Metaphysics of Morals* (1785) that the nature of ethics is such that it necessarily involves a conflict with self-interest.
49. Simons, "Be interested in the people you serve and your life will be happy."
50. The Canadian Competition Bureau, www.competitionbureau.gc.ca/.
51. We will return to this example again, and in greater detail, in chapter 7.
52. The Body Shop is also a good example of how you can get very severely criticized for not living up to the virtues that you trumpet.
53. *Australian Financial Review Magazine*, 7 July 1995, 16.
54. This has also been discussed on pages xv–xvi and will be discussed again at pages 67–9 under the heading "Good Ethics Is Good Business—Again."
55. St Thomas Aquinas (1224–1274). Questions 90–97 of his *Summa Theologiae* are referred to as the *Treatise on Law*. In the *Treatise on Law*, Aquinas argues that although one should focus on advancing the common good for its own sake (an ethical requirement), it is nevertheless the case that if one were trying to further one's own interest, the best way to do it would be to focus on trying to advance the common good, rather than by trying directly to advance one's own interest.
56. We have referred to these features more systematically earlier in this chapter, particularly in the section entitled "Defining Ethics." There is nothing unusual or peculiar about nominating these features as formal characteristics of an ethical opinion. See, for example, James Rachels, *The Elements of Moral Philosophy*, 2nd edn (New York: McGraw-Hill, 1993), 13; Lawrence M. Hinman, *Ethics: A Pluralistic Approach to Moral Theory*, 4th edn (Belmont, CA: Thomson Wadsworth, 2008), 4; Peter Singer, ed., *Ethics* (New York: Oxford University Press, 1994), 4, 10; Peter Singer, *Practical Ethics*, 2nd edn (New York: Cambridge University Press, 1993), 10, 12.
57. Ethical egoism is a view according to which the proper gauge for judging an action to be morally right is that it advances one's own interest: actions are right if they benefit *numero uno*. Psychological egoism is a view about how people do, in fact, behave and what they take into account. According to psychological egoism, people care most about themselves. Ethical egoism, but not psychological egoism, is a normative view, a view about how people should behave.
58. Milton Friedman offered this view in a number of publications, such as "The social responsibility of business is to increase its profits," *New York Times Magazine*, 13 September 1970, reprinted in T. Donaldson and P. Werhane, eds, *Ethical Issues in Business: A Philosophical Approach*, 2nd edn (Englewood Cliffs, NJ: Prentice Hall, 1983), 239–42; *Capitalism and Freedom* (Chicago: University of Chicago Press, 1962).
59. For a brief and clear discussion of egoism and self-interest, see Rachels, *The Elements of Moral Philosophy*, chaps 5 and 6.
60. Carol Gilligan, *In a Different Voice: Psychological Theory and Women's Development* (Cambridge, MA: Harvard University Press, 1982).
61. R.M. Boisjoly, "Personal integrity and accountability," *Accounting Horizons* 7 (1993): 59–69.

Chapter 2

1. Albert Z. Carr, "Is business bluffing ethical?," *Harvard Business Review*, January–February 1968.
2. Milton Friedman, *Capitalism and Freedom* (Chicago: University of Chicago Press, 1962).
3. T.J. Peters and R.H. Waterman, *In Search of Excellence* (Sydney: Harper and Row, 1984).
4. Ibid., 39.
5. John Ladd, "Morality and the ideal of rationality in formal organisations," *Monist* 54 (1970): 488–516.
6. Ibid., 50.
7. Peter Heckman, "Business and games," *Journal of Business Ethics* 11 (1992): 933–8.
8. As quoted in Timothy Blodgett, "Showdown on 'business bluffing,'" *Harvard Business Review*, May–June 1968, 162–70.
9. Ibid.
10. Ibid.
11. Thomas Nagel, "Ruthlessness in public life," in Stuart Hampshire, ed., *Public and Private Morality* (New York: Cambridge University Press, 1978), 75–92.
12. See Blodgett, "Showdown," 168–70.
13. Ibid., 169.

14. Lord Patrick Devlin, "Morals and the criminal law," originally published in 1959. The essay has been reprinted in a number of places. We have cited it from Richard A. Wasserstrom, *Morality and the Criminal Law* (Belmont, CA: Wadsworth, 1971), 24–48, at 46.
15. H.L.A. Hart, "Immorality and treason," first presented as a British radio broadcast on the BBC in 1959, then published in the *Listener* 62 (30 July 1959): 162–3. Reprinted in Wasserstrom, *Morality and the Criminal Law*, 49–54. Professor Hart explores this issue more fully in his book *Law, Liberty, and Morality* (London: Oxford University Press, 1963).
16. Gerald Dworkin, "Lord Devlin and the enforcement of morals," *Yale Law Journal* 75 (1966): 986–1005.
17. In this connection, see the sensible and timely argument of Max Charlesworth, "Ethical reflection and business practice," in C.A.J. Coady and C.J.G. Sampford, eds, *Business, Ethics and the Law* (Sydney: Federation Press, 1993), 187–205.
18. Sir Adrian Cadbury, "Ethical managers make their own rules," *Harvard Business Review*, September–October 1987, reprinted in E.K. Kellar, ed., *Ethical Insight, Ethical Action* (Washington: ICMA, 1988), 51–8. Sir Adrian's whole essay can be read as a discussion of the problem of dirty hands.
19. Bernard Williams, "Politics and moral character," in Stuart Hampshire, ed., *Public and Private Morality* (New York: Cambridge University Press, 1978), 55–74.
20. Ibid., 63.
21. Thomas More, *Utopia*, ed. G. Logan and R.M. Adams (Cambridge: Cambridge University Press, 1989), 36.
22. Raimond Gaita, *Good and Evil: An Absolute Conception* (London: Macmillan, 1991), 72–3.
23. See, for example, Williams's "Politics and moral character," in S. Hampshire, ed., *Public and Private Morality* (New York: Cambridge University Press, 1978); and in the same volume, Thomas Nagel, "Ruthlessness in public life," 75–92. See also Alan Donagan, *The Theory of Morality* (Chicago: University of Chicago Press, 1979), 180–8.
24. This example is quite like one offered by Bernard Williams in presenting a critique of utilitarianism—"A critique of utilitarianism," in J.J.C. Smart and Bernard Williams, *Utilitarianism: For and Against* (London: Cambridge University Press, 1973), 98–9—but that is not the point here.
25. See, for example, Julian Disney et al., *Lawyers*, 2nd edn (Sydney: Law Book Company, 1986), 660–5.
26. There have been recent changes to the specific requirements of this client privilege. For the point here, however, it does not matter.
27. This is a case in which we are using "ethical" and "moral" to mean different things. "Ethical" here has a narrow meaning, referring only to that which is required by the code of ethics of the profession.
28. See, for example, Williams, "Politics and moral character."
29. Mary Williams Walsh and Carl Hulse, "AIG bonuses of $50 million will be repaid," *New York Times*, 23 March 2009, http://www.nytimes.com/2009/03/24/business/24bonus.html?scp=26&sq=&st=nyt.
30. The Dodd-Frank Wall Street Reform and Consumer Protection Act can be accessed at: http://www.sec.gov/about/laws/wallstreetreform-cpa.pdf
31. For an indepth discussion of the subprime mortgage crisis, see P. Muolo and M. Padilla, *Chain of Blame: How Wall Street Caused the Mortgage and Credit Crisis* (Hoboken, NJ: John Wiley and Sons, 2010); and H. Davies, *The Financial Crisis: Who is to Blame?* (Cambridge, UK: Polity Press, 2010).
32. Albert Carr, "Is business bluffing ethical?," *Harvard Business Review* 46 (January–February 1968): 145.
33. Harry R. Wrage, manager of the Medinet Application Operation of the General Electric Company, quoted in Timothy B. Blodgett, "Showdown on 'Business Bluffing,'" *Harvard Business Review* 46 (May–June 1968): 164.

Chapter 3

1. Norman Bowie and Ronald Duska, *Business Ethics*, 2nd edn (Englewood Cliffs, NJ: Prentice Hall, 1990), 40. For a history of the concept and its background, see R. Edward Freeman, *Strategic Management: A Stakeholder Approach* (Boston: Pitman, 1984), chap. 2.
2. Dennis Pratt, *Aspiring to Greatness* (Sydney: Business and Professional Publishing, 1994), 58 and, more generally, chap. 1.
3. Freeman, *Strategic Management*, vi.
4. James E. Liebig, *Business Ethics: Profiles in Civic Virtue* (Golden, CO: Fulcrum, 1990), 217.
5. Kenneth Goodpaster, "Business ethics and stakeholder analysis," *Business Ethics Quarterly* 1 (1991): 53–71.
6. Perhaps this is not a good thing to do. Perhaps it could never be justified. Nevertheless, if it were the case, there would be no point in taking further account of the group whose interests were to be sacrificed. Nothing more could be learned about that group.

7. See M. Friedman, "The social responsibility of firms is to increase profits," *New York Times Magazine*, 13 September 1970, 122–6.
8. Robert Nozick, *Anarchy, State and Utopia* (Oxford: Blackwell, 1974), chap. 7.
9. Richard Titmuss, *Social Policy: An Introduction*, ed. Brian Abel-Smith and Kay Titmuss (London: Allen & Unwin, 1974), 137ff.
10. Information about this case is taken from Paul Barry, *The Rise and Fall of Alan Bond* (Sydney: Bantam, 1990), chap. 15.
11. Ibid., 171.
12. See J. Guttsman, "Canadian union agrees to concessions in GM deal," http://ca.reuters.com/article/domesticNews/idCAWNAB153320090308?sp=true; and M. Gollom, 2012, "CAW needs to be 'more flexible,' expert warns," CBC News, 15 August 2012, http://www.cbc.ca/news/canada/story/2012/08/14/caw-auto-industry-contract-talks.html.
13. I. MacLachlin, *Kill and Chill: Restructuring Canada's Beef Commodity Chain* (Toronto: University of Toronto Inc., 2001).
14. For comprehensive nationwide information on occupational health and safety in Canada, see Canadian Centre for Occupational Health and Safety (website), http://www.ccohs.ca/. For specific statistics on workplace injuries, see Canadian Centre for Occupational Health and Safety, http://www.ccohs.ca/oshanswers/information/injury_statistics.html#_1_1.
15. Andrew Buncombe, "US firms' war on workers: Where there's smoking, they're fired," *The Independent*, 29 January 2005, http://www.independent.co.uk/news/world/americas/us-firms-war-on-workers-where-theres-smoking-theyre-fired-488757.html.
16. CNN transcript of *Anderson Cooper 360°*, aired 7 December 2005, http://transcripts.cnn.com/TRANSCRIPTS/0512/07/acd.01.html.
17. Kris Maher, "Companies are closing doors on job applicants who smoke," *Wall Street Journal*, 21 December 2004, B6. See also Daniel Costello, "Costs make employers see smokers as a drag," *Los Angeles Times*, 28 January 2005, A-1, http://articles.latimes.com/2005/jan/28/health/he-nosmoke28.
18. Morley Safer, "Whose life is it anyway?," *CBS News*, 16 July 2006, http://www.cbsnews.com/stories/2005/10/28/60minutes/main990617.shtml.
19. Ibid.
20. Buncombe, "US firms' war on workers."
21. "FreshStart offers Weyco employees free access to online smoking cessation therapy," http://209.85.173.132/search?q=cache:CrlmM4guE2IJ: www.24-7pressrelease.com/pdf/2005/01/29/press_release_3050.pdf+Weyco+Godson&hl =en&ct=clnk&cd=3&gl=au&client=firefox-a.
22. Anderson Cooper, *Anderson Cooper 360°*.
23. Safer, "Whose life is it anyway?"
24. Ibid.
25. Buncombe, "US firms' war on workers."
26. Safer, "Whose life is it anyway?"
27. Buncombe, "US firms' war on workers."
28. For a list, see *100% Smoke-Free Employers*, http://smokinghurts.com/Smoke-FreeEmployers.htm.
29. Safer, "Whose life is it anyway?"
30. Ibid.
31. Cited in Bowie and Duska, *Business Ethics*, 90.
32. Canadian Human Rights Commission, 2009, Canadian Human Rights Commission's Policy on Alcohol and Drug Testing, http://www.chrc-ccdp.ca/pdf/padt_pdda_eng.pdf.
33. P. Bowal, "Employer Surveillance of Employees," *Law Now* 31, no. 1 (September–October 2006): 47
34. Ibid.
35. Hannah Clark, "Five ways—how to (legally) spy on employees," Forbes.com, 25 October 2006, http://www.forbes.com/2006/10/25/leadership-hewlett-packard-spying-lead-manage-cx_hc_1025fiveways.html.
36. SpectorSoft, http://www.spectorsoft.com/.
37. A useful summary of the case is David A. Kaplan, "A playbook for the HP hearings," *Newsweek*, 27 September 2006, http://www.newsweek.com/id/37880/page/1.
38. Lorraine Woellert, "HP's Hunsaker Papers," *Businessweek*, 4 October 2006, http://www.businessweek.com/technology/content/oct2006/tc20061003_396787.htm?chan=top+news_top+news+index_businessweek+exclusives.
39. Ibid.
40. Mark Trumbull, "HP board flap raises wider privacy issues," *Christian Science Monitor*, 14 September 2006, http://www.csmonitor.com/2006/0914/p01s03-usju.html?s=widep.
41. Ibid.
42. Links to HP memos can be found in Woellert, "HP's Hunsaker Papers."
43. Woellert, "HP's Hunsaker Papers."
44. Ibid.
45. Mark Trumbull, "The changing rules of corporate spy games," *Christian Science Monitor*, 25 September 2006, http://www.csmonitor.com/2006/0925/p02s01-usec.html.

46. Woellert, "HP's Hunsaker Papers."
47. Ibid.
48. Ibid.
49. Rob Kelley, "Charges against HP's Dunn dropped," CNNMoney.com, 14 March 2007, http://money.cnn.com/2007/03/14/technology/hpq/index.htm.
50. "Patricia Dunn: I am Innocent," Ousted Hewlett-Packard Chairwoman talks to Lesley Stahl, *60 Minutes*, 8 October 2006, http://www.cbsnews.com/stories/2006/10/05/60minutes/main2069430.shtml.
51. Sox First, http://www.soxfirst.com/50226711/patricia_dunn_everybody_does_it.php; David H. Holtzman, "Hubris at HP—and beyond," *Businessweek*, 11 October 2006, http://www.businessweek.com/technology/content/oct2006/tc20061011_581843.htm. The *60 Minutes* website no longer carries this passage.
52. Andrea James, "Boeing bosses spy on workers," seattlepi.com, 16 November 2007, http://seattlepi.nwsource.com/business/339881_boeingsurveillance16.html.
53. Andrew Charlesworth, "HP private eyes fined US$600,000," ITNews, 31 May 2008, http://mobile.itnews.com.au/Article.aspx?CIID=112791&type=News&page=0&showall=true.
54. David Lazarus, "Lesson learned by lenient sentences for HP defendants," *San Francisco Chronicle*, 16 March 2007, http://www.sfgate.com/cgi-bin/article.cgi?f=/c/a/2007/03/16/BUG9OOM1FL1.DTL.
55. David A. Kaplan, "Suspicions and spies in Silicon Valley," *Newsweek*, 18 September 2006, http://www.newsweek.com/id/45548.
56. Gabriel Madway, "Dunn: H-P's Hurd tried to get Keyworth to admit leak," *Marketwatch*, 27 September 2006, http://www.marketwatch.com/news/story/dunn-h-ps-hurd-tried-get/story.aspx?guid=%7B53A6C413-47D7-47D0-8583-5001AB57CD88%7D.
57. See "CALEA: The perils of wiretapping the internet," *Electronic Frontier Foundation* (website), http://www.eff.org/issues/calea. For further information on the Communications Assistance for Law Enforcement Act, see the *Ask CALEA* website, http://www.askcalea.net/.
58. David Brown, "Maker of Vioxx is accused of deception," *Washington Post*, 16 April 2008, http://www.washingtonpost.com/wp-dyn/content/article/2008/04/15/AR2008041502086.html.
59. Milanda Rout, "Drug company drew up doctor hit list," *Australian*, 1 April 2009, 1–2.
60. David Barboza, "Death sentences in milk cases," *New York Times*, 23 January 2009, A5.
61. For a comprehensive discussion of the Ford Explorer/Firestone case, see R.F. Hartley, *Business Ethics: Mistakes and Successes* (Hoboken, NJ: John Wiley & Sons, 2005).
62. The information for this case is drawn from "Mistral's ill wind," *Choice*, April 1992, 7–11.

Chapter 4

1. See Albert Z. Carr, "Is business bluffing ethical?," *Harvard Business Review*, January– February 1968. See also Milton Friedman, *Capitalism and Freedom* (Chicago: University of Chicago Press, 1962); and idem, "The social responsibility of business is to increase its profits," *New York Times Magazine*, 13 September 1970, reprinted in T. Donaldson & P. Werhane, eds, *Ethical Issues in Business: A Philosophical Approach*, 2nd edn (Englewood Cliffs, NJ: Prentice Hall, 1983), 239–42.
2. This distinction mirrors that made by Tönnies in 1887 between *Gesellschaft* and *Gemeinschaft*: "The corporation or joint stock company . . . which is liable only for itself, represents, in its exclusive concentration on profit making, the perfect type of all legal forms for an association based on rational will. This is because it is from its very origin a relationship of *Gesellschaft* (i.e. an enterprise association), without any admixture of elements of *Gemeinschaft* (community), and thus does not allow, as in other cases, any misconception as to its real character." Ferdinand Tönnies, *Community and Association*, trans. C.P. Loomis (London: Routledge and Kegan Paul, 1955), 227.
3. William S. Laufer, "Integrity, diligence, and the limits of good corporate citizenship," *American Business Law Journal* 34, no. 2 (Winter, 1996): 157–81.
4. See the United States Sentencing Commission website at http://www.ussc.gov/Guidelines/2011_Guidelines/Manual_HTML/1a1.htm.
5. Denning LJ in *H.L. Bolton (Engineering) Co. Ltd. v. T. J. Graham & Sons Ltd* [1951] 1 Q.B. 159 at 172, quoted in Paul Redmond, *Companies and Securities Law*, 2nd edn (North Ryde: Law Book Company, 1992), 214.
6. Enron Code of Ethics (July 2000), http://www.bennettlawfirm.com/enron.pdf.
7. Milton Friedman, "The social responsibility of business is to increase its profits," *New York Times Magazine*, 13 September 1970.
8. Christine Parker's *The Open Corporation* (Cambridge: Cambridge University Press, 2002) shows why the assumption is simplistic and inaccurate.

9. Mark Lawson, "Just don't invite the chief executive out to play golf," *Australian Financial Review*, 5 December 2002.
10. Mark Lawson, "The ethical dilemma of corporate generosity," *Australian Financial Review*, 5 December 2002.
11. Mel Wilson, "Corporate reputation and the triple bottom line: The social responsibilities of business," *Risky Business*, no. 2 (2001), http://www.pwc.com/extweb/manissue.nsf/DocID/ C00115084F24343E852569E600656A08.
12. Kate Legge, "Humble hero of the operating theatre," *Weekend Australian*, 23–24 June 2001, 10.
13. Colleen Ryan, "The hard yard," *Australian Financial Review Magazine*, July 2003, 18–25.
14. Ibid., 22.
15. Ibid.
16. Elaine Sternberg, *Just Business* (London: Warner Books, 1995), 42.
17. Elizabeth Vallance, *Business Ethics at Work* (Cambridge: Cambridge University Press, 1995), 9–10.
18. Milton Friedman and Rose Friedman, *Free to Choose* (London: Secker & Warburg, 1980), esp. chap. 4; and for a succinct rejoinder, Colin Grant, "Friedman fallacies," *Journal of Business Ethics* 10 (1991): 907–14.
19. For a highly readable discussion of these issues, see Thomas C. Schelling, *Choice and Consequence: Perspectives of an Errant Economist* (Cambridge: Harvard University Press, 1984).
20. Cf. John Finnis, *Natural Law and Natural Rights* (Oxford: Clarendon Press, 1980), 174–7.
21. See Edward Coker, "Adam Smith's concept of the social system," *Journal of Business Ethics* 9 (1990): 139–42; and Albert Z. Carr, "Is business bluffing ethical?," *Harvard Business Review*, January–February 1968.
22. Karl Marx, *Capital*, vol. 1 (New York: International Pubs, 1967; Foreign Languages Publishing House, 1959), chap. 32.
23. Dwight Lemke and Marshall Schminke, "Ethics in declining organizations," *Business Ethics Quarterly* 1 (1991): 235–48.
24. For a comprehensive account of the story of Michael Milken and the fall of Drexel, Burnham, Lambert, see D.G. Stone, *April Fools: An Insider's Account of the Rise and Collapse of Drexel Burnham* (New York: Donald I. Fine, 1990); and C. Bruck, *The Predators' Ball: The Inside Story of Drexel Burnham and the Rise of the Junk Bond Raiders* (New York: American Lawyer/Simon and Schuster, 1988.
25. *Sydney Morning Herald*, 13 November 1993, 33.
26. R. Behar, "Jungle fever: The Bre-X saga is the greatest gold scam ever," *Fortune Magazine*, 9 June 1997, http://money.cnn.com/magazines/fortune/fortune_archive/1997/06/09/227519/index.htm.
27. S. Maich, "The ghost of Bre-X rises," *Maclean's Magazine*, 8 June 2005, http://www.macleans.ca/columnists/article.jsp?id=3&content=20050613_107322_107322.

Chapter 5

1. See, for example, Robert Arrington, "Advertising and behavior control," *Journal of Business Ethics* 1, no. 1 (February 1982): 3–12; and Alan Goldman, "Ethical issues in advertising," in Tom Regan, ed., *Just Business: New Introductory Essays in Business Ethics* (New York: Random House, 1984), 235–69.
2. Dave Thompson "The big fat lie about battery life," *Sydney Morning Herald*, 6 February 2009, http://www.smh.com.au/news/digital-life/how-tos/the-big-fat-lie-about-battery-life/2009/02/06/1233423460353.html.
3. Richard De George has also suggested that advertising can be considered as a transaction: "the transaction is fair if both parties have adequate, appropriate information about the product, and if they enter into the transaction willingly and without coercion." Richard De George, *Business Ethics*, 6th edn (Upper Saddle River, NJ: Pearson Education, 2006), 336.
4. Julian Lee, "Furore over Coke myth-busting ad," *Sydney Morning Herald*, 15 October 2008, http://www.smh.com.au/news/health/coke-draws-the-fizz-for-mythbusting-ad/2008/10/14/1223750084672.html.
5. Julian Lee, "Kerry Armstrong Coke ad gets all-clear," *Sydney Morning Herald*, 27 November 2008, http://www.smh.com.au/news/national/kerry-armstrong-ad-gets-allclear/2008/11/27/1227491680882.html.
6. Lee, "Furore over Coke myth-busting ad."
7. De George, *Business Ethics*, 6th edn, 345.
8. CBC News Online, 11 May 2004, http://www.cbc.ca/news/background/genetics_modification/.
9. CBC News Online, 11 May 2004, http://www.cbc.ca/news/background/genetics_modification/.
10. This was announced by a spokesperson for the US Department of Consumer Affairs. Apparently over 60 per cent of email advertisements violate some law or other with respect to untrue or fraudulent or insufficiently informative claims.
11. Advertising Standards Canada, http://www.adstandards.com/en/AboutASC/ourHistory.aspx.

12. Canadian Radio-television and Telecommunications Commission, http://www.crtc.gc.ca/eng/backgrnd/brochures/b29903.htm.
13. CBC mandate, http://www.cbc.radio-canada.ca/about/mandate.shtml.
14. CBC Policies and Guidelines, Advertising Standards, http://cbc.radio-canada.ca/en/reporting-to-canadians/acts-and-policies/programming/advertising-standards/.
15. Canadian Marketing Association, http://www.the-cma.org/about.
16. Canadian Marketing Association, Code of Ethics and Standards of Practice, http://www.the-cma.org/regulatory/code-of-ethics.
17. International Advertising Association, "Advertising: It makes the difference," *Sydney Morning Herald*, 5 June 1993, 13.
18. CBC News, 22 August 2007, "Hoax camp ads outrage Torontonians," http://www.cbc.ca/news/canada/toronto/story/2007/08/22/camp-okutta.html.
19. Bowie and Duska, *Business Ethics*, 54.
20. *Adweek*, 15 April 2011, http://www.adweek.com/adfreak/car-dealers-sexist-ad-has-companion-piece-130630.
21. *Adweek*, 12 April 2011, http://www.adweek.com/adfreak/30-freakiest-ads-2010-124101.
22. This description is taken from the Advertising Standards Council's seventeenth report, 1993, 48.
23. Ibid., 49.
24. Catherine Lumby, "Sexist or Sexy," *Independent Monthly*, November 1993, 33.
25. Of course, such a view would also favour a much more liberal approach to what products or services should be legally available.
26. *Sydney Morning Herald*, 6 May 1993, 38.
27. http://www.cbc.ca/marketplace/2008/01/23/more_detail_about_the_health_c/.
28. http://www.healthcheck.org/page/what-health-check.
29. This is taken from David Braybrooke, *Ethics in the World of Business* (Totowa, NJ: Rowman & Allanheld, 1983), 94–5.
30. Le Winter's lost in the first instance, but the decision was reversed on appeal (Supreme Court of New York, Appellate Division, Second Department, 1939).
31. Christopher Elliott, 2008, "Unfair Fairs; Avoid the Bait-and-Switch" (2008), msnbc.com, http://www.msnbc.msn.com/id/27366920/ns/travel-travel_tips/t/unfair-fares-avoid-bait-and-switch/.
32. Ibid.
33. *Sydney Morning Herald*, 18 June 1993, 1.
34. John Millard (reporter), *The Investigators*, 2 March 1993, ABC Television.
35. Reported on the Saturn website, April 2004: http://www.saturn.com/aboutus2/news/ a02press1.jsp: "In the history of the study, the only other brand that earned both top achievements simultaneously was Lexus in 1994." Reported on the Saturn website, April 2004: http://www.saturn.com/aboutus2/news/a02press3.jsp. Further, "the no-haggle, no-hassle sales approach and respectful treatment of customers earned Saturn retailers the top spot in J. D. Power and Associates' sales satisfaction index for six of the past seven years." Reported on the Saturn website, April 2004: http://www.saturn.com/aboutus2/news/a01press4.jsp. Note: although those websites are no longer current, a number of sites (blogs and more) discuss this history; for example: http://thoughtindustry.blogspot.com/2008/05/saturns-cursed-brief-history.html (a blog by Craig Daitch) and http://www.carforums.net/showthread.php?t=27094.

Chapter 6

1. Supreme Court of the United States, "Wal-Mart Stores, Inc. v. Dukes et al.," Certiorari to the United States Court of Appeals for the Ninth Circuit, No. 10–277, argued 29 March 2011—decided 20 June 2011, http://www.supremecourt.gov/opinions/10pdf/10-277.pdf.
2. M. Burk, "Dukes v. Wal-Mart one year later: Where do women stand?," HuffingtonPost.com, http://www.huffingtonpost.com/martha-burk/post_3504_b_1601449.html.
3. Bronwyn Young, "Sex bias decision upheld," *Australian Financial Review*, 6 December 1989, 3.
4. Christopher Cornell, Fed-Ex Driver wins sex-harassment case," Human Resource Executive Online, 2 June 2004, http://www.hreonline.com/HRE/story.jsp?storyId=4222585&query=benefits.
5. See, for example, Ian Palmer, "Email abuse & misuse," *Insight*, http://www.insight-mag.com/insight/03/08/col-5-pt-1-WorkForce.asp; and the NSW Department of Commerce, Office of Industrial Relations, http://www.industrialrelations.nsw.gov.au/pubs/July2003/email.html.
6. Cathy Bolt, "Pregnancy sacking damages $12,000," *Australian Financial Review*, August 1993, 6.
7. Lesley Alderman, "When the stork carries a pink slip," *New York Times*, 27 March 2009, http://www.nytimes.com/2009/03/28/health/28patient.html?_r=1.

8. CBC News, "Pregnancy discrimination complaints on rise," 7 March 2012, http://www.cbc.ca/news/canada/new-brunswick/story/2012/03/07/nb-pregnancy-complaints-rights-commission.html.
9. The full New Brunswick Human Rights Act can be found at http://laws.gnb.ca/en/showfulldoc/cs/2011-c.171//20120705.
10. In Canada, each province maintains its own Human Rights Act that covers private sector businesses and organizations and provincial and municipal governments. Federally regulated activities such as broadcasting, telecommunications, extra-provincial transportation, uranium, and grains, among others, fall under the Canadian Human Rights Act. The full Canadian Human Rights Act can be found at http://laws-lois.justice.gc.ca/eng/acts/h-6/index.html.
11. Lesley Alderman, "When the stork carries a pink slip," 7.
12. *Sydney Morning Herald*, 9 September 1993, 34.
13. Patrick Kelly, "Conducting a glass ceiling self-audit now," *HR Magazine*, October 1993, 76.
14. Ibid., 77–8.
15. Statistics taken from Statistics Canada, Table 202-0102 – Average female and male earnings, and female-to-male earnings ratio, by work activity, 2010 constant dollars, annual.
16. Leonie Still, "Breaking the glass ceiling: Another perspective," *Women in Management Series*, paper no. 15, Faculty of Commerce, University of Western Sydney, Nepean, July 1992.
17. *Sydney Morning Herald*, 14 September 1993, 9.
18. Louise Story, "Reporting on the aspirations of young women," *New York Times*, 23 September 2005, http://www.nytimes.com/2005/09/23/national/23women-sidebar.html.
19. Louise Story, "Many women at elite colleges set career path to motherhood," *New York Times*, 20 September 2005, http://www.nytimes.com/2005/09/20/national/20women.html?_r=2.
20. Susan Pinker, *The Sexual Paradox* (London: Atlantic Books, 2008), 70.
21. Ibid., 161–2, 176–8.
22. L. Jenner, L. Mulligan-Ferry, and R. Soares, *2009 Catalyst Census: Financial Post 500 Women Board Directors* (Toronto: Catalyst Canada, 2010).
23. See Ontario Women's Justice Network, "Janzen: The Supreme Court of Canada recognizes sexual harassment in the workplace as a form of sex discrimination," July 2008, http://owjn.org/owjn_2009/legal-information/aboriginal-law/119.
24. The Accessibility for Ontarians with Disabilities Act (AODA) requires all managers and employees dealing with individuals with accessibility issues to have completed AODA training by 1 January 2012 or within a certain period after employment. The full AODA can be found at http://www.e-laws.gov.on.ca/html/source/regs/english/2011/elaws_src_regs_r11191_e.htm. One example of a service certified to provide such training is Accessibility Advantage, which can be found at http://www.aodatraining.org/.
25. American Civil Liberties Union, "HIV employment discrimination by Transportation Security Administration," 21 October 2011, http://www.aclu.org/hiv-aids/tsa-hiv-discrimination-case-profile.

Chapter 7

1. Government of Canada, Department of Justice, Federal Accountability Act, 2006, http://laws-lois.justice.gc.ca/eng/acts/F-5.5/index.html.
2. Norman Bowie and Ronald Duska, *Business Ethics*, 2nd edn (Englewood Cliffs, NJ: Prentice Hall, 1990), 37.
3. Mike Martin and Roland Schinzinger, *Ethics in Engineering*, 2nd edn (New York: McGraw-Hill, 1989), 43–4.
4. Martin Gansberg's article in the *New York Times* of 27 March 1964, "Thirty-eight who saw murder didn't call the police," can be found at http://www2.selu.edu/Academics/Faculty/scraig/gansberg.html.
5. Government of New Brunswick, 1982, Employment Standards Act, http://laws.gnb.ca/en/ShowTdm/cs/E-7.2.
6. Murray Brewster, "Vets department and board struggled for years to contain privacy leaks," *Winnipeg Free Press*, 16 February 2012.
7. John McMillan, "Legal protection of whistleblowers," in S. Prosser, R. Wear, and J. Nethercote, eds, *Corruption and Reform* (St Lucia, Qld: University of Queensland Press, 1990), 210.
8. See Roger Boisjoly's first-hand account of the decision to launch *Challenger* in the face of indications of high risk in "The Challenger disaster: Moral responsibility and the working engineer," in Deborah G. Johnson, *Ethical Issues in Engineering* (Englewood Cliffs, NJ: Prentice Hall, 1991), 6–14.
9. "Persons of the Year," *Time*, 30 December–6 January 2003, 34–57.
10. Ibid., 57.
11. Quentin Dempster, *Whistleblowers* (Sydney: ABC Books, 1997), 3.

12. See Howard Whitton, "Ethics and principled dissent in the Queensland public sector: A response to the Queensland whistleblower study," *Australian Journal of Public Administration* 54 (1995): 455–61.
13. Sissela Bok, "Blowing the whistle," in J. Fleishman et al., eds, *Public Duties: The Moral Obligations of Government Officials* (Cambridge: Cambridge University Press, 1982), 208–9.
14. Richard De George, *Business Ethics*, 6th edn (Upper Saddle River, NJ: Pearson Education, 2006), 300–12.
15. Norman Bowie, "Business codes of ethics: Window dressing or legitimate alternative to government regulation?," in Tom L. Beauchamp and Norman E. Bowie, eds, *Ethical Theory and Business* (Englewood Cliffs, NJ: Prentice Hall, 1979), 138–49; and Bowie and Duska, *Business Ethics*, 72–7.
16. Ross Webber, "Whistleblowing," *Executive Excellence*, July 1990; see Allen Westin, "Conclusion," in Allen Westin, ed., *Whistleblowing: Loyalty and Dissent in the Corporation* (New York: McGraw-Hill, 1981), 160–3.
17. Bowie and Duska, *Business Ethics*, 74.
18. A. Dyck, A. Morse, and L. Zingales, 2010, "Who blows the whistle on corporate fraud?," *Journal of Finance* 65, no. 6 (2010), http://www.nber.org/papers/w12882.pdf.
19. Michael Keeley and Jill Graham, "Exit, voice and ethics," *Journal of Business Ethics* 10 (1991): 350–1.
20. Bok, "Blowing the whistle," 215–17.
21. Allen Westin, ed., *Whistleblowing: Loyalty and Dissent in the Corporation* (New York: McGraw-Hill, 1981), 151–60, makes some suggestions about such protections that partly apply in Australia through industrial legislation—for example, laws against unfair dismissals.
22. National Society of Professional Engineers, Code of Ethics for Engineers, n.d., http://www.nspe.org/Ethics/CodeofEthics/index.html.
23. Donna Jacobs, "A whistle blown: A decade lost," *Ottawa Citizen*, 22 May 2006.
24. David Leigh, Luke Harding, and the *Guardian*, *WikiLeaks: Inside Julian Assange's War on Secrecy* (New York: Guardian Books, 2011).
25. Ashley Fantz, "Who is Rudolf Elmer, WikiLeaks' newest leaker?," CNN, 17 January 2011, http://news.blogs.cnn.com/2011/01/17/who-is-rudolf-elmer-wikileaks-newest-leaker/.
26. CBC News, "Dismissed RCMP officer ordered reinstated," Canadian Broadcasting Corporation, 19 March 2004.
27. http://fairwhistleblower.ca/.
28. The information in this case comes from Julian Cribb, "Committed to truth," *Australian*, 8 September 1993, 8.
29. Peter Woodford, "Health Canada muzzles oilsands whistleblower," *National Review of Medicine* 4, no. 8 (30 March 2007).
30. Graham Lanktree, "Oilsands whistleblower MD cleared," *National Review of Medicine* 5, no. 1 (15 January 2008).
31. T. MacCharles, "The high cost of whistleblowing," *Toronto Star*, 30 June 2007, http://www.thestar.com/news/article/231204--high-cost-of-whistleblowing. See also M. Kay, "RCMP whistleblowers should be honoured, says Commons committee," *Ottawa Citizen*, 6 September 2007, http://www.rcmpwatch.com/rcmp-whistleblowers-should-be-honoured-says-commons-committee/.
32. Joel Bakan, *The Corporation: The Pathological Pursuit of Profit and Power* (New York: Free Press, 2004).
33. Fred P. Clark, "Unfounded 'whistle blower' suit can kill a small defense company," *Aviation Week and Space Technology*, 2 March 1992, 65–6.
34. See, for example, William De Maria, "Quarantining dissent: The Queensland public sector ethics movement," *Australian Journal of Public Administration* 54 (1995): 443–54. Although De Maria's critique is directed at the public sector, it could equally be directed at the private sector. De Maria's article is rebutted by Howard Whitton, "Ethics and principled dissent in the Queensland public sector: A response to the Queensland whistleblower study"; compare Noel Preston, "Public sector ethics in Australia: A review," *Australian Journal of Public Administration* 54 (1995): 462–70.

Chapter 8

1. Andy Hoffman, "Sino-Forest clams up as probe continues," *Globe and Mail*, 16 August 2011.
2. Jacquie McNish and Andy Hoffman, "Sino-Forest CEO resigns amid OSC probe," *Globe and Mail*, 29 August 2011.
3. Andy Hoffman, "A business model shrouded in fog," *Globe and Mail*, 26 November 2011.
4. R.W. LeBlanc, "A black eye for Bay Street: With proper governance, the Sino-Forest scandal would never have happened," *Canadian Business* 88, no. 15 (2011): 12.
5. "A business model shrouded in fog," *Globe and Mail*, 26 November 2011.
6. "Top 10 crooked CEOs: Dennis Kozlowski," *Time*, 9 June 2009.

7. D. Hunter, *The Bubble and the Bear: How Nortel Burst the Canadian Dream* (Toronto: Doubleday, Canada, 2003).
8. "International people: Northern Telecom," *Financial Times*, 6 June 1995.
9. K. Warn, "Nortel faces insider trading allegations," *Financial Times*, 20 February 2001, 30.
10. Hunter, *The Bubble and the Bear.*
11. Jacquie McNish, "Why the smiling barracuda is moving on," *Globe and Mail*, 17 December 2011.
12. K.A. Kim and J.R. Nofsinger, *Corporate Governance*, 2nd edn (Upper Saddle River, NJ: Pearson Prentice Hall, 2007).
13. K. Eichenwald, *Conspiracy of Fools: A True Story* (New York: Broadway Books, 2005).
14. L.W. Jeter, *Disconnected: Deceit and Betrayal at WorldCom* (Hoboken, NJ: John Wiley and Sons, 2003).
15. B.L. Toffler, *Final Accounting: Ambition, Greed and the Fall of Arthur Andersen* (New York: Doubleday, 2003).
16. Milton Friedman, "The social responsibility of business is to increase its profits," *New York Times Magazine*, 13 September 1970, reprinted in T. Donaldson and P. Werhane, eds, *Ethical Issues in Business: A Philosophical Approach*, 2nd edn (Englewood Cliffs, NJ: Prentice Hall, 1983), 239–42.
17. K.A. Kim and J.R. Nofsinger, *Corporate Governance*, 2nd edn (Upper Saddle River, NJ: Pearson Prentice Hall, 2007).

Chapter 9

1. As quoted in Elizabeth Wolgast, *Ethics of an Artificial Person* (Stanford, CA: Stanford University Press, 1992), 23.
2. IPSOS, 2007, Canada Speaks, http://www.ipsos-na.com/news-polls/pressrelease.aspx?id=3333.
3. CPA letter, "Gallup survey shows accounting's image still rising," November 2005, http://www.aicpa.org/pubs/cpaltr/nov2005/gallup.htm; Flanagan, *Values, Codes of Ethics and the Law*, 24.
4. Lydia Saad, "Nurses shine, bankers slump in ethics ratings," Gallup, 24 November 2008, http://www.gallup.com/poll/112264/Nurses-Shine-While-Bankers-Slump-Ethics-Ratings.aspx.
5. Gwendolen B. White and Michael J. White, "Perceptions of accountants: What are they after Enron and WorldCom?," *Journal of College Teaching & Learning*, November 2006.
6. Cited by Flanagan, *Values, Codes of Ethics and the Law*, 24.
7. Philomena Leung and Barry Cooper, *Professional Ethics: A Survey of Australian Accountants* (Melbourne: ASCPA, 1995), 10. The authors sent their survey to 7,000 members and obtained usable responses from 1,500.
8. Ibid., 12, 18.
9. Adapted from Leung and Cooper, *Professional Ethics*, 16.
10. R.L. Whitelaw, as quoted in Mike W. Martin and Roland Schinzinger, *Ethics in Engineering*, 2nd edn (New York: McGraw-Hill, 1989), 168.
11. Ibid., 168–9.
12. As quoted in Jack Maurice, *Accounting Ethics* (London: Pitman Publishing, 1996), 30.
13. Adapted from the British Statement on the Ethical Responsibilities of Members in Business, as quoted in Maurice, *Accounting Ethics*, 31.
14. OnlineNewshour, "Enron: after the Collapse," http://www.pbs.org/newshour/bb/business/enron/player6.html.
15. See Barbara Ley Toffler with Jennifer Reingold, *Final Accounting: Ambition, Greed and the Fall of Arthur Andersen* (New York: Broadway Books, 2003).
16. Kurt Eichenwald, "Ex-accounting chief at Enron is indicted on 6 felony charges," *New York Times*, 23 January 2004, http://www.nytimes.com/2004/01/23/business/23enron.html?ex=1077339600&en=7bee0e9c177fec7a&ei=5070.
17. Kurt Eichenwald, "Audacious climb to success ended in a dizzying plunge," *New York Times*, 13 January 2002, http://query.nytimes.com/gst/fullpage.html?res=950CE4DD1738F930A25752C0A9649C8B63.
18. Frank Clarke and Graeme Dean, "Corporate collapses analysed," in *Collapse Incorporated* (North Ryde, NSW: CCH, 2001), 86.
19. Ibid., 72–6.
20. Eichenwald, "Ex-accounting chief at Enron is indicted"; Kristen Hays, "Causey may be key in Enron prosecutions," *Chicago Tribune*, 24 January 2004, http://www.chicagotribune.com/ business/sns-ap-enron-causey,1,7140173.story?coll=sns-business-headlines.
21. Joe Stinebaker, "Former Enron exec Causey in prison," *Chicago Tribune*, 3 January 2007, http://www.chicagotribune.com/sns-ap-enron-causey,0,5477225.story.
22. Joseph Kahn, "Californians call Enron documents the smoking gun," *New York Times*, 8 May 2002.
23. See "Summary of SEC actions and SEC related provisions pursuant to the Sarbanes-Oxley Act of 2002," 30 July 2003, http://www.sec.gov/news/press/2003-89a.htm.

24. IFAC, "Proposed revision to code of ethics for professional accountants," Exposure Draft, 2003, http://www.ifac.org/Guidance/EXD-Details.php?EDID=0027.
25. Clarke and Dean, "Corporate collapses analysed," 86.
26. Ibid., 91.
27. For example, the code of ethics of the New Zealand Institute of Chartered Accountants (Wellington: ICANZ, 2003) requires accountants to display integrity, objectivity and independence, competence, quality performance, and professional behaviour.
28. Michael Davis, "Introduction," in *Conflict of Interest in the Professions* (Oxford: Oxford University Press, 2001), 8.
29. A suggestion of systematic conflicts within the Scouts is made in Lewis Kamb, "Scouts who wear two hats," *Times Union*, 2 February 2009, http://www.timesunion.com/AspStories/story.asp?storyID=765958&category=REGION&TextPage=1.
30. Gardiner Harris, "Top psychiatrist didn't report drug makers' pay," *New York Times*, 4 October 2008, http://www.nytimes.com/2008/10/04/health/policy/04drug.html.
31. Judith Warner, "Diagnosis: Greed," *New York Times*, 9 October 2008, http://warner.blogs.nytimes.com/2008/10/09/diagnosis-greed/?th&emc=th.
32. Harris, "Top psychiatrist didn't report drug makers' pay."
33. Ibid.
34. Ibid.
35. Ibid.
36. "Merrill paying $1M fine in settlement with SEC," *Washington Post*, 30 January 2009, http://www.washingtonpost.com/wp-dyn/content/article/2009/01/30/AR2009013003161.html.
37. "Merrill Lynch to pay $1M settlement," *Business Journal*, 2 February 2009, http://www.bizjournals.com/triad/stories/2009/02/02/daily5.html.
38. Comments of Merrill Lynch spokesman Mark Herr reported in "Merrill paying $1M fine in settlement with SEC."
39. Kim Khan, "Merrill settles charges," *CNN Money*, 21 May 2002, http://money.cnn.com/2002/05/21/news/companies/merrill/.
40. Patrick McGeehan, "$100 Million Fine For Merrill Lynch," *New York Times*, 22 May 2002, http://query.nytimes.com/gst/fullpage.html?res=9904E7DC1038F931A15756C0A9649C8B63&scp=1&sq=Merill%20Lynch%20Spitzer%20fine&st=cse.
41. Ibid.
42. Khan, "Merrill settles charges."
43. McGeehan, "$100 million fine for Merrill Lynch."
44. Khan, "Merrill settles charges."
45. Remarks by Chairman Alan Greenspan, "Corporate governance," at the Stern School of Business, New York University, New York, 26 March 2002, http://www.federalreserve.gov/BoardDocs/Speeches/2002/200203262/default.htm.
46. To make the distinction clear, think of the rules of football. They are there to "constitute" the game of football, not to regulate the conduct of people kicking a ball around a paddock. Anyone can do the latter, but only those who know the rules of football can play the game. Sprinting, handball, and hockey are not football; each game is distinguished by the rules that constitute it. It makes no sense to say that the rules of football or hockey are oppressive or that the recipe for soufflé is over-regulated. These rules are the conditions that allow the activity—be it a game, cooking, or a professional activity—to happen.
47. See the discussion of the spirit of a "true and fair" account in F.L. Clarke, G.W. Dean, and K.G. Oliver, *Corporate Collapse* (Cambridge: Cambridge University Press, 1997), 246–7.
48. Ibid., 23.
49. See these discussions of this point: Frank Clarke and Graeme Dean, "Legislators and regulators have failed to get the principles right," *Australian Financial Review*, 7 November 2002, 71; Stephen Cohen, "Ethics is judgement, not rules," *Australian Financial Review*, 26 November 2002, 71; Stephen Cohen, "Regulations are not the answer," *Australian Financial Review*, 15 January 2003.
50. In "Legislators and regulators have failed to get the principles right," Frank Clarke and Graeme Dean make a point very similar to this one.
51. Michael West, "BT sues auditors for $60m," *Sydney Morning Herald*, 31 January 1996, 25.
52. Mark Westfield, "Longest running trial puts blowtorch on auditors," *Australian*, 9 September 1997, 25.
53. George Sutton, "Accountability brings with it all sorts of limits," *Australian*, 9 December 1994, 22.
54. Peter Jubb, "Confidentiality in a professional context with especial reference to the accounting profession in Australia," in M. Hoffman, J. Brown Kamm, R.E. Frederick, and E.S. Petry, eds, *The Ethics of Accounting and Finance* (London: Quorum Books, 1996), 77.
55. Ibid.

56. Clarke, Dean, and Oliver, *Corporate Collapse*, 254.
57. Ibid., 55.

Chapter 10

1. For an illuminating discussion of the supposed differences among types of codes, see Conal Condren, "Code types: Functions and failings and organizational diversity," *Business and Professional Ethics Journal* 14, no. 4 (1995): 69–90.
2. Isabelle de Pommereau, "Are towns really safer without traffic lights?" *Christian Science Monitor*, 12 September 2008, http://www.csmonitor.com/2008/0912/p07s03-woeu.html.
3. Ibid.
4. Bowie and Duska, *Business Ethics*, 85.
5. Adrian Lynch, "Get integrity back into management," *Rydges*, December 1985, 49.
6. For a fuller discussion of this general topic and of the role of a responsibility regime in promoting a culture of ethical excellence, see S. Cohen, "Promoting ethical judgment in an organisation context," forthcoming in the *Australian Journal of Professional and Applied Ethics*.
7. See Nice, David C., *Amtrak: The History and Politics of a National Railroad* (Boulder, CO: Lynne Reiner Publishers, 1998).
8. Aristotle, *Nicomachean Ethics*, Book V, chap. 10.
9. Analogously, it is sometimes argued that this has been exactly the case with IQ testing. This was initially developed in 1905, and revised in 1908, 1911, and 1916, in order to identify those who are intellectually challenged, indicated by their falling below a certain number on the IQ scale. However, it is, after all, a scale with high numbers as well as low numbers. So, the test began to be used as a way of discriminating at the higher levels as well. It was not designed to do this, and, so the argument goes, it does not do this at all well. It is not, in fact, a tool for this job. This is exactly the issue of "concept validity."
10. Onora O'Neill, *A Question of Trust* (Cambridge: Cambridge University Press, 2002), particularly chaps 3 and 4.
11. See Amanda Sinclair, "Codes in the workplace: Organisational versus professional codes," in Margaret Coady and Sidney Bloch, eds, *Codes of Ethics and the Professions* (Melbourne: Melbourne University Press, 1996), for a comparison of professional and organizational codes that involve some of the issues mentioned here.
12. Some qualification is required here. For example, in terms of their profession, chartered accountants advertise themselves as being better able to do a number of things (for example, income tax returns), perhaps, impliedly, not merely because of their expertise but also because of their commitment to a code of conduct. There are other examples as well, but as a general point, it does seem correct to say that the profession operates as a monopoly and so would usually have no reason to offer the presence of a code of ethics as competitive advertising.
13. Robert Howard, "Values make the company," *Harvard Business Review*, September–October 1990, 133–44.
14. Alan Farnham, "State your values, hold the hot air," *Fortune*, 19 April 1993, 54.
15. Ibid.
16. On enforcement of codes, see Ian Freckelton, "Enforcement of ethics," in Coady and Bloch, *Codes of Ethics and the Professions*, 130–65.
17. Norman Bowie, "Business codes of ethics: window dressing or legitimate alternative to government regulation?," in Tom L. Beauchamp and Norman E. Bowie, eds, *Ethical Theory and Business* (Englewood Cliffs, NJ: Prentice Hall, 1979), 234–9.
18. The full text of this letter can be read on the Ontario Securities Commission website: http://www.osc.gov.on.ca.
19. This is available at the ASX website: http://www.asx.com.au/about/CorporateGovernance_AA2.shtm.
20. Canadian Bankers Association, http://www.cba.ca/en/consumer-information/43-rights- responsibilities/78-voluntary-commitments-and-codes-of-conduct.
21. Walter W. Manley II, *Handbook of Good Business Practice* (London: Routledge, 1992), 4–13. According to Manley's research, the British managers found that codes help establish the ethical tone of the organization; state its values; facilitate the imparting of these values to employees; give a commonly accepted basis to a company's policies and employee understandings of them; underpin a company's strategic direction; prepare staff for external scrutiny and help avoid intrusive attention from interest groups and the media; set clear standards for dealings with other businesses and third parties; clarify the rights and responsibilities of the company, its management, and its employees; respond to government pressure for greater external regulation; improve a company's image and public confidence in it; reduce exposure to lawsuits; improve performance and profits; enhance corporate pride; build excellence across the company's operations; set benchmarks for performance; reassure shareholders

as to the company's integrity; sustain public confidence in the market system; foster a business culture of openness and free communication; facilitate the integration of the cultures of merged companies; and deter unethical behaviour throughout a company.

22. James A. Waters, "Catch 20.5: Corporate morality as an organizational phenomenon," in A.P. Iannone, ed., *Contemporary Moral Controversies* (New York: Oxford University Press, 1989), 152.
23. For an interesting and readable discussion of this point, see C.A.J. Coady, "Ethos and ethics in business," in Coady and Sampford, *Business, Ethics and the Law*, 149–71.
24. Honeywell, *Code of Ethics and Business Conduct* (Minneapolis: Honeywell, 1995), 4.
25. The guidelines require that (i) a code of ethics and organizational standards be developed; (ii) responsibility for ethics programs be vested in a senior executive; (iii) persons with a record of sharp practice or misconduct be excluded from positions of authority; (iv) employees be properly informed about the code of ethics and organizational standards; (v) monitoring, auditing, and safe reporting mechanisms be instituted; (vi) fair and firm disciplinary measures be taken against misconduct; and (vii) measures be taken to prevent recurrences of misconduct.
26. The issue of conformism to external pressures is a serious objection to organizational ethics programs. For a discussion of the problem, see C.A.J. Coady, "On regulating ethics," in Coady and Bloch, *Codes of Ethics and the Professions*, 269–87.
27. Ronald R. Sims, "The institutionalization of organizational ethics," *Journal of Business Ethics* 10 (1991): 504.
28. Ibid., passim; Waters, "Catch 20.5," 159–61.
29. Amanda Sinclair has argued that ethical cultures can be established through treating an organization as a single culture or as a number of co-existing subcultures, but we believe that ethical failure is more likely to result from fragmentation. See Sinclair's "Improving ethics through organisational culture: A comparison of two approaches," in Coady and Sampford, *Business, Ethics and the Law*, 128–48.

Chapter 11

1. See Andy Hoffman, "A big mess," *Globe and Mail*, 12 October 2009.
2. Naomi Klein, *No Logo* (Hammersmith, London: Flamingo, 2001).
3. Elizabeth Becker, "Animal fans' secret recipe is to boycott restaurant," *New York Times*, 6 January 2003.
4. A fuller argument is developed in Stephen Cohen and Damian Grace, "Ethics and sustainability: Looking beyond basic legal requirements," *Australian Master OHS and Environment Guide 2003* (Sydney: CCH, 2002).
5. De George, *Business Ethics*, 6th edn (Upper Saddle River, NJ: Pearson Prentice Hall, 2006), 345.
6. "The tragedy of the commons," *Science* 162 (December 1968): 1234–8.
7. Manuel Velasquez, *Business Ethics: Concepts and Cases*, 6th edn (Upper Saddle River, NJ: Pearson Prentice Hall, 2006), 226.
8. Manuel Velasquez provides an excellent discussion of this point in *Business Ethics*, 231–4.
9. William T. Blackstone, "Ethics and ecology," in William T. Blackstone, ed., *Philosophy and the Environmental Crisis* (Athens, GA: University of Georgia Press, 1974).
10. Hendrickson B. and Chun W., "The Canadian Climate Exchanges: The Future of Canadian Emissions Trading" in *Emissions Trading and Climate Change Bulletin*, McMillan, Bimch, Mendelsohn LLP, Toronto, 2007. http://www.mcmillan.ca/Files/CdnClimateExchanges_0507.pdf. See also King, M.R. *An Overview of Carbon Markets and Emissions Trading: Lessons for Canada*, Bank of Canada Discussion Paper, 2008. http://www.bankofcanada.ca/wp-content/uploads/2010/01/dp08-1.pdf.
11. The Kyoto Protocol refers to the protocol to the United Nations Framework Convention on Climate Change (UNFCCC) adopted in 1997 designed to combat global warming. The UNFCCC is an international environmental treaty with the goal of achieving moderation of greenhouse gases in the atmosphere in order to prevent dangerous interference with the global climate system. The UNFCCC went into force in 2005, and by 2011, 191 countries had ratified the protocol. Canada ratified the protocol, but later renounced it in late 2011.
12. B. Curry, and S. McCarthy, "Canada formally abandons Kyoto Protocol on Climate Change," *Globe and Mail*, 12 December 2011, http://www.theglobeandmail.com/news/politics/canada-formally-abandons-kyoto-protocol-on-climate-change/article4180809/.
13. Conference Board of Canada "GHG emissions per capita," http://www.conferenceboard.ca/hcp/details/environment/greenhouse-gas-emissions.aspx.
14. Michael Hoffman, "Business and environmental ethics," *Business Ethics Quarterly* 1, no. 2 (1991): 169–84.

15. Peter Singer, *Animal Liberation*, 2nd edn (New York: Thorsons, 1991), 6.
16. Thomas More, *Utopia*, ed. G. Logan and R.M. Adams (Cambridge: Cambridge University Press, 1989), 73.
17. See Raimond Gaita's excellent discussion in *The Philosopher's Dog* (Melbourne: Text Publishing, 2002).
18. Ted Trainer, for example, argues that economies based on ever-increasing consumption are both unsustainable and irrational. There are alternative possible economies not based on geometric consumption. For Trainer, affluence is the problem: *Abandon Affluence* (London: Zed Books, 1985).
19. See Trading Economics website: http://www.tradingeconomics.com/.
20. H. Daly and J. Cobb, *For the Common Good* (London: Greenprint, 1989), 450.
21. John Rawls, *A Theory of Justice* (Oxford: Clarendon Press, 1972), 289.
22. Ibid., 285–9.
23. For a list of explicit principles that give effect to Rawls's point, see Holmes Rolston III, "Just environmental business," in Tom Regan, ed., *Just Business* (New York: Random House, 1984), chap. 11.
24. Christopher Pearson, "Green errors began with DDT," *Weekend Australian*, 24–25 January 2004, 16.
25. Michael Crichton, "Remarks to the Commonwealth Club San Francisco," 15 September 2003, http://www.crichton-official.com/speeches/speeches_quote05.html.
26. This information may be accessed at http://www.shell.com/home/Framework?siteId= royal-en&FC2=/royal-en/html/iwgen/environment_and_society/making_it_happen/our_approach/zzz_lhn.html&FC3=/royal-en/html/iwgen/environment_and_society/making_it_happen/ our_approach/our_approach.html.
27. Mel Wilson, "Corporate reputation and the triple bottom line: The social responsibilities of business," *Risky Business*, no. 2 (2001), http://www.pwc.com/extweb/manissue.nsf/DocID/ C00115084F24343E852569E600656A08.
28. Accessed at http://www.igc.apc.org/habitat/agenda21/rio-dec.html. See also Wingspread Statement, http://www.gdrc.org/u-gov/precaution-3.html.
29. Wingspread Statement, http://www.gdrc.org/u-gov/precaution-3.html.
30. Ibid.
31. Frank Cross, "Paradoxical perils of the precautionary principle," *Washington and Lee Law Review* 53 (1996): 851.
32. Duff Wilson, "Fear in the fields: How hazardous wastes become fertilizer," *The Seattle Times*, 3 July 1997. Accessed at http://online.sfsu.edu/rone/Environ/fearinthefields1.htm
33. Quoted by Duff Wilson, "Fear in the fields—how hazardous wastes become fertilizer—spreading heavy metals on farmland is perfectly legal, but little research has been done to find out whether it's safe," *Seattle Times*, 3 July 1997, http://community.seattletimes.nwsource.com/archive/?date=19970704&slug=2547909. The series of articles by Duff Wilson may be accessed at http://seattletimes.nwsource.com/news/special/fear_fields.html.
34. See CBC Digital Archives, "Great Lakes pollution: What is the Sarnia Blob?" Last updated 14 February 2012, http://www.cbc.ca/archives/categories/environment/pollution/troubled-waters-pollution-in-the-great-lakes/what-is-the-sarnia-blob.html.
35. Jan Mayman, "The stink of Uncle Al," *Weekend Australian*, 11–12 May 2002, 19–22.
36. Ibid., 19.
37. Ibid.
38. For evidence presented at the inquiry, see http://www.parliament.wa.gov.au/parliament/commit.nsf/(InqByName)/AEED11314738B6B148256B610023EA99?opendocument.
39. Christine Parker, *The Open Corporation* (Melbourne: Cambridge University Press, 2000), 68–83.
40. Ibid., 77.
41. ISO statistics, http://www.ecology.or.jp/isoworld/english/analy14k.htm.
42. See the SustainAbility website for more on Elkington at http://www.sustainability.com/home.asp.
43. See http://www.globalreporting.org/about/brief.asp.
44. Information on the Valdez Principles is drawn from Rajib Sanyal and Joao Neves, "The Valdez Principles: Implications for corporate social responsibility," *Journal of Business Ethics* 10 (December 1991): 883–90. A decade earlier, American business had responded to another challenge—racial discrimination in South Africa—with the Sullivan Code. The Sullivan Code was initially a voluntary code designed to prevent American firms from exploiting non-white South Africans, and its success made it a model for the Valdez Principles.
45. Environment Canada website: http://www.ec.gc.ca/.
46. *Canada's Action on Climate Change*, Environment Canada website: http://www.climatechange.gc.ca/.
47. See Fisheries and Oceans Canada, Fisheries Act, http://www.dfo-mpo.gc.ca/habitat/role/141/1415/14151-eng.htm. See also Conservation Ontario,

Planning and Regulations, Conservation Authorities' Federal Fisheries Act Partnership, http://www.conservation-ontario.on.ca/planning_regulations/fisheries_act.html.

48. Canadian Fisheries, Oceans and Aquaculture Management, "Dredging the Sydney Harbour: Doing what HADD to be done," http://www.omrn-rrgo.ca/docs/CFOAM_seminar_announce_April2012.pdf.
49. *World Commission on Environment and Development, Our Common Future* (London: Oxford University Press, 1987.
50. Ecologically Sustainable Development Working Group Chairs, *Intersectoral Issues Report* (Canberra: AGPS, 1992), 3.
51. Ibid., 13.
52. Peter Kent, Notes for Remarks by the Honourable Peter Kent, P.C., M.P., Minister of the Environment, Joint Canada-Alberta Implementation Plan for Oil Sands Monitoring, Edmonton, Alberta, 3 February 2012.
53. Ibid.
54. Rowan Callick, "Green codes drawn up for doing business overseas," *Australian Financial Review*, 2 November 1995.
55. Cameron Forbes and Matthew Stevens, "BHP considers PNG mining solutions," *Australian*, 24 May 1994.
56. See details of acid rock drainage management at Ok Tedi in reports available at http://www.oktedi.com/component/search/acid%20rock?ordering=&searchphrase=all.
57. *BHP and Ok Tedi*, 8.
58. Ibid.
59. See *BHP Billiton Health Safety Environment & Community Report*, 2003, http://www.bhpbilliton.com/hsecReport/2003/home/home8.html.

Chapter 12

1. In a famous passage, Hobbes characterized such a life as "solitary, poor, nasty, brutish, and short." *Leviathan* (1651), part I, chap. 13.
2. Campbell writes, "Now in every human being there is a built-in human instinct system, without which we should not even come to birth. But each of us has also been educated to a specific local culture system." *Reflections on the Art of Living: A Joseph Campbell Companion*, selected and edited by Diane K. Osbon (New York: Harper Perennial, 1991), 126.
3. Here we follow John Kekes, *The Morality of Pluralism* (Princeton, NJ: Princeton University Press, 1993), 38–44.
4. Robert Armstrong et al., "Business ethics," in Anthony Milner and Mary Quilty, eds, *Australia in Asia: Comparing Cultures* (Melbourne: Oxford University Press, 1996), 24.
5. Ibid., 26. In a brief but pointed way, Armstrong et al. set out some of the core values of Japanese, Chinese, Thai, Indonesian, and Korean cultures.
6. Reported in "Excerpts from the International Press," *TI Newsletter*, March 1997, http://www.transparency.de/newsletter/.
7. Johann Lambsdorff, "The question of responsibility," 26 September 1997, http://gwdu19.gwdg.de/%7Ejlambsd/bribery/node4.htm.
8. Louise Williams, "Bre-X scam sparks attacks on foreigners," *Sydney Morning Herald*, 6 May 1997, 28.
9. Nicholas Cumming-Bruce, "Chief of state-owned firm in $62m graft case," *Sydney Morning Herald*, 25 January 1997, 22.
10. Amartya Sen, "Does business ethics make economic sense?," *Business Ethics Quarterly* 3 (1993): 50.
11. Robert Garran, "Nomura president falls on his sword," *Weekend Australian*, 15–16 March 1997, 53; "Nomura bosses resign en masse," *Australian*, 23 April 1997, 23. When the rest of the senior management of Nomura resigned in April 1997, they retained their rights as "advisers," with the power to continue to do business in the company's name. In this way, public honour was saved, but Nomura did not face a sudden loss of corporate knowledge and the individuals did not have to pay the full price of resignation.
12. For details of the Lockheed scandal, see Velasquez, *Business Ethics*, 207–8; Martin and Schinzinger, *Ethics in Engineering*, 261–2.
13. *Sydney Morning Herald*, 18 November 1996, 38.
14. Greg McArthur, "A gift for Mr. Hossain," *Globe and Mail Report on Business Magazine*, September 2011.
15. Certified Global Management Accountants, "Managing responsible business: A global survey on business ethics," http://www.cgma.org/Resources/Reports/DownloadableDocuments/CGMA%20Ethics%20Report%20FINAL.pdf.
16. "More top executives willing to pay bribes—survey," Reuters, 23 May 2012, http://ht.ly/b7o3G.
17. "Surveys on Business Ethics, 2011," *Business Ethics Briefing*, Issue 23, February 2012, http://www.ibe.org.uk/userfiles/surveys_2011.pdf.
18. Robert W. Armstrong, "An empirical investigation of international marketing ethics: problems encountered by Australian firms," *Journal of Business Ethics* 11 (1992): 161–71.
19. The Asian Intelligence Report, cited in "Indonesia 'most corrupt,'" business survey, *Sydney Morning Herald*, 31 March 1997, 7.

20. Hanbo, one of Korea's largest steelmakers and US$6 billion in debt, allegedly obtained loans it would not otherwise have gotten from government-controlled banks at the behest of the ruling New Korea Party. Hanbo chairman Chung Tae-soo has a history of bribing government officials. He was convicted of paying former president Roh Tae-woo US$23 million in bribes during his 1988–92 term.
21. "Dud loans dog Vietnam's banks," *Sydney Morning Herald*, 24 March 1997, 38.
22. On 7 March 1997, the *Australian Financial Review* reported on its front page that the east coast criminal milieu had assumed all the trappings of legitimate business in order to pursue criminal activities—such as money laundering—more efficiently. In the United States, the "mob" has infiltrated the securities industry. "Mob muscles into brokers' offices," *Sydney Morning Herald*, 24 March 1997, 38.
23. S.J. Vitell, S.L. Nwachukwu, and J.H. Barnes, "The effects of culture on ethical decision-making: An application of Hofstede's typology," *Journal of Business Ethics* 12 (1993): 753–60. They distinguish two types of culture: individualist and collectivist. In individualist cultures, it is acceptable to give primacy to the interests of individuals, their families, and their connections. In collectivist cultures, the individual's identity is determined by a group of some kind and the interests of the group are accorded primacy. Collectivist societies emphasize loyalty more than individualist ones. The authors suggest that in collectivist societies (they cite Japan), individuals are more likely to be guided by the norms and values of their industrial, business, or professional group. In contrast to this alignment, the individual in an individualist society (they cite the United States) is less influenced by organizational norms, even when formally stated, as in codes of ethics. Moreover, they suggest that business practitioners in individualistic societies are more likely than those in collectivist societies to consider themselves as more important stakeholders than other employees or the owners (754–6).
24. Alois A. Nugroho, "The myth of immoral business: a specific challenge of business ethics in Indonesia," *International Society of Business, Economics and Ethics Papers*, Tokyo 1996, http://www.nd.edu/~isbee/p_nugroh.htm.
25. Julius Tahija, "Swapping business skills for oil," *Harvard Business Review*, September–October 1993, 113.
26. "All employees are expected to comply with anti-trust/competition laws throughout the world, i.e., no price fixing, bid rigging, criminal collusion. Marketing and selling efforts must conform to highest ethical standards. . . . It is Honeywell's policy to comply with FCPA laws which prohibit the bribery of foreign government or political officials and establish mandatory internal record keeping standards. . . . No employee will provide or accept kickbacks. . . . No employee will give, offer or promise to give, or ask for or accept anything of value to or from an employee or other representative of any current or potential customer, supplier, or regulatory authority, in exchange for assistance or influence in a transaction." Honeywell, *Code of Ethics and Business Conduct* (Honeywell: Minnesota, 1995), 1–2.
27. Richard De George, *Competing with Integrity in International Business* (New York: Oxford University Press, 1993), 114.
28. Ibid, 46–56. De George also offers 10 "strategies" or counsels of perfection for dealing with corruption in international business. The first and probably hardest is to remain ethical, even if competitors do not. The others include using an imaginative response to ethical difficulty; avoiding overreaction and maintenance of a sense of proportion; developing background legal institutions at home and abroad; exposing unethical practices in the media where possible; combining with other parties to reform social, legal, and political institutions; and requiring strict accountability of MNCs and those who work within them. See also ibid., 114–20.
29. Ibid., 112.
30. Adapted from Herbert's report, reprinted in K. Woldring, ed., *Business Ethics in Australia and New Zealand* (Melbourne: Nelson, 1996), 191–2.
31. Verena Dobnik, "Nike accused of allowing 'boot camp factories,'" *Sydney Morning Herald*, 29 March 1997, 17.
32. See http://usas.org for information on United Students Against Sweatshops.
33. Peter Hancock, *Women Workers in Nike Factories in West Java* (Fitzroy: Community Aid Abroad, 1997).
34. On 3 December 1984, significant quantities of methyl isocyanate (MIC), a chemical used in the production of pesticides, escaped from a Union Carbide plant in Bhopal, India, killing approximately 4,000 people, injuring 200,000, and leaving tens of thousands with permanent disabilities and health problems. While several possible causes of the accident have been suggested, investigations indicate that many of the advanced safety features that were originally installed in the plant were either turned

off, in need of maintenance, or in serious disrepair. Lack of oversight by Union Carbide and a failure to adequately train its local employees were significant factors in the lead-up to the accident. For a complete chronology of the events following the disaster, see the Bhopal Information Centre, Chronology, http://www.bhopal.com/chronology. See also chapter 12 of R.F. Hartley, *Business Ethics: Mistakes and Successes*, 1st ed. (Hoboken, NJ: John Wiley and Sons, 2005).

35. Brad Norington, "The shoe fits here as well," *Sydney Morning Herald*, 18 April 1997, 15.
36. Chris Patten, "Synergy of robust rights and robust development," *Sydney Morning Herald*, 24 November 1993, 15.
37. This and other aspects of economic development and liberty are elaborated in Chris Patten, *East and West: The Last Governor of Hong Kong on Power, Freedom and the Future* (London: Pan Macmillan, 1998).
38. However, the costs can be overstated; see the argument that ethical knowledge is an asset in Norman E. Bowie and Paul Vaaler, "Some arguments for universal moral standards," in *International Society of Business, Economics and Ethics Papers* (Tokyo, 1996), http:// www.nd.edu/~isbee/ p_bowie.htm.
39. International Trade Union Confederation, "ITUC Survey 2012: Annual Survey of Violations of Trade Union Rights," http://survey.ituc-csi.org/.
40. "Canada imposes new sanctions on Myanmar," *Globe and Mail*, 14 November 2007.
41. Thomas Donaldson, "Multinational decision-making: Reconciling international norms," in Anthony Ellis, ed., *Ethics and International Relations* (Manchester: Manchester University Press, 1986), 127–40; idem, *The Ethics of International Business* (New York: Oxford University Press, 1989), chap. 5; idem, "The language of international corporate ethics," *Business Ethics Quarterly* 2 (1992): 271–81.
42. Donaldson, *The Ethics of International Business*, 84. Compare Donaldson's "The perils of multinationals' largess," *Business Ethics Quarterly* 4 (1994): 367–71.
43. As Donaldson puts it, "the corporation, if indeed it is a moral agent at all, has limited moral capacities and a decidedly non-human psychology. It is often taller and richer than most of us: but it is morally peculiar. It strives for nothing except economic objectives, or, if it [does strive for other objectives] its striving has none of the psychological characteristics of human moral striving. It does not weep at funerals, struggle with its appetite, or enjoy wedding parties." Donaldson, "The language of international corporate ethics," 275–6. Compare, for example, Robert Ewin, "The moral status of the corporation," *Journal of Business Ethics* 10 (1991): 755: "Because they are artificial people and not 'natural' people, corporations lack the emotional makeup necessary to the possession of virtues and vices. Their moral personality is exhausted by their legal personality."
44. Geraldine Brooks, "They hang writers don't they?," *Weekend Australian*, 30–31 December 1995, Features, 5.
45. Found at http://www.transparency.org/surveys/index.html.
46. Kevin Jackson, "Global distributive justice and the corporate duty to aid," *Journal of Business Ethics* 12 (1993): 550. See Donaldson's reply in "The perils of multinationals' largess."
47. George C. Brenkert, "Can we afford international human rights?," *Journal of Business Ethics* 11 (1992): 517.
48. These have been growing in number internationally. For ethical investment strategies, see A. Landier and V.B. Nair, *Investing for Change: Profit from Responsible Investment* (New York: Oxford University Press, 2009). See also H.K. Baker and J.R. Nofzinger, eds, *Socially Responsible Finance and Investing: Financial Institutions, Corporations, Investors, and Activists* (Hoboken, NJ: John Wiley and Sons, 2012).
49. For an elaboration of the argument from self-interest, see Bowie and Vaaler, "Some arguments for universal moral standards."
50. Donaldson, *The Ethics of International Business*, 75. Donaldson nominates 10 fundamental human rights: the right to freedom of physical movement; the right to ownership of property; the right to freedom from torture; the right to a fair trial; the right to non-discriminatory treatment; the right to physical security; the right to freedom of speech and association; the right to minimal education; the right to political participation; and the right to subsistence.
51. This criticism is discussed at length in Brenkert, "Can we afford international human rights?," 515–21.
52. Peter Drucker, *Post-Capitalist Society* (New York: Harper Business, 1993), 102.
53. As quoted in Sam North, "Human rights concerns pull Levi's out of China," *Sydney Morning Herald*, 8 May 1993, 15.
54. Robert Waterman, *Frontiers of Excellence* (Sydney: Allen & Unwin, 1994), 166–7. For a discussion of

the Levi's Aspiration Statement, its emphasis on ethics, and its attempt to globalize its values, see chapter 7 of Waterman, as well as Rhymer Rigby, "Jeans genius," *Management Today*, November 1996, 56–60. Rigby's article shows just how tough, in a business sense, Levi's is, but also just how seriously it takes ethics. In Bangladesh and Turkey, Levi's pays contractors to keep their children in school until they are 14 years old. This ensures that those who are potentially the main income-earners for families, children in sweatshops, are instead given an education and that, of course, Levi's is not open to charges of using child labour. According to Rigby, this is an expensive option for Levi's, but the company takes a long-term view and believes in adhering to its published ethical stance. Elaine Sternberg argues that Levi's can do these things legitimately because it is not in the position of a listed company, which must increase shareholder value and would not be at liberty to disperse profits in this manner. This point is a fair one, but it overlooks the fact that Levi's's shareholders choose to set an example through their corporation for shareholders in public companies.

55. Grand Metropolitan, *Report on Corporate Citizenship 1997* (London: Grand Metropolitan, 1997), 15.
56. Grand Met's model is based on corporate relationships with employees, government, investors, brand consumers, business partners, and communities.
57. Grand Metropolitan, *Report*, 19–20.
58. Friedman, "The social responsibility of business is to increase its profits."
59. Chris Marsden, "Corporate citizenship," unpublished discussion paper, BP Corporate Citizenship Unit, Business School, University of Warwick, 1997, 15.
60. Tahija, "Swapping business skills for oil," 5.
61. Ibid., 5–9.
62. Richard De George, "Entrepreneurs, multinationals, and business ethics," paper given at the International Society of Business, Economics and Ethics, Tokyo, 1996.
63. Ibid., 2.
64. Ibid.
65. Systems do not absolve individuals of personal responsibility for acting ethically. But not all corruption is of equal seriousness, and individuals cannot be required to display ethical behaviour out of proportion to the likely benefits. Although this cannot be required, it might still be freely given (for instance, by whistleblowers) and win our moral admiration and gratitude.
66. De George also argues that bribes harm those paying them: they suffer the injustice "but [do] not impose it on others." "Entrepreneurs, multinationals, and business ethics," 5. This is not strictly true: bribes impose a direct cost on customers and on those who must bear the costs of policing corruption. Bribery distorts markets, disadvantages competitors, and tends to drive up prices. This is not always the case, particularly in maturing economies, where, as Michael Backman argues, corruption "can enable bad government to be frustrated, and incompetent or slothful bureaucracies can be cut through." This does not answer the ethical objections, but as De George shows, even this requires discrimination. Backman, "Putting a kick back into business," *Australian Financial Review*, 27 October 1997, 15.
67. De George, "Entrepreneurs, multinationals, and business ethics," 4.
68. In 1996, in a first for Australia, WMC produced the report of an audit of the company's environmental performance. The audit identified problems and potential savings of which the company was previously unaware—for example, in water consumption. The CEO of WMC, Hugh Morgan, said the company had "a very strong self-interest in getting it right. I try to make it clear that this environmental activity is not a function of something imposed from outside. This is very much in our own self-interest." Mark Davis, "WMC compiles its own green report card," *Business Review Weekly*, 10 June 1996, 20–2.
69. Global Sullivan Principles, "History & Evolution," http://www.thesullivanfoundation.org/gsp/endorsement/history/default.asp.
70. Ibid.
71. GSP in Action, http://www.thesullivanfoundation.org/gsp/inAction/default.asp.
72. Global Sullivan Principles, http://www.thesullivanfoundation.org/gsp/principles/gsp/default.asp.
73. "Overview of the UN Global Compact," http://www.unglobalcompact.org/AboutTheGC/index.html.
74. "The Ten Principles" of the UN Global Compact, http://www.unglobalcompact.org/AboutTheGC/TheTenPrinciples/index.html.
75. The background history of the CRT is to be found at "Caux Round Table: History and Meetings," http://www.cauxroundtable.org/History.htm, extracted in part from Michael Henderson, *The Forgiveness Factor: Stories of Hope in a World of Conflict* (Salem, OR: Grosvenor Books, 1996), 181–93.

76. Ibid.
77. Charles M. Denny, one of the authors of the Caux Principles, as quoted in Henderson, *The Forgiveness Factor*.
78. J. Lambsdorff, TI Newsletter, September 1997, at http://archive.transparency.org/policy_research/surveys_indices/cpi/previous_cpi.
79. See Transparency International website: http://www.transparency.org/policy_research/surveys_indices/bpi/bpi_2008#faq.
80. *Lima Convention*, 2 November 1997, http://www.transparency.de/iace/council.html.

Appendices

1. William W. May (ed.), *Ethics in the Accounting Curriculum: Cases and Readings* (Sarasota, Florida: American Accounting Association, 1990). This model was adapted by the AAA from an eight-step model suggested by H. Q. Langenderfer and J. W. Rockness, "Integrating ethics into the accounting curriculum: Issues, problems and solutions," *Issues in Accounting Education*, 4, 1989, pp. 58–69.
2. Laura Nash, "Ethics without the sermon," *Harvard Business Review*, 59, November–December 1981, pp. 79–90.
3. Michael Rion, *The Responsible Manager: Practical Strategies for Ethical Decision Making* (San Francisco: Harper & Row, 1990), pp. 13–14, and then applied throughout the book.
4. Mary Guy, *Ethical Decision Making in Everyday Work Situations* (New York: Quorum Books, 1990), pp. 14–19, 28–30.
5. Excerpted by permission of the publisher, from *A Rock and a Hard Place* by Kent Hodgson © 1992, Kent Hodgson, AMACOM, division of American Management Association, New York, NY. All rights reserved. www.amacombooks.org
6. Philip G. Cottell Jr. & Terry M. Perlin, *Accounting Ethics: A Practical Guide for Professionals* (New York: Quorum Books, 1990), pp. 10, 12–13.
7. David Mathison, "Business ethics cases and decision models: A call for relevancy in the classroom," *Journal of Business Ethics*, 7, 1988, p. 780.
8. Anthony M. Pagano, "Criteria for ethical decision making in managerial situations," *Proceedings of the National Academy of Management*, New Orleans, 1987, pp. 1–12.
9. The CRT Principles may be found at http://www.cauxroundtable.org/index.cfm?&menuid=8. They are largely based on principles developed by the Minnesota Center for Corporate Responsibility.

Glossary

absolutism the view that there exists a universally correct moral position

accountability the requirement to justify decisions in terms of the delegated powers and authority of one's role

agent a person or entity that represents the interests of another party

aspirational desiring and striving to improve; to be better than the current state

bait advertising advertising a very limited number of items at a very low price as a means of attracting customers

bait-and-switch advertising advertising a product that is either unavailable or that seems to be a bargain, with the intention of substituting a more expensive item

Board of Directors elected by shareholders to represent them in overseeing the executive level of management to ensure that management does indeed act in the shareholders' best interests

bottom-up approach to ethical reasoning the moral judgments we make personally through moral intuition or reactions we have to particular situations

bribe the provision of money or gifts with the intention of influencing an individual with official, public, or legal decision-making responsibilities

business code an established set of principles or rules of behaviour that operates at the level of an individual business

categorical imperative an ethical principle developed by Immanuel Kant that requires, without exception, that a person "act only according to the maxim by which you can at the same time will that it should become universal law"

code an established set of principles or rules of behaviour

code of conduct an established set of specific and enforceable ethical prescriptions, which eliminate the uncertainty, variability, and necessity of judgment and discretion of a code of ethics

code of ethics a formal statement of an organization's ethical values and principles

compassion respect for the humanity of others

conflict of interest the presence in a person of competing (conflicting) professional, personal, and/or business interests

consequentialism a moral outlook that evaluates actions or behaviours according to the consequences of those outlooks or behaviours

constitutive rules rules about what constitutes, or defines, a practice

corporate governance the controls put in place to ensure that a corporation acts in an ethical, legal, and transparent manner in the best interests of its shareholders

cultural relativism the view that behaviours and values are relative to particular cultures; that behaviours are dependent on the accepted norms of the particular culture or society in which they take place

de facto value system a value system that exists in actual fact; it is in place and acted upon in good faith, even if not officially codified

de jure value system a value system that is formally codified

deontological (or **nonconsequentialism**) a moral outlook that evaluates actions or behaviours according to something other than the consequences of those behaviours

descriptive theories of ethics the non-judgmental empirical study of ethics in particular groups or societies

direct discrimination the intent to discriminate

dirty hands a situation in which, even if someone does the morally right thing, that person has also done something that is morally wrong. The moral wrongness does not evaporate simply in virtue of the rightness of the act.

ethical decision-making model a set of systematically organized trigger questions that take into account the differing perspective that anyone in an organization must be aware of in dealing with ethical issues

ethical defeat the admission that a person's actions have no positive ethical justification; that a person's actions are completely immoral

ethical dilemma a situation involving the conflict between moral imperatives where to comply with one necessitates the transgression of the other

ethical egoism identifying one's self-interest as the reference point for the moral world and the gauge of what is morally right and morally wrong

ethical empowerment the delegation of authority for ethical decision-making

ethical reasoning the reasoned application of ethical theory or theories to a given situation; the moral judgments we make personally through moral intuition or reactions we have to particular situations

ethical relativism the view that moral values are relative to particular environments; moral behaviours are dependent on the accepted ethical norms of the particular culture, society, or environment in which they take place

ethics the study of the theoretical foundations of moral principles governing individual behaviour and the practical application of those principles

fairness the part of justice that relates to equity; giving each individual their due

fiduciary relationship a legal or ethical relationship of confidence or trust between two or more parties where one person or party (the fiduciary) acts at all times in the best interests of another person or party

Foreign Corrupt Practices Act the 1977 US law prohibiting American corporations from making payments to foreign governments in order to advance their business interests; this was the first example of extraterritorial legislation governing citizens beyond the borders of the enacting jurisdiction

Generally Accepted Accounting Principles (GAAP) the common set of accounting principles, standards, and procedures that companies use to compile their financial statements. GAAP are a combination of authoritative standards (set by policy boards) and represent the commonly accepted ways of recording and reporting accounting information

glass ceiling an invisible barrier that prevents qualified people from rising above a certain level of rank or salary in business organizations

golden rule the maxim accepted by the vast majority, if not all, of the world's cultures and religions that states that one should treat others as one would like others to treat oneself

harassment continual pestering or bullying

honesty accountability to provide the truth to certain individuals based on context and relationship

incentive-based executive compensation the use of salary, bonuses, and long-term incentives to align managers' interests with shareholders' interests

indirect discrimination the result of some activity without being the aim of that activity

industry code an established set of principles or rules of behaviour that operates throughout a whole industry and sets the standard for firms and employees within that industry

internal whistleblowing blowing the whistle inside the organization—reporting the concern outside the normal channels of authority, but still not going public (not reporting outside the organization)

justice the inclusion and consideration of concepts such as equity, need, contributions, merits, social values, risks, and compassion in reaching an outcome

market for capital control the purchase of a firm that is underperforming relative to industry rivals in order to improve its strategic competitiveness

market for executive employment an external control that naturally motivates corporate executives to act in the best interests of the shareholders in order to maintain or increase their desirability in the external job market

monopoly a situation in which a single company or entity owns all or almost all of the market for a given type of product, commodity, or service

moral blindness failure to see that a moral issue exists at all

moral negligence failure to consider something that one should consider

moral pluralism the presence of a number of different, perhaps incompatible, moral principles; the view that there is no single moral theory or principle that should be accepted as preferable to others; different, diverse, and even mutually inconsistent ethical positions should be recognized and considered

moral recklessness failure to give adequate consideration to something; lack of attention due to haste or lack of due concern

negative advocacy focusing on attacking the credibility of the whistleblower in an attempt to divert attention from the problem issue being exposed by the whistleblower

negative externality the external cost of a transaction, not transmitted through prices, that is incurred by a party who was not involved as either a buyer or seller of the goods or services causing the cost or benefit

negative option billing the practice in which a good or service is automatically provided to the customer without the customer having requested it, placing the onus on the customer to cancel the good or service or be billed accordingly

negative rights rights that require or involve only freedom from interference

nonconsequentialism (or **deontology**) a moral outlook that evaluates actions or behaviours according to something other than the consequences of those behaviours

oligopoly a state of limited competition in which the market is shared by a few dominant producers or sellers

positive rights rights that require assistance or provision in order to be exercised

practical reasoning reasoning for the purpose of action, or for doing something

prescriptive theories of ethics theories that allow for the judgment of an act as right or wrong; recommending and forbidding certain types of conduct

principal a person or entity first in rank of importance or level of ownership

principal-agent problem represents the conflict of interest between the principal and the agent

private morality the morality and moral requirements and considerations present in one's personal affairs, whether or not those affairs are private

professional code an established set of principles or rules of behaviour that operates throughout a whole profession and sets the standard for its practitioners

professional ethics the application of ethical principles to professional practice

psychological egoism the stance that people are always motivated by self-interest and selfishness

public morality the morality and moral requirements and considerations present when one has a public persona, role, or position

the public trust the reliance of the public on the integrity of the public sector or of a given profession or professional

puffery untruths or exaggerations that are assumed to be recognized as such by people who are exposed to them

reflective equilibrium the state of a person's beliefs, reached by interplay between principles and judgments, when his or her moral principles and moral judgments are in harmony

relativism the view that moral values are relative to particular environments; moral behaviours are dependent on the particular culture, society, or environment in which they take place

sexual harassment continual pestering, bullying, or unwanted attention of a sexual nature, often associated with an abuse of power

shareholder an owner of shares in a company

social licence an intangible permission endowed by a society rooted in its beliefs, customs, traditions, and practices

stakeholder the broad constituency served by business. As such, they have a deemed interest in what a firm does in order to earn profits.

teleopathy becoming fixated on goals far from the original mission or outside the original mandate

top-down approach to ethical reasoning general or universal moral principles, which are inflexible and non-negotiable are applied to specific situations, in order to determine the ethically justifiable decision

trustworthiness the ability to receive a truth or responsibility and sustain the confidence of others that you will not use it lightly or inappropriately

utilitarianism the contention that the greatest good comes from choosing the alternative that provides the greatest aggregate level of satisfaction

utility level of satisfaction or happiness

virtue ethics a moral outlook that bases the rightness of an action on a comparison to the response of a moral person or person with the requisite moral character

voluntary code of conduct a set of non-legislated commitments made by a company or organization to influence or control behaviour in the interest of protecting the industry, its customers, and other stakeholders

whistleblowing making public matters that organizations have ignored or wish to keep hidden but which constitute a significant wrong or an immediate danger

Bibliography

Accessibility for Ontarians with Disabilities Act (AODA): http://www.e-laws.gov.on.ca/html/source/regs/english/2011/elaws_src_regs_r11191_e.htm.

Advertising Standards Canada: http://www.adstandards.com/en/AboutASC/ourHistory.aspx.

Alderman, Lesley. "When the stork carries a pink slip." *New York Times*, 27 March 2009.

American Civil Liberties Union. "HIV employment discrimination by Transportation Security Administration," 21 October 2011, http://www.aclu.org/hiv-aids/tsa-hiv-discrimination-case-profile.

Aquinas, St Thomas. *Treatise on Law*. South Bend, IN: Regnery/Gateway, 1979.

Aristotle. *The Ethics of Aristotle*, trans. J.A.K. Thomson et al. Harmondsworth, UK: Penguin Books, 1976.

Armstrong, Robert W. "An empirical investigation of international marketing ethics: Problems encountered by Australian firms." *Journal of Business Ethics* 11 (1992): 161–71.

Armstrong, Robert, et al. "Business ethics." In Anthony Milner and Mary Quilty, eds, *Australia in Asia: Comparing Cultures*. Melbourne: Oxford University Press, 1996.

Arrington, Robert. "Advertising and behavior control." *Journal of Business Ethics* 1, no. 1 (February 1982): 3–12.

Asian Intelligence Report. Cited in "Indonesia 'most corrupt,'" business survey, *Sydney Morning Herald*, 31 March 1997, 7.

Backman, Michael. "Putting a kick back into business." *Australian Financial Review*, 27 October 1997, 15.

Bakan, Joel. *The Corporation: The Pathological Pursuit of Profit and Power*. New York: Free Press, 2004.

Baker, H.K., and J.R. Nofzinger, eds. *Socially Responsible Finance and Investing: Financial Institutions, Corporations, Investors, and Activists*. Hoboken, NJ: John Wiley and Sons, 2012.

"Bank of America CEO subpoenaed over Merrill Lynch bonuses," 20 February 2009: http://www.syracuse.com/news/index.ssf/2009/02/bank_of_america_ceo_subpoenaed.html.

Barboza, David. "Death sentences in milk cases." *New York Times*, 23 January 2009.

Barker, Geoffrey. "Dead fish, ethics and Ok Tedi." *Australian Financial Review*, 9 October 1995.

———. "Ethics: The glove that tempers the iron fist." *Australian Financial Review Magazine*, 7 July 1995, 14–20.

Barry, Paul. *The Rise and Fall of Alan Bond*. Sydney: Bantam, 1990.

BBC. "Stand-off over Sir Fred's pension." BBC News, 27 February 2009: http://news.bbc.co.uk/2/hi/uk_news/politics/7912651.stm.

Becker, Elizabeth. "Animal fans' secret recipe is to boycott restaurant." *New York Times*, 6 January 2003.

Beder, Sharon. "Engineers, ethics and etiquette." *New Scientist*, 25 September 1993, 36–41.

Behar, R. "Jungle fever: The Bre-X saga is the greatest gold scam ever." *Fortune Magazine*, 9 June 1997, http://money.cnn.com/magazines/fortune/fortune_archive/1997/06/09/227519/index.htm.

Bhopal Information Centre. Chronology, http://www.bhopal.com/chronology.

Blackstone, William T. "Ethics and ecology." In William T. Blackstone, ed., *Philosophy and the Environmental Crisis*. Athens, GA: University of Georgia Press, 1974.

Blodgett, Timothy. "Showdown on 'business bluffing,'" *Harvard Business Review*, May–June 1968, 162–70.

Boisjoly, Roger. "The Challenger disaster: Moral responsibility and the working engineer." In Deborah G. Johnson, *Ethical Issues in Engineering*, 6–14. Englewood Cliffs, NJ: Prentice Hall, 1991.

———. "Personal Integrity and Accountability." In *Accounting Horizons*, 1993, 59–69.

Bok, Sissela. "Blowing the whistle." in J. Fleishman et al., eds, *Public Duties: The Moral Obligations of Government Officials*. Cambridge: Cambridge University Press, 1982.

Bolt, Cathy. "Pregnancy sacking damages $12,000." *Australian Financial Review*, August 1993, 6.

Bowal, P. 2006, "Employer Surveillance of Employees." *Law Now* 31, no. 1 (September/October 2006): 47

Bowie, Norman. "Business codes of ethics: Window dressing or legitimate alternative to government regulation?" In Tom L. Beauchamp and Norman E. Bowie, eds, *Ethical Theory and Business*. Englewood Cliffs, NJ: Prentice Hall, 1979.

Bowie, Norman, and Ronald Duska. *Business Ethics*, 2nd edn. Englewood Cliffs, NJ: Prentice Hall, 1990.

Bowie, Norman E., and Paul Vaaler. "Some arguments for universal moral standards." In *International Society of Business, Economics and Ethics Papers*. Tokyo, 1996: http://www.nd. edu/~isbee/ p_bowie.htm.

Braybrooke, David. *Ethics in the World of Business*. Totowa, NJ: Rowman and Allanheld, 1983.

Brenkert, George C. "Can we afford international human rights?" *Journal of Business Ethics*, 11 (1992): 517.

Brewster, Murray. "Vets department and board struggled for years to contain privacy leaks." *Winnipeg Free Press*, 16 February 2012.

Brooks, Geraldine. "They hang writers don't they?" *Weekend Australian*, 30–31 December 1995, Features, 5.

Brown, David. "Maker of Vioxx is accused of deception." *Washington Post*, 16 April 2008.

Bruck, C. *The Predators' Ball: the Inside Story of Drexel Burnham and the Rise of the Junk Bond Raiders*. New York: American Lawyer/Simon and Schuster, 1988.

Buncombe, Andrew. "US firms' war on workers: Where there's smoking, they're fired." *Independent*, 29 January 2005.

Business Journal. "Merrill Lynch to pay $1m settlement," 2 February 2009.

Cadbury, Sir Adrian. "Ethical managers make their own rules." *Harvard Business Review*, September–October 1987, reprinted in E.K. Kellar, ed., *Ethical Insight, Ethical Action*. Washington: ICMA, 1988.

"CALEA: The perils of wiretapping the internet." *Electronic Frontier Foundation* (website), http://www.eff.org/issues/calea.

Callick, Rowan. "Green codes drawn up for doing business overseas." *Australian Financial Review*, 2 November 1995.

Campbell, Joseph. *Reflections on the Art of Living: A Joseph Campbell Companion*, ed. Diane K. Osbon. New York: Harper Perennial, 1991.

Canadian Bankers Association. "Voluntary commitments and codes of conduct": http://www.cba.ca/en/consumer-information/43-rights- responsibilities/78-voluntary-commitments-and-codes-of-conduct.

Canadian Centre for Occupational Health and Safety, http://www.ccohs.ca/.

Canadian Code of Advertising Standards: http://www.adstandards.com/en/standards/canCodeOfAdStandards.pdf.

Canadian Competition Bureau: http://www.competition-bureau.gc.ca/.

Canadian Fisheries, Oceans and Aquaculture Management. "Dredging the Sydney Harbour: Doing what HADD to be done," http://www.omrn-rrgo.ca/docs/CFOAM_seminar_announce_April2012.pdf.

Canadian Human Rights Commission. Canadian Human Rights Commission's Policy on Alcohol and Drug Testing, 2009, http://www.chrc-ccdp.ca/pdf/padt_pdda_eng.pdf.

Canadian Marketing Association: http://www.the-cma.org/about.

Canadian Marketing Association. Code of Ethics and Standards of Practice: http://www.the-cma.org/regulatory/code-of-ethics.

Canadian Radio-television and Telecommunications Commission: http://www.crtc.gc.ca/eng/backgrnd/brochures/b29903.htm.

Carey, Lorraine. "Profits and principles: The operationalisation of corporate ethics in Australian enterprises." PhD thesis, University of Canberra, 2007.

Carr, Albert Z. "Is business bluffing ethical?" *Harvard Business Review*, January–February 1968.

"Caux Round Table: History and Meetings, " 2 November 1997: http://www.cauxroundtable.org/History.htm.

CBC Digital Archives. "Great Lakes pollution: What is the Sarnia Blob?" Last updated 14 February 2012, http://www.cbc.ca/archives/categories/environment/pollution/troubled-waters-pollution-in-the-great-lakes/what-is-the-sarnia-blob.html.

CBC Mandate: http://www.cbc.radio-canada.ca/about/mandate.shtml.

CBC News. "Dismissed RCMP officer ordered reinstated," 19 March 2004, http://www.cbc.ca/news/canada/edmonton/story/2004/03/19/ed_stenhouse20040319.html.

———. "Hoax camp ads outrage Torontonians," 22 August 2007, http://www.cbc.ca/news/canada/toronto/story/2007/08/22/camp-okutta.html.

CBC News Online. "Genetically modified foods: A primer," 11 May 2004, http://www.cbc.ca/news/background/genetics_modification/.

CBC Policies and Guidelines, Advertising Standards: http://cbc.radio-canada.ca/en/reporting-to-canadians/acts-and-policies/programming/advertising-standards/.

Certified Global Management Accountants. "Managing responsible business: A global survey on business ethics," http://www.cgma.org/Resources/Reports/DownloadableDocuments/CGMA%20Ethics%20Report%20FINAL.pdf.

Charlesworth, Andrew. "HP private eyes fined US$600,000." ITNews, 31 May 2008.

Charlesworth, Max. "Ethical reflection and business practice." In C.A.J. Coady and C.J.G. Sampford, eds, *Business, Ethics and the Law*, 187–205. Sydney: Federation Press, 1993.

Charter, February 1994. "Financial Reports Review Program," 55–6.

Choice, April 1992. "Mistral's ill wind," 7–11.

Cicero. *De officiis*, trans. Walter Miller. Cambridge, MA, and London: Loeb, 1913.

Clark, Andrew. "Thain says sorry for $1.2m furniture bill." *Guardian*, 27 January 2009: http://www.guardian.co.uk/business/2009/jan/27/merrill-lynch-john-thain-citigroup.

Clark, Fred P. "Unfounded 'whistle blower' suit can kill a small defense company." *Aviation Week and Space Technology*, 2 March 1992, 65–6.

Clark, Hannah. "Five ways—How to (legally) spy on employees." Forbes.com, 25 October 2006.

Clarke, F.L., G.W. Dean, and K.G. Oliver. *Corporate Collapse*. Cambridge: Cambridge University Press, 1997.

Clarke, Frank, and Graeme Dean. "Legislators and regulators have failed to get the principles right." *Australian Financial Review*, 7 November 2002, 71.

Coady, C.A.J. "Ethos and ethics in business." In C.A.J. Coady and C.J.G. Sampford, eds, *Business, Ethics and the Law*. Sydney: Federation Press, 1993.

———. "On regulating ethics." In Margaret Coady and Sidney Bloch, eds, *Codes of Ethics and the Professions*, 269–87. Melbourne: Melbourne University Press, 1996.

Cohen, Stephen. "Ethics is judgement, not rules." *Australian Financial Review*, 26 November 2002, 71.

———. "'Good ethics is good business'—revisited." *Business and Professional Ethics Journal* 18, no. 2 (1999): 57–68.

———. *The Nature of Moral Reasoning: The Framework and Activities of Ethical Deliberation, Argument, and Decision-Making*. Melbourne: Oxford University Press, 2004.

———. "Regulations are not the answer." *Australian Financial Review*, 15 January 2003.

Cohen, Stephen, and Damian Grace. "Ethics and sustainability: Looking beyond basic legal requirements." *Australian Master OHS and Environment Guide 2003*. Sydney: CCH, 2002.

Coker, Edward. "Adam Smith's concept of the social system." *Journal of Business Ethics* 9 (1990): 139–42.

Condren, Conal. "Code types: Functions and failings and organizational diversity." *Business and Professional Ethics Journal* 14, no. 4 (1995): 69–90.

Conference Board of Canada. "GHG Emissions per Capita," http://www.conferenceboard.ca/hcp/details/environment/greenhouse-gas-emissions.aspx.

Connolly, Kate. "I'm no monster, says dungeon father in attack on 'biased' media." *Guardian*, 8 May 2008.

Conservation Ontario, Planning and Regulations, Conservation Authorities' Federal Fisheries Act Partnership, http://www.conservation-ontario.on.ca/planning_regulations/fisheries_act.html.

Cooper, Anderson. *Anderson Cooper 360°*, CNN transcript, aired 7 December 2005: http://transcripts.cnn.com/TRANSCRIPTS/0512/07/acd.01.html.

Cornell, Christopher. "Fed-Ex driver wins sex-harassment case." Human Resource Executive Online, 2 June 2004, http://www.hreonline.com/HRE/story.jsp?storyId=4222585&query=benefits.

Costello, Daniel. "Costs make employers see smokers as a drag." *Los Angeles Times*, 28 January 2005, A-1.

Cottell, Philip G., Jr, and Terry M. Perlin. *Accounting Ethics: A Practical Guide for Professionals*. New York: Quorum Books, 1990.

CPA letter. "Gallup survey shows accounting's image still rising," November 2005.

Cribb, Julian. "Committed to truth." *Australian*, 8 September 1993, 8.

Crichton, Michael. "Remarks to the Commonwealth Club San Francisco," 15 September 2003: http://www.crichton-official.com/speeches/speeches_quote05.html.

Cross, Frank. "Paradoxical perils of the precautionary principle." *Washington and Lee Law Review* 851 (1996): 53.

Cumming-Bruce, Nicholas. "Chief of state-owned firm in $62m graft case." *Sydney Morning Herald*, 25 January 1997, 22.

Curry, B., and S. McCarthy. "Canada formally abandons Kyoto Protocol on Climate Change." *Globe and Mail*, 12 December 2011, http://www.theglobeandmail.com/news/politics/canada-formally-abandons-kyoto-protocol-on-climate-change/article4180809/.

Daly, H., and J. Cobb. *For the Common Good*. London: Greenprint, 1989.

Dancy, Jonathan. *Moral Reasons*. Oxford: Blackwell, 1993.

Davies, H. *The Financial Crisis: Who is to Blame?* Cambridge, UK: Polity Press, 2010.

Davis, Mark. "WMC compiles its own green report card." *Business Review Weekly*, 10 June 1996, 20–2.

Davis, Michael. Introduction to *Conflict of Interest in the Professions*. Oxford: Oxford University Press, 2001.

De George, Richard. *Business Ethics*. 2nd edn. New York: Macmillan, 1986.

———. *Business Ethics*. 6th edn. Upper Saddle River, NJ: Pearson Education, 2006.

———. *Competing with Integrity in International Business*. New York: Oxford University Press, 1993.

———. "Entrepreneurs, multinationals, and business ethics." Paper given at the International Society of Business, Economics and Ethics, Tokyo, 1996.

De Maria, William. "Quarantining dissent: The Queensland public sector ethics movement." *Australian Journal of Public Administration* 54 (1995): 443–54.

Dempster, Quentin. *Whistleblowers*. Sydney: ABC Books, 1997.

de Pommereau, Isabelle. "Are towns really safer without traffic lights?" *Christian Science Monitor*, 12 September 2008.

Devlin, Lord Patrick. "Morals and the criminal law." In Richard A. Wasserstrom, *Morality and the Criminal Law*. Belmont, CA: Wadsworth, 1971.

Disney, Julian, et al. *Lawyers*. 2nd edn. Sydney: Law Book Company, 1986.

Dobnik, Verena. "Nike accused of allowing 'boot camp' factories." *Sydney Morning Herald*, 29 March 1997, 17.

"Dodd-Frank Wall Street Reform and Consumer Protection Act," http://www.sec.gov/about/laws/wallstreetreform-cpa.pdf.

Donagan, Alan. *The Theory of Morality*. Chicago: University of Chicago Press, 1979.

Donaldson, Thomas. *The Ethics of International Business*. New York: Oxford University Press, 1989.

———. "The language of international corporate ethics." *Business Ethics Quarterly* 2 (1992): 271–81.

———. "Multinational decision-making: Reconciling international norms." In Anthony Ellis, ed. *Ethics and International Relations*, 127–40. Manchester: Manchester University Press.

Dowd, Maureen. "Wall Street's socialist jet-setters." *New York Times*, 27 January 2009, A31.

Drucker, Peter. *Post-Capitalist Society*. New York: Harper Business, 1993.

———. "What is 'business ethics'?" *Public Interest* 63 (1981): 18–36.

Dworkin, Gerald. "Lord Devlin and the enforcement of morals." *Yale Law Journal* 75 (1966): 986–1005.

Dyck, A., A. Morse, and L. Zingales. "Who blows the whistle on corporate fraud?," *Journal of Finance* 65, no. 6 (2010), http://www.nber.org/papers/w12882.pdf.

Dylan, Bob. "The Wicked Messenger." *John Wesley Harding*. Columbia, 1967.

Ebertz, Roger P. "Is reflective equilibrium a coherentist model?" *Canadian Journal of Philosophy* 23 (1993).

Ecologically Sustainable Development Working Group Chairs. *Intersectoral Issues Report*. Canberra: AGPS, 1992.

Eichenwald, Kurt. "Audacious climb to success ended in a dizzying plunge." *New York Times*, 13 January 2004.

———. *Conspiracy of Fools: A True Story*. New York: Broadway Books, 2005).

———. "Ex-accounting chief at Enron is indicted on 6 felony charges." *New York Times*, 23 January 2004.

Elias, David. "Accidental hero defeats David Tweed." *Sydney Morning Herald*, 24 October 2003.

———. "Tweed finds profit preying on old folk." *Sydney Morning Herald*, 30 December 2004.

Elliott, Christopher. "Unfair fairs: Avoid the Bait-and-Switch," 2008, msnbc.com: http://www.msnbc.msn.com/id/27366920/ns/travel-travel_tips/t/unfair-fares-avoid-bait-and-switch/.

Enron Code of Ethics (July 2000), http://www.bennettlawfirm.com/enron.pdf.

Ewin, Robert. "The moral status of the corporation." *Journal of Business Ethics* 10 (1991): 749–56.

Fantz, Ashley. "Who is Rudolf Elmer, WikiLeaks' newest leaker?" CNN, 17 January 2011: http://news.blogs.cnn.com/2011/01/17/who-is-rudolf-elmer-wikileaks-newest-leaker/.

Farnham, Alan. "State your values, hold the hot air." *Fortune*, 19 April 1993, 54.

Finnis, John. *Natural Law and Natural Rights*. Oxford: Clarendon Press, 1980.

Fisheries and Oceans Canada. Fisheries Act, http://www.dfo-mpo.gc.ca/habitat/role/141/1415/14151-eng.htm.

Fitzgerald, Barry. "BHP in deal on Ok Tedi compo." *Age*, 8 May 1997.

Flanagan, Jack. *Values, Codes of Ethics and the Law*. Sydney: Institute of Chartered Accountants in Australia, 2006.

Forbes, Cameron, and Matthew Stevens. "BHP considers PNG mining solutions." *Australian*, 24 May 1994.

Frankena, William. *Ethics*. 2nd edn. Englewood Cliffs, NJ: Prentice Hall, 1973.

Freckelton, Ian. "Enforcement of ethics." In Margaret Coady and Sidney Bloch, eds, *Codes of Ethics and the Professions*. Melbourne: Melbourne University Press, 1996.

Freeman, R. Edward. *Strategic Management: A Stakeholder Approach*. Boston: Pitman, 1984.

Friedman, Milton. *Capitalism and Freedom*. Chicago: University of Chicago Press, 1962.

———. "The social responsibility of business is to increase its profits." *New York Times Magazine*, 13 September 1970, reprinted in T. Donaldson and P. Werhane, eds, *Ethical Issues in Business: A Philosophical Approach*, 239–42. 2nd edn. Englewood Cliffs, NJ: Prentice Hall, 1983.

Friedman, Milton, and Rose Friedman. *Free to Choose*. London: Secker and Warburg, 1980.

Gaita, Raimond. *Good and Evil: An Absolute Conception*. London: Macmillan, 1991.

———. *The Philosopher's Dog*. Melbourne: Text Publishing, 2002.

Gansberg, Martin. "Thirty-eight who saw murder didn't call the police." *New York Times*, 27 March 1964.

Garran, Robert. "Nomura bosses resign en masse." *Australian*, 23 April 1997, 23.

———. "Nomura president falls on his sword." *Weekend Australian*, 15–16 March 1997, 53.

Gilligan, Carol. *In a Different Voice: Psychological Theory and Women's Development*. Cambridge, MA: Harvard University Press, 1982.

Global Sullivan Principles. The Leon H. Sullivan Foundation: http://www.thesullivanfoundation.org/gsp/default.asp.

Goldman, Alan. "Ethical issues in advertising." In Tom Regan, ed., *Just Business: New Introductory Essays in Business Ethics*. New York: Random House, 1984.

Gollom, M. "CAW Needs to be 'more flexible,' expert warns." CBC News, 15 August 2012, http://www.cbc.ca/news/canada/story/2012/08/14/caw-auto-industry-contract-talks.html.

Goodpaster, Kenneth. "Business ethics and stakeholder analysis." *Business Ethics Quarterly* 1 (1991).

Government of Canada, Department of Justice. Federal Accountability Act, 2006: http://laws-lois.justice.gc.ca/eng/acts/F-5.5/index.html.

Government of New Brunswick, Employment Standards Act, 1982: http://laws.gnb.ca/en/ShowTdm/cs/E-7.2.

Grace, Damian. "Errant corporations, diffuse responsibilities, and the environment: Ethical issues in the Orica case study." *Journal of Environmental Management* 90, no. 4 (April 2009).

Graham, Duncan. "$92,000 damages for porn in workplace harassment." *Sydney Morning Herald*, 22 April 1994, 3.

Grand Metropolitan. *Report on Corporate Citizenship*. London: Grand Metropolitan, 1997.

Grant, Colin. "Friedman fallacies." *Journal of Business Ethics* 10 (1991): 907–14.

Grant-Taylor, Tony. "Greyhound hardly shareholder's best friend." *Sydney Morning Herald*, 25 March 1994, 21, 25.

Guttsman, J. "Canadian Union Agrees to Concessions in GM Deal." Reuters, 8 March 2009, http://ca.reuters.com/article/domesticNews/idCAWNAB153320090308?sp=true.

Guy, Mary. *Ethical Decision Making in Everyday Work Situations*. New York: Quorum Books, 1990.

Hancock, Peter. *Women Workers in Nike Factories in West Java*. Fitzroy: Community Aid Abroad, 1997.

Hardin, Garrett. "The tragedy of the commons." *Science* 162 (December 1968): 1234–8.

Harris, Gardiner. "Top psychiatrist didn't report drug makers' pay." *New York Times*, 4 October 2008.

Hart, H.L.A. "Immorality and treason." In Richard Wasserstrom, ed., *Morality and the Criminal Law.* Belmont, CA: Wadsworth, 1971.

———. *Law, Liberty, and Morality.* London: Oxford University Press, 1963.

Hartley, R.F. *Business Ethics: Mistakes and Successes*. 1st ed. Hoboken, NJ: John Wiley and Sons, 2005.

Hays, Kristen. "Causey may be key in Enron prosecutions." *Chicago Tribune*, 24 January 2004.

Heckman, Peter. "Business and games." *Journal of Business Ethics* 11 (1992): 933–8.

Henderson, Michael. *The Forgiveness Factor: Stories of Hope in a World of Conflict.* Salem, OR: Grosvenor Books, 1996.

Herbert, Bob. Report on fire at Kadar Industrial Toy Company. In K. Woldring, ed., *Business Ethics in Australia and New Zealand*, 191–2. Melbourne: Nelson, 1996.

Hinman, Lawrence M. *Ethics: A Pluralistic Approach to Moral Theory*. 4th edn. Belmont, CA: Thomson Wadsworth, 2008.

Hobbes, Thomas. *Leviathan.* New York: Oxford University Press (Oxford World's Classics), 1996.

Hodgson, Kent. *A Rock and a Hard Place: How to Make Ethical Business Decisions When the Choices Are Tough.* New York: American Management Association, 1992.

Hoffman, Andy. "A big mess." *Globe and Mail*, 12 October 2009.

———. "A business model shrouded in fog." *Globe and Mail*, 26 November 2011.

———. "Sino-Forest clams up as probe continues." *Globe and Mail*, 16 August 2011.

Hoffman, Michael. "Business and environmental ethics." *Business Ethics Quarterly* 1, no. 2 (1991): 169–84.

Holtzman, David H. "Hubris at HP—and beyond." *Businessweek*, 11 October 2006.

Honeywell. *Code of Ethics and Business Conduct.* Minneapolis: Honeywell, 1995.

Howard, Robert. "Values make the company." *Harvard Business Review*, September–October 1990, 133–44.

Hunter, D. *The Bubble and the Bear: How Nortel Burst the Canadian Dream.* Toronto: Doubleday, Canada, 2003.

Institute of Business Ethics. "Surveys on Business Ethics, 2011." *Business Ethics Briefing*, no. 23 (February 2012), http://www.ibe.org.uk/userfiles/surveys_2011.pdf.

International Advertising Association. "Advertising. It makes the difference." *Sydney Morning Herald*, 5 June 1993, 13.

International Trade Union Confederation. "ITUC Survey 2012: Annual Survey of Violations of Trade Union Rights," http://survey.ituc-csi.org/.

Irving, Mark. "Women in workplace porn case get $92,000." *Australian*, 22 April 1994, 3.

Jackson, Kevin. "Global distributive justice and the corporate duty to aid." *Journal of Business Ethics* 12 (1993): 550.

Jacobs, Donna. "A whistle blown: A decade lost." *Ottawa Citizen*, 22 May 2006.

James, Andrea. "Boeing bosses spy on workers." seattlepi.com, 16 November 2007.

Jenner, L., L. Mulligan-Ferry, and R. Soares. *2009 Catalyst Census: Financial Post 500 Women Board Directors.* Toronto: Catalyst Canada, 2010.

Jeter, L.W. *Disconnected: Deceit and Betrayal at WorldCom.* Hoboken, NJ: John Wiley and Sons, 2003.

Jonsen, Albert, and Stephen Toulmin. *The Abuse of Casuistry.* Berkeley: University of California Press, 1988.

Jubb, Peter. "Confidentiality in a professional context with especial reference to the accounting profession in Australia." In M. Hoffman, J. Brown Kamm, R.E. Frederick and E.S. Petry, eds, *The Ethics of Accounting and Finance.* London: Quorum Books, 1996.

Kahn, Joseph. "Californians call Enron documents the smoking gun." *New York Times*, 8 May 2002.

Kamb, Lewis. "Scouts who wear two hats." *Times Union*, 2 February 2009.

Kant, Immanuel. *Foundations of the Metaphysics of Morals*, trans. L.W. Beck. New York: Macmillan, 1990.

Kaplan, David A. "A playbook for the HP hearings." *Newsweek*, 27 September 2006.

———. "Suspicions and spies in Silicon Valley." *Newsweek*, 18 September 2006.

Kay, M. "RCMP whistleblowers should be honoured, says Commons committee." *Ottawa Citizen*, 6 September 2007, http://www.rcmpwatch.com/rcmp-whistleblowers-should-be-honoured-says-commons-committee/.

Keeley, Michael, and Jill Graham. "Exit, voice and ethics." *Journal of Business Ethics* 10 (1991).

Kekes, John. *The Morality of Pluralism*. Princeton, NJ: Princeton University Press, 1993.

Kelley, Rob. "Charges against HP's Dunn dropped." CNNMoney.com, 14 March 2007.

Kelly, Patrick. "Conducting a glass ceiling self-audit now." HR *Magazine*, October 1993.

Kent, Peter. "Notes for Remarks by the Honourable Peter Kent, P.C., M.P., Minister of the Environment." Joint Canada-Alberta Implementation Plan for Oil Sands Monitoring, Edmonton, Alberta, 3 February 2012.

Khan, Kim. "Merrill settles charges." *CNN Money*, 21 May 2002.

Kim, K.A., and J.R. Nofsinger. *Corporate Governance*. 2nd ed. Upper Saddle River, NJ: Pearson Prentice Hall, 2007.

Klein, Naomi. *No Logo*. Hammersmith, London: Flamingo, 2001.

Ladd, John. "Morality and the ideal of rationality in formal organizations." *Monist* 54 (1970): 488–516.

Lambsdorff, Johann. "The question of responsibility," 26 September 1997: http://gwdu19.gwdg.de/%7Ejlambsd/ bribery/node4.htm.

———. TI *Newsletter*, September 1997: http://www.transparency.de/newsletter/997index.html.

Landier, A., and V.B. Nair. *Investing for Change: Profit from Responsible Investment*. New York: Oxford University Press 2009.

Lanktree, Graham. "Oilsands whistleblower MD cleared." *National Review of Medicine* 5, no. 1 (15 January 2008).

Laufer, William S. "Integrity, diligence, and the limits of good corporate citizenship." *American Business Law Journal* 34, no. 2 (Winter 1996): 157–81.

Lawson, Mark. "The ethical dilemma of corporate generosity." *Australian Financial Review*, 5 December 2002.

———. "Just don't invite the chief executive out to play golf." *Australian Financial Review*, 5 December 2002.

Lawson, Mark, and Ian Howarth. "WMC mauled in Savage engagement." *Australian Financial Review*, 27 July 1993, 24.

Lazarus, David. "Lesson learned by lenient sentences for HP defendants." *San Francisco Chronicle*, 16 March 2007.

LeBlanc, R.W. "A black eye for Bay Street: With proper governance, the Sino-Forest scandal would never have happened." *Canadian Business* 88, no. 15 (2011): 12.

Lee, Julian. "Furore over Coke myth-busting ad." *Sydney Morning Herald*, 15 October 2008.

———. "Kerry Armstrong Coke ad gets all-clear." *Sydney Morning Herald*, 27 November 2008.

Legge, Kate. "Humble hero of the operating theatre." *Weekend Australian*, 23–24 June 2001.

Leigh, David, Luke Harding, and the *Guardian*. *WikiLeaks: Inside Julian Assange's War on Secrecy*. New York: Guardian Books, 2011.

Lemke, Dwight, and Marshall Schminke. "Ethics in declining organizations." *Business Ethics Quarterly* 1 (1991): 235–48.

Leung, Philomena, and Barry Cooper. *Professional Ethics: A Survey of Australian Accountants*. Melbourne: ASCPA, 1995.

Lewis, Michael. "The irresponsible investor." *New York Times*, 6 June 2004.

Liebig, James E. *Business Ethics: Profiles in Civic Virtue*. Golden, CO: Fulcrum, 1990.

Lima Declaration, 2 November 1997: http://www.transparency.de/iacc/council.html.

Lumby, Catherine. "Sexist or Sexy." *Independent Monthly*, November 1993.

Lynch, Adrian. "Get integrity back into management." *Rydges*, December 1985.

McArthur, Greg. "A gift for Mr. Hossain." *Globe and Mail Report on Business Magazine*, September 2011.

MacCharles, T. 2007, "The high cost of whistleblowing." *Toronto Star*, 30 June 2007, http://www.thestar.com/news/article/231204--high-cost-of-whistleblowing.

McDonald, Paula, Kerriann Dear, and Sandra Backstrom. "Expecting the worst: Circumstances surrounding pregnancy discrimination at work and progress to formal redress." *Industrial Relations Journal* 39, no. 3 (2008): 233.

McGeehan, Patrick. "$100 million fine for Merrill Lynch." *New York Times*, 22 May 2002.

McGuiness, Padraic P. "Elusive ethics." *Sydney Morning Herald*, 17 November 1994, 20.

MacLachlin I. *Kill and Chill: Restructuring Canada's Beef Commodity Chain*. Toronto: University of Toronto Incorporated, 2001.

McMillan, John. "Legal protection of whistleblowers." In S. Prosser, R. Wear, and J. Nethercote, eds, *Corruption and Reform*. St Lucia, Qld: University of Queensland Press, 1990.

McNish, Jacquie. "Why the smiling barracuda is moving on." *Globe and Mail*, 17 December 2011.

McNish, Jacquie, and Andy Hoffman. "Sino-Forest CEO resigns amid OSC probe." *Globe and Mail*, 29 August 2011.

Madway, Gabriel. "Dunn: H-P's Hurd tried to get Keyworth to admit leak." *Marketwatch*, 27 September 2006.

Maher, Kris. "Companies are closing doors on job applicants who smoke." *Wall Street Journal*, 21 December 2004.

Maich, S. "The ghost of Bre-X rises." *MacLean's Magazine*, 8 June 2005, http://www.macleans.ca/columnists/article.jsp?id=3andcontent=20050613_107322_107322.

"Managing in Asia: Ethics and other issues." *Far Eastern Economic Review*, 16 September 1993, 33–53.

Manley II, Walter W. *Handbook of Good Business Practice*. London and New York: Routledge, 1992.

Manley II, Walt W., and William A. Shrode. *Critical Issues in Business Conduct*. New York: Quorum Books, 1990.

Marsden, Chris. "Corporate citizenship." Discussion paper, BP Corporate Citizenship Unit, Business School, University of Warwick, 1997.

Martin, Mike, and Roland Schinzinger. *Ethics in Engineering*. 2nd edn. New York: McGraw-Hill, 1989.

Marx, Karl. *Capital*. Vol. 1. New York: International Publishing, 1967.

Mathison, David. "Business ethics cases and decision models: A call for relevancy in the classroom." *Journal of Business Ethics* 7 (1988): 777–82.

Maurice, Jack. *Accounting Ethics*. London: Pitman Publishing, 1996.

May, William W., ed. *Ethics in the Accounting Curriculum: Cases and Readings*. Sarasota, FL: American Accounting Association, 1990.

Mayman, Jan. "The stink of uncle Al." *Weekend Australian*, 11–12 May 2002.

Media Research Centre of Alaska, 20 February 2009: http://mediaresearchak.org/gallup_poll.htm.

Mellor, Bill. "Integrity and ruined lives." *Time*, 21 October 1991.

Meredith, Paul. "Ethical Framework." *Charter*, November 2006.

Mill, J.S. *Utilitarianism*. Indianapolis: Bobbs-Merrill, 1957.

More, Thomas. *Utopia*, ed. G. Logan and R.M. Adams. Cambridge: Cambridge University Press, 1989.

Muolo, P., and M. Padilla. *Chain of Blame: How Wall Street Caused the Mortgage and Credit Crisis*. Hoboken, NJ: John Wiley and Sons, 2010.

Nagel, Thomas. "Ruthlessness in public life." In Stuart Hampshire, ed., *Public and Private Morality*, 75–92. New York: Cambridge University Press, 1978.

Nash, Laura. "Ethics without the sermon." *Harvard Business Review* 59 (November–December 1981): 79–90.

National Society of Professional Engineers. Code of Ethics for Engineers, n.d.: http://www.nspe.org/Ethics/CodeofEthics/index.html.

Norington, Brad. "Nike protests urged over 'appalling' work conditions." *Sydney Morning Herald*, 1 April 1997, 6.

———. "The shoe fits here as well." *Sydney Morning Herald*, 18 April 1997, 15.

North, Sam. "Human rights concerns pull Levi's out of China." *Sydney Morning Herald*, 8 May 1993, 15.

Nozick, Robert. *Anarchy, State and Utopia*. Oxford: Blackwell, 1974.

Nugroho, Alois A. "The myth of immoral business: A specific challenge of business ethics in Indonesia." International Society of Business, *Economics and Ethics Papers*. Tokyo, 1996: http://www.nd.edu/~isbee/p_nugroh.htm.

O'Neill, Onora. *A Question of Trust*. Cambridge: Cambridge University Press, 2002.

OnlineNewshour. "Enron: After the collapse," 27 February 2009: http://www.pbs.org/newshour/bb/business/enron/player6.html.

Ontario Women's Justice Network. "Janzen: The Supreme Court of Canada Recognizes sexual harassment in the workplace as a form of sex discrimination," July 2008, http://owjn.org/owjn_2009/legal-information/aboriginal-law/119.

Pagano, Anthony M. "Criteria for ethical decision making in managerial situations." *Proceedings of the National Academy of Management*, 1–12. New Orleans, 1987.

Palmer, Ian. "Email abuse and misuse." *Insight*, July 2003: http://www.insight-mag.com/ insight/03/08/col-5-pt-1-WorkForce.asp.

Parker, Christine. *The Open Corporation*. Cambridge: Cambridge University Press, 2002.

Paterson, Tony. "Josef Fritzl: The making of a monster." *Independent*, 3 May 2008.

Patten, Chris. *East and West: The Last Governor of Hong Kong on Power Freedom and the Future*. London: Pan Macmillan, 1998.

———. "Synergy of robust rights and robust development." *Sydney Morning Herald*, 24 November 1993, 15.

Pearson, Christopher. "Green errors began with DDT." *Weekend Australian*, 24–25 January 2004.

"Persons of the Year." *Time*, 30 December–6 January 2003, 34–57.

Peters, T.J., and R. H. Waterman. *In Search of Excellence*. Sydney: Harper and Row, 1984.

Pincoffs, Edmund L. *Quandaries and Virtues*. Lawrence: University of Kansas Press, 1986.

Pinker, Susan. *The Sexual Paradox*. London: Atlantic Books, 2008.

Pratt, Dennis. *Aspiring to Greatness*. Sydney: Business and Professional Publishing, 1994.

Preston, Noel. "Public sector ethics in Australia: A review." *Australian Journal of Public Administration* 54 (1995): 462–70.

Rachels, James. *The Elements of Moral Philosophy*. 2nd edn. New York: McGraw-Hill, 1993.

Rawls, John. *A Theory of Justice*. Cambridge, MA: Harvard University Press, 1971.

Redmond, Paul. *Companies and Securities Law*. 2nd edn. North Ryde: Law Book Company, 1992.

Reuters. "More top executives willing to pay bribes—survey." 23 May 2012, http://ht.ly/b7o3G.

Rigby, Rhymer. "Jeans genius." *Management Today*, November 1996, 56–60.

Rion, Michael. *The Responsible Manager: Practical Strategies for Ethical Decision Making*. San Francisco: Harper and Row, 1990.

Rolston III, Holmes. "Just environmental business." In Tom Regan, ed., *Just Business*. New York: Random House, 1984.

Rout, Milanda. "Drug company drew up doctor hit list." *Australian*, 1 April 2009.

Ryan, Colleen. "The hard yard." *Australian Financial Review Magazine*, July 2003.

Ryle, Gerard. "Industrial waste sold as fertilizer." *Sydney Morning Herald*, 6 May 2002.

Saad, Lydia. "Nurses shine, bankers slump in ethics ratings." Gallup, 24 November 2008, http://www.gallup.com/poll/112264/Nurses-Shine-While-Bankers-Slump-Ethics-Ratings.aspx.

Safer, Morley. "Whose life is it anyway?" CBS News, 16 July 2006: http://www.cbsnews.com/stories/2005/10/28/60minutes/main990617.shtml.

St Anne, Christine. "Share predator targets Suncorp: Bank issues warning." *InvestorDaily*, 27 May 2008.

Sanyal, Rajib, and Joao Neves. "The Valdez Principles: Implications for corporate social responsibility." *Journal of Business Ethics*, 10 December 1991, 883–90.

Schelling, Thomas C. *Choice and Consequence: Perspectives of an Errant Economist*. Cambridge: Harvard University Press, 1984.

Securities and Exchange Commission. "Summary of SEC actions and SEC related provisions pursuant to the Sarbanes-Oxley Act of 2002," 30 July 2003: http://www.sec.gov/news/press/2003-89a.htm.

Sen, Amartya. "Does business ethics make economic sense?" *Business Ethics Quarterly* 3 (1993): 50.

Simons, Paul. "Be interested in the people you serve and your life will be happy." Fourth annual lecture, St James Ethics Centre, Sydney, November 1994.

Sims, Ronald R. "The institutionalization of organization ethics." *Journal of Business Ethics* 10 (1991).

Sinclair, Amanda. "Codes in the workplace: Organizational verses professional codes." In Margaret Coady and Sidney Bloch, eds, *Codes of Ethics and the Professions*. Melbourne: Melbourne University Press, 1996.

———. "Improving ethics through organisational culture." In C.A.J. Coady and C.J.G. Sampford, eds, *Business, Ethics and the Law*. Sydney: Federation Press, 1993.

Singer, Marcus G. *Generalization in Ethics*. New York: Russell and Russell, 1971.

Singer, Peter. *Animal Liberation*. 2nd edn. New York: Thorsons, 1991.

———, ed. *Ethics*. New York: Oxford University Press, 1994.

———. *Practical Ethics*. 2nd edn. New York: Cambridge University Press, 1993.

Smart, J.J.C., and Bernard Williams. *Utilitarianism: For and Against*. London: Cambridge University, 1973.

Smith, Adam. *An Enquiry into the Nature and Causes of the Wealth of Nations*. New York: Modern Library, 1937.

———. *The Theory of Moral Sentiments*. Indianapolis: Liberty Press, 1982.

Smith, M. "Western's code of conduct for its employees." *Australian Financial Review*, 10 November 1993, 21.

Smith, M., and I. Howarth. "WMC cuts back power of managing director." *Australian Financial Review*, 1 September 1993, 20.

Social Philosophy and Policy 11, no. 1 (1994).

Sternberg, Elaine. *Just Business*. London: Warner Books, 1995.

Still, Leonie. "Breaking the glass ceiling: Another perspective." *Women in Management Series*, paper no. 15, Faculty of Commerce, University of Western Sydney, Nepean, July 1992.

Stinebaker, Joe. "Former Enron exec Causey in prison." *Chicago Tribune*, 3 January 2007.

Stone, D.G. *April Fools: An Insider's Account of the Rise and Collapse of Drexel Burnham*. New York: Donald I. Fine, 1990.

Story, Louise. "Many women at elite colleges set career path to motherhood." *New York Times*, 20 September 2005.

———. "Reporting on the aspirations of young women." *New York Times*, 23 September 2005.

Sutton, George. "Accountability brings with it all sorts of limits." *Australian*, 9 December 1994, 22.

Sydney Morning Herald. "Dud loans dog Vietnam's banks," 24 March 1997, 38.

———. "I'm no monster, says dungeon dad," 8 May 2008.

———. "Mob muscles into brokers' offices," 24 March 1997, 38.

Tahija, Julius. "Swapping business skills for oil." *Harvard Business Review*, September–October 1993, 113.

The Ten Principles of the United Nations Global Compact: http://www.unglobalcompact.org/AboutTheGC/TheTenPrinciples/index.html.

Thompson, Dave. "The big fat lie about battery life." *Sydney Morning Herald*, 6 February 2009.

Titmuss, Richard. *Social Policy: An Introduction*, ed. Brian Abel-Smith and Kay Titmuss. London: Allen and Unwin, 1974).

Toffler, Barbara Ley, and Jennifer Reingold. *Final Accounting: Ambition, Greed and the Fall of Arthur Andersen*. New York: Broadway Books, 2003.

Tönnies, Ferdinand. *Community and Association*, trans. C.P. Loomis. London: Routledge and Kegan Paul, 1955.

"Top 10 Crooked CEOs: Dennis Kozlowski." *Time*, 9 June 2009.

Trainer, Ted. *Abandon Affluence*. London: Zed Books, 1985.

Transparency International website, www.transparency.org.

Treadgold, Tim. "Lady Bountiful turns nasty." *Business Review Weekly*, 1 October 1993, 24–8.

Trumbull, Mark. "The changing rules of corporate spy games." *Christian Science Monitor*, 25 September 2006.

———. "HP board flap raises wider privacy issues." *Christian Science Monitor*, 14 September 2006.

United States Sentencing Commission website: http://www.ussc.gov/Guidelines/2011_Guidelines/Manual_HTML/1a1.htm.

Vallance, Elizabeth. *Business Ethics at Work*. Cambridge: Cambridge University Press, 1995.

Velasquez, Manuel, *Business Ethics*. 3rd edn. Englewood Cliffs, NJ: Prentice Hall, 1992.

———. *Business Ethics: Concepts and Cases*. 6th edn. Upper Saddle River NJ: Pearson Prentice Hall, 2006.

Vitell, S.J., S.L. Nwachukwu, and J.H. Barnes. "The effects of culture on ethical decision-making: An application of Hofstede's typology." *Journal of Business Ethics* 12 (1993): 753–60.

Walsh, Marry Williams, and Carl Hulse. "A.I.G. bonuses of $50 million will be repaid." *New York Times*, 23 March 2009.

Warn, K. "Nortel faces insider trading allegations." *Financial Times*, 20 February 2001, 30.

Warner, Judith. "Diagnosis: greed." *New York Times*, 9 October 2008.

Washington Post. "Merrill paying $1m fine in settlement with SEC," 30 January 2009.

Waterman, Robert. *Frontiers of Excellence*. Sydney: Allen and Unwin, 1994.

Waters, James A. "Catch 20.5: Corporate morality as an organizational phenomenon." In A.P. Iannone, ed., *Contemporary Moral Controversies*. New York: Oxford University Press, 1989.

Webber, Ross. "Whistleblowing." *Executive Excellence*, July 1990.

West, Michael. "BT sues auditors for $60m." *Sydney Morning Herald*, 31 January 1996, 25.

Westfield, Mark. "Longest running trial puts blowtorch on auditors." *Australian*, 9 September 1997, 25.

Westin, Allen, ed. *Whistleblowing: Loyalty and Dissent in the Corporation*. New York: McGraw-Hill, 1981.

White, Gwendolen B., and Michael J. White. "Perceptions of accountants: What are they after Enron and WorldCom?" *Journal of College Teaching and Learning* 3, no. 11 (November 2006).

Whitton, Howard. "Ethics and principled dissent in the Queensland public sector: A response to the Queensland whistleblower study." *Australian Journal of Public Administration* 54 (1995): 455–61.

Williams, Bernard. "A critique of utilitarianism." In J.J.C. Smart and Bernard Williams, *Utilitarianism: For and Against*. London: Cambridge University, 1973.

———. "Politics and moral character." In Stuart Hampshire, ed., *Public and Private Morality*. London: Cambridge University Press, 1978.

Williams, Louise. "Bre-X scam sparks attacks on foreigners." *Sydney Morning Herald*, 6 May 1997, 28.

Wilson, Catherine. *Moral Animals*. New York: Oxford University Press, 2004.

Wilson, Duff. "Fear in the fields—How hazardous wastes become fertilizer—Spreading heavy metals on farmland is perfectly legal, but little research has been done to find out whether it's safe." *Seattle Times*, 3 July 1997.

Wilson, Mel, "Corporate reputation and the triple bottom line: The social responsibilities of business." *Risky Business*, no. 2 (2001).

Woellert, Lorraine. "HP's Hunsaker papers." *Businessweek*, 4 October 2006.

Wolgast, Elizabeth. *Ethics of an Artificial Person*. Stanford, CA: Stanford University Press, 1992.

Wood, Leonie. "Whistleblowers face a conundrum." *Age*, 6 April 2009.

Woodford, Peter. "Health Canada muzzles oilsands whistleblower." *National Review of Medicine* 4, no. 8 (30 March 2007).

World Commission on Environment and Development. *Our Common Future*. London: Oxford University Press, 1987.

Young, Bronwyn. "Sex bias decision upheld." *Australian Financial Review*, 6 December 1989, 3.

Index